D0176424

THE VISTA HIGHER LEARNING

Introductory Spanish

Pocket Dictionary & Language Guide

Boston, Massachusetts

Copyright © 2005 by Vista Higher Learning

All rights reserved.

No part of this work may be reproduced or distributed in any form or by any means, electronic or mechanical, including photocopying and recording, or by any information storage or retrieval system without prior written permission from Vista Higher Learning, 31 St. James Avenue, Boston, MA 02116-4104.

ISBN 1-59334-387-6

Library of Congress Control Number: 2004106252

5 6 7 8 9 B 09 08 07 06

CONTENTS

Introduction 1

Spanish-English Dictionary 3

English-Spanish Dictionary 115

Useful Expressions 213

Verb Conjugation Tables 264

Reference Section

- Academic Subjects 286
- Animals 288
- The Human Body and Health 290
- Useful Classroom Expressions 296
- Countries and Nationalities 298
- Currencies 303
- Expressions and Sayings 304
- False Friends 309
- Foods 312
- Holidays 317
- Weights and Measures 321
- Spanish Names 325
- Numbers 333
- Occupations 334

Introduction

The Vista Higher Learning Introductory Spanish Pocket Dictionary & Language Guide was created to complement your Vista Higher Learning introductory Spanish textbook. Its Spanish-English and English-Spanish dictionaries contain all of the active words and expressions taught in these texts:

- ***VISTAS***
- ***AVENTURAS***
- ***PANORAMA***
- ***INVITACIONES: Primera parte y Segunda parte***

Besides active vocabulary, the dictionaries also incorporate several thousand additional words, expressions, and idioms chosen because of their high-frequency and their usefulness to students who are using these Vista Higher Learning introductory textbooks to learn Spanish.

The dictionaries are followed by *Useful Expressions*, a storehouse of contextualized sentences illustrating new vocabulary, idioms, and grammatical structures that can help you make your Spanish more natural and expressive. These sentences are related to the themes presented in your Vista Higher Learning textbook. Verb conjugation tables containing all of the verbs taught in your textbook follow the *Useful Expressions* section.

The Pocket Dictionary & Language Guide then closes with the *Reference* section. It contains lists of specialized vocabulary on a variety of topics, such as country names, adjectives of nationality, academic subjects, foods, numbers, sayings, false friends, and so forth.

We hope that you will find the ***Vista Higher Learning Introductory Spanish Pocket Dictionary & Language Guide*** to be a useful language learning resource and that it will help you to increase your Spanish language skills in a productive, enjoyable fashion.

The Vista Higher Learning Editorial Staff

Note on Alphabetization

For purposes of alphabetization, the Spanish language contains one more letter, **ñ**, than English. **Ñ** follows **n**; therefore, the word **dañar**, for example, appears after **danza**.

Abbreviations Used in This Dictionary

adj.	adjective	*L.A.*	Latin America
adv.	adverb	*loc.*	set expression
art.	article	*m.*	masculine
aux.	auxiliary	*n.*	noun
conj.	conjunction	*obj.*	object
def.	definite	*p.p.*	past participle
dem.	demonstrative	*pl.*	plural
d.o.	direct object	*poss.*	possessive
f.	feminine	*prep.*	preposition
fam.	familiar	*pron.*	pronoun/pronominal
form.	formal		
i.	intransitive	*recip.*	reciprocal
impers.	impersonal	*refl.*	reflexive
indef.	indefinite	*sing.*	singular
inf.	infinitive	*subj.*	subject/subjunctive
interj.	interjection	*t.*	transitive
i.o.	indirect object	*v.*	verb
irreg.	irregular		

Español-Inglés
Spanish–English

A

a *prep.* at; to
a la(s) + (*time*) at + (*time*)
abadía *f.* abbey
abajo *adv.* down
¡Abajo! Down (with it/him/her/them)!
abatido/a *adj.* dejected
abeja *f.* bee
abeto *m.* fir tree
abierto *p.p. of* **abrir** opened
abierto/a *adj.* open
abogado/a *m. f.* lawyer
abonar *v.t.* (*soil*) to fertilize
abono *m.* fertilizer
abortar *v.i.* to have a miscarriage
abortar de manera provocada to have an abortion
aborto *m.* (espontáneo) miscarriage; (provocado) abortion
abrazar *v.t.* to hug; to embrace
abrazarse *v. pron. (recip.)* to hug; to embrace each other
abrazo *m.* hug; embrace
abrebotellas *m.* bottle opener
abrelatas *m. sing.* can opener
abreviar *v.t.* to abbreviate
abreviatura *f.* abbreviation
abridor *m.* opener
abrigo *m.* coat; overcoat; jacket
abril *m.* April
abrillantador (para pisos/suelos) *m.* (*floor*) polish
abrillantar *v.t.* to polish
abrir *v.t.* to open
abrirse *v. pron.* to open
La ventana se abrió de golpe. The window opened suddenly.
absorbente *adj.* absorbent
absorber *v.t.* to absorb
absurdo/a *adj.* absurd
abuelo/a *m.* grandfather; *f.* grandmother
abuelos *m., pl.* grandparents
aburrido/a *adj.* bored; boring
aburrir *v.t.* to bore
Este libro me aburre. This book bores me.
aburrirse *v. pron.* to get bored
Espero que hoy no se aburran. I hope you don't get bored today.
acá *adv.* here
¡Ven acá! Come here!
acabar *v.t.* to finish
Acabé la tarea. I'm done with my homework.
acabar de (+ *inf.*) *v.i.* to have just done something
Acabo de limpiar. I've just finished cleaning.
acampada *f.* camp; camping
ir de acampada to go camping
acampar *v.i.* to camp
acantilado *m.* cliff
acariciar *v.t.* to caress; (*hair, pet*) to stroke, to pet
acaso: por si acaso *loc.* just in case
accesorio *m.* accessory
accidentado/a *adj.* (*terrain*) rugged; (*person*) hurt, injured

accidente *m.* accident
accidente laboral industrial accident
acción *f.* action
...de acción action (*genre*)
accionar *v.t.* (*machine*) to operate; to activate
aceite *m.* oil
aceite de oliva olive oil
aceituna *f.* olive
acelerador *m.* accelerator (*pedal*)
acelerar *v.t.* to accelerate
¡Acelera! Hurry up!
aceptar *v.t.* to accept
acera *f.* sidewalk
acerca de *prep.* about
Leí un artículo acerca de Sevilla. I read an article about Seville.
acercarse (a) *v. pron.* to approach, to come closer (to)
acero *m.* steel
acero inoxidable stainless steel
ácido *m.* acid
ácido fólico folic acid
ácido/a *adj.* acid; (*flavor*) tart, tangy
acogedor(a) *adj.* cozy
acolchado/a *adj.* padded
acompañar *v.t.* to go with, to accompany
acondicionado *adj.* conditioned
aconsejar *v.t.* to advise
acontecimiento *m.* event
acordar (o:ue) *v.t.* to agree
acordarse (de) (o:ue) *v. pron.* to remember
acostarse (o:ue) *v. pron.* to go to bed
acostumbrarse (a) *v. pron.* to be accustomed to
acrobacia *f.* acrobatics
acróbata *m., f.* acrobat
activar *v.t.* to activate
actividad *f.* activity
activo/a *adj.* active
acto *m.* act
en el acto *loc.* immediately, right away
acto seguido *adv.* immediately after
actor *m.* actor
actriz *f.* actor
actual *adj.* current, present
actualidades *f., pl.* news; current events
acuarela *f.* watercolor (*painting*)
acuario *m.* aquarium
acuático/a *adj.* aquatic
acuerdo *m.* agreement
de acuerdo con according to
llegar a un acuerdo to reach an agreement
adaptación *f.* adaptation
adaptarse (a) *v. pron.* to adapt; to adjust (to)
adelantar (a un vehículo) *v.t.* to pass (*a vehicle*)
adelante *adv.* forward, ahead
La librería Porté está un poco más adelante. The Porté Bookshop is a little farther ahead.
adelgazar *v.i.* to lose weight; to slim down
además (de) *adv.* furthermore; besides; in addition (to)

adentro *adv.* inside
aderezar *v.t.* (*food*) to season; (*salad*) to dress
aderezo *m.* seasoning; dressing
adicción *f.* addiction
adicional *adj.* additional
adicto/a *m., f.* addict; *adj.* addicted
adiós *m.* good-bye
aditivo *m.* additive
adivinanza *f.* riddle
adivinar *v.t.* to guess
adjetivo *m.* adjective
administración *f.* management, administration
administración de empresas business administration
administrar *v.t.* (*business*) to manage; to run
adolescencia *f.* adolescence
adolescente *m., f.* teenager, adolescent
adolorido/a *adj.* sore
¿adónde? *adv.* (*destination*) (to) where?
adornar *v.t.* to decorate; (*food*) to garnish
adorno *m.* ornament, decoration
de adorno for decoration
Se puso un lazo de adorno en el pelo. She wore a ribbon in her hair for decoration.
adquirir (i:ie) *v.t.* to acquire
adquisición *f.* acquisition
adrede *adv.* intentionally, on purpose
aduana *f.* customs
adulación *f.* flattery
adulador(a) *m., f.* flatterer
adular *v.t.* to flatter
advertencia *f.* warning
advertir (i:ie) *v.t.* to warn; to notice
Por fin alguien advirtió mi presencia. Finally someone noticed I was there.
aéreo/a *adj.* air
correo aéreo air mail
aeróbico/a *adj.* aerobic
aerolínea *f.* airline
aeroplano *m.* airplane
aeropuerto *m.* airport
afectado/a *adj.* affected
afectar *v.t.* to affect
afeitarse *v. pron.* to shave (*oneself*)
afición *f.* hobby
aficionado/a *adj.* fan
aficionarse (a) *v. pron.* to become a fan (of); (*hobby*) to take up
afinar *v.t.* (*musical instrument*) to tune
afirmativo/a *adj.* affirmative
africano/a *adj./m., f.* African
afuera *adv.* outside
afueras *f., pl.* suburbs; outskirts
agachar *v.t.* (*head*) lower
agacharse *v. pron.* to squat
agencia *f.* office; agency
agencia de viajes travel agency
agente *m., f.* agent
agente de viajes travel agent
agosto *m.* August
agotado/a *adj.* (*person, supplies*) exhausted; (*commerce*) out of stock; (*tickets*) sold out

agotamiento *m.* exhaustion
agotarse *v. pron.* (*provisions, supplies*) to run out
agradable *adj.* (*person*) pleasant, nice; (*situation*) enjoyable
agradecer (c:zc) *v.t.* to thank, to be grateful
Te agradezco tu ayuda. Thank you for your help.
agradecido/a *adj.* grateful
agrícola *adj.* agricultural
labor agrícola farm labor
agricultor(a) *m., f.* farmer
agricultura *f.* agriculture, farming
agridulce *adj.* bittersweet
agrio/a *adj.* sour
agrupar *v.t.* to group
agruparse *v. pron.* to get into groups
agua (el) *f.* water
agua bendita holy water
agua dulce fresh water
agua mineral mineral water
agua potable drinking water
agua salada salt water
aguacate *m.* avocado
aguafiestas *m., f.* party pooper
aguantar *v.t.* to endure, to put up with; (*Spain*) to hold
aguante *m.* endurance
águila (el) *f.* eagle
aguja *f.* needle
agujerear *v.t.* (*material*) to make holes; (*ear*) to pierce
agujero *m.* hole
ahijado/a *m.* godson; *f.* goddaughter
ahogado/a *adj.* drowned
ahogar *v.t.* to drown
Ahoga sus dudas leyendo. He drowns his doubts by reading.
Ahoga sus penas trabajando. She drowns her sorrow with work.
ahogarse *v. pron.* to drown
Se ahogó en el río. He drowned in the river.
ahora *adv.* now
ahora mismo right now
de ahora en adelante from now on
ahorrador(a) *adj.* frugal
ahorrar (dinero) *v.t.* to save (*money*)
ahorros *m.* savings
aire *m.* air
aire acondicionado air conditioning
al aire libre in the open air
aislante *adj.* insulating
aislar *v.t.* to isolate; to insulate
ajedrecista *m., f.* chess player
ajedrez *m.* chess
ajo *m.* garlic
al (*contraction of* a + el) to the, at the
al contado in cash
al (+ *inf.*) upon, on
Al llegar a San Juan, fuimos a la playa. Upon arriving in San Juan, we went to the beach.
ala (el) *f.* wing
ala delta (*vehicle*) hang glilder; (*sport*) hang gliding
practicar el ala delta to hang glide

alardear (de) *v.i.* (*Spain*) to boast (about)
Alardeaba de haber ganado. He was boasting about having won.
alarmante *adj.* alarming
albahaca *f.* basil
albañil *m.* builder; bricklayer
albañilería *f.* (*profession*) building; bricklaying
albaricoque *m.* apricot
alberca *f.* (*Mexico*) swimming pool
albergue *m.* hostel
albergue juvenil youth hostel
alcachofa *f.* artichoke
alcalde, alcaldesa *m., f.* mayor
alcaldía *f.* city hall
alcoba *f.* (*L.A.*) bedroom
alcohol *m.* alcohol
alcohólico/a *adj.* alcoholic
aldea *f.* village
alegrarse (de) *v. pron.* to be happy
alegre *adj.* happy; joyful
alegría *f.* joy; happiness
alejado/a *adj.* remote
alemán *m.* (*language*) German
alemán, alemana *adj./m., f.* German
alérgico/a *adj.* allergic
aleta *f.* (*fish*) fin; (*swiming*) flipper
alfabeto *m.* alphabet
alfombra *f.* carpet; rug
alga (el) *f.* seaweed
algarabía *f.* rejoicing, jubilation; noisy commotion
algo *pron.* something; anything
algodón *m.* cotton
de algodón (made of) cotton
alguien *pron.* someone; somebody; anyone
algún, alguno/a(s) *adj.* any; some
alguna vez ever
aliento *m.* breath
dar aliento to encourage
alimentación *f.* diet
alimentar *v.t.* to feed
alimentarse *v. pron.* to feed oneself
alimento *m.* food
aliñar *v.t.* (*food*) to season; (*salad*) to dress
aliño *m.* seasoning; dressing
aliviar *v.t.* to ease; alleviate; (*pain*) to relieve
aliviar el estrés/la tensión to relieve/reduce stress/tension
aliviarse *v. pron.* (*pain*) to let up; (*person*) to get better
alivio *m.* relief
allí *adv.* there
allí mismo right there
alma (el) *f.* soul
almacén *m.* department store
almacenamiento *m.* storage
almacenar *v.t.* to store
almeja *f.* clam
almendra *f.* almond
almendro *m.* almond tree
almíbar *m.* syrup
almohada *f.* pillow
almorzar (o:ue) *v.i.* to have lunch
almuerzo *m.* lunch
¿Aló? *interj.* Hello? (*on the telephone*)
alojado/a *adj.* guest
alojamiento *m.* lodging

alojar (a alguien) *v.t.* to lodge, to put up
alojarse *v. pron.* (*hotel*) to stay
alpinismo *m.* (*mountain*) climbing
alpinista *m., f.* (*mountain*) climber
alquilar *v.t.* to rent
alquiler *m.* rent (*payment*)
alrededor (de) *prep.* around
Hay una muralla alrededor de la ciudad vieja. There is a wall around the old city.
alrededor *adv.* around
una mesa con cuatro sillas alrededor a table with four chairs around it
alrededores *m., pl.* outskirts, surrounding area
en los alrededores de Barcelona on the outskirts of Barcelona
altavoz *m.* loudspeaker
alternador *m.* alternator
alternativa *f.* alternative
altillo *m.* attic
alto/a *adj.* tall; high
alto *m.* halt, stop
señal de alto stop (*sign*)
altura *f.* height
aluminio *m.* aluminum
de aluminio (*made*) of aluminum
alumno/a *m., f.* (*elementary school*) pupil, student
ama: el ama *m., f.* **de casa** housekeeper; caretaker; housewife; home-maker
amable *adj.* nice; friendly; kind
amanecer *m.* dawn
al amanecer at dawn
amanecer (c:zc) *v. impers.* to dawn; (*person*) to wake up (*in the morning*)
Amanecí con dolor de cabeza. I woke up with a headache.
amapola *f.* poppy
amante *m., f.* lover; fan; *adj.* loving
amantes del jazz jazz lovers
su amante esposa his loving wife
amante de la buena conversación fond of good conversation
amar *v.t.* to love
amargo/a *adj.* bitter
amarillento/a *adj.* yellowish
amarillo/a yellow
amarse *v. pron.* (*recip.*) to love each other
ambición *f.* ambition
ambicionar *v.t.* to aspire to
ambicioso/a *adj.* ambitious
ambientador *m.* air freshener
ambiente *m.* (*natural*) environment; (*created by people, decoration*) atmosphere
ambos/as *adj.* both
Sujetó la pelota con ambas manos. He held down the ball with both hands.
ambulancia *f.* ambulance
amenaza *f.* threat
amenazar *v.t.* to threaten
amígdala *f.* tonsil
amigo/a *m., f.* friend
hacer amigos to make friends

amistad *f.* friendship
amistades *m., pl.* friends
Martina tiene muchas amistades en Cartagena. Martina has lots of friends in Cartagena.
amistoso/a *adj.* friendly
amor *m.* love
amortiguador *m.* shock absorber
amueblado/a *adj.* furnished
amueblar *v.t.* to furnish
analfabeto/a *m., f.* illiterate person; *adj.* illiterate
analista *m., f.* analyst
anaranjado/a *adj.* (*color*) orange
anarquía *f.* anarchy
anárquico/a *adj.* anarchic
anatomía *f.* anatomy
anatómico/a *adj.* anatomical
ancho/a *adj.* wide
anchoa *f.* anchovy
anciano/a *adj.* elderly; *m.* elderly man; *f.* elderly woman
andar en bicicleta to ride bikes
andar en patineta to skateboard
anestesia *f.* anesthesia
anestesiar *v.t.* anesthetize
anestesiólogo/a *m., f.* anesthesiologist
anfitrión *m.* host
anfitriona *f.* hostess
anglosajón, anglosajona *adj./m., f.* Anglo-Saxon
anguila *f.* eel
ángulo *m.* angle
anillo *m.* ring
anillo de bodas wedding ring
anillo de compromiso engagement ring
animado/a *adj.* (*person*) in good spirits; (*party*) lively
animal *m.* animal
animar *v.t.* to cheer up; to encourage
animarse *v. pron.* to cheer up
aniversario (de bodas) *m.* (wedding) anniversary
anoche *adv.* last night
anormal *adj.* abnormal
ansia *f.* longing
ansiar *v.t.* to crave for, to long for
anteayer *adv.* the day before yesterday
antepasado/a *m., f.* ancestor
antes *adv.* before
antes de *prep.* before
antes (de) que *conj.* before
antibiótico *m.* antibiotic
anticipación *f.* anticipation; (*business*) advance
con anticipación ahead of time; beforehand
anticonceptivo *m.* contraceptive
anticuado/a *adj.* old-fashioned
antideportivo *adj.* unsportsmanlike
antídoto *m.* antidote
antifaz *m.* mask
antigüedades *f., pl.* antiques; antiquities
antiguo/a *adj.* old; ancient
antipatía *f.* dislike
antipático/a *adj.* unpleasant, irritating, hasty
antojo *m.* whim
antología *f.* anthology
antorcha *f.* torch

anular *v.t.* to cancel
anunciar *v.t.* to announce; to advertise
anuncio *m.* (*newspaper*) advertisement
anzuelo *m.* hook
morder el anzuelo (*loc.*) to swallow the bait; to bite
añil *adj.* indigo
año *m.* year
el año pasado last year
añoranza *f.* yearning
añorar (a alguien) *v.t.* to long for (someone); to miss (someone)
apagar *v.t.* (*TV, radio*) to turn off; (*fire*) to put out, to extinguish
apagón *m.* power failure, blackout
aparato *m.* appliance
aparato circulatorio circulatory system
aparato digestivo digestive system
aparato doméstico household appliance
aparato respiratorio respiratory system
aparecer (c:zc) *v.i.* to appear
apartamento *m.* apartment
apellido *m.* last name
apenas *adv.* hardly; scarcely; barely; just
Apenas le conozco. I barely know him.
Apenas te oigo. I can hardly hear you.
aperitivo *m.* appetizer
apilar *v.t.* to stack
apio *m.* celery
aplaudir *v.t./v.i.* to applaud, to clap
aplauso *m.* applause
aplazamiento *m.* postponement
aplazar *v.t.* to postpone, to put off
apodo *m.* nickname
apoyar *v.t.* to support
apoyo *m.* support
apreciar *v.t.* to appreciate
aprecio *m.* esteem
aprender (a + *inf.*) *v.t.* to learn
apresurarse *v. pron.* to hurry
aprobado *m.* passing grade, C
aprobar (o:ue) *v.i.* to pass
aprovechar *v.t.* to make good use of
aprovecharse (de) *v. pron.* to take advantage (of)
aptitud *f.* aptitude, competence
apto/a *adj.* fit (*to practice a profession*); suitable
No es apto para ejercer la psicología. He's not fit to practice psychology.
apuñalar (a alguien) *v.t.* to stab (somebody)
apurarse *v. pron.* to hurry; to rush
aquel, aquella, aquellos/as *dem. adj.* that (over there); those (over there)
aquél, aquélla, aquéllos/as *dem. pron.* that (over there); those (over there)
aquello *dem. neuter pron.* that; that thing; that fact
aquí *adv.* here
aquí está here (he/she/it) is

aquí estamos en... here we are in . . .
aquí mismo right here
árabe *m.* (*language*) Arabic
árabe *adj.* Arabian; *m., f.* Arab
araña *f.* spider; (*light*) chandelier
árbitro/a *m.* referee; umpire
árbol *m.* tree
árbol frutal fruit tree
árbol genealógico family tree
arboleda *f.* grove
arbusto *m.* shrub, bush
archipiélago *m.* archipelago
archivar *v.t.* to file
archivo *m.* file
arcilla *f.* clay
arco *m.* arch; (*sport*) bow
arco iris *m.* rainbow
ardilla *f.* squirrel
arena *f.* sand
arete *m. (L.A.)* earring
argumentar *v.t.* to argue
argumento *m.* (*reasoning*) argument; (*literature, film*) plot
arisco/a *adj.* unfriendly
aristocracia *f.* aristocracy
aristócrata *m., f.* aristocrat
arma (el) *f.* weapon, arm
armar (un rompecabezas) *v.t.* to assemble (a puzzle)
armario *m.* closet
aroma *m.* scent
arqueólogo/a *m., f.* archaeologist
arquitecto/a *m., f.* architect
arrancar *v.t.* (*car*) to start; (*sheet of paper*) to tear out
arrastrar *v.t.* to drag
arrastrarse (por el piso/suelo) *v. pron.* to crawl (on the ground)
arrecife *m.* reef
arreglado/a *adj.* tidy
arreglar *v.t.* to fix; to arrange; to neaten; to straighten up
El profesor arregló la situación. The professor fixed the situation.
La modista me arregló el vestido. My dressmaker fixed my dress.
arreglarse *v. pron.* to do oneself up; to get ready
Tarda mucho en arreglarse. He/She takes forever getting ready.
arrepentido/a *adj.* repentant, feeling sorry
arrepentirse *v. pron.* to be sorry; to regret
arrestado/a *adj.* arrested; under arrest
estar arrestado/a to be under arrest
arrestar *v.t.* to arrest
arresto *m.* arrest
arriba *adv.* up
¡Manos arriba! Hands up!
Me miró de arriba abajo. He/She looked me up and down.
arriesgarse *v. pron.* to take the risk
arroba *f.* @ symbol
arrogante *adj.* arrogant
arroz *m.* rice
arte *m.* art
arteria *f.* artery
artes *f., pl.* arts

artes marciales martial arts
artesanía *f.* craftsmanship; crafts
articulación *f.* joint, articulation
artículo *m.* article; item
artículos *m., pl.* (*business*) goods
artículos de cocina kitchenware
artículos de deporte sporting goods
artículos de piel leather goods
artículos de punto knitwear
artista *m., f.* artist
artístico/a *adj.* artistic
arveja *m.* pea
asa (el) *f.* (*cup, serving dish*) handle
asado *m.* roast
asado de cordero roast lamb
asado *p.p. of* **asar** roasted; **asado/a** *adj.* roast(ed)
castañas asadas roasted chesnuts
asador *m.* barbecue
asar *v.t.* to roast
ascender *v.t.* (*temperature, prices*) to rise; *v.i.* (*employee*) to be promoted
ascenso *m.* rise; (*at work*) promotion
ascensor *m.* elevator
asco *m.* nausea
¡Qué asco! How revolting! How disgusting!
asegurar *v.t.* to assure, to guarantee
asegurarse *v. pron.* to make sure
asesinato *m.* murder; assassination
asesino/a *adj./m., f.* murderer; assassin
asfalto *m.* asphalt
así *adv.* thus; so (*in such a way*); like this
Debe hacerse así. It must be done like this.
así así so-so
asiático/a *adj.* Asiatic; *m., f.* Asian
asiduo/a *m., f.* (*client*) regular; *adj.* frequent
asiento *m.* seat
asiento delantero front seat
asiento trasero rear seat
asignación *f.* (*Mexico*) homework
asistencia *f.* assistance
asistencia médica health care
asistir (a) *v.i.* to attend
asociación *f.* association
asociar *v.t.* (*ideas, words*) to associate
asociarse (con) *v. pron.* to collaborate (with)
asombroso/a *adj.* amazing, astonishing
aspecto *m.* appearance
áspero/a *adj.* (*surface, skin*) rough
aspiradora *f.* vacuum cleaner
aspirante *m., f.* candidate; applicant
aspirina *f.* aspirin
asqueroso/a *adj.* (*food, smell*) disgusting, revolting; (*place*) filthy

Esta cocina está asquerosa. This kitchen is filthy.

astrología *f.* astrology

astrólogo/a *m., f.* astrologist

astronauta *m., f.* astronaut

astronomía *f.* astronomy

astrónomo/a *m., f.* astronomer

astuto/a *adj.* shrewd

asumir *v.t.* to assume

atajo *m.* short cut

ataque *m.* attack

ataque al corazón heart attack

ataque cardíaco heart attack

ataque de nervios panic attack

atardecer *m.* dusk

al atardecer at dusk, at twilight

ataúd *m.* coffin

ateísmo *m.* atheism

atención *f.* attention; care

atender *v.i.* to pay attention

atender a los clientes to take care of clients

atentado *m.* assault, attack; crime

atentado terrorista terrorist attack; assassination attempt

atentar (contra) *v.t.* to attempt to assassinate (*somebody*); to attack (*something*)

ateo/a *adj.* atheistic; *m., f.* atheist

aterrizaje *m.* landing

aterrizar *v.i.* to land

atleta *m., f.* athlete

atlético/a *adj.* athletic

atletismo *m.* athletics; track and field

atontado/a *adj.* stunned, dazed

atracar *v.t.* (*bank*) to hold up; (*person*) to mug

atracción *f.* attraction

atraco *m.* robbery, holdup

atractivo/a *adj.* attractive

atractivo *m.* attraction; appeal, charm

No entiendo su atractivo. I don't understand his appeal.

atraer *v.t. irreg.* (**yo atraigo**) to attract

atragantarse *v. pron.* to choke

atrás *adv.* behind

atravesar *v.t.* to cross

atreverse *v. pron.* to dare

atrevido/a *adj.* (*dress*) daring, provocative; (*person*) brave; daring, cheeky.

¿No te da miedo viajar sola? Eres muy atrevida. You're not afraid of traveling all by yourself? You're really brave.

atrevimiento *m.* nerve

atropellar (a alguien con un vehículo) *v.t.* to run over (someone with a vehicle)

atroz *adj.* atrocious, awful

atún *m.* tuna

audición *f.* hearing; (*test*) audition

auditorio *m.* auditorium; audience; theater

auge *m.* peak

estar en auge to be on the increase

aula *f.* classroom; lecture hall

aula magna main lecture hall

aumentar *v.t.* to increase

aumentar de peso to gain weight

aumento *m.* increase
aumento de sueldo (*pay*) raise
aunque *conj.* although, even though
auricular *m.* headphone; (*telephone*) receiver
ausencia *f.* absence
ausentarse *v. pron.* to go away
ausente *adj.* absent
australiano/a *adj./m., f.* Australian
auténtico/a *adj.* real
autobús *m.* bus
autodidacta *m., f.* self-taught person; autodidact
auto(e)stop *m.* hitchhiking
hacer auto(e)stop to hitchhike
auto(e)stopista *m., f.* hitchhiker
autógrafo *m.* autograph
automático/a *adj.* automatic
automóvil *m.* automobile
automovilismo *m.* motor racing
automovilista *m., f.* motorist
autonomía *f.* autonomy
autónomo/a *adj.* (*government*) autonomous; *m., f.* (*work*) self-employed worker, freelancer
autopista *f.* highway; freeway, expressway
autor(a) *m., f.* author
autor intelectual *(L.A.)* mastermind (*of a crime*)
autoritario/a *adj.* authoritarian
autoritarismo *m.* authoritarianism
autorretrato *m.* self-portrait
auxiliar *v.t.* to help
¡Auxilio! *interj.* Help!
avance *m.* advance
avanzado/a *adj.* advanzed
avanzar *v.i.* to advance; to move forward
avaricia *f.* avarice
avaricioso/a *adj.* greedy, avaricious
avaro/a *m., f.* miser
ave (el) *f.* bird
avellana *f.* hazelnut
avellano *m.* hazel tree
avenida *f.* avenue
aventura *f.* adventure
...de aventuras adventure (*genre*)
aventurero/a *adj.* adventurous; *m., f.* adventurer
avergonzado/a *adj.* embarrassed
avergonzar (o:ue) *v.t.* to shame, to embarrass
avergonzarse (o:ue) *v. pron.* to be ashamed
avería *f.* (*Spain*) (*automobile, mechanical*) breakdown
averiado/a *adj.* (*Spain*) broken down, out of order
averiarse *v. pron.* (*Spain*) to break down
averiguar *v.t.* to find out; to check
aversión *f.* aversion, dislike
avestruz *m.* ostrich
avión *m.* airplane
viajar en avión to travel by plane
avioneta *f.* light aircraft
avisar *v.t.* to warn, to inform
aviso *m.* warning, notice
avispa *f.* wasp
axila *f.* armpit

¡Ay! *interj.* Oh!, Ouch!, Yikes!
¡Ay, qué dolor! Ouch, it hurts!/Oh, what pain!
ayer *adv.* yesterday
ayudar (a) *v.t.* to help (to)
ayudarse *v. pron. (recip.)* to help each other
ayunar *v.i.* to fast
ayuno *m.* fast
ayunas: **salir en ayunas** to go out without breakfast
ayuntamiento *m.* city hall
azafrán *m.* saffron
azar *m.* chance; coincidence
al azar at random, randomly
azúcar *m.* sugar
azucarero *m.* sugar bowl
azul *adj./m.* blue
azul celeste sky blue
azul marino navy blue
azulado/a *adj.* bluish
azulejo *m.* (*ceramic*) tile

B

babero *m.* bib
bacalao *m.* cod, codfish
bahía *f.* bay
bailar *v.t.* to dance
bailarín, bailarina *m., f.* dancer
baile *m.* dance
bajar *v.i.* to go down
bajar(se) de (un vehículo) *v. pron.* to get off/out of (a vehicle)
bajo/a *adj.* (*person*) short; (*volume, light, temperature*) low
Por favor, hablen más bajo. Please speak quietly.
bajo/a *prep.* under
bajo cero below zero
bajo control under control
bajo ningún pretexto under no circumstances
bajo juramento under oath
balanza *f.* (*for weighing*) scale
balcón *m.* balcony
baldosa *f.* (*floor*) tile
ballena *f.* whale
ballet *m.* ballet
balneario *m.* spa, resort
baloncesto *m.* basketball
balonmano *m.* handball
banana *f.* banana
banco *m.* bank; bench
banda *f.* (*music*) band
banda sonora sound track
bandera *f.* flag
banquero/a *m., f.* banker
bañarse *v. pron. (refl.)* to bathe; to take a bath; to shower
bañera *f.* bathtub
baño *m.* bathroom
baraja (de cartas/naipes) *f.* deck (of cards)
barato/a *adj.* cheap
barba *f.* beard
barbero *m.* barber
barbudo/a *adj.* bearded
barco *m.* ship
barra (de pan) *f.* (*Spain*) loaf (of bread)
barrer (el suelo/el piso) *v.t.* to sweep the floor
barriga *f.* stomach
barrio *m.* neighborhood
barro *m.* mud
barroco/a *adj.* baroque
báscula *f.* scale

bastante *adj.* enough; sufficient; rather
bastar *v.i.* to be enough
Con esto basta y sobra. This is more than enough.
Con ocho basta. Eight is enough.
Dos semanas no bastan para completarlo. Two weeks are not enough to finish it.
bastón *m.* walking stick
basura *f.* trash
basurero *m.* garbage dump; garbage can
basurero/a *m., f.* garbage collector
bata *f.* robe
bata de baño bathrobe
batidor *m.* whisk
batidora *f.* (*Spain*) blender, mixer
batir *v.t.* to whisk; to beat
batir un récord mundial to break a world record
baúl *m.* trunk
bautizar *v.t.* to baptize; to name
bautizo *m.* baptism
bazo *m.* spleen
bebé *m., f.* baby
beber *v.t./v.i.* to drink
bebida *f.* drink
bebida alcohólica *f.* alcoholic beverage
beca *f.* grant; scholarship
béisbol *m.* baseball
belleza *f.* beauty
bello/a *adj.* beautiful
bellas artes *f., pl.* (fine) arts
bendecir *v.t. irreg.* (**yo bendigo**) to bless
bendición *f.* blessing
beneficiarse *v.t.* to benefit
beneficio *m.* benefit
beneficioso/a *adj.* beneficial
benigno *adj.* benign
berenjena *f.* eggplant
bermellón *m.* vermilion
berrinche *m.* tantrum
besar *v.t.* to kiss
besarse *v. pron.* (*recip.*) to kiss each other
beso *m.* kiss
betabel *f.* (*Mexico*) (*sugar*) beet
biblioteca *f.* library
bibliotecario/a *m., f.* librarian
bicarbonato *m.* baking soda
bicicleta *f.* bicycle
bien *adj.* good; well
bienes raíces *m., pl.* real estate
bienestar *m.* well-being
bienvenida *f.* welcome
dar la bienvenida to welcome
bienvenido/a *adj.* welcome
bigote(s) *m.* (*pl.*) moustache
bikini *m.* bikini
bilingüe *adj.* bilingual
bilingüismo *m.* bilingualism
billete *m.* (*Spain*) ticket; paper money
billete de ida y vuelta round-trip ticket
Vale muchos billetes. It costs a lot of money.
billón *m.* trillion
Un billón es un millón de millones. One trillion is a million millions.
biodiversidad *f.* biodiversity
biogenética *f.* genetic engineering

biografía *f.* biography
biográfico/a *adj.* biographical
biología *f.* biology
biólogo/a *m., f.* biologist
biosfera *f.* biosphere
bisabuelo/a *m.* great-grandfather; *f.* great-grandmother
bisagra *f.* hinge
bisnieto/a *m.* great-grandson; *f.* great-granddaughter
bistec *m.* steak
bisturí *m.* scalpel
blanco/a *adj.* white
bluejeans *m., pl.* (*L.A.*) jeans
blusa *f.* blouse
boca *f.* mouth
  boca abajo face-down
  boca arriba face-up
bocina *f.* (*automobile*) horn
boda *f.* wedding
  boda concertada arranged marriage
bodega *f.* (*house*) cellar; (*store*) wine cellar
boina *f.* beret
boletín *m.* bulletin, report
  boletín de notas school report
  boletín informativo newsletter
boleto *m.* (*L.A.*) ticket
boliche *m.* bowling
bolígrafo *m.* pen
bolsa *f.* purse; bag
  la Bolsa the stock market
bolsillo *m.* pocket
  libro de bolsillo paperback book
bolsista *m., f.* stockbroker
bolsita *f.* (*diminutive*) small bag
  bolsita de té teabag
bolso *m.* shoulder bag
bomba *f.* bomb
bombero/a *m., f.* firefighter
bonito/a *adj.* pretty
bordar *v.t.* to embroider
bordo: a bordo aboard, on board
  ¡Todos a bordo! All aboard!
borracho/a *adj.* drunk
borrador *m.* eraser
borrar *v.t.* to erase
bosque *m.* forest
  bosque nuboso cloud forest
  bosque tropical tropical forest; rain forest
bota *f.* boot
  botas de agua rubber boots
  botas de montar riding boots
botánica *f.* botany
botánico/a *m., f.* botanist; *adj.* botanical
botar *v.t.* (*L.A.*) to throw away
botella *f.* bottle
  botella de vino bottle of wine
botiquín *m.* medicine cabinet
  botiquín de primeros auxilios first-aid kit
botón *m.* button
  botón de rebobinado rewind button
botones *m., sing.* bellhop
boxeador(a) *m., f.* boxer
boxear *v.i.* to box
boxeo *m.* boxing
bragas *f., pl.* (*Spain*) panties
brasier *m.* (*L.A.*) bra
brazo *m.* arm
  Es su brazo derecho. He's her right-hand man.
breve *adj.* brief; short

en breve *adv.* shortly, soon
brevedad *f.* brevity
brillar *v.i.* to shine
brillo (para zapatos) *m.* (*shoe*) polish
brindar *v.t. (drink)* to toast
brindis *m.* toast
brisa *f.* breeze
brócoli *m.* broccoli
broma *f.* joke
  broma pesada practical joke
  bromas aparte joking aside
  en broma in jest, as a joke
  hacer bromas to make jokes
bromista *m., f.* joker
bronce *m.* bronze
bronceado/a *adj.* sun-tanned
bronceador *m.* suntan lotion
broncear *v.t.* to tan
broncearse *v. pron.* to (get a) tan
buceador(a) *m., f.* (*underwater*) diver
bucear *v.i.* to scuba dive
budista *adj./m., f.* Buddhist
buen, bueno/a *adj.* good
  Buen viaje. Have a good trip.
  Buena idea. Good idea.
  Buenas noches. Good evening.; Good night.
  Buenas tardes. Good afternoon.
  buenísimo/a *adj. (superlative)* extremely good
  ¿Bueno? Hello? (*on telephone*)
  (No) Es bueno que ... It's (not) good that ...
  (No) Es bueno que corras. It's (not) good that you run.
  Buenos días. Good morning.
bueno *adv.* well
bufanda *f.* scarf
búho *m.* owl
buitre *m.* vulture
bujía *f.* spark plug
bulevar *m.* boulevard
bulto *m.* bundle, package
buque *m.* boat, ship
burbuja *f.* bubble
buscar *v.t.* to look for
búsqueda *f.* search
buzón *m.* mailbox

C

caballero *m.* gentleman
caballo *m.* horse
  montado/a a caballo on horseback
cabaña *f.* cabin
cabello *m.* hair
caber *v.i. irreg.* **(yo quepo)** to fit
  Esta mesa no cabe aquí. This table doesn't fit here.
  Esta falda no me cabe. This skirt doesn't fit me.
  no cabe duda (de) que... there's no doubt that...
cabeza *f.* head
cable *m.* cable
  echarle un cable a alguien *idiom.* to help somebody out
cada *adj.* each
cadáver *m.* corpse
cadena *f.* chain
  cadena perpetua life imprisonment; life sentence
cadena *f.* channel (TV)
cadera *f.* hip
caer *v.t. irreg.* **(yo caigo)** to fall
caerse *v. pron. irreg.* **(yo me caigo)** to fall (down)

café *m.* (*place*) café, coffee shop; (*drink*) coffee; (*color*) brown
cafeína *f.* caffeine
cafetera *f.* coffee maker
cafetería *f.* cafeteria
caída *f.* fall
  caída libre free fall
caído *p.p. of* **caer** fallen; **caído/a** *adj.* fallen
caja *f.* box; cash register
  caja de música music box
  caja fuerte safe
cajero/a *m., f.* cashier
  cajero automático automatic teller machine (ATM)
calabaza *f.* pumpkin
calamar *m.* squid
calavera *m.* skull
calcetín *m.* sock
calculadora *f.* calculator
calcular *v.t.* to calculate, to work out
cálculo *m.* calculation, estimate
caldo *m.* broth, soup
  caldo de patas (Ecuador) beef soup
  caldo de gallina chicken soup
  caldo de res beef soup
calefacción *f.* heating
calendario *m.* calendar
calentador *m.* heater
calentar (e:ie) *v.t.* to heat
calentarse (e:ie) *v. pron.* to warm up
calidad *f.* quality
caliente *adj.* hot
calificación f. grade
calificar *v.t.* to grade
calificarse *v. pron.* to qualify
callado/a *adj.* (*person*) quiet
calle *m.* street
callejón *m.* alley
  callejón sin salida dead end, blind alley
calor *m.* heat
caloría *f.* calorie
calvo/a *adj.* bald
calzado *m.* shoes
calzar *v.t.* to take size . . . shoes
  Calzo un 38. I take size 38.
calzarse *v. pron.* to put one's shoes on
calzoncillos *m., pl.* men's underwear
  calzoncillos largos long underwear
cama *f.* bed
cámara *f.* camera
  cámara digital *f.* digital camera
  cámara de video video camera
camarero/a *m.* waiter; *f.* waitress
camarón *m.* shrimp
camarote *m.* (*ship*) cabin
cambiar (de/en) *v.t.* to change
  cambiar de casa to move
  cambiar de marcha to shift gears
cambio *m.* change; exchange rate
  a cambio de in exchange for
  cambio de marchas gearshift
  cambio de moneda currency exchange
  cambio de velocidades gearshift

en cambio on the other hand
camello *m.* camel
camerino *m.* (*theater*) dressing room
camilla *f.* stretcher
caminar *v.i.* to walk
camino *m.* road, path
De camino a casa, me perdí. On my way home, I got lost.
camión *m.* truck
camionero/a *m., f.* truck driver
camioneta *f.* pickup truck
camisa *f.* shirt
camiseta *f.* t-shirt
campana *f.* bell
campeón, campeona *m., f.* champion
campeonato *m.* championship
campestre *adj.* rural
campo *m.* countryside; field
la gente del campo country people
campo de fútbol soccer field
campo de golf golf course
cana *f.* gray hair
echar una cana al aire *idiom.* to let one's hair down
canadiense *adj./m., f.* Canadian
canal *m.* (TV) channel
canario *m.* canary
cancha *f.* court, field
canción *f.* song
candidato/a *m., f.* candidate
candidato a la presidencia presidential candidate
canela *f.* cinnamon
cangrejo *m.* crab
canguro *m.* kangaroo
cansado/a (*de + inf.*) *adj.* tired (of + *gerund*)
Estoy cansado de esperar. I'm tired of waiting.
cansancio *m.* fatigue
cansarse *v. pron.* to tire oneself out
cantante *m., f.* singer
cantar *v.t.* to sing
cantidad *f.* amount
cantimplora *f.* water bottle, canteen
caña *f.* cane
caña de azúcar sugar cane
caña de pescar fishing rod
cañería *f.* pipe
capacitación *f.* training
capilla *f.* chapel
capital *m.* (*finance*) capital
capital *f.* capital city
capítulo *m.* chapter
capó *m.* (*car*) hood
capricho *m.* whim
cápsula *f.* capsule
capturar *v.t.* to capture
cara *f.* face
cara a cara face to face
¡Caramba! *interj.* Darn! Shoot! Gosh!
caracol *m.* snail
caradura *adj./m., f.* cheeky (*person*)
¡Qué cara más dura tienes! You've got some nerve!
caravana *f.* trailer
carbohidrato *m.* carbohydrate
carbón *m.* coal
carburador *m.* carburator
cárcel *f.* prison, jail
cardiología *f.* cardiology
carencia *f.* lack, (*supplies, food*) shortage

caribeño/a *adj./m., f.* Caribbean (person)
caricia *f.* caress
caries *f.* (*sing. or pl.*) cavity, cavities
cariño *m.* affection
cariñoso/a *adj.* affectionate, loving
carisma *m.* charisma
carne *f.* meat
carne de res beef
carne picada/molida ground beef
carnicería *f.* butcher shop
carnicero/a *m., f.* butcher
carnívoro/a *adj.* carnivorous; *m., f.* carnivore
caro/a *adj.* expensive
carpeta *f.* folder
carpintería *f.* carpenter's workshop; (*activity*) carpentry
carpintero/a *m., f.* carpenter
carrera *f.* (*profession*) career; (*sports*) race
a la carrera on the run
carrera ciclista bicycle race
carrera contra reloj time trial
carrera de caballos horse race
carrera de fondo long-distance race
carrera de obstáculos obstacle course
carrera de relevos relay race
carrera pedestre foot race
Está en la cima de su carrera. She's at the peak of her career.
carretera *f.* highway
carretilla *f.* wheelbarrow
carril *m.* (*highway*) lane
carro *m.* (*L.A.*) automobile, car; (*Spain*) cart
carro de bomberos fire engine
carro de carreras racecar
carro deportivo sports car
carroza *f.* (*carnival*) float
carta *f.* letter; (*playing*) card
cartel *m.* poster
cartera *f.* wallet
cartero/a *m., f.* mail carrier
casa *f.* house; home
casa de apartamentos apartment building
en casa at home
casado/a *adj.* married
casar *v.t.* to marry
casarse (con) *v. pron.* to get married (to)
cascanueces *m., sing.* nutcracker
casco *m.* helmet
casero/a *adj.* (*meal*) homemade, home style
casi *adv.* almost
caso *m.* case
el caso es que the thing is that
en caso de in case of
caspa *f.* dandruff
castaña *f.* chestnut
castaño/a *adj.* (*hair, eyes*) brown
castellano *m.* (*language*) Spanish, Castilian
castellano/a *adj./m., f.* Castilian
castigar *v.t.* to punish

castigo *m.* punishment
castillo *m.* castle
casualidad *f.* chance, coincidence
por (pura) casualidad by (sheer) chance
¡Qué casualidad! What a coincidence!
catarata *f.* waterfall
catarro *m.* cold
catástrofe *f.* catastrophe
catastrófico/a *adj.* catastrophic
catedral *f.* cathedral
como una catedral (*fam.*) huge, enormous
una mentira como una catedral a whopper of a lie
catedrático/a *m., f.* professor; department head
categoría *f.* category
de categoría fine, first-rate, excellent
un restaurante de categoría a first-rate restaurant
un escritor de poca categoría a second-rate writer
católico/a *adj./m., f.* Catholic
catorce fourteen
cava *m.* sparkling wine
caverna *f.* cavern
cavernícola *adj./m., f.* cave dweller; caveman
caza *f.* (*sport*) hunting
cazador(a) *m., f.* hunter
cazar *v.t.* to hunt
cazuela *f.* casserole
cebolla *f.* onion
cebra *f.* zebra
paso cebra (*Spain*) crosswalk
ceder *v.t.* to give in; to give way
ceder el paso to yield (the right of way)
Discutieron hasta que el más sensato cedió. They argued until the most sensible one gave in.
cederrón *m.* CD-ROM
cedro *m.* cedar
ceja *f.* eyebrow
celebrar *v.t.* to celebrate
celos *m., pl.* jealousy
Tiene celos de su hermanita. She is jealous of her little sister.
celoso/a *adj.* jealous
célula *f.* cell
celular *adj.* (*phone*) cellular
celulitis *f.* cellulite
cementerio *m.* cemetery
cemento *m.* cement
cena *f.* dinner, supper
cenar *v.i.* to have dinner, to dine
¿Qué hay para cenar? What's for dinner?
cenicero *m.* ashtray
ceniza *f.* ash
censo *m.* census
censura *f.* censorship; censure
censurar *v.t.* to censor; to censure
centro *m.* center; (*city*) downtown
centro comercial shopping mall/center
centro de gravedad center of gravity

centro de atención center of attention
cepillar *v.t.* to brush
cepillarse (el pelo/los dientes) *v. pron.* to brush one's hair/teeth
cepillo *m.* brush
cepillo de dientes toothbrush
cepillo de pelo hairbrush
cera *f.* wax
cerámica *f.* pottery
ceramista *m., f.* ceramist
cerca de *adv.* near
cercano/a *adj.* near; (*relative*) close
Cercano Oriente Near East
cerdo *m.* (*animal*) pig; (*meat*) pork
cereales *m., pl.* cereal; grains
cerebro *m.* brain
cereza *f.* cherry
cerezo *m.* cherry tree
cerilla *f.* match
cero *m.* zero
cerrado *p.p. of* **cerrar** closed
cerrado/a *adj.* closed
cerrajero/a *m., f.* locksmith
cerrajería *f.* locksmith's shop
cerrar (e:ie) *v.t.* to close
cerrarse (e:ie) *v. pron.* to close
La puerta se cerró lentamente. The door closed slowly.
cerrojo *m.* (*lock*) bolt
correr/echar el cerrojo to bolt the door
certeza *f.* certainty
cerveza *f.* beer
césped *m.* grass
cesta *f.* basket
ceviche *m.* marinated fish dish
ceviche de camarón marinated shrimp
chal *m.* shawl
chaleco *m.* vest
champán *m.* champagne
champiñón *m.* mushroom
champú *m.* shampoo
chantaje *m.* blackmail
chantajear *v.t.* to blackmail
chantajista *m., f.* blackmailer
chaqueta *f.* jacket
charlatán, charlatana *m., f.* chatterbox; *adj.* talkative
chau *fam.* bye
cheque *m.* (*bank*) check
cheque de viajero traveler's check
cheque en blanco blank check
chequeo (médico) *m.* (*L.A.*) physical exam
chévere *adj., fam.* terrific, great, cool
chicle *m.* chewing gum
chico/a *m.* boy; *f.* girl
chimenea *f.* chimney; fireplace
chino *m.* (*language*) Chinese
chino/a *adj./m., f.* Chinese
chismes *m., pl.* gossip
chiste *m.* joke
chistoso/a *adj.* funny, amusing
chocar (con, contra) *v.i.* to crash, to collide; to run into; to hit (*a car*); to dislike **(me choca)**
chocolate *m.* chocolate
chofer/chófer *m.* chauffeur, driver

choque *m.* collision; (crash) car accident
chuleta *f. (food)* chop
chuleta de cerdo pork chop
cibercafé *m.* cybercafé
cicatriz *f.* scar
cicatrizar *v.i.* to scar, to heal
ciclismo *m.* cycling
ciclista *m., f.* cyclist
ciego/a *adj.* blind
a ciegas *adv.* blindly
cielo *m.* sky; heaven
¡Cielos! Good heavens!
cien(to) one hundred
cientos de miles hundreds of thousands
por ciento percent
Es cien por cien(to) algodón. It's pure cotton.
ciénaga *f.* swamp
ciencia *f.* science
(...de) ciencia ficción science-fiction (*genre*)
ciencias exactas exact sciences
científico/a *adj.* scientific; *m., f.* scientist
cierto/a *adj.* certain; true
(No) Es cierto. It's (not) true.
por cierto by the way
ciervo *m.* deer
cifra *f.* (*arithmetic*) figure, number
cigüeña *f.* stork
cilindro *m.* cylinder
cima *f.* top, summit; peak
cimientos *m., pl.* (*house, building*) foundations
cinco five
cincuenta fifty
cine *m.* movie theater; movies
cine mudo silent movies
cine negro film noir
cineasta *m., f.* filmmaker, director
cinta *f.* (*audio*) tape; ribbon
Siempre lleva una cinta en el pelo. She always wears a ribbon in her hair.
cinta caminadora *f.* treadmill
cintura *f.* waist
cinturón *m.* belt
cinturón de seguridad seat belt
ciprés *m.* cypress
circo *m.* circus
circuito *m.* (*electric*) circuit
circuito en serie series circuit
circuito cerrado closed circuit
circulación *f.* circulation; traffic
circulación sanguínea blood circulation
círculo *m.* circle
ciruela *f.* plum
cirugía *f.* surgery
cirujano/a *m., f.* surgeon
cisne *m.* swan
cita *f.* date; appointment
cítrico/a *adj.* citrus
ciudad *f.* city
ciudad natal hometown
ciudadanía *f.* citizenship
ciudadano/a *m., f.* citizen
civilización *f.* civilization
civilizado/a *adj.* civilized
claro/a *adj.* clear; (*color*) light
¡Claro! *interj.* Of course!

¡Claro que sí! *(fam.)* Of course!
clase *f.* class
clase de ejercicios aeróbicos aerobics class
clase alta/baja upper/lower class
clase media middle class
clase trabajadora working class
clásico/a *adj.* classical
clausura *f.* closing
ceremonia de clausura closing ceremony
clavado *m.* (*L.A.*) (*high*) dive
clavel *m.* carnation
clavícula *f.* clavicle
clavo *m.* nail
dar en el clavo *idiom.* to hit the nail on the head
cliente/a *m., f.* customer
clientela *f.* clientele, customers
clima *m.* climate
climatizado/a *adj.* (*place, room*) air-conditioned
climatología *f.* climatology
clínica *f.* clinic
cloaca *f.* sewer
cloro *m.* chlorine
clorofila *f.* chlorophyll
clóset *m.* closet
coartada *f.* alibi
cobarde *adj.* coward
cobardía *f.* cowardice
cobertizo *m.* shed
cobija *f.* (*L.A.*) blanket
cobrar *v.t. (check)* to cash; (*rent*) to charge for; (*salary*) to earn
El dueño de mi casa no me cobra la electricidad. My landlord doesn't charge me for electricity.
Cobro una miseria. I earn a pittance.
cobre *m.* copper
cocer (o:ue) (c:z) *v.t.* to boil, to cook
cocer a fuego lento to simmer
coche *m.* (*Spain*) car; automobile
coche bomba car bomb
coche cama sleeper, sleeping car
cocina *f.* kitchen; (*Spain*) stove
cocinar *v.t.* to cook
cocinero/a *m., f.* cook; chef
coco *m.* coconut
codo *m.* elbow
codorniz *f.* quail
cofre *m.* (*car*) hood
cohete *m.* rocket
cohete espacial space rocket
coincidencia *f.* coincidence
¡Qué coincidencia! What a coincidence!
coincidir *v.i.* to coincide, to match up
cojín *m.* cushion
cojo/a *adj.* (*person*) lame
col *f.* (*Spain*) cabbage
cola *f.* line; (*animal*) tail
cola de caballo pony tail
hacer cola to line up; to stand in line
colaboración *f.* collaboration
colaborar *v.i.* to collaborate
colador *m.* colander

colar (o:ue) *v.t.* to strain, to drain; **colar café** (*L.A.*) to make coffee
colarse (o:ue) (en una fiesta) *v. pron.* to crash (a party)
colchón *m.* mattress
colchón de agua water bed
colchón de muelles spring mattress
coleccionar *v.t.* to collect (*as hobby*)
coleccionismo *m.* collecting
coleccionista *m., f.* collector
colegio *m.* school
colesterol *m.* cholesterol
colgar (o:ue) *v.t.* to hang
colibrí *m.* humming bird
cólico *m.* colic
collar *m.* necklace
colmillo *m.* fang; (*in humans*) eye tooth
colmo: ¡Esto es el colmo! *loc.* That's the last straw!
colocación *f.* placing; arrangement
colocar *v.t.* to place, to put; to arrange
colonia *f.* cologne
colonización *f.* colonization, settling
colonizar *v.t.* to colonize
colono *m.* colonist; settler
coloquio *m.* discussion, talk
color *m.* color
colorear *v.t.* to color
columna *f.* column
columna vertebral spinal column, spine
combustible *m.* fuel
comedia *f.* comedy; play
comedor *m.* dining room
comenzar (e:ie) *v.t./v.i.* to begin
comer *v.t./v.i.* to eat; to have lunch
comercial *adj.* (*movie*) commercial; (*district, operation*) business-related; *m.* (*L.A.*) commercial, advertisement
comestible *adj.* edible
comestibles *m., pl.* groceries
cometa *f.* kite; *m.* comet
comida *f.* food; meal
comida basura junk food
comida rápida fast food
comienzo *m.* beginning
a comienzos de at the beginning of
al comienzo at first, in the beginning
comisaría (de policía) *f.* police station
como *prep.* like, as
Anda despacio como una tortuga. She walks as slowly as a turtle.
Es tan alto como su padre. He's as tall as his father.
Quiero un carro como el tuyo. I want a car like yours.
¿cómo? *adv.* how?; what?
¿Cómo es...? What's . . . like?
¿Cómo está Ud.? *form.* How are you?
¿Cómo estás? *fam.* How are you?
¿Cómo les fue...? *pl.* How did . . . go for you?
¿Cómo se llama Ud.? (*form.*) What's your name?

¿Cómo te llamas (tú)? (*fam.*) What's your name?
cómoda *f.* chest of drawers, dresser
cómodo/a *adj.* comfortable
compañerismo *m.* camaraderie
compañero/a *m., f.* companion; partner; mate
compañero/a de clase classmate
compañero/a de cuarto roommate
compañía *f.* company; firm
El perro me hace compañía. My dog keeps me company.
comparación *f.* comparison
en comparación con compared to/with
comparar *v.t.* to compare
compartir *v.t.* to share
compás *m.* (*tool*) compass; (*music*) beat, rhythm
competencia *f.* (*L.A.*) competition, contest
competente *adj.* competent
competidor(a) *m., f.* competitor
competir (e:i) *v.i.* to compete
competitivo/a *adj.* competitive
complejo/a *adj.* complex
completamente *adv.* completely
complicar *v.t.* to complicate, to make difficult
cómplice *m., f.* accomplice
comportamiento *m.* behavior
comportarse *v. pron.* to behave oneself
compositor(a) *m., f.* composer
compra(s) *f.* buy, purchase
ir de compras to go shopping
la lista de la compra the shopping list
una buena/mala compra a good/bad buy
comprar *v.t.* to buy
comprender *v.t.* to understand
comprensión *f.* understanding
comprobar *v.t.* **(o:ue)** to check
comprometerse (a/con) *v. pron.* to promise (to); to get engaged (to)
Se comprometió a limpiar todas las ventanas. He promised to clean all the windows.
compromiso *m.* commitment; engagement
computación *f.* computer science
computadora *f.* computer
computadora portátil portable computer; laptop
común *adj.* common, shared
comunicación *f.* communication
comunicar *v.t.* to communicate
comunicarse (con) *v. pron.* to communicate (with)
comunidad *f.* community
con *prep.* with
Con él/ella habla. This is he/she. (*on the telephone*)
con tal (de) que provided (that)
conciencia *f.* conscience
a conciencia *adv.* conscientiously
concierto *m.* concert
concordar (con) *v.i.* to agree (with)

concreto *m.* (*L.A.*) concrete
concursar *v.i.* (*contest*) to participate, to take part
concurso *m.* contest; game show
condensar *v.t.* to condense
conducir (c:zc) *v.i.* to drive
conducta *f.* conduct, behavior
conductor(a) *m., f.* chauffeur; driver
conejo *m.* rabbit
conferencia *f.* lecture
confiado/a *adj.* (*person*) trusting
confianza *f.* confidence; trust
en confianza *adv.* in confidence
No le tengo mucha confianza. I don't trust him much.
Es una persona de confianza. She's a trustworthy/reliable person.
confiar (en alguien) *v.t.* to trust (somebody)
Confía en mí. Trust me.
confirmación *f.* confirmation
confirmar *v.t.* to confirm
confirmar una reservación to confirm a reservation
confort *m.* comfort
confortable *adj.* comfortable
confundido/a *adj.* confused
confundir *v.t.* to confuse
confusión *f.* confusion
confuso/a *adj.* (*idea, text*) confused, hazy
Su explicación fue muy confusa. His explanation was very confused.
congelador *m.* freezer
congestionado/a *adj.* (*medicine*) congested; stuffed-up
congreso *m.* conference
conmemoración *f.* commemoration, remembrance
en conmemoración de in memory of
conmemorar *v.t.* to commemorate
conmigo with me
conocer (c:zc) *v.t.* to know; to be acquainted with; to meet
conocido/a *adj.* (well-)known; familiar
conquista *f.* conquest
conquistador(a) *m., f.* conqueror
conquistar *v.t.* to conquer
consecuencia *f.* consequence
en consecuencia *adv.* consequently, as a result, therefore; (*to act*) accordingly
conseguir (e:i) *v.t.* to get; to obtain
consejero/a *m., f.* counselor; advisor
consejo *m.* advice
dar consejos to give advice
consenso *m.* consensus
consentido/a *adj.* spoiled (person)
consentimiento *m.* consent, permission
consentir (e:ie) *v.t.* to consent to, to permit
conserje *m., f.* (*hotel*) receptionist

conservación *f.* (*culinary*) preserving; (*environment*) conservation, protection
conservador(a) *adj./m., f.* conservative
conservar *v.t.* (*culinary*) to preserve; to conserve
considerado/a *adj.* (*person*) considerate
constelación *f.* constellation
constitución *f.* constitution
constructor(a) (de obras) *m., f.* builder, building contractor
construir (y) *v.t.* to build
consulado *m.* consulate
consultar *v.t.* (*dictionary, facts*) to look up
consultorio *m.* doctor's office
consumidor(a) *m., f.* consumer
consumir *v.t.* consume
consumir alcohol to consume alcohol
consumo *m.* consumption, intake
contabilidad *f.* accounting
contador(a) *m., f.* accountant
contagiar *v.t.* (*disease*) to pass on
contagio *m.* contagion
contagioso/a *adj.* contagious
contaminación *f.* pollution; contamination
contaminación del aire/del agua air/water pollution
contaminado/a *m., f.* polluted
contaminar *v.t.* to pollute
contar (o:ue) *v.t.* to count; to tell
Contamos contigo. We count on you.
contemplar *v.t.* to contemplate, to gaze at
contemporáneo/a *adj.* contemporary
contentarse (con) *v. pron.* to be pleased (with), to be happy (with)
contento/a *adj.* happy; content
contestadora *f.* answering machine
contestar *v.t.* to answer
contigo with you
Contigo o sin ti. With or without you.
continuar *v.t.* **(yo continúo)** to continue
La novela continúa en el segundo tomo. The novel continues in the second volume.
contra *prep.* against
dos contra uno two against one
Estoy totalmente en contra. I'm totally against it.
Chocó contra un árbol. He crashed into a tree.
contradecir (a alguien) *v.t. irreg.* **(yo contradigo)** to contradict (somebody)
contradecirse *v. pron. irreg.* **(yo me contradigo)** to contradict oneself
contradicción *f.* contradiction
contraponer *v.t. irreg.* **(yo contrapongo)** to contrast
contrario *m.* contrary, opposite; *adj.* opposite
al contrario *adv.* on the contrary, quite the opposite

contrarreloj *adj.* timed
a contrarreloj against the clock
contraseña *f.* password
contratar *v.t.* to hire
contrato *m.* contract; lease
contrincante *m., f.* opponent
control *m.* control
control de natalidad birth control
control remoto remote control
controlar *v.t.* to control
convencer (c:z) *v.t.* to convince
convento *m.* convent
conversación *f.* conversation
conversar *v.i.* to talk, to converse, to chat
convertirse (e:ie) (en) *v. pron.* to become; to turn into
convertirse en rana to turn into a frog
convertirse en realidad to come true
convicción *f.* conviction
convincente *adj.* convincing
convivencia *f.* coexistence
convivir *v.i.* (*people*) to live together; (*ideas, ideologies*) to coexist
copa *f.* wineglass; goblet
copiar *v.t.* to copy
coqueta *f.* flirt, coquette
coquetear *v.i.* to flirt
corazón *m.* heart
corbata *f.* tie
corcho *m.* cork
cordero *m.* lamb
cordillera (montañosa) *f.* (mountain) range
cordón *m.* shoelace
coro *m.* choir, chorus
corpulento/a *adj.* (*person*) hefty
correa *m.* belt
corrección *f.* correction; correctness
correcto/a *adj.* correct
corredor(a) (de bolsa) *m., f.* stockbroker
corregir (e:i) (g:j) *v.t.* to correct
correo *m.* post office; mail
correo electrónico e-mail
correr *v.i.* to run; to jog
correspondencia *f.* mail
corrido *p.p. of* **correr** run
corrida (de toros) *f.* bullfight
corriente *f.* (*electricity*) current
corriente alterna alternating current, AC
corriente continua direct current, DC
corriente eléctrica electric current
contra corriente aginst the tide
estar al corriente to be up to date
ponerse al corriente to catch up
seguirle la corriente (a alguien) to humor (somebody), to play along with (somebody)
cortacésped *f.* lawnmower
cortar *v.t.* to chop; to slice; to cut
cortar el pasto to mow the lawn
corte *f.* cut; (*L.A.*) court (of law)

corte longitudinal lengthwise section
Corte Suprema Supreme Court
corte transversal cross section
cortés *adj.* courteous
cortesía *f.* courtesy
cortina *f.* curtain
correr las cortinas to draw the curtains
corto/a *adj.* short (*in length*)
cortocircuito *m.* short circuit
cosa *f.* thing
cosecha *f.* harvest
cosechar *v.t.* to harvest
coser *v.t.* to sew
costa *f.* coastline, coast
costar (o:ue) *f.* to cost
costar un ojo de la cara *idiom* to cost an arm and a leg
costero/a *adj.* coastal
costilla *f.* rib
costumbre *f.* habit, custom
cotillear *v.i.* (*Spain*) to gossip
cotilleo *m.* (*Spain*) gossip
cráneo *m.* skull
cráter *m.* crater
creador(a) *m., f.* creator
crear *v.t.* to create
creativo/a *adj.* creative
crecer (c:zc) *v.i.* to grow
creciente *adj.* increasing, growing
crecimiento *m.* growth
crédito *m.* credit
creer (en) *v.t.* to believe (in); to think
Creo que no. I don't think so.
no creer not to believe
creído *p.p. of* **creer** believed
crema *f.* cream
crema antiarrugas anti-wrinkle cream
crema de afeitar shaving cream
crema hidratante moisturizer
cremallera *f.* zipper
cremoso/a *adj.* creamy
crepúsculo *m.* (*evening*) twilight; (*morning*) dawn
criar *v.t.* (*children*) to raise, to bring up
crimen *m.* crime; murder
crisis *f.* crisis
crisis de los cuarenta midlife crisis
crisis nerviosa nervous breakdown
crisis respiratoria respiratory failure
cristal *m.* crystal; glass
cristalería *f.* glassware
cristiano/a *adj./m., f.* Christian
criticar *v.t.* to criticize
crítico/a *m., f.* critic
crítico de arte art critic
cronometrar *v.t.* to time
cronómetro *m.* chronometer; stopwatch
cruce *m.* crossroads
crucero *m.* cruise
crucigrama *m.* crossword
cruda *f.* (*Mexico*) hangover
tener cruda to have a hangover
crudo/a *adj.* (*food*) raw
crujiente *adj.* crunchy; (*bread*) crusty

cruz *f.* cross
Cruz Roja Red Cross
cruzar *v.t.* to cross
cuaderno *m.* notebook
cuadra *f.* (city) block
cuadrado *m.* square
cuadrilátero *m.* (*boxing*) ring; (*baseball*) home run
cuadro *m.* picture
cuadros, (de) *m., pl.* plaid
una falda de cuadros a plaid skirt
¿cuál(es)? *pron.* which?; which one(s)?; what?
¿Cuál te gusta más? Which one do you like best?
¿Cuál es la fecha (de hoy)? What is the date (today)?
cuando *conj.* when
Cuando estoy triste, canto. When I'm sad, I sing.
de cuando en cuando *loc.* every so often
de vez en cuando *loc.* now and then; from time to time
¿cuándo? *adv.* when?
¿Cuándo terminas? When do you finish?
No sé cuándo termina. I don't know when he finishes.
cuanto: cuanto antes as soon as possible
Envíemela cuanto antes. Send it to me as soon as possible.
¿cuánto/a? *adv.* how much?
¿Cuánto cuesta? How much does it cost?
¿Cuánto tiempo hace que esperas? How long have you been waiting?
¿cuántos/as? *adv.* how many?
¿Cuántos años tienes? How old are you?
cuarenta forty
cuarto *m.* room
cuarto de baño bathroom
cuarto/a *adj., m.* fourth
cuatro four
cuatrocientos/as four hundred
cubertería *f.* cutlery
cubierto *p.p. of* **cubrir** covered
cubiertos *m., pl.* silverware
cubrir *v.t.* to cover
cucaracha *f.* cockroach
cuchara *f.* (*table or large*) spoon
cucharita *f.* teaspoon
cucharón *m.* ladle
cuchillo *m.* knife
cuello *m.* neck
cuenta *f.* bill; account
a fin de cuentas all things considered, after all
A fin de cuentas, es mejor esperar que irse. All things considered, it's better to wait than to leave.
A fin de cuentas, ¿a quién le importa? After all, who cares?
cuenta corriente checking account
cuenta de ahorros savings account
en resumidas cuentas to make a long story short
por mi cuenta on my own
cuentakilómetros *m., sing.* odometer, speedometer
cuento *m.* short story

cuerda *f.* rope
cuero *m.* leather
cuerpo *m.* body
cuestión *f.* issue, matter
Es un experto en cuestiones de historia medieval. He's an expert in matters of medieval history.
cuestionar *v.t.* to question
cuestionarse *v. pron.* to ask oneself
Tenemos que cuestionarnos si es válida la conclusión. We have to ask ourselves if the conclusion is valid.
cuidado *m.* care; *interj.* Watch out!
cuidar *v.t.* to take care of
cuidarse *v. pron.* to take care of oneself
culpa *f.* fault
echar la culpa a alguien to blame someone
tener la culpa to be to blame
culpable *adj.* guilty; *m., f.* guilty person
culpar *v.t.* to blame
cultivar *v.t.* to grow
cultura *f.* culture
Tiene mucha cultura. She's a highly educated person.
culturismo *m.* bodybuilding
cumpleaños *m., sing.* birthday
cumplir años *v.t.* to have a birthday
¿Cuántos años cumples? How old are you?
cumplir (con) *v.i.* (*duty*) to carry out
Cumplí con mi deber. I did my duty.
cuna *f.* cradle
cuñado/a *m.* brother-in-law; *f.* sister-in-law
cura *f.* cure; *m.* priest
curar *v.t.* to cure
curita *f.* adhesive bandage
currículum *m.* (*Spain*) résumé; curriculum vitae
curso *m.* course
curva *f.* curve, bend
curva peligrosa sharp bend
custodiar *v.t.* to guard
cutis *m.* skin, complexion
limpieza de cutis skin cleansing

D

dados *m., pl.* (*game*) dice
dama *f.* lady
damas (chinas) *f., pl.* (*game*) checkers
danza *f.* dance
dañar *v.t.* to damage; to harm; to break down
dañarse *v. pron.* to get damaged; (*food*) to go bad
dañino/a *adj.* harmful
daño *m.* damage, harm
dar *v.t. irreg.* **(yo doy)** to give
dar a luz (a) to give birth (to)
dar de comer to feed
dar direcciones to give directions
dar en el clavo *idiom* to hit the nail on the head
dar lo mismo to not matter
dar un consejo to give advice
dar un paseo to go for a walk
dar vuelta to turn

Me da lo mismo si vienes o no. It doesn't matter to me if you come or not.

dardos *m., pl.* (*game*) darts

darse con *v. pron. irreg.* to bump into; to run into

darse cuenta de (que) to realize, to become aware of

Gustavo se dio cuenta de que tenía que salir por la puerta de atrás. Gustavo realized he would have to leave by the back door.

darse prisa to hurry (up); to rush

darse vuelta to turn

de *prep.* of; from

¿de quién(es)? whose?

¿De dónde eres? *fam.* Where are you from?

¿De dónde es Ud.? *form.* Where are you from?

¿De parte de quién? Who is calling? (*on telephone*)

de ida y vuelta roundtrip

de repente suddenly, all of a sudden

debajo de *prep.* below; under

debate *m.* debate

debatir *v.t.* to debate

deber (+ *inf.*) *v. aux.* to have to; should; must

Deberías salir más temprano. You should leave earlier.

deber *m.* responsibility; obligation; duty

Tu deber es esperar aquí. Your duty is to wait here.

deberes *m., pl.* homework

debido *adj.* appropriate

a su debido tiempo in due course

con el debido respeto with all due respect

debido a (que) *loc.* due to, owing to (the fact that); because of

No hubo partido debido a la lluvia. There was no match because of the rain.

débil *adj.* weak

década *f.* decade

la década de los sesenta the sixties

decadencia *f.* decadence; decline

decaer *v. irreg.* (**yo decaigo**) to decay, to decline; to deteriorate

decano/a *m., f.* (*university*) dean

decepcionado/a *adj.* disappointed

decepcionarse *v.t.* to be disappointed

decidido *p.p. of* **decidir** decided

decidido/a *adj.* (*person*) determined

decidir (+ *inf.*) *v.t.* to decide

decidirse *v. pron.* to make up one's mind

¡Decídete de una vez! Come on, make up your mind!

décimo/a *adj.* tenth

decir *m.* a saying

Es sólo un decir. It's just a manner of speaking.

decir *v.t.* **(e:i)** to say; to tell

¿Diga? Hello? (*on the telephone*)
No me diga(s). You don't say.
decisión *f.* decision
tomar una decisión to make a decision
declarar *v.t.* to declare; to say
decorado *m.* (*theater*) set
decorar *v.t.* to decorate; (*food*) to garnish
dedicación *f.* dedication
dedicar *v.t.* to dedicate
dedicatoria *f.* dedication
dedo *m.* finger; (*del pie*) toe
defecto *m.* fault, defect
defectuoso/a *adj.* faulty, defective
defender *v.t.* to defend, to protect
defensa *f.* defense
defensa personal self-defense
deficiencia *f.* deficiency, shortcoming
déficit *m.* deficit
definición *f.* definition
definir *v.t.* to define
deforestación *f.* deforestation
defunción *f.* death
dejar *v.t.* to let; to quit; to leave (behind); to drop off; to allow
dejar una propina to leave a tip
dejar de (+ *inf.*) *v.i.* to stop (*doing something*)
del (*contraction of* de + el) of the; from the
delantal *m.* apron
delante de *prep.* in front of
deleite *m.* delight
delfín *m.* dolphin
delgado/a *adj.* thin; slender
delicioso/a *adj.* delicious
delincuencia *f.* crime, delinquency
delincuente *m., f.* criminal
delineante *m.* draftsman, *f.* draftswoman
delinear *v.t.* to deliniate; to outline
delito *m.* crime, offense
demás (lo/los/las) *pron.* the rest
demasiado *adv.* too much
democracia *f.* democracy
demócrata *m., f.* democrat
democrático/a *adj.* democratic
demostración *f.* proof
demostrar *v.t.* to prove
densidad *f.* density
dentadura *f.* teeth
dentadura postiza false teeth
tener buena/mala dentadura to have good/bad teeth
dentista *m., f.* dentist
dentro *adv.* (*space*) inside
dentro de within
Llámame dentro de dos horas. Call me within two hours.
denuncia *f.* report
denunciar *v.t.* (*crime*) to report
departamento *m.* department
depender (de) *v.t.* to depend (on)
Eso no depende de mí. That doesn't depend on me.
dependiente/a *m., f.* clerk
depilarse *v.t.* (*eyebrows*) to pluck; (*legs*) to shave, to wax

deporte *m.* sport
deportista *m., f.* sports person
deportivo/a *adj.* sports-loving, sports-related
depositar *v.t.* to deposit
depósito *m.* tank
depósito de gasolina gas tank
depredador(a) *adj.* predatory
depredador *m.* predator
depresión *f.* depression
deprimido/a *adj.* depressed
deprimirse *v. pron.* to get depressed
derecha *f.* right
a la derecha (de) to the right (of)
derecho/a *adj.* straight
derecho *adv.* straight (ahead)
(todo) derecho straight ahead
Siga (todo) derecho. Keep on going straight.
derechos *m., pl.* rights
deriva *f.* drift
a la deriva adrift
dermatólogo/a *m., f.* dermatologist
derramar *v.t.* (*liquid*) to spill
derramarse *v. pron.* (*liquid*) to spill over, to run over
derrame *m.* spillage; (*medical*) hemorrhage
derretir *v.t.* to melt
El calor derritirá la mantequilla. The heat will melt the butter
derretirse *v. pron.* to melt
El helado se derritió. The ice cream melted.
derrota *f.* defeat
derrotar *v.t.* to defeat, to beat (*an opponent*)
desactivar *v.t.* to defuse
desafiar *v.t.* to challenge
desafinado/a *adj.* out of tune
desafío *m.* challenge
desafortunadamente *adv.* unfortunately
desagradecido/a *adj.* ungrateful
desagüe *m.* wastepipe, drainpipe
desanimado/a *adj.* downhearted
desaparecer *v.t.* to disappear
desaparecido/a *adj.* missing
desaparición *f.* disappearance
desarreglado/a *adj.* unkempt, messy
desarrollar *v.t.* to develop
desarrollo *m.* development
desastre *m.* disaster
desastre natural natural disaster
desastroso/a *adj.* disastrous
desatascar *v.t.* to unblock, to clear
desayunar *v.t.* to have breakfast
desayuno *m.* breakfast
descafeinado/a *adj.* decaffeinated
descalificación *f.* (*sports*) disqualification
descalificar *v.* (*sports*) to disqualify
descalzarse *v. pron.* to take off one's shoes
descampado *m.* open ground

en un descampado in/on open ground
descansar *v.i.* to rest
descanso *m.* rest
descapotable *adj./m.* (*automobile*) convertible
descarga *f.* (*electricity*) discharge
descarga eléctrica electric shock
descargar *v.t.* to download
descarrilamiento *m.* derailment
descarrilar *v.t.* to derail
descender *v.i.* to descend
descendiente *m., f.* descendant
descenso *m.* descend; (*temperatures, prices*) fall, decline, decrease
descifrar *v.t.* to decipher, to decode
descompuesto/a *adj. (L.A.)* not working; out of order
desconfiado/a *adj.* distrustful
desconfiar (de alguien) *v.i.* distrust
descontar *v.t.* to discount; to give a discount
descremado/a *adj.* (*dairy products*) skimmed
describir *v.t.* to describe
descrito/a *p.p.* of **describir** described
descubierto *p.p. of* **descubrir** discovered
descubrimiento *m.* discovery
descubrir *v.t.* to discover
descuento *m.* discount
desde *prep.* from; *conj.* since
Les llamé desde Japón. I called them from Japan.
¿Desde cuándo lo sabes? Since when have you known it?
desear *v.t.* to wish, to desire
desechable *adj.* disposable
desechar *v.t.* (*leftovers*) to throw away
desembocadura *f.* (*river*) mouth
desempacar *v.t./intrans.* to unpack
desempleo *m.* unemployment
desengañar *v.t.* to disillusion
desengaño *m.* disappointment
desenvolver (o:ue) *v.t.* to unwrap
deseo *m.* desire, wish
desértico/a *adj.* pertaining to the desert, desert-like
desesperación *f.* desperation
desesperado/a *adj.* desperate
desesperanza *f.* despair
desesperar *v.t.* to exasperate
La lentitud del tren le desesperó. The slowness of the train exasperated him.
desesperarse *v. pron.* to despair, to give up hope
No te desesperes; todo saldrá bien. Don't give up hope; everything will be fine.
desfavorable *adj.* unfavorable
desfile *m.* parade
desgraciado/a *adj.* unhappy, unfortunate; *m., f.* wretch
desgracia *f.* misfortune
desgraciadamente *adv.* unfortunately

deshelar (e:ie) *v.t.* to defrost
deshelarse (e:ie) *v. pron.* (*ice*) to melt; (*river, lake*) to thaw
deshidratar *v.t.* to dehydrate
deshielo *m.* thaw
deshonesto/a *adj.* dishonest
desierto *m.* desert
desigualdad *f.* inequality
desilusionado/a *adj.* disappointed
desinfectante *adj./m.* disinfectant
desinfectar *v.t.* to disinfect
desintoxicación *f.* detoxification
desintoxicar *v.t.* to detoxify
desmayarse *v. pron.* to faint
desnatado/a *adj.* (*dairy products*) skimmed
desobedecer *v.t.* to disobey
desodorante *m.* deodorant
desordenado/a *adj.* disorderly
despacio *adv.* slowly
despedida *f.* farewell; good-bye
despedir (e:i) *v.* to fire
despedirse (de) (e:i) *v. pron.* to say good-bye (to)
despegar *v.i.* (*airplane, rocket*) to take-off
despegue *m.* (*airplane, rocket*) takeoff
despeinado/a *adj.* disheveled, unkempt
despejado/a *adj.* (*sky*) clear
despensa *f.* pantry
despertador *m.* alarm clock
despertarse (e:ie) *v. pron.* to wake up
despistado/a *adj.* absent-minded, forgetful; *m., f.* scatterbrain
desplazamiento *m.* movement; trip
desplazarse *v. pron.* to move (*from one place to another*); to travel
después (de) *adv.* afterwards; then
después de after
después de que after
destacar *v.t.* to emphasize, to stress
destino *m.* destination, destiny
destornillador *m.* screwdriver
destrucción *f.* destruction
destruir (y) *v.t.* to destroy
desventaja *f.* disadvantage
desvestirse (e:i) *v. pron.* to get undressed, to undress
detalle *m.* detail
detallista *adj./m., f.* perfectionist
detención *f.* arrest
detener *v.t. irreg.* **(yo detengo)** (*vehicle*) to stop; (*person*) to arrest
detenido *p.p. of* **detener** arrested
detenido/a *adj.* detained; under arrest
estar detenido to be under arrest
detractor(a) *m., f.* detractor; critic
detrás de *adv.* behind
devolución f. (*purchase*) return; (*money*) refund
devolver (o:ue) *v.t.* to take back; to return (*merchandise*)
día *m.* day
día de fiesta holiday

día laborable work day
diabetes *f.* diabetes
diabético/a *adj./m., f.* diabetic
diagnosticar *v.t.* to diagnose
diagnóstico *m.* diagnostic
diálogo *m.* dialogue
diamante *m.* diamond
diapositiva *f.* slide
diario *m.* diary; newspaper
diario/a *adj.* daily
diarrea *f.* diarrhea
dibujar *v.t.* to draw
dibujo *m.* drawing
dibujos animados *m., pl.* (*animated*) cartoons
diccionario *m.* dictionary
dicho *m.* saying
dicho *p.p. of* **decir** said
diciembre *m.* December
dictador(a) *m., f.* dictator
dictadura *f.* dictatorship
diecinueve nineteen
dieciocho eighteen
dieciséis sixteen
diecisiete seventeen
diente *m.* tooth
dieta *f.* diet
a dieta on a diet
comer una dieta equilibrada to eat a balanced diet
diez ten
diferencia *f.* difference
a diferencia de in contrast to, unlike
diferente *adj.* different
difícil *adj.* hard; difficult
dificultad *f.* difficulty, hardship
dificultar *v.t.* to make difficult
difunto/a *m., f.* deceased (*person*)
Diga. Hello. (*on telephone*)
diligencia *f.* errand
dimisión *f.* resignation
dimitir *v.i.* to resign
dinamita *f.* dynamite
dinamitar *v.t.* to dynamite
dinastía *f.* dynasty
dinero *m.* money
dinosaurio *m.* dinosaur
Dios *m.* God
¡Dios me libre! *loc.* Heaven forbid!
diplomático/a *adj.* diplomatic, tactful; *m., f.* diplomat
dirección *f.* address
dirección electrónica *f.* e-mail address
direcciones *f., pl.* directions
directo *adj.* (*fly*) direct, nonstop
en directo *adv.* (*radio, TV*) live
director(a) *m., f.* director; (*musical*) conductor
dirigir *v.t.* to direct
disciplina *f.* discipline; (*university*) subject
disco *m.* (computer) disk
disco compacto compact disc; CD
discoteca *f.* disco(teque)
discreto/a *adj.* discreet, discrete
discriminación *f.* discrimination
disculpa *f.* apology
pedir disculpas to apologize
disculpar *v.t.* to excuse
disculparse (por) *v. pron.* to apologize for
discurso *m.* speech
discusión *f.* argument

discutir *v.t.* to argue; to discuss
diseñador(a) *m., f.* designer
diseño *m.* design
disfraz *m.* costume
disfrazarse de... to wear a... costume
disfrutar (de) *v.t.* to enjoy; to reap the benefits (of)
disfunción *f.* dysfunction
disgusto: a disgusto *adv.* against one's will
Fui, pero a disgusto. I went, but against my will.
disimular *v.t.* to hide; to conceal; to pretend
disminución *f.* decrease
disminuir (y) *v.i.* (*number*) to decrease; *v.t.* (*price, speed*) to reduce
Ha disminuido el número de parados. The number of unemployed people has decreased.
Debes disminuir la velocidad. You have to reduce your speed.
disparar *v.t./v.i.* to shoot, to fire
disparo *m.* shot, gunshot
disponibilidad *f.* availability
disponible *adj.* available
distancia *f.* distance
distinguido/a *adj.* distinguished
distinguir *v.t.* **(yo distingo)** to distinguish
distribución *f.* distribution
distribuir (y) *v.t.* to distribute
divergencia *f.* difference
divergente *adj.* (*opinions*) differing
divergir (e:i) (g:j) *v.i.* to differ
diversión *f.* fun activity; entertainment; recreation
divertido/a *adj.* fun
divertir (e:ie) *v.t.* to entertain
Pepe nos divirtió con sus historias. Pepe entertained us with his stories.
divertirse (e:ie) *v. pron.* to have fun
divisar *v.t.* to sight
divorciado/a *adj.* divorced
divorciarse (de) *v. pron.* to get divorced (from)
divorcio *m.* divorce
divulgación *f.* spreading
divulgar *v.t.* (*news, information*) to spread
El chismoso divulgó la noticia por toda la universidad. The gossip spread the news around the whole university.
doblar *v.t.* (*paper, clothes*) to fold; (*corner*) to turn; (*movie*) to dub
doble *adj.* double
doce twelve
docena *f.* dozen
doctor(a) *m., f.* doctor; physician
doctorado *m.* doctorate; Ph.D.
documental *m.* documentary
documentar *v.t.* to document; to provide evidence for
Estos artículos no documentan nada. These do not provide any evidence.
documentarse *v. pron.* to do research

Tuve que documentarme muy bien para escribir la tesis. I had to do a lot of research to write the thesis.

documento *m.* document
documentos de viaje travel documents

dólar *f.* dollar

doler (o:ue) *v.i.* to hurt
Me duele mucho. It hurts a lot.

dolor *m.* ache; pain
dolor de cabeza headache

doméstico/a *adj.* domestic

dominar *v.t.* to dominate; to master
Aún no domino muy bien el español. I haven't quite mastered Spanish yet.

dominarse *v. pron.* to restrain, to control oneself

domingo *m.* Sunday

dominó *m.* (*game*) dominoes; (*game piece*) domino

don/doña *title of respect used with a person's first name* Mr.; sir/Mrs.; ma'am

dona *f.* donut

donante *m., f.* donor

donde *conj.* where
Están donde las dejaste. They are where you left them.

¿dónde? *adv.* where
¿Dónde está...? Where is...?
¿Dónde están las llaves? Where are the keys?

donjuán *m.* womanizer

dorado/a *adj.* gold, golden

dormir (o:ue) *v.i.* to sleep

dormirse (o:ue) *v. pron.* to go to sleep; to fall asleep; to oversleep
Llego un poco tarde; me dormí. I'm a bit late; I overslept.

dormitorio *m.* bedroom

dos two
dos veces twice; two times

doscientos/as two hundred

drama *m.* drama; play

dramático/a *adj.* dramatic

dramaturgo/a *m., f.* playwright

droga *f.* drug

drogadicto/a *adj.* drug-addicted; *m., f.* drug addict

ducha *f.* shower

ducharse *v. pron.* to shower; to take a shower

duda *f.* doubt
poner en duda to question, to doubt
Nadie pone en duda su talento. Nobody questions his talent.
sin duda undoubtedly, without a doubt

dudar *v.t.* to doubt
no dudar not to doubt

dueño/a *m., f.* owner; landlord

dulce *adj.* sweet

dulces *m., pl.* sweets; candy

duna *f.* dune

duradero/a *adj.* lasting

durante *prep.* during

durar *v.i.* to last
¿Cuánto dura la película? How long is the movie?
El dinero no duró mucho. The money didn't last long.

¿Dura más la piel? Does leather last longer?
durazno *m. (L.A.)* peach
duro/a *adj.* hard

E

e *conj.* (*used instead of* **y** *before words beginning with* **i** *and* **hi**) and
Javier e Inés Javier and Inés
masaje e hidratación massage and moisturizing
ebrio/a *adj.* inebriated, drunk
echar *v.t.* to throw
echar chispas *idiom* to be hopping mad
echar la casa por la ventana *loc.* to go overboard, to pull out all the stops
echar una carta al buzón to put a letter in the mailbox; to mail
echarle flores a alguien *idiom* to flatter someone
eclipse *m.* eclipse
ecología *f.* ecology
ecológico/a *adj.* ecological; (*food*) organic
ecologista *m., f.* environmentalist, ecologist
economía *f.* economics
ecosistema *m.* ecosystem
ecoturismo *m.* ecotourism
ecuador *m.* equator
cruzar el ecuador to cross the equator
ecuatoriano/a *adj.* Ecuadorian
edad *f.* age
edad de piedra Stone Age
edad media Middle Ages
No nos dijo su edad. He didn't tell us his age.
edificio *m.* building
edificio de apartamentos apartment building
educado/a *adj.* polite, well-mannered
educador(a) *m., f.* educator
efectivo *m.* (*money*) cash
en efectivo (in) cash
efecto *m.* effect
bajo los efectos del alcohol under the influence of alcohol
efectos especiales special effects
efecto invernadero greenhouse effect
efecto secundario side effect
en efecto in fact
eficacia *f.* effectiveness
eficaz *adj.* effective
eficiencia *f.* efficiency
eficiente *adj.* efficient
egoísmo *m.* selfishness
egoísta *adj.* selfish
ejemplo *m.* example
ejercicio *m.* exercise
ejercicios aeróbicos aerobic exercise
ejercicios de estiramiento stretching exercises
ejercicios de portugués Portuguese exercises
hacer ejercicio to exercise, to work out
ejército *m.* army
el *m., sing., def. art.* the
él *pron. m. sing.* he; him
elástico/a *adj.* elastic
elección, elecciones *f.* election

electorado *m.* electorate
electricista *m., f.* electrician
electrocutarse *v. pron.* to be electrocuted
electrodoméstico *m.* electric appliance
electrólisis *f.* electrolysis
electrónica *f.* electronics
elefante *m.* elephant
elegante *adj.* elegant
elegir (e:i) (g:j) *v.t.* to elect
elemental *adj.* (*course, level*) elementary
Elemental, amigo Watson. Elementary, my dear Watson.
elevado/a *adj.* (*quantity*) large; (*price*) high
un elevado número de personas a large number of people
un precio elevado a high price
eliminación *f.* elimination
eliminar *v.t.* to eliminate
ella *pron. fem. sing.* she; her
ellos/as *pron. m., f. pl.* they; them
Dáselo a ellos. Give it to them.
elocuencia *f.* eloquence
elocuente *adj.* eloquent
elogiar *v.t.* to praise
elogio *m.* praise
embajada *f.* embassy
embalse *m.* reservoir
embarazada *adj.* pregnant
embarcadero *m.* jetty, wharf
embarcar *v.i.* (*passengers*) to board (*a ship*)
embargo: sin embargo however; yet
embotellamiento (de tráfico) *m.* (*Spain*) traffic jam
embrague *m.* clutch (*pedal*)
embriagado/a *adj.* inebriated, drunk
embudo *m.* funnel
emergencia *f.* emergency
emigración *f.* emigration
emigrante *m., f.* emigrant
emigrar *v.i.* emigrate
emitir *v.t.* to broadcast
emocionado/a *adj.* excited
emocionante *adj.* exciting
empacar *v.t.* to pack
empacharse *v. pron.* to get an upset stomach
empatar *v.i.* (*sports*) to tie
empate *m.* (*sports*) tie
empeorar *v.t.* to get worse; to make worse
Esto empeora la situación. This makes the situation worse.
empezar (e:ie) *v.t.* to begin; to start
para empezar to begin
empleado/a *m., f.* employee
empleo *m.* job, employment
empobrecer (c:zc) *v.t.* to impoverish, to make poor
Las guerras empobrecen los países. Wars impoverish countries.
empobrecerse (c:zc) *v. pron.* to become impoverished, poor
empresa *f.* company; firm; business
empresario/a *m., f.* entrepreneur
empujar *v.t.* to push
en *prep.* in; on

en caso (de) que in case (that)
en cuanto *conj.* as soon as
en qué in what; how
¡En marcha! Forward ho/march!
¿En qué puedo servirles? How may I help you?
en resumidas cuentas *loc.* to make a long story short, in short
en un dos por tres *idiom* in a jiffy
enamorado/a (de) *adj.* in love (with); beloved
enamorarse (de) *v. pron.* to fall in love (with)
encantado/a *adj.* delighted; pleased to meet you
encantador(a) *adj.* charming
encantar *v.t.* to like very much; (*inanimate things*) to love; to enchant
encanto *m.* charm
encarcelar *v.t.* to imprison, to jail
encargar *v.t.* to order
encargo *m.* order
encendedor *m.* lighter
encender *v.t.* to light, to turn on
encerar *v.t.* to polish, to wax
encía *f.* (*dental*) gum
encima de *adv.* on top of
por encima *adv.* (*read*) superficially
encontrar (o:ue) *v.t.* to find
encontrarse (o:ue) *v. pron.* to meet each other; to run into each other; to find each other
encuesta *f.* poll; survey
energía *f.* energy
energía (nuclear/solar) (nuclear/solar) energy
enero *m.* January
énfasis *m.* emphasis
enfatizar *v.t.* to emphasize
enfermarse *v. pron.* to get sick
enfermedad *f.* illness
enfermería *f.* health center
enfermero/a *m., f.* nurse
enfermo/a *adj.* sick
enfocar *v.t.* (*a topic*) to focus on, to look at
El programa enfoca el problema de la falta de vivienda. The program looks at the problem of homelessness.
enfoque *m.* approach
enfrentamiento *m.* clash
enfrentar *v.t.* to confront, to face
Hay que enfrentar la realidad. It's necessary to face reality.
enfrentarse (con) *v. pron.* to confront
El ejército se enfrenterá con el enemigo. The army will confront the enemy.
enfrente *prep.* across from, in front of
enfrente de *adv.* opposite; facing
El ayuntamiento está enfrente de la catedral. The town hall is opposite the cathedral.
enfríar *v.t.* to chill

engañar *v.t.* to deceive, to cheat on
engaño *m.* deception
engordar *v.i.* to gain weight
que no engorda *adj.* non-fattening
engreído/a *adj.* conceited
enigma *m.* enigma, mystery
enigmático/a *adj.* enigmatic, mysterious
enloquecer (c:zc) *v.i.* to go crazy
ennegrecer (c:zc) *v.t.* to blacken
ennegrecerse (c:zc) *v. pron.* to go black, (*sky, clouds*) to darken
enojado/a *adj.* mad; angry; upset
enojar *v.t.* to annoy, to make angry
enojarse (con) *v. pron.* to get angry (with)
enredadera *f.* climbing plant
enriquecer (c:zc) *v.t.* to enrich, to make rich
La lectura enriquece la imaginación. Reading enriches imagination.
enriquecerse (c:zc) *v. pron.* to get rich
ensalada *f.* salad
ensaladera *f.* salad bowl
ensayar *v.t.* to rehearse
ensayo *m.* essay; rehearsal
enseguida *adv.* right away
enseñanza *f.* learning
enseñar *v.t.* to teach; to show
ensuciar *v.t.* to dirty; to get (something) dirty
entender (e:ie) *v.t.* to understand
entierro *m.* burial
entonces *adv.* then
entrada *f.* entrance; (*Spain*) ticket
entrar (en) *v.i.* to enter, to come in
entre *prep.* between; among
entre tú y yo between you and me
entre la multitud among the crowd
entre semana on weekdays
entregar *v.t.* to turn in, to deliver
entremeses *m., pl.* hors d'oeuvres; appetizers
entrenador(a) *m., f.* trainer; coach
entrenamiento *m.* coaching; training
El boxeo requiere mucho entrenamiento. Boxing requires a lot of training.
El entrenamiento duró seis horas. The training lasted six hours.
entrenarse *v. pron.* to practice; to train
entretener *v.t. irreg.* (**yo entretengo**) to entertain
entretenerse *v. pron. irreg.* (**yo me entretengo**) to amuse oneself; to hang about
No te entretengas camino a la escuela. Don't mess around on the way to school.
entretenido/a *adj.* entertaining
entrevista *f.* interview

entrevistador(a) *m., f.* interviewer
entrevistar *v.t.* to interview
entusiasmado/a *adj.* enthusiastic
entusiasmo *m.* enthusiasm
envase *m.* container
envejecer (c:zc) *v.i.* to age, to grow old
envejecimiento *m.* aging
enviar *v.t.* to send; to mail
Te enviaré los libros por correo. I'll mail you the books.
envidioso/a *adj.* envious, jealous
envolver (o:ue) *v.t.* to wrap
papel de envolver wrapping paper
enyesar *v.t.* (*medicine*) to put in a cast
El médico me enyesó el brazo. The doctor put my arm in a cast.
Tengo el brazo enyesado. My arm is in a cast.
equilibrado/a *adj.* balanced
equipado/a *adj.* equipped
equipaje *m.* luggage
equipo *m.* team
equipo local home team
equipo visitante visiting team
equipo de técnicos team of technicians
equitación *f.* (horse) riding
equivalencia *f.* equivalence
equivaler *v.i.* to be equivalent to
equivocación *f.* mistake
equivocado/a *adj.* mistaken; wrong
equivocarse *v. pron.* to make a mistake, to be mistaken
¿Me equivoco al pensar que mientes? Am I mistaken in thinking you're lying?
Nos equivocamos de camino. We went the wrong way.
eres *fam.* you are
ermita *f.* chapel
ermitaño/a *m., f.* hermit
eructar *v.i.* to belch, to burp
eructo *m.* belch, burp
erupción *f.* eruption
hacer erupción (*volcano*) to erupt
es he/she/it is; *form.* you
Es de... He/She is from...
Es la una. It's one o'clock.
Es obvio que... It's obvious that...
escalada *f.* (*mountaineering*) climb, ascent
escalador(a) *m., f.* (*mountaineering*) climber
escalar *v.t.* to climb
escalar montañas to climb mountains
escalera *f.* stairs; stairway
escalera de incendios fire escape
escalera mecánica escalator
escalofrío *m.* shiver
tener escalofríos to be shivering; to have the chills
escalón *m.* step, stair
escandaloso/a *adj.* loud; outrageous

escapada *f.* getaway
escaparate *m.* (*Spain*) shop window
escarcha *f.* frost
escayola *f.* (*Spain*) plaster cast
escayolar *v.* (*Spain*) *trans.* to put in a cast
escenario *m.* stage
escoba *f.* broom
escoger (g:j) *v.t.* choose
esconder *v.t.* to hide
escondidillas *f.* hide-and-seek
escondite, (al) *m.* hide-and-seek
escorpión *m.* scorpion
escribir *v.t./v.i.* to write
escribir a máquina to type
escribir un mensaje electrónico to write an e-mail message
escribir una (tarjeta) postal to write a postcard
escribir una carta to write a letter
escrito *p.p. of* **escribir** written
por escrito *adv.* in writing
escritor(a) *m., f.* writer
escritorio *m.* desk
escuchar *v.t.* to listen (to)
escuchar la radio to listen to the radio
escuchar música to listen to music
escuela *f.* school
escuela pública *f.* public school
escuela de niños/as *f.* all-boys/girls school
esculpir *v.t.* to sculpt
escultor(a) *m., f.* sculptor
escultura *f.* sculpture
escurrir *v.t.* (*dishes*) to drain; (*clothes*) to wring out
ese, esa, esos, esas *dem. adj.* that (by you); those (by you)
ése, ésa, ésos, ésas *dem. pron.* that (one by you); those (by you)
esfera *f.* sphere
esforzarse (o:ue) *v. pron.* to try hard
Debes esforzarte más. You must try harder.
esfuerzo *m.* effort
esgrima *f.* (*sport*) fencing
esgrimidor(a) *m., f.* fencer
esmeralda *f.* emerald
esnob *adj.* snobby; *m., f.* snob
esnobismo *m.* snobbery
esnórkel *m.* snorkel
eso *dem. pron. neuter.* that (by you)
esófago *m.* esophagus
espacio *m.* space
espagueti *m.* spaghetti
espalda *f.* back
No me importa que hablen a mis espaldas. I don't mind them talking behind my back.
España *f.* Spain
español *m.* (*language*) Spanish
español(a) *adj./m., f.* Spanish
espárrago *m.* asparagus
espátula *f.* spatula
especialista *m., f.* specialist
especialización *f.* major (field of study or interest); specialization
especializarse *v. pron.* to specialize
especie *f.* (*biology*) species; type

especie en peligro de extinción endangered species
especie protegida protected species
espectacular *adj.* spectacular
espectáculo *m.* show
espectador(a) *m., f.* spectator
espejo *m.* mirror
esperanza *f.* hope
esperanza de vida life expectancy
esperar (+ *inf.*) *v.t.* to wait (for); to hope; to wish; to expect
espina *f.* (*fish*) bone; (*plant*) thorn
espinaca *f.* spinach
espolvorear *v.t.* (*sugar*) to sprinkle
esponja *f.* sponge
esponjoso/a *adj.* (*pastry*) spongy, soft; (*fabric*) fluffy
espontáneo/a *adj.* spontaneous
esposo/a *m.* husband; *f.* wife; *m., f.* spouse
espuma *f.* foam
esqueleto *m.* skeleton
esquema *m.* outline
esquí (acuático) *m.* (water) skiing
esquiador(a) *m., f.* skier
esquiar *v.i.* to ski
esquina *f.* corner
establecer (c:zc) *v.t.* to establish
establecer una marca mundial to set a world record
establo *m.* stable
estación *f.* station; season
estación de autobuses bus station
estación del metro subway station
estación de tren train station
estacionamiento *m.* parking lot; parking; parking space
estacionar *v.t.* to park
estacionarse *v. pron.* to park
estadio *m.* stadium
estado *m.* state
estado civil marital status
Estados Unidos *m. pl.* (EE.UU.; E.U.) United States
estadounidense *adj./m., f.* from the United States
estafador(a) *m., f.* fraud, con artist
estafar *v.t.* to defraud
estampado/a *adj.* print(ed), patterned
estampilla *f.* stamp
estancia *f.* stay
Nuestra estancia en La Coruña fue magnífica. Our stay in La Coruña was magnificent.
estanque *m.* pond (*man-made*)
estante *m.* bookcase; bookshelf, bookshelves
estar *v.i.* to be
Está bien. That's fine. It's okay.
(no) está nada mal it's not at all bad
estar a (veinte kilómetros) de aquí to be (twenty kilometers) from here
estar a dieta to be on a diet
estar a régimen to be on a diet

estar aburrido/a to be bored
estar afectado/a (por) to be affected (by)
estar bajo control to be under control
estar cansado/a to be tired
estar contaminado/a to be polluted
estar de acuerdo (con) to be in agreement with
estar de acuerdo to agree
no estar de acuerdo to disagree
estar de moda to be in fashion
estar de vacaciones *f., pl.* to be on vacation
estar de vuelta to be back
estar en buena forma to be in good shape
estar en las nubes to be daydreaming
estar enfermo/a to be sick
estar listo/a to be ready
estar perdido/a to be lost
estar roto/a to be broken
estar seguro/a to be sure
estar torcido/a to be twisted; to be sprained
estatua *f.* statue
este *m.* east
al este to the east
este, esta, estos, estas *dem. adj.* this; these
éste, ésta, éstos, éstas *dem. pron.* this (one); these
Éste/Ésta es... This is... *(introducing someone)*
estéreo *m.* stereo
estéril *adj.* sterile
esterilizar *v.t.* to sterilize
esteticista *m., f.* beautician
estetoscopio *m.* stethoscope
estiércol *m.* manure
estilo *m.* style; (*swimming*) stroke, style
algo por el estilo something like that
estilo braza (*Spain*) breaststroke
estilo espalda backstroke
estilo libre freestyle
estilo mariposa butterfly
estilo pecho (*L.A.*) breaststroke
estiramiento *m.* stretching
estirar *v.t.* to stretch
esto *dem. pron. neuter* this; this thing
estómago *m.* stomach
estornudar *v.i.* to sneeze
estrecho/a *adj.* narrow, tight
estrella *f.* star
estrella *m., f.* **de cine** movie star
estrella fugaz shooting star
estrellado/a *adj.* starry
estrenar *v.t.* to wear for the first time; to début
estreno *m.* (*film, play*) premiere
estreñido/a *adj.* constipated
estreñimiento *m.* constipation
estrés *m.* stress
estresado/a adj. under stress
estresante *adj.* (*situation*) stressful
estropear *v.t.* to damage
estropearse *v. pron.* (*automobile*) to break down
estudiante *m., f.* student
estudiantil *adj.* student
estudiar *v.t.* to study

estudioso/a *adj.* studious
estufa *f. (L.A.)* stove
estupendo/a *adj.* stupendous
etapa *f.* stage; step
las etapas de la vida the stages of life
ética *f.* ethics
ético/a *adj.* ethical
euforia *f.* euphoria, elation
eufórico/a *adj.* euphoric
Europa *f.* Europe
europeo/a *adj.* European
evadir *v.t.* (*danger, problem*) to avoid; (*taxes*) to evade
evadirse *v. pron.* (*responsibility, prison*) to escape
Luis se evadió de la responsabilidad. Luis escaped responsibility.
evaluación *f.* assessment; test
evaluar *v.t.* to assess; to test
evasión *f.* escape
evitar *v.t.* to avoid
evolución *f.* evolution
evolucionar *v.i.* to evolve
exageración *f.* exaggeration
exagerar *v.t.* to exaggerate
No exageres el valor de las cosas. Do not exagerate the value of things.
examen *m.* test; exam
examen médico physical exam
excavadora *f.* power shovel, excavator
excavar *v.t.* to dig, to excavate
excelente *adj.* excellent
exceso *m.* excess; too much
en exceso in excess, too much
excursión *f.* hike; tour; excursion
Vamos de excursión. We're going hiking.
excursionista *m., f.* hiker
exhibición de arte *f.* art exhibition
exigir (g:j) *v.t.* to demand
éxito *m.* success
tener éxito to succeed
éxodo *m.* exodus
experiencia *f.* experience
experimentar *v.t.* to experiment; to try out
expiración *f.* expiration
expirar *v.t.* (*time period, contract*) to expire
explicar *v.t.* to explain
explorar *v.t.* to explore
explorar un pueblo to explore a town
explorar una ciudad to explore a city
explosivo/a *adj.* explosive
exponer *v.t. irreg.* **(yo expongo)** (*art*) to exhibit
exportación *f.* exportation
exportar *v.t.* to export
exposición *f.* exhibition
expresión *f.* expression
expresivo/a *adj.* expressive
exprimidor *m.* juicer
expulsar *v.t.* to expel
expulsión *m.* expulsion
extinción *f.* extinction
extinguir *v.t.* **(yo extingo)** (*fire*) to extinguish, to put out
Los bomberos extinguieron el incendio. The firefighters put out the blaze.

extinguirse *v. pron.* **(yo me extingo)** to become extinct; to die out
Su entusiasmo se está extinguiendo poco a poco. Her enthusiasm is dying little by little.
extranjero/a *adj.* foreign; *m., f.* foreigner
en el extranjero abroad
extrañar (algo o a alguien) *v.t.* to miss
extrañarse (de) *v. pron.* to be surprised, to find strange
Me extraña que no te hayas quejado. I'm surprised that you haven't complained.
extraño/a *adj.* strange, odd
Es extraño (que...) It's strange (that...)
Es extraño que tosas tanto. It's strange that you cough so much.
extravagante *adj.* flamboyant
extremidades *f., pl.* (*anatomy*) extremities
extrovertido/a *adj.* extroverted

F

fábrica *f.* factory
fabricación *f.* manufacture
fabricación en serie mass production
fabricante *m., f.* manufacturer
fabricar *v.t.* to manufacture, to produce
fabricar en serie to mass produce
fabuloso/a *adj.* fabulous
fachada *f.* façade
fácil *adj.* easy
facilitar *v.t.* to facilitate, to make easier
faisán *m.* pheasant
falda *f.* skirt
fallecer (c:zc) *v.i.* to pass away
fallecido/a *m., f.* deceased
fallecimiento *m.* death
falta *f.* lack; (*spelling*) mistake
falta de recursos lack of resources
falta de ortografía spelling mistake
faltar *v.t.* to lack; to need
familia *f.* family
familiar *adj.* family; (*known*) familiar
Este lugar me resulta familiar. This place looks familiar.
familiares *m., pl.* relatives
famoso/a *adj.* famous; *m., f.* famous person, celebrity
fango *m.* mud
faringe *f.* pharynx
farmacia *f.* pharmacy
farmacia de guardia 24-hour pharmacy
faro *m.* (*automobile*) headlight
fascinar *v.t.* to fascinate; to love; to be fascinated by
fatigado/a *adj.* weary
fatigarse *v. pron.* to wear oneself out
favorable *adj.* favorable
favorito/a *adj.* favorite
fax *m.* fax (*machine*)
fe *f.* faith
febrero *m.* February
fecha *f.* date

fecha de caducidad expiration date
fecundación *f.* fertilization
fecundar *v.t.* to fertilize
felicidad *f.* happiness
¡Felicidades! Congratulations! (*for an event such as a birthday or anniversary*)
felicitar *v.t.* to congratulate
¡Felicitaciones! Congratulations! (*for an event such as an engagement or a good grade on a test*)
feliz *adj.* happy
¡Feliz cumpleaños! Happy birthday!
fenomenal *adj.* fantastic, great, phenomenal
fenómeno *m.* phenomenon
feo/a *adj.* ugly
ferrocarril *m.* railroad
fértil *adj.* fertile
fertilidad *f.* fertility
fertilizante *m.* fertilizer
festejar *v.t.* to celebrate
festejo *m.* celebration
festival *m.* festival
fiambre *m.* cold cut
fiambrera *f.* (*Spain*) lunch box
fianza *f.* bail
ficha *f.* (*game*) counter, game piece
fidelidad *f.* fidelity; faithfulness
fiebre *f.* fever
fiel *adj.* faithful; loyal
fiesta *f.* party
dar una fiesta to throw a party
fijo/a *adj.* set; fixed; permanent; steady
precio fijo fixed price
trabajo fijo permanent job
fila *f.* row
filatelia *f.* philately, stamp collecting
filmoteca *f.* film library
filología *f.* philology
filólogo/a *m., f.* philologist
filosofar *v.i.* to philosophize
filosofía *f.* philosophy
filósofo/a *m., f.* philosopher
fin *m.* end
fin de semana weekend
a fin de *conj.* in order to
a fines de at the end of
al fin *loc.* at last
al fin y al cabo *loc.* after all
por fin *adv.* at last
final *m.* **end**
al final at the end
a finales de at/toward the end of
finalmente *adv.* finally
financiar *v.t.* to finance
fingir (g:j) *v.t.* to pretend
Fingía no saberlo. She pretended not to know it.
firma *f.* signature
firmar *v.t.* to sign (*a document*)
física *f.* physics
físico/a *m., f.* physicist
flaco/a *adj.* skinny
flamenco/a *adj., m.* (*music*) flamenco
flan (de caramelo) *m.* baked (caramel) custard
flecha *f.* arrow
flexible *adj.* flexible

flexionar *v.t.* to flex
flor *f.* flower
florería *f.* (*L.A.*) flower shop
florero *m.* vase
florero/a *m., f.* (*L.A.*) florist
florista *m., f.* (*Spain*) florist
floristería *f.* (*Spain*) flower shop
flotar *v.i.* to float
fluir (y) *v.i.* to flow
foca *f.* seal
folklórico/a *adj.* folk; folkloric
folleto *m.* brochure
fondo *m.* (*street, corridor*) end; (*sea*) bottom
  a fondo *adv.* completely
  al fondo (de) *adv.* at the end (of)
fondos *m., pl.* (*money*) funds
fonética *f.* phonetics
fonología *f.* phonology
fontanería *f.* (*Spain*) *f.* plumbing
fontanero/a *m., f.* (*Spain*) plumber
forense *m., f.* forensic scientist
forma *f.* shape
  estar en buena/mala forma to be in good/bad shape
formación *f.* training
  formación profesional vocational training
formal *adj.* formal
formar *v.t.* to train
formulario *m.* form
  (re)llenar el formulario fill out the form
fortaleza *f.* fortress
fortuna *f.* fortune
  por fortuna *adv.* fortunately
fósforo *m.* match
fósil *m.* fossil
fosilizarse *v. pron.* to fossilize, to become fossilized
foto(grafía) *f.* photograph
fotocopiadora *f.* photocopier
fotocopiar *v.t.* to photocopy
fotosíntesis *f.* photosynthesis
fracasado/a *adj.* failed, unsuccessful
fracasar *v.i.* to fail
fracaso *m.* failure
frambuesa *f.* raspberry
francés *m.* (*language*) French
francés, francesa *adj./m., f.* French
Francia *f.* France
frase *f.* phrase; sentence
frazada *f.* (*L.A.*) blanket
frecuencia *f.* frequency
  con (mucha) frecuencia frequently, regularly
frecuentemente *adv.* frequently
fregadero (de la cocina) *m.* (kitchen) sink
fregar *v.* (*Spain*) *trans.* to mop
fregona *f.* (*Spain*) mop
frenar *v.i.* to brake
freno *m.* brake
  freno de mano handbrake
frente *f.* (*anatomy*) forehead
fresa *f.* strawberry
fresco/a *adj.* cool, fresh
frijol *m.* bean
frío/a *adj.* cold; chilled
  Sírvase frío. Serve chilled.
fritada *f.* fried dish (*pork, fish, etc.*)
frito/a *adj.* fried
frontera *f.* border, frontier

fronterizo/a *adj.* border
fruta *f.* fruit
frutería *f.* fruit store
frutilla *f.* (*L.A.*) strawberry
fucsia *adj.* fuchsia
fuego *m.* fire
  fuegos artificiales *m., pl.* fireworks
fuente *f.* platter, serving dish; fountain
  fuente de fritada platter of fried food
fuera *adv.* outside
fuerte *adj.* strong
fuga *f.* (*prison*) escape; (*gas, water*) leak
fugarse *v. pron.* to escape, to flee, to run away
fugitivo/a *m., f.* fugitive
fumar *v.t.* to smoke
  no fumar not to smoke
  Prohibido fumar. No smoking.
función *f.* show, function
funcionar *v.i.* to work; to function
  Funciona a la perfección. It works perfectly.
funeral *m.* funeral
furioso/a *adj.* furious
fusible *m.* (*electricity*) fuse
fútbol *m.* soccer
  fútbol americano football
futbolista *m., f.* soccer player; football player
futuro/a *adj./m.* future
  en el futuro (cercano) in the (near) future
  futura mamá mother-to-be
  un trabajo sin futuro a job with no prospects

G

gacela *f.* gazelle
gafas (oscuras/de sol) *f. pl.* (sun)glasses
galardón *m.* award, prize
galardonado/a *m., f.* award-winner
galardonar *v.t.* to award
galaxia *f.* galaxy
galería *f.* gallery
galleta *f.* cookie
gallo *m.* rooster
gana *f.* desire
  de buena/mala gana *adv.* willingly/unwillingly
ganadería *f.* ranching, cattle raising
ganadero/a *m., f.* rancher, cattle farmer
ganar *v.t.* to win; (*money*) to earn
  ganarse la vida *idiom* to make a living, to earn one's living **Mario se gana la vida escribiendo guiones de telenovela.** Mario makes his living writing soap opera scripts.
ganga *f.* bargain
garaje *m.* garage
garantía *f.* guarantee, warranty
garantizar *v.t.* to guarantee
garbanzo *m.* chickpea
gardenia *f.* gardenia
garganta *f.* throat
gas *m.* gas
  gas lacrimógeno tear gas
gasolina *f.* gasoline

gasolinera *f.* gas station
gastar *v.t.* (*money*) to spend
gasto *m.* expense
gastronomía *f.* gastronomy
gatillo *m.* (*firearm*) trigger
apretar el gatillo to pull the trigger
gato/a *m., f.* cat
géiser *m.* geyser
gelatina *f.* gelatine
gemelo/a *m., f.* twin
generoso/a *adj.* generous
genética *f.* genetics
genético/a *adj.* genetic
gente *f.* people
buena gente *idiom* nice person, nice guy, nice gal
geografía *f.* geography
geólogo/a *m., f.* geologist
geometría *f.* geometry
geométrico/a *adj.* geometric(al)
geranio *m.* geranium
gerente *m., f.* manager
gimnasia *f.* gymnastics
gimnasia rítmica rhythmic gymnastics
gimnasio *m.* gymnasium
gimnasta *m., f.* gymnast
ginecólogo/a *m., f.* gynecologist
girar *v.t./intrans.* to turn
Gire a la izquierda en la próxima esquina. Turn left at the next corner.
No gires la cabeza. Don't turn your head.
girasol *m.* sunflower
giro *m.* turn
giro bancario bank draft
giro postal money order
globo *m.* balloon
glotón, glotona *adj.* gluttonous; greedy
gobernar (e:ie) *v.t.* to govern, to rule
gobierno *m.* government
golf *m.* golf
golfista *m., f.* golfer
golpe *m.* blow; coup; hit
Dio unos golpes en la mesa. He pounded on the table several times.
de golpe *adv.* suddenly
Ocurrió de golpe. It happened suddenly.
goma *f.* (*pencil*) eraser
de goma (made of) rubber
gordo/a *adj.* fat
gorra *f.* cap (*with a visor*)
gorra de béisbol baseball cap
gorrión *m.* sparrow
gorro *m.* cap (*without a visor*)
gorro de lana wool cap, ski cap
gota *f.* drop
gótico/a *adj.* Gothic
gozar (de) *v.t.* to enjoy
Mi padre goza de una salud de hierro. My father has a strong constitution.
grabadora *f.* tape recorder
grabar *v.t.* to record
gracias *f., pl.* thank you; thanks
Gracias por todo. Thanks for everything.
Gracias una vez más. Thanks again.
(Muchas) gracias. Thank you (very much). Thanks (a lot).

gracioso/a *adj.* funny
graduación *f.* graduation
graduar *v.t.* (*temperature, etc.*) to adjust, to regulate
graduarse (en/de) *v. pron.* (*university*) to graduate (from/in)
gran, grande *adj.* big; great; large
Es un gran amigo. He's a great friend.
granada *f.* (*fruit*) pomegranate; (*military*) grenade
granero *m.* barn
grano *m.* grain, seed, bean; (*medical*) blemish, pimple
ir al grano *idiom* to get to the point
grasa *f.* fat
gratis *adj.* free of charge
grave *adj.* (*illness, wound, problem*) serious
gravedad *f.* gravity
gravísimo/a *adj. (superlative)* extremely serious; grave
griego *m.* (*language*) Greek
griego *adj./m., f.* Greek
grifo *m.* faucet
grillo *m.* cricket
gripe *f.* flu
gris *adj./m.* gray
gritar *v.i.* to scream
grito *m.* yell, shout
grosero/a *adj.* rude, ill-mannered, impolite, rough
grúa *f. (machinery)* crane
grupo *m.* group
guagua *f.* bus
guantes *m., pl.* gloves
guapo/a *adj.* handsome; good-looking
guarda forestal *m., f.* ranger
guardabarros *m.* (*automobile*) fender
guardar *v.t.* to save (on a computer)
guardería *f.* nursery school, day-care center
guardia *m., f.* guard, police officer
estar de guardia (*doctor*) to be on duty, to be on call
guardia de seguridad security guard
guerra *f.* war
guía *m., f.* guide
guía de teléfonos phone book
Lo puedo usar de guía. I can use it as a guide.
guiñar (el ojo) *v.t.* to wink
guión *m.* script, screenplay
guionista *m., f.* scriptwriter, screenwriter
guisante *m.* pea
guisar *v.i. (Spain)* to cook
guiso *m.* stew
guitarra *f.* guitar
gusano *m.* worm
gustar *v.i.* to be pleasing to; to like
Me gusta. I like it.
Me gustaría. I would like it.
¿Te gusta(n)...? Do you like...?
¿Te gustaría (+ *inf.*)...? Would you like to...?
gusto *m.* pleasure; (*senses*) taste
El gusto es mío. The pleasure is mine.
Gusto de (+ *inf.*)... It's a pleasure to . . .

H

haber *v. impers. irreg.* **(no) hay** *sing.* there is (not); *pl.* there are (not)
Hay (mucha) contaminación. It's (very) smoggy.
Hay (mucha) niebla. It's (very) foggy.
hay que it is necessary (that)
Hay que pensar antes de hablar. Think before you speak.
No hay de qué. You're welcome.
No hay duda (de) que... There's no doubt that...
haber *v. aux. irreg.* (*in compound verbs*) to have
Yo no lo he hecho. I haven't done it.
hábil *adj.* skillful
habilidad *f.* skill
habitación *f.* room
habitación doble double room
habitación individual single room
hablar *v.i.* to talk; to speak
hacer *v.t. irreg.* **(yo hago)** to do; to make
hacer amigos to make friends
hacer berrinches to throw tantrums
hacer cola to stand in line
hacer diligencias to do errands; to run errands
hacer ejercicio to exercise, to work out
hacer ejercicios aeróbicos to do aerobics
hacer ejercicios de estiramiento to do stretching exercises
hacer el papel (de) to play the role of
hacer gimnasia to work out; to exercise,
hacer juego (con) (*clothing*) to match (with), to go well (with)
hacer la cama to make the bed
hacer las maletas to pack (one's suitcases)
hacer quehaceres domésticos to do household chores
hacer travesuras to get into trouble
hacer turismo to go sightseeing
hacer un picnic to have a picnic
hacer un viaje to go on/take a trip
hacer una excursión to go on a hike; to go on a tour
hacer una fiesta to throw a party
hacer una maestría to pursue a Master's degree
hacer *v. impers.* (*weather*)
Hace buen/mal tiempo. The weather is good/bad. It's good/bad weather.
Hace (mucho) calor. It's (very) hot.
Hace fresco. It's cool.
Hace (mucho) frío. It's (very) cold.
Hace (mucho) sol. It's (very) sunny.

Hace (mucho) viento. It's (very) windy.
hacer *v. impers.* (*time*)
hace dos semanas two weeks ago
hacerse *v. pron. irreg.* **(yo me hago)** to become
hacerse daño to hurt oneself
hacerse el sordo to pretend not to hear
hacerse rico to become rich
hacha (el) *f.* ax
hacia *prep.* toward
hada (el) *f.* fairy
hada madrina fairy godmother
hallar *v.t.* to find
hallazgo *m.* find, discovery
Aquel restaurante fue un verdadero hallazgo. That restaurant was a real find.
halterofilia *f.* (*sport*) weightlifting
hamaca *f.* hammock
hambre (el) *f.* hunger
hambriento/a *adj.* hungry
hamburguesa *f.* hamburger
harina *f.* flour
harina de otro costal *idiom* another kettle of fish
hartarse *v. pron.* to get fed up; (*food*) to fill oneself
hasta *prep.* until, toward
hasta ahora until now
Hasta la vista. See you later.
Hasta luego. See you later.
Hasta mañana. See you tomorrow.
Hasta pronto. See you soon.
hasta (que) *conj.* until
hasta que lleguen until they arrive
hebreo *m.* (*language*) Hebrew
hebreo *adj./m., f.* Hebrew
hecho *p.p. of* **hacer** done
de hecho in fact
heladería *f.* ice cream shop
helado *m.* ice cream
helado/a *adj.* iced
helicóptero *m.* helicopter
hembra *f.* female
hemisferio *m.* hemisphere
hemorragia *f.* hemorrhage
herbívoro/a *adj.* herbivorous; *m., f.* herbivore
heredar *v.t.* to inherit
heredera *f.* heiress
heredero *m.* heir
hereditario/a *adj.* hereditary
herencia *f.* inheritance
herida *f.* wound
herido/a *adj./m., f.* injured
Hubo un herido de gravedad. One person was seriously injured.
hermanastro/a *m.* stepbrother; *f.* stepsister
hermano/a *m.* brother, *f.* sister
hermano/a mayor/menor older/younger brother/sister
hermanos *m., pl.* brothers and sisters
hermético/a *adj.* airtight
hermoso/a *adj.* beautiful
héroe *m.* hero
heroina *f.* heroine
herramienta *f.* tool
hervido/a *adj.* boiled
hervir (e:ie) *v.t.* to boil
hidráulico/a *adj.* hydraulic

hiedra *f.* ivy
hielo *m.* ice
quebrar/romper el hielo *loc.* break the ice
hierba *f.* grass
hierbas *f., pl.* herbs
hierro *m.* iron
hígado *m.* liver
higo *m.* fig
higuera *f.* fig tree
hijastro/a *m.* stepson; *f.* stepdaughter
hijo/a *m.* son; *f.* daughter
hijo/a único/a only child
hijos *m., pl.* children
hilera *f.* row
hilo *m.* thread
de hilo (made of) linen
hilo dental dental floss
hindú *adj./m., f.* Hindu
hipérbole *f.* hyperbole
hípica *f.* equestrian sports
hipo *m.* hiccups
hipódromo *m.* hippodrome
hipoteca *f.* mortgage
hipotecar *v.t.* to mortgage
hipótesis *f.* hypothesis
hipotético/a *adj.* hypothetical
hispano/a *adj./m., f.* Hispanic
historia *f.* history; story
historiador(a) *m., f.* historian
hockey *m.* hockey
hockey sobre césped (*L.A.*) field hockey
hockey sobre hielo ice hockey
hockey sobre hierba (*Spain*) field hockey
hoguera *f.* bonfire
hoja *f.* (*plant*) leaf; (*paper*) sheet
hoja de vida (*Colombia*) résumé
hola *interj.* hello; hi
hombre *m.* man
hombre de negocios businessman
hombre del tiempo weatherman
hombre lobo werewolf
hombre rana frogman, diver
hombrera *f.* shoulder pad
hombro *m.* shoulder
homenaje *m.* tribute, homage
homenajear *v.t.* to pay homage
honesto/a *adj.* honest
hora *f.* hour
¿A qué hora...? At what time...?
horario *m.* schedule
horario fijo fixed schedule
horario flexible flexible schedule
horizonte *m.* horizon
hormiga *f.* ant
hormigón *m.* (*Spain*) concrete
hormona *f.* hormone
hornear *v.t.* to bake
pan recién horneado freshly baked bread
hornillo *m.* portable electric stove
horno *m.* oven
horno de microondas microwave oven
horror *m.* horror
...de horror horror
hortensia *f.* hydrangea
horticultor(a) *m., f.* horticulturalist
horticultura *f.* horticulture

hospedar *v.t.* to provide accommodation
hospital *m.* hospital
hospitalario/a *adj.* hospitable
hospitalidad *f.* hospitality
hostal *m.* inn; hostel
hotel *m.* hotel
hoy *adv.* today
hoy día *adv.* nowadays
Hoy es... Today is . . .
huelga *f.* strike
huelguista *m., f.* striker
huella *f.* footprint; mark
huella dactilar fingerprint
huerta *f.* orchard
huerto *m.* vegetable garden
hueso *m.* bone; (*fruit*) pit
huésped *m., f.* guest
huevo *m.* egg
huida *f.* escape
huir (y) *v.i.* to flee, to escape
Huir de la injusticia. Escape injustice.
humanidades *f., pl.* humanities
humanismo *m.* humanism
humanista *m., f.* humanist
humectante *m.* moisturizer
humedad *f.* humidity
húmedo *adj.* humid; damp
humilde *adj.* humble
en mi humilde opinión in my humble opinion
humillado/a *adj.* humiliated
humo *m.* smoke
humor m. mood
de buen/mal humor in a good/bad mood
huracán *m.* hurricane

I

iceberg *m.* iceberg
ida *f.* (*travel*) one way
boleto/billete de ida one-way ticket
idea *f.* idea
idealista *adj.* idealist
idioma *m.* language
iglesia *f.* church
ignorancia *f.* ignorance
ignorante *adj.* ignorant
igual *adj.* equal, same, like
dos y dos igual a cuatro two and two equals four
Es igual que su madre. She's like her mother.
Son las dos iguales. They are both the same.
¿Blanco o negro? –Me da igual. ¿Black or white? – It's all the same to me.
igualdad *f.* equality
igualmente *adv.* likewise
¡Que te diviertas! –Igualmente. Have fun! –Likewise.
ilegible *adj.* illegible
ilusionado/a *adj.* thrilled
ilustrar *v.t.* to illustrate
imaginar *v.t.* to imagine
imaginarse *v. pron.* to imagine
imán *m.* magnet
imitación *f.* imitation
imitar *v.t.* to imitate
impaciencia *f.* impatience
impacientarse *v. pron.* to get impatient
Se impacientó con el retraso del autobús. She got impatient over the delay of the bus.
impaciente *adj.* impatient
impedir (e:i) *v.t.* to prevent

impensable *adj.* unthinkable
imperio *m.* empire
impermeable *adj.* waterproof
impermeable *m.* raincoat
importación *f.* importation
importante *adj.* important
(No) Es importante que... It's (not) important that...
Es importante que vengas a clase. It's important that you come to class.
importar *v.i.* to be important to; to matter
No importa. It doesn't matter.
imposible *adj.* impossible
(No) Es imposible (que...) It's (not) impossible (that...)
Es imposible que tenga sed. It's impossible that she's thirsty.
impostor(a) *m., f.* impostor
imprenta *f.* print shop
impresora *f.* printer
imprimir *v.t.* to print
improbable *adj.* improbable
(No) Es improbable (que...) It's (not) improbable (that...)
Es improbable que llueva. It probably won't rain.
impuesto *m.* tax
inadvertido/a *adj.* unnoticed
inauguración *f.* inauguration
inaugurar *v.t.* to inaugurate
incendio *m.* fire
incertidumbre *f.* uncertainty
incógnito *adj.* unknown
de incógnito *adv.* incognito
incomprensible *adj.* incomprehensible
incomprensión *f.* lack of understanding
inconcebible *adj.* inconceivable
inconveniente *m.* drawback
increíble *adj.* incredible
incremento *m.* increase
independiente *adj.* independent
independizarse *v. pron.* to become independent
indicar *v.t.* to indicate, to show
índice *m.* rate
índice de mortalidad mortality rate
índice de natalidad birth rate
indicio *m.* evidence
indígena *adj.* indigenous, native
indiscreto/a *adj.* indiscreet, tactless
individual *adj.* individual; (*room*) private; *m.* (*sport*) singles
individualidad *f.* individuality
inefable *adj.* indescribable
inesperado/a *adj.* unexpected
inexplicable *adj.* inexplicable
infarto *m.* heart attack
infección *f.* infection
influir (en) (y) *v.i.* to influence
Los poemas de Darío influyeron en otros poetas. Darío's poems influenced other poets.
información *f.* information
informal *adj.* casual
informar *v.t.* to inform
informarse *v. pron.* to get information
informe *m.* report; (*written work*) paper
infusión (de hierbas) *f.* herbal tea

ingeniero/a *m., f.* engineer
ingerir (e:ie) *v.t.* to ingest
ingestión *f.* ingestion
Inglaterra *f.* England
ingle *f.* groin
inglés *m.* (*language*) English
inglés, inglesa *adj./m., f.* English
ingrávido/a *adj.* weightless
injusto/a *adj.* unfair
inmaduro/a *adj.* (*person*) immature
inmediatamente *adv.* immediately
inmigración *f.* immigration
inmigrante *m., f.* immigrant
inmigrar *v.i.* to immigrate
inmunizar (a alguien contra algo) *v.t.* to immunize
inmunológico/a *adj.* immunological
innovación *f.* innovation
innovador(a) *adj.* innovative; *m., f.* innovator
innovar *v.t.* to innovate
inodoro *m.* toilet
inolvidable *adj.* unforgettable
inquietante *adj.* worrying
inquietar(se) *v. pron.* to worry
inquieto/a *adj.* worried
inscribirse *v. pron.* to register, to enroll
Quiere inscribirse en la clase de astronomía. She intends to register for the astronomy class.
inscripción *f.* registration, enrollment
insecto *m.* insect
insípido/a *adj.* (*food*) bland; (*person, work*) insipid
insistencia *f.* insistence
insistir (en) *v.i.* to insist (on)
(insistir en *+inf.*) Insistió en invitarme. He insisted on inviting me.
(insistir en que *+ subj.*) Insiste en que vayamos todos. He insists on all of us going.
insociable *adj.* unsociable
insólito/a *adj.* unusual
insomnio *m.* insomnia
insoportable *adj.* unbearable
inspector(a) *m., f.* inspector
inspector(a) de aduanas customs inspector
inspirar *v.t.* to inspire
instalación *f.* installation
instalaciones deportivas sports facilities
instalar *v.t.* (*equipment*) to install
instalarse *v. pron.* to settle, install oneself
Se instaló delante de la tele y no se movió. He settled in front of the TV and didn't budge.
institución *f.* institution
instrumento *m.* (*medical, musical*) instrument
insulina *f.* insulin
inteligente *adj.* intelligent
intentar *v.* to try
intento *m.* attempt; try
intercambiar *v.t.* exchange
intercambio *m.* exchange
interés *m.* interest
interesante *adj.* interesting

interesar *v.i.* to be interesting to; to interest
interesarse (en) *v. pron.* to take an interest (in)
Siempre se interesa en los resultados. He's always interested in the results.
intermedio *adj.* intermediate
intermitente *m.* (*automobile*) turn signal
internacional *adj.* international
Internet *m.* Internet
interpretación *f.* (*oral translation*) interpreting
interpretar *v.t.* to play (a role), to perform
intérprete *m., f.* interpreter
interrumpir *v.t.* to interrupt
intersección *f.* intersection
intervención *f.* intervention, participation
intervención quirúrgica operation
intestino *m.* intestine
intestino delgado small intestine
intestino grueso large intestine
intimar (con alguien) *v.i.* to get close (to someone)
intimidad *f.* privacy
intolerante *adj.* intolerant
intriga *f.* intrigue
intrigado/a *adj.* intrigued, in suspense
inundación *f.* flood
inundar *v.t.* to flood
inútil *adj.* useless
inválido/a *adj.* (*person*) disabled
invernadero *m.* greenhouse
inverosímil *adj.* unlikely, improbable; unrealistic
invertebrado/a *adj./m.* invertebrate
invertir (e:ie) *v.t.* to invest
investigador(a) *m., f.* researcher; investigator
investigar *v.t.* to research
invierno *m.* winter
invitado/a *m., f.* guest
invitar *v.t.* to invite
involuntario *adj.* involuntary
inyección *f.* injection
inyectar *v.t.* to inject
ir *v.i. irreg.* to go
ir a (+ *inf.*) to be going to *(do something)* **Voy a leer un rato.** I'm going to read for a while.
ir a exceso de velocidad to speed
ir a la playa to go to the beach
ir de campamento to go camping
ir de compras to go shopping
ir de excursión (a las montañas) to (go on a) hike (in the mountains)
ir de pesca to go fishing
ir de vacaciones to go on vacation
ir en auto(móvil) to go by auto(mobile); to go by car
ir en autobús to go by bus
ir en avión to go by plane
ir en barco to go by ship/boat
ir en metro to go by subway
ir en motocicleta to go by motorcycle

ir en taxi to go by taxi
ir en tren to go by train
¡Vamos! Let's go!; Come on!
ironía *f.* irony
irónico/a *adj.* ironic
irresponsable *adj.* irresponsible
irse *v. pron. irreg.* to go away; to leave **No te vayas, aún es temprano.** Don't leave; it's still early.
irse de pinta (*idiom*) (*Mexico*) to play hooky
irse de vacaciones to go on vacation
italiano *m. (language)* Italian
italiano/a *adj./m., f.* Italian
itinerario *m.* itinerary
izquierdo/a *adj.* left; *m., f.* left
a la izquierda (de) to the left (of)

J

jabón *m.* soap
jabonera *f.* soap dish
jamás *adv.* never; not ever
jamón *m.* ham
Januká *m.* Chanukah
japonés *m.* (*language*) Japanese
japonés, japonesa *adj./m., f.* Japanese
jarabe para la tos *m.* cough syrup
jardín *m.* garden, (back) yard
jardinería *f.* gardening
jardinero/a *m., f.* gardener
jarra *f.* pitcher
jarrón *m.* vase
jeans *m., pl.* jeans
jefe/a *m., f.* boss
jerarquía *f.* hierarchy
jerárquico/a *adj.* hierarchical
jerarquizado/a *adj.* hierarchical
jerez *m.* (*wine*) sherry
jeringa *f.* syringe
jirafa *f.* giraffe
joroba *f.* hump
jorobado/a *adj.* hunchbacked
jota *f.* (*playing cards*) jack
joven *adj.* young; *m., f.* youth, young person
joyas *f.* jewels
joyería *f.* jewelry store
joyero/a *m., f.* jeweler; *m.* jewelry box
jubilado/a *m., f.* retired person
jubilarse *v. pron.* to retire (from work)
judío/a *adj.* Jewish; *m., f.* Jew
juego *m.* game
juego limpio/sucio fair/foul play
juegos *m. pl.* games
juegos de azar gambling
juegos de mesa board games
Juegos Olímpicos Olympic Games
Juegos Paralímpicos Paralympics
jueves *m., sing.* Thursday
juez *m., f.* judge
jugador(a) *m., f.* player; gambler
jugar (u:ue) *v.t./v.i.* to play
jugar a las cartas to play cards
jugo *m.* juice

jugo de fruta fruit juice
jugoso/a *adj.* juicy
juguete *m.* toy
juguetería *f.* toy store
juicio *m.* judgment; trial
julio *m.* July
junio *m.* June
jungla *f.* jungle
junta *f.* board, committee
junta directiva board of directors
juntarse *v. pron.* to get together
juntos/as *adj./adv.* together
jurado *m.* jury
jurar *v.i.* to swear
justicia *f.* justice
justo/a *adj.* fair
juvenil *adj.* youthful
juventud *f.* youth
juzgar *v.t.* to judge

K

kilo(gramo) *m.* kilo(gram)
kilómetro *m.* kilometer

L

la *f., sing. art., def.* the
la *d.o. pron. f., sing.* her, it, you
labio *m.* lip
laboratorio *m.* laboratory
lacio/a *adj.* (*hair*) straight
ladera *f.* hillside, mountainside, slope
El primer grupo subió por la ladera norte. The first group ascended the northern slope.
lado *m.* side
al lado de beside; next to
por un lado..., por otro lado... on (the) one hand..., on the other hand . . .
ladrar *v.i.* to bark
ladrido *m.* bark
ladrillo *m.* brick
ladrón, ladrona *m., f.* thief; robber; burglar
lagarto *f.* lizard
lago *m.* lake
lágrima *f.* tear
lamentar *v.t.* to regret
lámpara *f.* lamp
lana *f.* wool
de lana (made of) wool
lancha *f.* motorboat
langosta *f.* lobster
langostino *m.* prawn
lanzado *p.p. of* **lanzar** thrown
lanzado/a *adj.* (*person*) impulsive, impetuous
lanzamiento *m.* launch, throw
lanzamiento de bala *(L. A.)* shotput
lanzamiento de disco discus throw
lanzamiento de jabalina javelin throw
lanzamiento de peso *(Spain)* shotput
lanzar *v.t.* to throw; to launch
La NASA lanzó un cohete a Saturno. NASA launched a rocket to Saturn.
lápiz *m.* pencil
lápiz labial lipstick
largo/a *adj.* long (*in length*)
a la larga in the long run
laringe *f.* larynx
larva *f.* larva
las *f., pl. art., def.* the

las *d.o. pron. f., pl.* them
lástima f. shame, pity
Es una lástima (que...) It's too bad (that...); It's a shame (that...)
Es una lástima que no te puedas quedar. It's a pity that you can't stay.
lastimar *v.t.* to hurt
lastimarse *v. pron.* to injure oneself; to get hurt
lastimarse el pie to injure one's foot
lata *f.* (*tin*) can
¡Qué lata! *loc.* What a drag!
latido *m.* heartbeat
latín *m.* (*language*) Latin
latino/a *adj./m., f.* Latin
latir *v.i.* (*heart*) to beat
lavabo *m.* (bathroom) sink
lavadora *f.* washing machine
lavandería *f.* laundromat
lavaplatos *m., sing.* dishwasher
lavar (el suelo) *v.t.* to wash (the floor)
lavar los platos to do (wash) the dishes
lavarse *v. pron.* to wash (oneself)
lavarse la cara to wash one's face
lavarse las manos to wash one's hands
lavarse los dientes to brush one's teeth
lazo *m.* bow; ribbon
lazos *m., pl.* ties
lazos familiares family ties
le *i.o. pron. sing.* to/for him, her, *form.* you
lección *f.* lesson
leche *f.* milk
lechuga *f.* lettuce
lector *m., f.* reader
leer *v.t.* to read
leer correo electrónico to read e-mail
leer un periódico to read a newspaper
leer una revista to read a magazine
legado *m.* legacy
legal *adj.* legal
legalizar *v.t.* to legalize
leído *p.p. of* **leer** read
lejano/a *adj.* distant; remote; far-off
un pariente lejano a distant relative
lejía *f.* bleach
lejos de *adv.* far from
lengua *f.* tongue; language
lenguas extranjeras *f., pl.* foreign languages
lentamente *adv.* slowly
lenteja *f.* lentil
lentes *m., pl.* eyeglasses, lenses
lentes de contacto contact lenses
lentes (de sol/oscuros/negros) (sun)glasses
lento/a *adj.* slow
leña *f.* firewood
leño *m.* log
león *m.* lion
leopardo *m.* leopard
les *i.o. pron. pl.* to/for them, *form* you

letra *f.* (*alphabet*) letter; handwriting; (*song*) lyrics
Tienes una letra ilegible. Your handwriting is illegible.
letra de imprenta printing
Escriba su nombre completo en letra de imprenta. Print your full name.

letra mayúscula capital letter
letra minúscula lowercase letter
letrero *m.* sign
levadura *f.* yeast
levantar *v.t.* to lift
levantar pesas to lift weights
levantarse *v. pron.* to get up
ley *f.* law
la ley del más fuerte the survival of the fittest
leyenda *f.* legend
liberación *f.* liberation
liberal *adj./m., f.* liberal
liberar *v.t.* to free, to release
libertad *f.* liberty, freedom
la Estatua de la Libertad the Statue of Liberty
libertad condicional parole
libertad de expresión freedom of speech
libra *f.* pound
libre *adj.* free
librería *f.* bookstore
libro *m.* book
libro de bolsillo paperback
libro de consulta reference book
licencia *f.* license
licencia de conducir/manejar driver's license
licor *m.* liqueur, liquor
licuadora *f.* (*L.A.*) blender
licuar *v.t.* to blend
líder *m., f.* leader
liderar *v.t.* to lead
liderazgo *m.* leadership
ligar *v.i.* (*Spain*) to pick up boys/girls
ligero/a *adj.* (*weight/food*) light
lima *f.* (*tool*) file; nail file
limitar *v.t.* to limit; to restrict
límite *m.* limit
limón *m.* lemon, lime
limonada *f.* lemonade
limonero *m.* lemon tree
limosna *f.* alms, charity
vivir de limosnas to live by begging
limpiaparabrisas *m. sing.* windshield wiper
limpiar *v.t.* to clean
limpiar la casa to clean the house
limpio/a *adj.* clean
limusina *f.* limousine
lindo/a *adj.* pretty
línea *f.* line
en línea in-line
línea discontinua broken line
lingüista *m., f.* linguist
lingüística *f.* linguistics
lingüístico/a *adj.* linguistic
linterna *f.* flashlight
líquido/a *adj./m.* liquid
lirio *m.* lily
lista *f.* list
lista de espera waiting list
lista de éxitos best-seller list

pasar lista to call roll
listo/a *adj.* smart; ready
estar listo/a to be ready
ser listo/a to be smart
literal *adj.* literal
Es una traducción demasiado literal; no suena natural. It's too literal a translation; it doesn't sound natural.
literario/a *adj.* literary
literatura *f.* literature
litro *m.* liter
liviano/a *adj.* light
llamada *f.* call
llamada telefónica telephone call
llamar *v.t.* to call
llamar a cobro revertido to call collect
llamar la atención (a) to attract attention (to)
llamar por teléfono to call on the phone
llamarse *v. pron.* to be called; to be named
Me llamo... My name is...
llanta *f.* tire
llanura *f.* prairie
llave *f.* key
llave maestra master key
llavero *m.* key chain
llegada *f.* arrival
llegar *v.i.* to arrive
llegar a ser to become
llegar tarde to be late
llenar *v.t.* to fill; (*form*) (*L.A.*) to fill out
llenar el tanque to fill the tank
llenar un formulario to fill out a form
lleno/a *adj.* full
llevar *v.t.* to carry, to take (someone somewhere); (*clothes*) to wear **¿Qué es eso que llevas puesto?** What's that you're wearing?
llevar una vida sana to lead a healthy lifestyle
llevarse *v. pron.* to take
Puedes llevártelo. You can take it.
llevarse bien/mal (con) to get along well/badly/poorly (with)
llorar *v.i.* to cry
lloriquear *v.i.* to whine
llorón, llorona *adj./m., f.* crybaby
llover (o:ue) *v. impers.* to rain
llover a cántaros *idiom* to pour, to rain cats and dogs
Llueve. It's raining.
lluvia *f.* rain
lluvia ácida acid rain
lo *d.o. pron.* it, him, *form.* you
Dilo. Say it.
Díselo. Say it to him.
lo pasamos de película we had a great time
lo que what; that which
lobo *m.* wolf
loco/a *adj.* crazy
loco de remate stark raving mad
locomotora *f.* locomotive
locura *f.* madness
locutor(a) *m., f.* (*TV, radio*) announcer

lograr *v.t.* to achieve
logro *m.* achievement
lombriz *f.* earthworm
lomo *m.* flank steak
  lomo a la plancha grilled flank steak
lona *f.* canvas
lonchera *f.* (*L.A.*) lunch box
longevidad *f.* longevity
loro *m.* parrot
los *m., pl. art., def.* the
los *d.o. pron. m. pl.* them, *form.* you
lucha *f.* fight, struggle
luchar (por/contra) *v.i.* to fight, to struggle (for/against)
lucir (c:zc) *v.* to look good
luego *adv.* afterwards, then; later
  desde luego *idiom* of course
  ¡Hasta luego! See you later.
  Y luego qué. And then what?
lugar *m.* place
lujo *m.* luxury
lujoso/a *adj.* luxurious
luna *f.* moon
  luna de miel honeymoon
lunar *m.* mole, beauty mark; polka dot
  una corbata de lunares a polka-dot tie
lunes *m., sing.* Monday
lupa *f.* magnifying glass
luz *f.* light, electricity
  Apaga la luz. Turn out the light.
  la luz del sol sunlight

M

maceta *f.* flower pot
macho *m.* male
madera *f.* wood
madrastra *f.* stepmother
madre *f.* mother
madrina *f.* godmother
madrugada *f.* early morning
madrugar *v.i.* to get up early
madurez *f.* maturity; middle age
maduro/a *adj.* (*person*) mature; (*fruit*) ripe
maestría *f.* (*L.A.*) Master's degree
maestro/a *m., f.* (*elementary school*) teacher
magia *f.* magic
mágico/a *adj.* magical
magma *m.* magma
magnesio *m.* magnesium
magnífico/a *adj.* magnificent
mago/a *m., f.* magician
maíz *m.* corn
mal *adv.* bad, ill
maleducado/a *adj.* rude, bad-mannered
maleta *f.* suitcase
maletero *m.* (*Spain*) (*automobile*) trunk
malgastar *v.t.* to waste
  No malgastes tu tiempo en tonterías. Don't waste your time with stupid little things.
maligno *adj.* (*tumor*) malignant
malo/a *adj.* bad; mean
  ¡Mala suerte! Unlucky!
  ¡Qué película más mala! What a terrible movie!
  (No) Es malo que... It's (not) bad that...

No es malo que lo digas. It's not bad that you say it.
mamá *f.* mom
mami *f.* mom
mamífero *m.* mammal
manantial *m.* (*water*) spring
mandar *v.t.* to order; to send; to mail
mandarina *f.* tangerine
manejar *v.i.* to drive
manera *f.* way
de ninguna manera by no means; no way
manga *f.* sleeve
manguera *f.* hose
manicomio *m.* mental hospital
manicura *f.* manicure
manifestación *f.* demonstration
manifestante *m., f.* demonstrator
manillar *m.* (*Spain*) (*bike*) handlebars
maniquí *m.* mannequin
mano *f.* hand
manta *f.* blanket
mantel *m.* tablecloth
mantener (e:ie) *v.t. irreg.* **(yo mantengo)** to maintain, to support; to keep
Mantengan la calma. Stay calm.
Mantener las apariencias. Keep up appearances.
¿Quién va a mantener a la familia? Who's going to support the family?
mantenerse en forma (e:ie) *v. pron. irreg.* **(yo me mantengo)** to stay in shape
mantequilla *f.* butter
manzana *f.* apple
mañana *f.* morning, a.m.; *adv.* tomorrow
a las dos de la mañana at two in the morning, at two a.m.
mañanitas *f. pl.* birthday song
mapa *m.* map
mapa de carreteras road map
maquillador(a) *m., f.* makeup artist
maquillaje *m.* makeup
maquillar *v.t.* to apply makeup
maquillarse *v. pron.* to put on makeup
máquina *f.* machine
máquina de afeitar razor
máquina de coser sewing machine
máquina de escribir typewriter
mar *m.* sea, ocean
en alta mar on the high sea
maratón *m.* marathon
maravillosamente *adv.* marvelously
maravilloso/a *adj.* marvelous
marca *f.* mark; (*commerce*) brand, brand name; (*sport*) record
Es una marca de prestigio. It's a well-known brand.
Superó su marca. She beat her own record.
marcador *m.* (*sports*) scoreboard
marcapasos *m., sing.* pacemaker
marcar *v.t.* (*telephone*) to dial; (*sports*) to score

Marca el 007. Dial 007.
¿Quién marcó el gol de la victoria? Who scored the winning goal?

marea *f.* tide
marea alta/baja high/low tide
marea negra oil slick

mareado/a *adj.* dizzy; nauseated

marearse *v. pron.* to get dizzy
¿Te mareas en barco? Do you get seasick?

maremoto *m.* seaquake; tidal wave

margarina *f.* margarine

margarita *f.* daisy

marinero *m.* sailor

mariposa *f.* butterfly

mariscada *f.* assorted seafood

mariscos *m., pl.* shellfish; seafood

mármol *m.* marble

marrón *adj./m.* brown

martes *m., sing.* Tuesday

martillo *m.* hammer

marzo *m.* March

más *adv./ pron.* more **¿Quieres más?** Would you like some more?
más de (+ *number)* more than **Hay más de diez personas.** There are more than ten people.
más o menos so so
más... que more... than **más grande que una casa** bigger than a house
más tarde later

masa *f.* dough

masaje *m.* massage

masajista *m.* masseur; *f.* masseuse

máscara *f.* mask

mascarilla *f.* mask

masticar *v.t.* to chew

matar *v.t.* to kill
matar dos pájaros de un tiro *loc.* to kill two birds with one stone

matarse *v. pron.* to kill oneself
Se mata estudiando. She studies like crazy.

matemáticas *f., pl.* mathematics

matemático/a *m., f.* mathematician

materia *f.* matter; (*school*) subject; course
materia inorgánica inorganic matter
¿Qué materia enseña la Srta. López? What subject does Miss López teach?

materialista *adj.* materialistic

materno/a *adj.* (*relative*) maternal

matrícula *f.* (*education*) registration, matriculation; (*automobile*) registration number, license plate
matrícula de honor (*grade*) distinction, magna cum laude

matricularse *v. pron.* (*education*) to register, to enroll

matrimonio *m.* marriage

máximo/a *m.* maximum, top

mayo *m.* May

mayonesa *f.* mayonnaise

mayor *adj.* older
el/la mayor the oldest; the eldest
mayordomo *m.* butler
mayoría *f.* majority
me *pron.* me
Dámelo. Give it to me.
mecánico/a *m., f.* mechanic
mecanismo *m.* mechanism
mecanógrafo/a *m., f.* typist
mecedora *f.* rocking chair
mecer (c:z) *v.t.* to rock
medalla *f.* medal
mediano/a *adj.* medium
medianoche *f.* midnight
medias *f., pl.* pantyhose, stockings
medicamento *m.* medication
medicina *f.* medicine
medición *f.* measurement
médico/a *m., f.* doctor; physician
médico de cabecera family doctor
médico de familia family doctor
médico/a de guardia doctor on call, doctor on duty
médico/a *adj.* medical
tratamiento médico medical treatment
medida *f.* measurement, size
medio/a *m.* half
medio ambiente *m.* environment
medio/a hermano/a *m.* half-brother; *f.* half-sister
mediocre *adj.* mediocre
mediodía *m.* noon, midday
medios *m., pl.* means; resources
los medios de comunicación (the) media; means of comunication
medir (e:i) *v.t.* to measure
meditación *f.* meditation
meditar *v.i.* to meditate
médula *f.* marrow
medusa *f.* jellyfish
megáfono *m.* megaphone
mejilla *f.* cheek
mejillón *m.* mussel
mejor *adj.* better; best
el/la mejor *m., f.* the best
lo mejor the best (thing)
Es mejor que… It's better that…
Es mejor que vayas. It's better that you go.
mejor que *adj.* better than
mejora *f.* improvement
mejorar *v.t.* to improve
mejorarse *v. pron.* to get better
mellizo/a *m., f.* twin
melocotón *m.* (*Spain*) peach
melón *m.* melon
membrana *f.* membrane
memoria *f.* memory
de memoria *adv.* by heart
Se sabe el poema de memoria. He knows the poem by heart.
memorizar *v.t.* to memorize
mendigo/a *m., f.* beggar
menopausia *f.* menopause
menor *adj.* younger
el/la menor *m., f.* the youngest
menos *adv.* less
a menos que *conj.* unless **Iré a menos que llueva.** I'll go unless it rains.

menos cuarto/quince quarter to/of **Son las dos menos cuarto/quince.** It's a quarter to/of two.
menos de (+ *number)* less/fewer than **Tengo menos de una hora.** I have less than an hour.
menos... que less... than **¿Qué es menos interesante que hablar?** What's less interesting than talking?
por lo menos at least
mensaje *m.* message
mensaje electrónico e-mail message
mensualidad *f.* (*monthly payment*) installment
menta *f.* mint
mentalidad *f.* mentality
mentir (e:ie) *v.i.* to lie
mentira *f.* lie
parecer mentira *idiom* to be hard to believe; to be incredible
Aunque parezca mentira, sólo tiene diez años. It's hard to believe, but he's only ten.
mentiroso/a *adj.* liar
menú *m.* menu
menudo/a *adj.* tiny, minute
a menudo *adv.* frequently, often
mercadillo *m.* street market
mercado *m.* market
mercado al aire libre open-air market
mercurio *m.* mercury
merecer (c:zc) *v.t.* to deserve
merendar (e:ie) *v.i.* to snack (in the afternoon); to have an afternoon snack
merienda *f.* afternoon snack
mérito *m.* merit
merluza *f.* (*fish*) hake
mermelada *f.* jam
mes *m.* month
mesa *f.* table
mesa de noche night table
mesero/a *m.* waiter; *f.* waitress
meseta *f.* plateau
mesita *f.* end table
mesita de noche night stand
meta *f.* objective, goal
metabolismo *m.* metabolism
metabolizar *v.t.* to metabolize
metáfora *f.* metaphor
metafórico/a *adj.* metaphoric
metal *m.* metal
metamorfosis *f.* metamorphosis
meteorito *m.* meteorite
meteorólogo/a *m., f.* meteorologist
meter *v.t.* to put (into)
meter la pata put one's foot in one's mouth
metereología *f.* meteorology
metódico/a *adj.* methodical
método *m.* method
metro *m.* meter; subway
mexicano/a *adj./m., f.* Mexican
México *m.* Mexico
mezclar *v.t.* to mix, to toss
mezquita *f.* mosque
mí *pron.* me
¿Para mí? For me?
mi(s) *poss.* my
micrófono *m.* microphone
microonda *f.* microwave
microondas, (el) *m.* microwave (oven)

microscopio *m.* microscope
miedo *m.* fear
No tengas miedo. Don't be afraid.
miel *f.* honey
miembro *m.* member; (*body*) limb
mientras *adv.* while
mientras tanto meanwhile
miércoles *m., sing.* Wednesday
mil *m.* one thousand
a las mil y una very late
Anoche llegó a las mil y una. Last night he arrived very late.
Mil perdones. I'm extremely sorry.
milagro *m.* miracle
milla *f.* mile
millón *m.* million
mil millones a billion (*US*)
millones (de) millions (of)
mimbre *m.* wicker
mina *f.* mine
mineral *m.* mineral
minería *f.* mining industry
minero/a *m., f.* miner
minifalda *f.* miniskirt
mínimo/a *adj./m.* minimum
como mínimo at least
ministro/a *m., f.* (*government*) minister
minoría *f.* minority
minúsculo/a *adj.* minute, tiny
minuto *m.* minute
mío/a(s) *poss.* my, (of) mine
miope *adj.* myopic
miopía *f.* myopia
mirar *v.t.* to watch, to see, to look at
mirar (la) televisión to watch television
misil *m.* missile
mismo/a *adj.* same
misterioso/a *adj.* mysterious
mitad *f.* half, middle
mitin *m.* political meeting
mochila *f.* backpack
moda *f.* fashion
ir a la moda *v.* to be fashionably dressed or trendy
de moda in fashion
módem *m.* modem
modernizar *v.t.* to modernize
moderno/a *adj.* modern, trendy
modificar *v.t.* to modify
modista *f.* dressmaker
modo *m.* way, manner; (*verb tense*) mood **¿el modo subjuntivo o el indicativo?** the subjunctive or the indicative mood?
de ningún modo by no means
de todos modos anyway; in any case
moho *m.* mold
mojado/a *adj.* wet
mojar *v.t.* to wet, to get wet
mojarse *v. pron.* to get (oneself) wet
Salí sin paraguas y me mojé toda. I went out without an umbrella and I got all wet.
molestar *v.t.* to bother, to annoy; to disturb
No le molestes, está estudiando. Don't disturb him, he's studying.

Deja de molestarme, estoy pensando. Stop bothering me, I'm thinking.
Este ruido me molesta. This noise annoys me.
molestia *f.* inconvenience, bother
No es ninguna molestia. It's no bother at all.
molesto/a *adj.* upset
molino *m.* (*machine, factory*) mill
momento *m.* moment
monarca *m., f.* monarch
monarquía *f.* monarchy
monasterio *m.* monastery
mondadientes *m.* toothpick
moneda *f.* coin
monedero *m.* coin purse
monitor *m.* (*computer*) monitor
monitor(a) *m., f.* trainer, coach, instructor
monitor de esquí ski instructor
monja *f.* nun
monje *m.* monk
mono *m.* monkey
monólogo *m.* monologue
montacargas *m.* forklift
montaña *f.* mountain
montar *v.t.* (*bike*) to ride; (*machine, furniture*) to assemble
montar a caballo to ride a horse
¿Aún no has montado el escritorio? You still haven't assembled the desk?
monumento *m.* monument
mora *f.* blackberry
morado/a *adj.* purple
moral *f.* moral
moralidad *f.* morality
morder (o:ue) *v.t.* to bite
mordisco *m.* bite
moreno/a *adj.* brunet(te), dark-skinned, tanned
morfología *f.* morphology
moribundo/a *adj.* moribund, dying
morir (o:ue) *v.i.* to die
Me muero por ir. I'm dying to go.
Me muero por un beso. I'm dying for a kiss.
mortalidad *f.* mortality
mosca *f.* fly
mosquitero *m.* mosquito net
mostaza *f.* mustard
mostrar (o:ue) *v.t.* to show
moto *f.* motorcycle
motocicleta *f.* motorcycle
motociclismo *m.* motorcycling
motociclista *m., f.* motorcyclist
motor *m.* motor, engine
móvil *adj.* mobile
movilidad *f.* mobility
mozo/a (*L.A.*) *m.* waiter; *f.* waitress
muchacho/a *m.,* boy; *f.* girl
muchísimo/a *adj. (superlative)* very much
Muchísimas gracias. Thank you very much.
mucho/a(s) *adj.* many; a lot of; much; *adv.* a lot
muchas veces many times; a lot
Mucho gusto. Pleased/Nice to meet you.

mudanza *f.* move
mudar *v.t.* to move, to change
Las serpientes mudan de piel cada año. Snakes change their skin each year.
mudarse *v. pron.* to move (from one house to another)
¿Cuántas veces te has mudado este año? How many times have you moved this year?
mudo/a *adj.* mute
muebles *m., pl.* furniture
muela *f.* molar, back tooth; *(generic)* tooth **Me sacaron una muela.** I had a tooth pulled.
muela del juicio wisdom tooth
muelle *m.* spring
muerte *f.* death
muerto/a *p.p. of* **morir** died; *adj.* dead
Estoy muerto de hambre. I'm starving.
muestra *f.* sample
mujer *f.* woman
mujer de negocios businesswoman
mujer policía female police officer
mujeriego *m.* womanizer
multa *f.* fine, ticket
multitud *f.* crowd
mundial *adj.* worldwide
mundo *m.* world
municipal *m.* municipal
muñeca/o *m., f.* doll; *f.* wrist
muralla *f.* wall
murciélago *m. (animal)* bat
muro *m.* wall
músculo *m.* muscle
musculoso/a *adj.* muscular
museo *m.* museum
música *f.* music
poner la música muy alta to play loud music
musical *adj.* musical
músico/a *m., f.* musician
muslo *m.* thigh
musulmán, musulmana *adj./m., f.* Muslim
muy *adv.* very
Muy amable. That's very kind of you.
Muy bien, gracias. Very well, thank you/thanks

N

nacer (c:zc) *v.i.* to be born
nacimiento *m.* birth
nación *f.* nation
Naciones Unidas United Nations **Ése es el edificio de las Naciones Unidas.** That's the UN building.
nacional *adj.* national
nacionalidad *f.* nationality
nacionalismo *m.* nationalism
nacionalista *adj.* nationalist
nada *pron./adv.* nothing, (not) anything
De nada. You're welcome.
No está nada mal. It's not bad at all.
No me gustan nada. I don't like them at all.
nada mal not bad at all
nadador(a) *m., f.* swimmer
nadar *v.i.* to swim

nadie *pron.* no one, nobody, not anyone, anybody
No lo sabe nadie. Nobody knows it.
naipe *m.* playing card
naranja *f.* orange
naranjo *m.* orange tree
nariz *f.* nose
narrador(a) *m., f.* narrator
nata *f.* (*Spain*) cream; (*on boiled milk*) skin
natación *f.* swimming
natación sincronizada synchronized swimming
natalidad *f.* birthrate
natural *adj.* natural
naturaleza *f.* nature
naturalmente *adv.* naturally; of course
navaja *f.* jackknife, penknife
navegar *v.i.* to sail
navegar (en Internet/la red) to surf (the Internet/Web)
Navidad *f.* Christmas
necesario/a *adj.* necessary
(No) Es necesario que... It's (not) necessary that...
No es necesario que te quedes. It's not necessary that you stay.
neceser *m.* toilet kit
necesidad *f.* necessity
necesitar (+ *inf.*) *v.t.* to need
nectarina *f.* nectarine
negación *f.* refusal
negar (e:ie) *v.t.* to deny
no negar not to deny
negarse (e:ie) *v. pron.* to refuse
negativo/a *m.* negative
negocios *m., pl.* business, commerce
negro/a *adj./m.* (*color*) black
nervio *m.* nerve
nervioso/a *adj.* nervous
neumático *m.* tire
neurona *f.* neuron
nevar (e:ie) *v. impers.* to snow
Nieva. It's snowing.
ni *conj.* nor
ni... ni *conj.* neither... nor
Ni tú ni yo. Neither you nor I.
niebla *f.* fog
nieto/a *m.* grandson; *f.* granddaughter
nieve *f.* snow
ningún, ninguno/a(s) *adj.* no; none; not any
ningún problema no problem
ninguna parte, (a) nowhere
niñero/a *m., f.* baby-sitter
niñez *f.* childhood
niño/a *m., f.* child, kid
de niño/a as a child
niño/a mimado/a spoiled child, brat
nitrógeno *m.* nitrogen
nivel *m.* level
no *adv.* no; not
No es así. That's not the way it is.
No muy bien. Not very well.
No, no vengo. No, I'm not coming.
Vienes, ¿no? You're coming, right?
¿Vienes o no? Are you coming or not?
noche *f.* night, evening
de la noche in the evening,

at night, P.M. **a las diez de la noche** at ten P.M.
por la noche at night
nogal *m.* walnut tree
nombre *m.* name
en mi nombre in my name
en nombre de on behalf of, in the name of
nombre de pila first name
nórdico/a *adj.* Nordic; *m., f.* Northern European
norte *m.* north
al norte to the north
norteamericano/a *adj./m., f.* (North) American
nos *pron.* us, ourselves, each other
Nos vemos. See you.
nosotros/as *pron.* we, us
entre nosotros/as between us; off the record
nota *f.* (*school*) grade, mark, note
notar *v.t.* to notice
noticias *f., pl.* news
noticiero *m.* newscast
novatada *f.* practical joke
hacer una novatada (a alguien) *v.* to haze (somebody)
novato/a *adj.* inexperienced, new
novecientos/as nine hundred
noveno/a *adj./m.* ninth
noventa ninety
noviembre *m.* November
novillo *m.* steer
hacer novillos *(Spain)* to play hooky
novio/a *m.,* boyfriend; *f.* girlfriend
nube *f.* cloud
nublado/a *adj.* cloudy
Está (muy) nublado. It's (very) cloudy.
nuclear *adj.* nuclear
núcleo *m.* nucleus
nuera *f.* daughter-in-law
nuestro/a(s) *poss.* our
nueve nine
nuevo/a *adj.* new
de nuevo again
nuez *f.* walnut
número *m.* number; (*shoe*) size
nunca *adv.* never; not ever
nutrición *f.* nutrition
nutricionista *m., f.* nutritionist

Ñ

ñame *m.* yam

O

o *conj.* or
o... o *conj.* either... or
O te quedas o te vas. Either you stay or you go.
obedecer (c:zc) *v.t.* to obey
obesidad *f.* obesity
obeso/a *adj.* obese
objetivo/a *m.* objective; aim, goal
objeto *m.* object; purpose
¿Cuál es el objeto de esta discusión? What's the purpose of this argument?
obligar *v.t.* to force, to oblige; to make
(a alguien a + *inf.*)
No le obligues a estudiar. Don't force him to study.

(a alguien a que + *subj.*) No me obligues a que lo diga. Don't make me say it.
obra *f.* (*of art, literature, music, etc.*) work
obra maestra masterpiece
observación *f.* observation
observador(a) *adj.* observant
observatorio *m.* observatory
observar *v.t.* to observe
obtener (e:ie) *v.t. irreg.* **(yo obtengo)** to obtain; to get
obvio/a *adj.* obvious
Es obvio (que...) It's obvious (that...)
océano *m.* ocean; sea
ochenta eighty
ocho eight
ochocientos/as eight hundred
ocio *m.* leisure time
ocioso/a *adj.* idle
ocre *m.* ocher
octavo/a *adj./m.* eighth
octubre *m.* October
oculista *m., f.* optician
ocupación *f.* occupation
ocupado/a *adj.* busy
ocurrir *v. impers.* to occur; to happen
Ocurrió lo inesperado. The unexpected happened.
odiar *v.t.* to hate
oeste *m.* west
al oeste to the west
ofender *v.t.* to offend
ofenderse *v. pron.* to take offense
ofensa *f.* insult
oferta *f.* offer
oficina *f.* office
oficio *m.* trade
ofrecer (c:zc) *v.t.* to offer
ofrenda *f.* offering
oftalmólogo/a *m., f.* ophthalmologist
oído *m.* (*sense of*) hearing; inner ear
oído *p.p. of* **oír** heard
oír (y) *v.t./v.i. irreg.* **(yo oigo)** to hear
oiga(n) *form., sing. pl.* listen (*in conversation*)
oír decir que *idiom* to have heard that **He oído decir que te casas.** I've heard that you are getting married.
oye *fam., sing.* listen (*in conversation*)
¡Ojalá! *interj.* I hope so!
Ojalá (que) I hope (that); I wish (that)
Ojalá que vuelva pronto. I hope/Hopefully he comes back soon.
Ojalá no llueva mañana. I hope/wish it doesn't rain tomorrow.
ojo *m.* eye
ola *f.* wave
oler (a) *v.i. irreg.* to smell (like)
Huele a humo aquí. It smells like smoke here.
olfato *m.* (*sense*) smell
olimpiada/olimpiadas *f./f., pl.* Olympic Games, Olympics
Olimpiadas Especiales Special Olympics
olímpico/a *adj.* Olympic
olla *f.* cooking pot
olla a presión pressure cooker

olor *m.* smell, odor
el olor de la primavera the smell of spring
olor corporal body odor
olvidar *v.t.* to forget
ombligo *m.* navel
omoplato *m.* scapula
once eleven
oncólogo/a *m., f.* oncologist
onda *f.* (*physics, radio*) wave
onza *f.* ounce
opaco/a *adj.* opaque
ópera *f.* opera
operación *f.* operation
opinar *v.t.* to express an opinion
opinión *f.* opinion
en mi opinión in my opinion
oportunidad *f.* opportunity
optimista *adj./m., f.* optimist, optimistic
orden *m.* order, sequence; *f.* order, command
A sus órdenes. At your service.
ordenado/a *adj.* orderly; well-organized
ordenador *m.* (*Spain*) computer
ordinal *adj.* ordinal
orégano *m.* oregano
oreja *f.* (*outer*) ear
organización *f.* organization; arrangement
organizar *v.t.* to organize; to arrange
órgano *m.* organ
órganos de los sentidos sensory organs
orgullo *m.* pride
orgulloso/a *adj.* proud
original *adj.* original
originalidad *f.* originality
orilla *f.* shore, (river)bank
La casa está a orillas del mar. The house is on the seashore.
orina *f.* urine
orinar *v.i.* to urinate
oro *m.* gold
orquesta *f.* orchestra
ortografía *f.* spelling
ortográfico/a *adj.* spelling
os *fam., pl.* you
¿Os gusta? Do you like it?
osito *m.* teddy bear
oso/a *m., f.* bear
Osa Mayor Big Dipper
Osa Menor Little Dipper
ostra *f.* oyster
otoño *m.* autumn, fall
otro/a *adj.* other; another
otra vez again
oveja *f.* sheep
OVNI (Objeto Volador No Identificado) *m.* UFO (Unidentified Flying Object)
oxidarse *v. pron.* to rust
óxido *m.* rust
oxígeno *m.* oxygen
oyentes *m., pl.* listeners

P

paciencia *f.* patience
paciente *adj./m., f.* patient
pacifista *adj./m., f.* pacifist
padecer de (c:zc) *v.i.* (*disease*) to suffer from
Padece del corazón. He has heart problems.
padecimiento *m.* suffering

padrastro *m.* stepfather
padre *m.* father; priest
padres *m., pl.* parents
padrino *m.* godfather
pagar *v.t.* to pay
  pagar a plazos to pay in installments
  pagar al contado to pay in cash
  pagar en efectivo to pay in cash
  pagar la cuenta to pay the bill
página *f.* page
  página principal home page
país *m.* country
  país desarrollado developed country
  país en vías de desarrollo developing country
paisaje *m.* landscape; countryside
pájaro *m.* bird
pala *f.* shovel
palabra *f.* word
palacio *m.* palace
paladar *m.* palate
palanca *f.* lever
paleontología *f.* paleontology
paleontólogo/a *m., f.* paleontologist
pálido/a *adj.* pale, pallid
palmera *f.* palm tree
palo *m.* stick; (*golf*) club
  de tal palo, tal astilla *loc.* like father, like son
paloma *f.* dove
pan *m.* bread
  pan integral whole-wheat bread
  pan tostado toasted bread; toast
panadería *f.* bakery
páncreas *m.* pancreas
pandilla *f.* gang
pandillero/a *m., f.* gang member
pantaletas *f., pl.* (*Venezuela*) panties
pantalla *f.* screen
pantalones *m., pl.* pants
  pantalones cortos shorts
pantano *m.* (*natural*) marsh, swamp; (*man-made*) reservoir
pantorrilla *f.* (anatomy) calf
pantuflas *f., pl.* slippers
pañuelo *m.* handkerchief
papa *f.* (*L.A.*) potato
  papas fritas fried potatoes; French fries
papá *m.* dad
papás *m., pl.* parents
papel *m.* paper; *m.* role
  papel de aluminio tinfoil
  papel higiénico toilet paper
  hacer un buen/mal papel *idiom* to make a good/bad impression
papelera *f.* wastebasket
papi *m.* daddy
paquete *m.* package
par *m.* pair
  un par de días a couple of days
  un par de zapatos a pair of shoes
para *prep.* for; in order to
  para que so that
parabrisas *m., sing.* windshield

paracaídas *m., sing.* parachute
paracaidismo *m.* parachuting
paracaidista *m., f.* parachutist
parachoques *m., sing.* bumper
parada *f.* (*train, bus*) stop
parador *m.* lodging
paraguas *m.* umbrella
paragüero *m.* umbrella stand
parar(se) *v.i.* to stop
pararrayos *m.* lightning rod
parásito *m.* parasite
parecer (c:zc) *v.i.* to seem; to appear
  al parecer *adv.* apparently, seemingly
parecerse (c:zc) (a alguien/a algo) *v. pron.* to look like (*somebody/something*); to be alike
  ¿A quién se parece? Who does he/she look like?
pared *f.* wall
pareja *f.* partner; (married) couple
  ¿Cuántas parejas vienen a cenar? How many couples are coming for dinner?
parientes *m., pl.* relatives
párpado *m.* eyelid
parque *m.* park
  parque acuático water park
  parque de atracciones (*Spain*) amusement park
  parque de diversiones (*L.A.*) amusement park
  parque natural nature reserve
párrafo *m.* paragraph
parrilla *f.* grill
  a la parrilla grilled, broiled
parte *f.* part
  de parte de on behalf of
participación *f.* participation
participante *m., f.* competitor
participar *v.t.* to participate
particular *adj.* private
partida *f.* departure
partido *m.* (*sports*) game, match; (*politics*) party
partir *v.t.* to cut; *v.i.* to leave
  a partir de from, starting (on)
pasa *f.* raisin
pasado *p.p. of* **pasar** passed
pasado/a *adj.* last; past
  el pasado lunes last Monday
pasaje *m.* ticket
  pasaje de ida y vuelta roundtrip ticket
pasajero/a *m., f.* passenger
pasamanos *m.* handrail, bannister
pasaporte *m.* passport
pasar *v.i.* to go by; to pass
  pasar la aspiradora to vacuum
  pasar por el banco to go by the bank
  pasar por la aduana to go through customs
  pasar tiempo to spend time
  pasarlo bien/mal to have a good/bad time
  pasarlo de película to have a great time
pasarse (el alto/el semáforo en rojo) *v. pron.* to run a red light
pasatiempo *m.* pastime; hobby
pasear *v.i.* to take a walk; to stroll

pasear en bicicleta to ride a bicycle
pasear por la ciudad/el pueblo to walk around the city/town
paseo *m.* stroll, walk
pasillo *m.* hallway
paso *m.* step; way
paso a nivel railroad crossing
paso de peatones (*L.A.*) crosswalk
ceder el paso to yield (the right of way)
pasta de dientes *f.* toothpaste
pastel *m.* cake; pie
pastel de chocolate chocolate cake
pastel de cumpleaños birthday cake
pastelería *f.* pastry shop
pastilla *f.* pill; tablet
pasto *m.* lawn, grass
patata *f.* (*Spain*) potato
patatas fritas fried potatoes, French fries
tortilla de patatas potato omelet
paterno/a *adj.* (*relative*) paternal
patilla *f.* sideburn
patinaje *m.* skating
patinaje artístico figure skating
patinaje sobre hielo ice skating
patinaje sobre ruedas roller skating
patinar *v.i.* to skate
patinar en hielo to ice skate
patinar en línea to rollerblade; to skate in-line
patio *m.* patio; yard
patrimonio *m.* heritage
patrocinador(a) *m., f.* sponsor
patrocinar *v.t.* to sponsor
patrón *m.* boss, owner
pavo *m.* turkey
payaso/a *m., f.* clown
paz *f.* peace
peatón *m.* pedestrian
peca *f.* freckle
pecho *m.* chest; breast
pechuga (de pollo) *f.* (chicken) breast
pecoso/a *adj.* freckled
pedagogía *f.* pedagogy
pedagógico/a *adj.* pedagogical
pedagogo/a *m., f.* pedagogue
pedal *m.* pedal
pedal del acelerador gas pedal
pedal del embrague clutch pedal
pedal del freno brake pedal
pedante *adj.* pedantic
pedazo *m.* piece
pedicura *f.* pedicure
pedir (e:i) *v.t.* to ask (for); to request; (*food*) to order
pedir prestado to borrow
pedir un préstamo to apply for a loan
pegar *v.t.* to hit; to glue; to stick
peinado *m.* hairstyle; hairdo
Su nuevo peinado le sienta bien. Her new hairdo suits her.
peinarse *v. pron.* to comb one's hair

peine *m.* comb
pelapapas *m.* peeler
pelar *v.t.* to peel
peldaño *m.* step, stair
pelea *f.* quarrel, fight
pelearse *v. pron.* to quarrel, to fight
Siempre se pelean por lo mismo. They always quarrel over the same thing.
película *f.* movie
peligro *m.* danger
peligroso/a *adj.* dangerous
pelirrojo/a *adj.* red-headed, red-hair
pelo *m.* hair
pelota *f.* ball; baseball
peluca *f.* wig
peludo/a *adj.* hairy
peluquería *f.* beauty salon
peluquero/a *m., f.* hairdresser
pena *f.* ache, grief, pity
No vale la pena. It's not worth the trouble.
pendiente *adj.* (*problem, matter*) unresolved
estar pendiente to be waiting
Estoy pendiente de que el jefe me llame. I'm waiting for the boss to call me.
tener (un asunto) pendiente to have (an) unfinished (matter)
pendientes *m.* (*Spain*) earrings
penicilina *f.* penicillin
península *f.* peninsula
penitenciaría *f.* penitentiary
pensar (e:ie) (en) *v.t.* to think (about)
pensar (+ *inf.*) to intend/plan (*to do something*)
Pienso llamarle mañana. I intend to call him tomorrow.
pensión *f.* boardinghouse; retirement pension
pensionista *m., f.* pensioner, retired person
peor *adj.* worse; worst
el/la peor the worst
lo peor the worst (thing)
peor que *adv.* worse than
pepino *m.* cucumber
pequeño/a *adj.* small
pera *f.* pear
percha *f.* hanger
perchero *m.* coat hanger
perder (e:ie) *v.t.* to lose; to miss
perdido *p.p. of* **perder** lost; **perdido/a** *adj.* lost
Perdón. Pardon me.; Excuse me.
perdonar *v.t.* to forgive
peregrinación *f.* pilgrimage
peregrino/a *m., f.* pilgrim
perejil *m.* parsley
pereza *f.* laziness
perezoso/a *adj.* lazy
perfecto/a *adj.* perfect
perfil *m.* profile
perforadora *f.* (*tool*) drill
perforar *v.t.* to drill; to perforate
perfume *m.* perfume
perfumería *f.* perfumery
perico *m.* parakeet
perímetro *m.* perimeter
periódico *m.* newspaper
periodismo *m.* journalism
periodista *m., f.* journalist
periquito *m.* parakeet

permanecer (c:zc) *v.i.* to remain; to stay
permiso *m.* permission
Con permiso. Pardon me., Excuse me.
Con su permiso, tengo que irme. If you'll excuse me, I have to leave.
permiso de trabajo work permit
permitir *v.t.* to permit, to allow
pero *conj.* but
perro/a *m., f.* dog
perseguir (e:i) *v.t. irreg.* **(yo persigo)** to pursue; to chase
persiana *f.* blind
persistente *adj.* persistent
persistir *v.i.* to persist
persona *f.* person
personaje *m.* character
personaje principal main character
personalidad *f.* personality
pertenecer (c:zc) (a) *v.t.* to belong to
pertenencias *f., pl.* belongings
pesa *f.* weight
pesadilla *f.* nightmare
pesado/a *adj.* heavy; annoying
pesar *m.* sorrow
a pesar de despite, in spite of
pesar *v.t.* to weigh
pesarse *v. pron.* to weigh oneself
pesca *f.* fishing
pescadería *f.* fish market
pescado *m.* (*cooked*) fish
pescador(a) *m., f.* fisherman/fisherwoman
pescar *v.i.* to fish
pesimista *adj.* pessimist, pessimistic
peso *m.* weight
pestaña *f.* eyelash
pesticida *m.* pesticide
pétalo *m.* petal
petrificado/a *adj.* petrified
pez *m.* (*live*) fish
pez gordo big shot
picante *adj.* spicy
pico *m.* beak
pie *m.* foot
piedra *f.* stone
piel *f.* skin
de piel (made) of leather
pierna *f.* leg
pijama *m., f.* pajamas
píldora *f.* pill
pimienta *f.* black pepper
pimiento *m.* bell pepper
pinacoteca *f.* art gallery
pinar *m.* pine forest
pinchar *v.t.* (*tire*) to go flat
pingüino *m.* penguin
pino *m.* pine tree
pintada *f.* graffiti
Hay pintadas de pandillas en la pared. There is gang graffiti on the wall.
pintalabios *m.* lipstick
pintar *v.t.* to paint
pintarse *v. pron.* to put on makeup
pintor(a) *m., f.* painter
pintoresco/a *adj.* picturesque
pintura *f.* painting; picture
piña *f.* pineapple
piñata *f.* container filled with candies

piragua *f.* canoe
piragüismo *m.* (*sport*) canoeing
piragüista *m., f.* canoeist
pirámide *f.* pyramid
piropear *v.t.* to make flattering comments
piropo *m.* flattering comment
piscina *f.* swimming pool
  piscina climatizada indoor pool
piso *m.* (*of a building*) floor, story; (*L.A.*) floor; (*Spain*) apartment
pista *f.* track; clue
  Dame una pista. Give me a clue.
  pista cubierta indoor track
  pista de aterrizaje landing strip
  pista de atletismo sports track
  pista de baile dance floor
  pista de esquí ski slope
  pista de hielo ice rink
  pista de hierba grass court
  pista de patinaje skating rink
  pista de tenis tennis court
  pista de tierra batida clay court
pizarra *f.* blackboard
pizarrón *m.* blackboard
pizca *f.* (*quantity*) pinch, little bit
placa (de matrícula) *f.* license plate
placer *m.* pleasure; delight
  Ha sido un placer. It's been a pleasure.
plagiar *v.t.* to plagiarize
plagio *m.* plagiarism
plancha *f.* (*appliance*) iron; griddle
  a la plancha grilled
planchar (la ropa) *v.t.* to iron (clothes)
plan *m.* plan
planeta *m.* planet
planetario *m.* planetarium
plano *m.* (*architecture*) blueprint; city map
plano/a *adj.* (*surface*) flat
planta *f.* plant; (*building*) floor
  planta baja ground floor
plantado/a: dejar plantado/a (a alguien) to stand (somebody) up
plástico *m.* plastic
  de plástico (*made*) of plastic
plata *f.* silver
plátano *m.* banana; plantain
plateado/a *adj.* silver
platillo *m.* dish
plato *m.* plate; (*meal*) dish, course
  plato principal main dish/main course
playa *f.* beach
plaza *f.* city or town square
  plaza de toros bullring
  plaza mayor town square
plazo *m.* (*time*) period, (*payments*) installment
plegable *adj.* folding
plegar *v.t.* to fold
plomería *f.* (*L.A.*) plumbing
plomero/a *m., f.* (*L.A.*) plumber
plomo *m.* lead
pluma *f.* pen; feather
pluralidad *f.* plurality
pluralismo *m.* plurarism

población *f.* population
poblar (o:ue) *v.t.* to populate
pobre *adj.* poor
pobreza *f.* poverty
poco/a *adj.* little; few
poder *m.* power
poder (o:ue) *v. aux.* to be able to; can
poderoso/a *adj.* powerful
podio *m.* podium
poema *m.* poem
poesía *f.* poetry
poeta *m., f.* poet
polémica *f.* controversy
polémico/a *adj.* controversial, polemical
El aborto es aún un tema polémico. Abortion is still a controversial topic.
polen *m.* pollen
policía *f.* police (force); *m., f.* police officer
polideportivo *m.* sports center
política *f.* politics
político/a *m., f.* politician; *adj.* political
pollo *m.* chicken
pollo asado roast chicken
polvo *m.* dust
pomelo *m.* (*Argentina, Spain*) grapefruit
ponchar *v.t.* to go flat
poncharse (una llanta) *v. pron.* to have a flat tire
ponchera *f.* punchbowl
poner *v.t. irreg.* **(yo pongo)** to put; to place; *v.i.* to turn on (*electrical appliances*)
poner a uno al día/al corriente *idiom* to bring someone up to date
poner el árbol to decorate the tree
poner en libertad (a alguien) to release (*somebody*)
poner la mesa to set the table
poner una inyección to give an injection
ponerse *v. pron. irreg.* **(yo me pongo)** to put on; to wear
ponerse (+ *adj.*) *v. pron. irreg.* **(yo me pongo)** to become (+ *adj.*)
ponerse elegante to dress up
Te has puesto muy elegante esta noche. You have dressed up tonight.
ponerse rojo/a to blush
por *prep.* for; for the sake of; for; by; in; through; due to; in exchange for
por aquí around here
por avión by plane
por ejemplo for example
por eso that's why; therefore
por favor please
por fin finally
por la mañana in the morning
por la noche at night
por la tarde in the afternoon; in the evening
por lo menos at least
por lo visto apparently
¿por qué? why?
por supuesto of course
por teléfono by phone; on the phone
por último finally

porcentaje *m.* percentage
porche *m.* porch
porción *f.* serving
porque *conj.* because
portaaviones *m., sing.* aircraft carrier
portarse *v. pron.* to behave oneself
portarse bien/mal to behave well/badly, to behave/misbehave
portátil *adj.* portable
portavoz *m., f.* spokesperson
portero/a *m., f.* doorman, porter
porvenir *m.* future
poseer *v.t.* to own
posesión *f.* possession
posesivo/a *adj.* possessive
posible *adj.* possible
lo antes posible as soon as possible
(no) es posible it's (not) possible
postal *f.* postcard
postre *m.* dessert
potencia *f.* power
pozo *m.* well
práctica *f.* practice
practicar *v.i.* to practice
practicar deportes to play sports
práctico/a *adj.* handy; useful
precaución *f.* precaution
precio *m.* price
precio fijo fixed/set price
predecir (e:i) *v.t. irreg.* **(yo predigo)** to predict, to foretell
predicción f. prediction
predicción del tiempo weather forecast
prefabricado/a *adj.* prefabricated
prefabricar *v.t.* to prefabricate
preferir (e:ie) *v.t.* to prefer
pregunta *f.* question
preguntar *v.t.* to ask (*a question*)
premiar *v.t.* to award
premio *m.* prize; award
prenda *f.* garment
Colgaron las prendas en el armario. They hung up the garments in the wardrobe.
prender *v.t.* to turn on
prensa *f.* press
preocupado/a (por) *adj.* worried (about)
preocuparse (por) *v. pron.* to worry (about)
No se/te preocupe(s). Don't worry.
preparar *v.t.* to prepare
prepararse *v. pron.* to get ready
preparativos *m., pl.* preparations
los preparativos del viaje/para la boda the travel/wedding preparations
preparatoria *f.* high school
preposición *f.* preposition
presa *f.* prey
presentación *f.* introduction
presentador(a) *m., f.* presenter
presentar *v.t.* to introduce; (*performance*) to put on; to present
Le presento a... *form.* I would like to introduce (*name*) to you.

Te presento a... *fam.* I would like to introduce (*name*) to you.
presidiario/a *m., f.* convict
presión *f.* pressure
las presiones de la vida diaria pressures of daily life
presión sanguínea blood pressure
preso/a *m., f.* prisoner
prestación *f.* fringe benefits
prestado/a *adj.* borrowed
préstamo *m.* loan
prestar *v.t.* to lend; to loan
presumido/a *adj.* vain
presupuesto *m.* budget
pretencioso/a *adj.* pretentious
pretexto *m.* excuse
prevención *f.* prevention
prevenir (e:ie) *v.t. irreg.* **(yo prevengo)** to prevent
primaria *f.* grammar school
primavera *f.* spring
primer, primero/a *adj.* first
en primer lugar *adv.* first of all
primitivo/a *adj.* primitive
primo/a *m., f.* cousin
primogénito/a *m., f.* firstborn
principal *adj.* main
príncipe *m.* prince
princesa *f.* princess
prisa *f.* haste; hurry
a toda prisa as fast as possible
¡De prisa! Hurry!
sin prisa pero sin pausa slowly but surely
prisión *f.* prison
probable *adj.* probable
(no) es probable it's (not) probable
probador *m.* dressing room
probar (o:ue) *v.t.* to taste; to try
probarse (o:ue) *v. pron.* (*clothes*) to try on
problema *m.* problem
prodigio/a *m., f.* prodigy
prodigioso/a *adj.* exceptional
productos *m., pl.* products
productos alimenticios foodstuffs
productos lácteos dairy (products)
profesión *f.* profession
profesor(a) *m., f.* teacher; professor
profesor(a) particular tutor
profundidad *f.* depth
profundo/a *adj.* deep
programa *m.* program
programa de computación software
programa de entrevistas talk show
programador(a) *m., f.* computer programmer
prohibido *p.p. of* **prohibir** prohibited
prohibido adelantar (*traffic sign*) no passing
prohibido el paso (*traffic sign*) no entry
prohibir *v.t.* to prohibit; to forbid
prolífico/a *adj.* prolific
promedio *m.* average
promesa *f.* promise
prometer *v.t.* to promise
pronombre *m.* pronoun

pronto *adj.* soon
propagar *v.t.* to propagate, to spread, to disseminate
Algunos periódicos propagan rumores. Some papers disseminate rumors.
propagarse *v. pron.* to propagate, to spread
El rumor se propagaba rápidamente. The rumor was propagating rapidly.
propenso/a a *adj.* prone to
propiedad *f.* property
propietario/a *m., f.* owner, proprietor
propina *f.* tip
propio/a *adj.* own
proponer *v.t. irreg.* **(yo propongo)** to propose
propósito *m.* intention; purpose
a propósito *adv.* on purpose, deliberately
a propósito by the way
buenos propósitos good intentions
propuesta *f.* proposal
protección *f.* protection
proteger (g:j) *v.t.* to protect
proteína *f.* protein
protesta *f.* protest
protestante *adj./m., f.* Protestant
protestar *v.i.* to protest
provecho *m.* benefit
¡Buen provecho! Enjoy your meal!
provisiones *f., pl.* provisions, supplies
provocación *f.* provocation
provocado/a *adj.* induced
provocar *v.t.* to cause; to provoke
próximo/a *adj.* next
proyección *f.* projection
proyectar *v.t.* to project
proyectil *m.* missile
proyecto *m.* project
prueba *f.* test; quiz
prueba de aptitud aptitude test
prueba de la alcoholemia sobriety test
prueba de nivel placement test
(p)sicología *f.* psychology
(p)sicólogo/a *m., f.* psychologist
(p)siquiatra *m., f.* psychiatrist
pubertad *f.* puberty
publicar *v.t.* to publish
público *m.* audience
pueblo *m.* town
puente *m.* bridge
puente colgante suspension bridge
puerta *f.* door
puerta principal front door
puerta trasera back door
puerto *m.* port, harbor
Puerto Rico *m.* Puerto Rico
puertorriqueño/a *adj./m., f.* Puerto Rican
pues *conj.* well; *adv.* then
puesto *m.* position; job; *p.p. of* **poner** put
puesta *f.* **de sol** sunset
pulgar *m.* thumb
pulmón *m.* lung
pulpo *m.* octopus
pulsera *f.* bracelet

punto *m.* point, period
en punto (*time*) on the dot, exactly, sharp
puntual *adj.* punctual
puñal *m.* dagger
puñalada *f.* stab
puño *m.* fist
pupila *f.* pupil
pupitre *m.* student desk
puro/a *adj.* pure; *adv.* sheer; *m.* cigar
aceite puro de oliva pure olive oil
pura casualidad sheer coincidence

Q

que *pron.* that; who; *conj.* that; (*in exclamations*) what; how
¡Qué alto eres! How tall you are!
¡Qué dolor! What pain!
¡Qué extraño! How strange!
¡Qué grande! How big!
¡Qué gusto (+ *inf.*)! What a pleasure to . . . !
¡Qué lata! *loc.* What a drag!
¡Qué ropa más bonita! What pretty clothes!
¡Qué sorpresa! What a surprise!
¿qué? *adv.* what?
¿Qué día es hoy? What day is it?
¿Qué hay de nuevo? What's new?; What's happening?
¿Qué hora es? What time is it?
¿Qué les parece? What do you (*pl.*) think?
¿Qué pasa? What's happening?; What's going on?
¿Qué pasó? What happened?; What's wrong?
¿Qué precio tiene? What is the price?
¿Qué tal? How are you?; How is it going?
¿Qué tal...? How is/are . . . ?
¿Qué talla lleva/usa? What size do you take?
¿Qué tiempo hace? What's the weather like?
quedar *v.i.* to be left over; (*clothing*) to fit; to be located; to be left behind
Ese vestido te queda muy bien. That dress fits you nicely.
¿Dónde queda la panadería? Where's the bakery (located)?
quedar embarazada to get pregnant
quedarse *v. pron.* to stay
¡Quédate! Stay!
quedarse calvo to go bald
quedarse embarazada to get pregnant
quedarse soltero/a to stay single
quedarse viudo/a to be widowed
quehaceres *m., pl.* chores
quehaceres domésticos household chores
queja *f.* complaint
quejarse (de) *v. pron.* to complain (about)

quemado/a *adj.* burned; (*figurative*) burned out
quemados *m., pl.* dodge ball
quemar *v.t.* to burn
No quemes la ropa vieja. Don't burn old clothes.
querer (e:ie) *v.t.* to want; to love
Quisiera un café. I would like a coffee.
No quiero. I don't want to.
querido/a *adj.* beloved
queso *m.* cheese
quien *pron.* who; whom
Ella es quien me lo dijo. She's the one who told me.
¿quién(es)? who?; whom?
¿Quién es...? Who is . . . ?
¿Quién habla? Who is speaking? (*telephone*)
química *f.* chemistry
químico/a *adj.* chemical; *m., f.* chemist
quince fifteen
quinceañero/a *m., f.* fifteen-year-old; teenager
(fiesta de) quinceañera young woman's fifteenth birthday celebration
quincena *f.* two weeks, fortnight
quinientos/as five hundred
quinto/a *adj./m.* fifth
quirófano *m.* operating room
quitar *v.t.* to take away
El policía me quitó los documentos. The police officer took away my documents.
quitar la mesa to clear the table
quitarse *v. pron.* (*clothes*) to take off
Quítate esos zapatos. Take those shoes off.
quizás *adv.* perhaps

R

rábano *m.* radish
rabino/a *m., f.* rabbi
racismo *m.* racism
racista *adj./m., f.* racist
radio *f.* (*medium*) radio; m. (*set*) radio
radiografía *f.* X-ray
radioyente *m., f.* radio listener
raíz *f.* root
rallador *m.* grater
rama *f.* branch
rana *f.* frog
rápido/a *adj.* fast
comida rápida fast food
rápido *adv.* quickly
¡Ven rápido! Come quickly!
raqueta *f.* (*sports*) racket
rascacielos *m.* skyscraper
rastrillo *m.* rake
rasuradora *f.* razor
rato *m.* while **Espera un rato, por favor.** Wait a while, please.
ratos libres *m., pl.* spare/free time
ratón *m.* mouse
ratón de biblioteca bookworm
raya *f.* stripe
de rayas striped
una camisa de rayas a striped shirt

rayo *m.* lightning bolt
raza *f.* race
razón *f.* reason
Lo hice por dos razones. I did it for two reasons.
Tienes razón. You're right.
No tienes razón. You're wrong.
reacción *f.* reaction
reaccionar *v.i.* to react
real *adj.* royal
realeza *f.* royalty
realizar *v.t.* to carry out; to make
rebaja *f.* sale
de rebaja reduced
rebanada *f.* slice
una rebanada de pan a slice of bread
rebelde *adj.* rebellious
rebobinar *v.t.* to rewind
Apriete el botón de rebobinar. Push the rewind button.
recado *m.* (*phone*) message
dejar un recado to leave a message
recaudar (fondos) *v.t.* to raise (money)
receloso/a *adj.* distrustful
recepción *f.* front desk
receta *f.* prescription; (*cooking*) recipe
recetar *v.t.* (*medication*) to prescribe
rechazar *v.t.* to reject
rechazo *m.* rejection
recibir *v.t.* to receive; to get
recibirse *v. pron.* to graduate
recibo *m.* receipt; bill
el recibo del teléfono the phone bill
reciclaje *m.* recycling
reciclar *v.t.* to recycle
recién *adv.* just
recién casado/a newlywed
recién nacido/a newborn (baby)
recién pintado/a wet paint
recipiente *m.* container
recital *m.* (*music, poetry*) recital
recoger (g:j) *v.t.* to pick up
recoger la mesa *v.t.* to clear the table
recomendable *adj.* advisable
recomendar (e:ie) *v.t.* to recommend
reconocer (c:zc) *v.t.* to recognize
reconocimiento *m.* recognition
récord *m.* (*sports*) record
recordar (o:ue) *v.t.* to remember
recorrer *v.t.* to tour around an area
recreo *m.* recess
rectángulo *m.* rectangle
rectificar *v.t.* to rectify
recuerdo *m.* souvenir
recuerdos *m., pl.* regards
recurso *m.* resource
recurso natural natural resource
red *f.* net; network; Web
reducir (c:zc) *v.t.* to reduce
reemplazar *v.t.* to replace
reflexionar *v.i.* to reflect
reforma *f.* reform

reformar *v.t.* to reform
reforzar (o:ue) *v.t.* to reinforce
refrán *m.* saying
refrescante *adj.* refreshing
refresco *m.* soft drink, soda
refrigerador *m.* refrigerator
refrigerar *v.t.* to refrigerate
refuerzo *m.* reinforcement
regadera *f.* watering can
regalar *v.t.* to give (a gift)
regalo *m.* gift, present
regañar *v.t.* to scold, to reprimand
regar *v.t.* (*plants*) to water
regatear *v.i.* to bargain
régimen *m.* diet
Está a régimen. She's on a diet.
región *f.* region; area
regla *f.* rule; ruler
regresar *v.i.* to return
regular *adj.* regular; so so; OK
regular *v.t.* to regulate
regularización *f.* regularization
reído *p.p. of* **reír** laughed
reina *f.* queen
reinar *v.i.* to reign
reino *m.* kingdom
reírse (e:i) *v.i.* **(yo río)** to laugh
reírse (e:i) (de) *v. pron.* **(yo me río)** to laugh (about)
rejuvenecer (c:zc) *v.t.* to rejuvenate
rejuvenecimiento *m.* rejuvenation
relación *f.* relationship
relajación *f.* relaxation
relajarse *v. pron.* to relax
relámpago *m.* lightning bolt
religión *f.* religion
religioso/a *adj.* religious
rellenar *v.t.* (*culinary*) to stuff; (*document*) (*Spain*) to fill out
relleno *m.* stuffing
relleno/a (de) *adj.* stuffed (with)
Me encantan los chiles rellenos de queso rallado. I love chilies stuffed with grated cheese.
reloj *m.* clock; watch
remar *v.i.* to row
remedio *m.* remedy
remero/a *m., f.* rower
remo *m.* oar
remolacha *f.* beet
remolino *m.* whirlpool; whirlwind
remover (o:ue) *v.t.* to stir
renacentista *adj.* Renaissance
renacimiento *m.* Renaissance
rencor *m.* grudge, resentment, hard feelings
Todavía siente rencor por lo que le hicieron. She still resents what they did to her.
rencoroso/a *adj.* resentful
renglón *m.* line
papel con renglones lined paper
renovación *f.* renewal, updating, renovation
renovar (o:ue) *v.t.* to renew, to change, to renovate
renunciar (a) *v.t.* to resign (from)
repelente *m.* (*for insects*) repellent
repente: de repente *adv.* suddenly

repetir (e:i) *v.t.* to repeat
repollo *m.* (*L.A.*) cabbage
reportaje *m.* report
reportero/a *m., f.* reporter; journalist
reposar *v.i.* to rest
Tenía que reposar por varias semanas después de la operación. He had to rest for several weeks after the operation.
reposo *m.* rest
represa *f.* dam
representante *m., f.* representative
represión *f.* repression
reprimir *v.t.* to repress
Tuvo que reprimir la emoción. He had to repress his emotion.
reprimirse *v. pron. (refl.)* to control oneself
reproducir (c:zc) *v.t.* to repeat, to reproduce
Es difícil reproducir los resultados. It's difficult to reproduce the results.
reproducirse (c:zc) *v. pron. (biology)* to reproduce; to happen again
Es improbable que se reproduzcan tales circunstancias. It's unlikely that such circumstances will happen again.
reproductor de DVD DVD player
reptil *m.* reptile
resaca *f.* (*Spain*) hangover
tener resaca to have a hangover
rescatar *v.t.* to rescue
rescate *m.* rescue
reservación *f.* reservation
hacer una reservación to book
reservado/a *adj.* reserved
resfriado *m. (illness)* cold
residencia *f.* residence
residencia de ancianos home for the elderly
residencia estudiantil dormitory
residente *adj./m., f.* resident
residir *v.i.* to live, to reside
resistencia *f.* resistance
resistir *v.t.* to resist
resolución *f.* (*problem*) solution; (*conflict*) settlement
resolver (o:ue) *v.t.* to resolve; to solve
respaldar *v.t.* (*person, decision*) to back, to support
respecto: con respecto a with regard to, regarding
respetar *v.t.* to respect
respeto *m.* respect
respiración *f.* breathing, respiration
respiración boca a boca mouth-to-mouth resuscitation
respirar *v.i.* to breathe
responder *v.t.* to respond, to answer
responsable *adj.* responsible
respuesta *f.* answer
restaurante *m.* restaurant
restaurar *v.t.* to restore
restos *m., pl.* leftovers

resuelto *p.p. of* **resolver** resolved
resultado *m.* result
resumen *m.* summary
en resumen in summary
resumir *v.t.* to summarize
resumiendo summarizing
retar (a alguien a + *inf.*) *v.t.* to challenge (somebody to + *inf.*)
Me retó a imitarle. He challenged me to imitate him.
reto *m.* challenge
El gran reto de nuestro siglo es acabar con la pobreza. The great challenge of our century is to end poverty.
retórica *f.* rhetoric
retórico/a *adj.* rhetorical
retraído/a *adj.* withdrawn
retrasarse *v.i.* to be late
retraso *m.* delay
retrato *m.* portrait, photograph of people
retrovisor *m.* rearview mirror
reumatismo *m.* rheumatism
reunión *f.* meeting
revelar *v.t.* to reveal; (*photography*) to develop
revés: al revés *adv.* the other way around; backward(s)
revisar *v.t.* to check
revisar el aceite to check the oil
revisión *f.* (*Spain*) (medical) checkup
revista *f.* magazine
rey *m.* king
rezar *v.i.* to pray
riachuelo *m.* stream, brook
rico/a *adj.* rich; (*food*) tasty, delicious
ridículo/a *adj.* ridiculous
Es ridículo (que...) It's ridiculous (that...)
Es ridículo que llores. It's ridiculous that you cry.
rincón *m.* (*inside*) corner
rinoceronte *m.* rhinoceros
riñón *m.* kidney
río *m.* river
riquísimo/a *adj. (superlative)* extremely delicious
risa *f.* laughter
morirse/partirse de risa to die laughing
robar *v.t.* to rob; to steal
roble *m.* oak tree
robo *m.* robbery; theft
rocío *m.* dew
rodaja *f.* slice
hamburguesa con queso y rodajas de cebolla a hamburger with cheese and sliced onions
rodaje *m.* (*cinema*) filming, shooting
rodar *v.t.* (*cinema*) to shoot, to film
rodilla *f.* knee
rogar (o:ue) *v.t.* to beg; to plead
rojizo/a *adj.* reddish
rojo/a *adj./m.* red
al rojo vivo red-hot
La situación está al rojo vivo. The situation is at the boiling point.
románico/a *adj.* Romanesque
romano/a *adj./m., f.* Roman
romanticismo *m.* Romanticism

romántico/a *adj./m., f.* romantic
romero *m.* rosemary
rompecabezas *m., sing.* (jigsaw) puzzle
rompeolas *m.* breakwater
romper (con) *v.t./v.i.* to break; to break up (with)
romper el hielo *loc.* break the ice
¿Han roto? Have they broken up?
romperse *v. pron.* to break
Se rompió la pierna. He broke his leg.
ron *m.* rum
roncar *v.i.* to snore
ronquido *m.* snore
ropa *f.* clothing; clothes
ropa deportiva sportswear
ropa interior underwear
ropero *m.* wardrobe
rosa *f.* rose
rosado/a *adj./m.* pink
rosal *m.* rosebush
roto/a *adj.* broken
rubí *m.* ruby
rubio/a *m., f.* blond(e)
rueda *f.* wheel
rueda de recambio spare tire
rueda de repuesto spare tire
rugido *m.* roar
rugir (g:j) *v.i.* to roar
ruido *m.* noise
ruidoso/a *adj.* noisy
ruleta *f.* roulette
rumor *m.* rumor
ruta *f.* route
rutina *f.* routine
rutina diaria daily routine

S

sábado *m.* Saturday
sábana *f.* sheet
saber *v.t. irreg.* **(yo sé)** to know; to know how (to); *m.* knowledge
no sé I don't know
saber (a) to taste like
Sabe a limón. It tastes like lemon.
sabiduría *f.* wisdom
sabihondo/a *adj./m., f.* know-it-all
sabio/a *adj.* learned, wise; *m., f.* wise person
sabor *m.* flavor
sabrosísimo/a *adj.* (*superlative*) extremely delicious
sabroso/a *adj.* tasty; delicious
sacacorchos *m.* corkscrew
sacar *v.t.* to take out
sacar buenas notas to get good grades
sacar fotos to take pictures/photographs
sacar la basura to take out the trash
sacar al perro a pasear to take out (walk) the dog
sacar(se) una muela to extract a tooth; to pull a tooth
saco *m.* bag, sack
saco de dormir sleeping bag
sacudir *v.t.* to shake; to dust
sacudir el polvo to dust
sacudir los muebles to dust the furniture
saga *f.* saga

sagrado/a *adj.* sacred
sal *f.* salt
sala *f.* living room; room
  sala de emergencia emergency room
salado/a *adj.* salty
salario *m.* salary
salchicha *f.* sausage
salero *m.* salt shaker
salida *f.* departure; exit
  callejón sin salida dead-end street
  salida del sol sunrise
salir *v.i. irreg.* **(yo salgo)** to leave; to go out
  salir con to go out with; to date (*someone*)
  salir de to leave from
  salir para to leave for (*a place*)
salirse (en) *v. pron.* to get off (at)
salmón *m.* salmon
salón *m.* hall; salon; classroom
  salón de actos auditorium
  salón de belleza beauty salon
salsa *f.* sauce
saltar *v.i.* to jump
saltear *v.t.* to sauté
salto *m.* jump
  salto alto (*L.A.*) high jump
  salto de altura (*Spain*) high jump
  salto de longitud (*Spain*) long jump
  salto largo (*L.A.*) long jump
  salto mortal somersault
salud *f.* health
saludable *adj.* healthy
saludar *v.t.* to greet, to say hello
saludarse *v. pron.* to greet each other, to say hello to each other
  ¿No se saludan? They don't say hello to each other?
saludo *m.* greeting
  Saludos. (*in a letter*) Best wishes.
  saludos a... greetings to...
  Saludos a tu padre. Give my regards to your father.
salvaje *adj.* (*animal, flower*) wild
salvamento *m.* rescue
salvar *v.t.* to save
salvavidas *m., f.* lifeguard; *m.* life jacket
salvia *f.* sage
sandalia *f.* sandal
sandía *m.* watermelon
sándwich *m.* sandwich
sangre *f.* blood
sanguíneo/a *adj.* blood
sano/a *adj.* healthy
sapo *m.* toad
sarampión *m.* measles
sardina *f.* sardine
sartén *f.* frying pan
sastre *m.* tailor
satisfecho/a *adj.* satisfied
sauna *f.* sauna
savia *f.* (*botany*) sap
se *pron.* himself, herself, itself, *form.* yourself, themselves, yourselves
se one; on one; on us
  Se hizo... He/She/It became...

Se nos dañó el auto. The car broke down on us.
Se nos ponchó/pinchó una llanta. We got a flat tire.
Se pueden comprar boletos aquí. One can buy tickets here.
secador *m.* hairdryer
secadora *f.* clothes dryer
secar *v.t.* to dry
secarse *v. pron.* to dry (oneself)
sección *f.* section
sección de (no) fumar *f.* (non) smoking section
seco/a *adj.* dry
secretario/a *m., f.* secretary
secuencia *f.* sequence
secuestrar *v.t.* (*person*) to kidnap; (*airplane*) to hijack
secuestro *m.* kidnapping; hijack
secundaria, (escuela) *f.* high school
sed *f.* thirst
seda *f.* silk
de seda (made of) silk
sedentario/a *adj.* sedentary; related to sitting
sediento/a *adj.* thirsty
sedimentación *f.* sedimentation
sedimento *m.* sediment
seducir (c:zc) *v.t.* to seduce; to captivate
seductor(a) *adj.* seductive; *m.* seducer, *f.* seductress
seguir (e:i) *v.t.* **(yo sigo)** to follow; to continue
según *prep.* according to
segundo/a *adj./m.* second
en segundo lugar *adv.* secondly
seguro *m.* insurance; safe
seguro médico medical insurance
seguro/a *adj.* sure; safe
(No) Es seguro (que)... It's (not) sure (that)...
No es seguro que lo tenga. He may not have it.
No estoy seguro. I'm not sure
seis six
seiscientos/as six hundred
seleccionar *v.t.* to select
selecto/a *adj.* select
sello *m.* stamp
selva *f.* jungle
semáforo *m.* traffic signal; street light
semana *f.* week
semana entrante/que viene next week
la semana pasada last week
Semana Santa Holy Week
semántica *f.* semantics
semejante *adj.* similar
semestre *m.* semester
semilla *f.* seed
seminario *m.* seminar
senado *m.* senate
sencillo/a *adj.* simple; (*person*) modest
sendero *m.* trail; trailhead
sensatez *f.* good sense
sensato/a *adj.* sensible
sensibilidad *f.* sensitivity
sensible *adj.* sensitive
sentar (e:ie) *v.i.* (*clothes*) to suit

Esa chaqueta te sienta bien. That jacket suits you.
sentarse (e:ie) *v. pron.* to sit down
sentido *m.* sense
sentido común common sense
sentido del orden sense of order
sentimental *adj.* sentimental
sentir (e:ie) *v.t.* to feel; to be sorry; to regret
Lo siento. I'm sorry.
sentirse (e:ie) *v. pron.* to feel
Me siento bien/mal. I feel good/bad.
señal *f.* sign
señal de alto stop sign
señal de tráfico traffic sign
señor (Sr.) *m.* Mr.; sir
señora (Sra.) *f.* Mrs.; ma'am
señorita (Srta.) *f.* Miss
separado/a *adj.* separated
separar *v.t.* to separate
separarse (de) *v. pron.* to separate (from)
septiembre *m.* September
séptimo/a *adj./m.* seventh
sequía *f.* drought
ser *m.* being
ser humano human being
ser vivo living being
ser *v. irreg.* to be
Es la una. It's one o'clock.
sea lo que sea *loc.* be that as it may
ser aficionado/a (a) to be a fan (of)
ser alérgico/a (a) to be allergic (to)
ser gratis to be free of charge
Son las... It's... o'clock.
serio/a *adj.* serious
serpentina *f.* streamer
serpiente *f.* snake
serpiente de cascabel rattlesnake
serrar *v.t.* to saw
servicio *m.* service
servilleta *f.* napkin
servir (e:i) *v.i.* to serve; to help
sesenta sixty
setecientos/as seven hundred
setenta seventy
seto *m.* hedge
seudónimo *m.* pseudonym, pen name
sexismo *m.* sexism
sexto/a *adj./m.* sixth
sí *adv.* yes
si *(conj.)* if
SIDA (síndrome de inmunodeficiencia adquirida) *m.* AIDS
sido *p.p. of* **ser** been
sidra *f.* cider
siempre *adv.* always
siempre que (+ *subj.*) whenever **Voy siempre que puedo.** I go whenever I can.
siempre y cuando (+ *subj.*) provided (that) **Iré siempre y cuando vengas conmigo.** I'll go provided you come with me.
sien *f.* (*anatomy*) temple
sierra *f.* saw
siesta *f.* afternoon nap
siete seven

siglo *m.* century
significar *v.t.* to mean
siguiente *adj.* next, following
silbar *v.i.* to whistle
silbato *m.* whistle
silenciador *m.* (*automobile*) muffler
silencio *m.* silence
silla *f.* seat; chair
  silla de ruedas wheel chair
sillón *m.* armchair
silvestre *adj.* (*flower, plant*) wild
simbiosis *f.* symbiosis
simbolizar *v.t.* symbolize
similar *adj.* similar
simpático/a *adj.* (*person*) nice; likeable
sin *prep.* without
  sin (+ *inf.*) without (+ *-ing*)
  sin hablar without talking
  sin que *conj.* without
  sin ton ni son *adv.* without rhyme or reason
sinagoga *f.* sinagogue
sinfín *m.* a great many, a lot
  Aún tiene un sinfín de cosas que hacer. He still has a lot of things to do.
sinfonía *f.* symphony
sinfónica *f.* symphony orchestra
sinfónico/a *adj.* symphonic
sino *conj.* but
  No una sino dos. Not one but two.
sinónimo/a *m.* synonym; *adj.* synonymous
sintaxis *f.* syntax
síntoma *m.* symptom
sinvergüenza *m., f.* shameless person; scoundrel
sistema *m.* system
  sistema inmunológico immune system
sitio *m.* place; site
  sitio web website
situado/a *p.p. of* **situar** located
sobrar *v.t.* to be left over
  Sobró mucho dinero. There was a lot of money left over.
sobras *m., pl.* leftovers
sobre *m.* envelope; *prep.* on; over
sobreestimar *v.t.* overestimate
sobrehumano/a *adj.* superhuman
sobrenombre *m.* nickname
sobresaliente *adj.* outstanding; *m.* (*grade*) excellent
sobresalir *v.i. irreg.* **(yo sobresalgo)** to excel, to stand out
sobrevalorar *v.t.* to overvalue; to overrate
sobrino/a *m.* nephew; *f.* niece
sobrio/a *adj.* sober
sociable *adj.* sociable
socializar *v.i.* to socialize
sociedad *f.* society
sociología *f.* sociology
sociólogo/a *m., f.* sociologist
socorrer *v.t.* to help
socorro *m.* help; *interj.* Help!
sodio *m.* sodium
sofá *m.* couch; sofa
sofocar *v.t.* (*fire*) to suffocate, to put out; (*weather*) to be stifling
  El calor me sofoca. The heat is stifling.

sofoco *m.* suffocation
sol *m.* sun
solamente *adv.* only
solar *adj.* solar
solario *m.* solarium
soldado *m., f.* soldier
soldadura *f.* weld
soldar (o:ue) *v.t.* to weld
soleado/a *adj.* sunny
soler (o:ue) + *inf.* *v.i.* usually; to be accustomed to
Suelo desayunar sólo café con leche. I usually just have coffee with milk for breakfast.
Suelo ir los domingos. I usually go on Sundays.
solicitar (empleo) *v.t.* to apply (for a job)
solicitud (de trabajo) *f.* (job) application
sollozar *v.i.* to sob
sollozo *m.* sob
solo *adj.* alone
sólo *adv.* only
Sólo sé que estoy solo. I only know that I'm alone.
soltar (o:ue) *v.t.* to release; to let go
soltero/a *adj.* single; unmarried
soltura *f.* ease, agility
solución *f.* solution
solucionar *v.t.* to solve
sombra *f.* shade, shadow
sombrero *m.* hat
sombrilla *f.* sunshade, beach umbrella
someterse a *v. pron.* (*test, examination*) to undergo
sonar (o:ue) *v.t.* to ring; (*alarm*) to go off
sonreído *p.p. of* **sonreír** smiled
sonreír (e:i) *v.i.* to smile
sonrisa *f.* smile
soñar (o:ue) *v.t.* to dream; *v.i.* **soñar con algo** to dream about something
soñar despierto to daydream
sopa *f.* soup
soportar *v.t.* to support, to withstand, to endure
No lo soporto más. I can't take it any more.
soprano *m., f.* soprano
sorbete *m.* sorbet
sorbo *m.* sip
sordo/a *adj.* deaf
sorprender *v.t.* to surprise
sorprenderse *v. pron.* to be surprised
Se sorprendió al verme. He was surprised to see me.
sorpresa *f.* surprise
por sorpresa *adv.* by surprise
sortija *f.* ring
soso/a *adj.* (*culinary*) bland, tasteless; (*person*) boring, dull
sospecha *f.* suspicion
sospechar (algo) *v.t.*; **(de alguien)** *v.i.* to suspect
sospechoso/a *adj.* suspicious
sostener (e:ie) *v.t. irreg.* **(yo sostengo)** support
sótano *m.* basement; cellar
soy I am
Soy yo. It's me. That's me.
soy de… I'm from…
su(s) *poss.* his; her; *form.* your; their

suave *adj.* (*to the touch*) soft; (*taste*) mild
subir *v.t.* to go up
subir(se) a *v.t.* to get on/into (a vehicle)
subirse a los árboles *v.* to climb trees
subirse a los columpios *v.* to go on the swings
subirse a los juegos *v.* to go on rides
subjetivo/a *adj.* subjective
submarino *m.* submarine
subrayado *adj.* underlined
subrayar *v.t.* to underline
subterráneo/a *adj.* underground, subterranean
sucesivamente *adv.* successively
y así sucesivamente and so forth
sucio/a *adj.* dirty
sucre *m.* Ecuadorian currency
sudado/a *adj.* sweaty
sudamericano/a *adj./m., f.* South American
sudar *v.i.* to sweat
suegro/a *m.* father-in-law; *f.* mother-in-law
sueldo *m.* salary, wage
suelo *m.* floor
sueño *m.* sleep
suerte *f.* luck
suéter *m.* sweater
sufrir *v.t.* to suffer **Sufre muchas presiones.** He's under a lot of pressure. **sufrir una enfermedad** to suffer an illness **Sufre una grave enfermedad.** He has a serious illness.
sugerencia *f.* suggestion
sugerir (e:ie) *v.t.* to suggest
suicidarse *v. pron.* to commit suicide
suicidio *m.* suicide
sujetador *m.* (*Spain*) *m.* bra
sumamente *adv.* extremely
suministrador(a) *m., f.* supplier
suministrar *v.t.* to supply
suministro *m.* supply; *m., pl.* supplies
suntuoso/a *adj.* sumptuous
superar *v.t.* to exceed, to go beyond; to overcome **La realidad supera la ficción.** Truth is stranger than fiction.
superarse *v. pron.* to better oneself
supermercado *m.* (super)market
superstición *f.* superstition
supersticioso/a *adj.* superstitious
supervisar *v.t.* to supervise
supervivencia *f.* survival
superviviente *m., f.* survivor
suponer *v.t. irreg.* **(yo supongo)** to suppose; to assume
sur *m.* south
al sur to the south
surtido *m.* assortment; variety
suspender *v.t.* (*examination*) to fail; (*performance*) to cancel
suspenso *m.* (*grade*) fail, F
sustancia *f.* substance
sustantivo *m.* noun
sustituir (y) *v.t.* to replace **Sustituyeron el azúcar por la miel.** They replaced the sugar with honey.
sustituto/a *m., f.* substitute

suyo/a(s) *adj./pron. poss.* (of) his; her; (of) hers; (of) its; *form.* your, (of) yours; their (of)

T

tabaco *m.* tobacco
tablero *m.* blackboard; board
tablero de anuncios bulletin board
tablero de control control panel
taburete *m.* stool
tacaño/a *adj.* stingy
tachadura *f.* crossing out, correction
tachar *v.t.* to cross out, to delete
tacto *m.* (*sense*) touch
tal *adv.* such **Nunca te dije tal cosa.** I never told you any such thing.
Son tal para cual. They are two of a kind.
tal vez *adv.* maybe
tales como such as
talentoso/a *adj.* talented
talla *f.* size
talla grande large
tallar *v.t.* (*wood, stone*) to carve
taller *m.* workshop
taller de mecánica mechanic's workshop
taller mecánico mechanic's repairshop
talón *m.* heel
tamaño *m.* size
también *adv.* also; too
tampoco *adv.* neither; not either
tan *adv.* so
tan pronto como as soon as
tan... como as . . . as
tanque *m.* tank
tanto *adv.* so much
No es para tanto. It's no big deal.
por lo tanto therefore
tanto... como as much ... as
tantos/as... como as many . . . as
tapa *f.* lid; (*Spain*) bar snack
ir de tapas (*Spain*) to go out and have a snack in a bar
tapar *v.t.* to cover
tapete (verde) *m.* (*games*) card table
tapiz *m.* tapestry
taquilla *f.* box office, ticket office
tardar (en) *v.i.* to be late (in) **El autobús tardó en llegar.** The bus was late (in arriving).
a más tardar at the very latest **Llévamelo el jueves a más tardar.** Bring it to me on Thursday at the very latest.
tarde *adv.* late
tarde *f.* afternoon; evening; p.m.
a las tres de la tarde at three in the afternoon, at three p.m.
tarea *f.* homework
tarjeta *f.* (post)card
tarjeta de crédito credit card
tarjeta de invitación invitation
tarjeta de Navidad Christmas card

tarjeta postal postcard
tartamudear *v.i.* to stutter, to stammer
tatarabuelo/a *m.* great-great grandfather; *f.* great-great grandmother
tauromaquia *f.* bullfighting
taxi *m.* taxi(cab)
taza *f.* cup; mug
tazón *m.* bowl
te *pron. fam.* you
Te presento a... Let me/I would like to introduce you to . . .
té *m.* tea
té helado iced tea
teatro *m.* theater
techo *m.* (*L.A.*) roof, ceiling; (*Spain*) ceiling
teclado *m.* keyboard
técnico/a *m., f.* technician
teja *f.* (*roof*) tile
tejado *m.* (*Spain*) roof
tejido *m.* weaving; (*anatomy*) tissue
tela *f.* fabric
tela metálica wire netting
telaraña *f.* spiderweb
teleadicto/a *m., f.* couch potato
teléfono (celular) *m.* (cellular) telephone
telenovela *f.* soap opera
telescopio *m.* telescope
teletrabajo *m.* telecommuting
televisión *f.* television
televisión por cable cable television
televisor *m.* television set
tema *m.* subject; theme
temática *f.* subject matter
temático/a *adj.* thematic, according to subject
temer *v.t.* to fear
temperamento *m.* temperament
temperatura *f.* temperature
templo *m.* temple
temporada *f.* season
temprano *adj.* early
tenazas *f., pl.* tongs
tendedero *m.* clothesline
colgar la ropa en el tendedero to hang clothes on the line
tendencia *f.* tendency
tender (e:ie) *v.t.* (*clothes*) to hang out
tendón *m.* tendon
tenedor *m.* fork
tener (e:ie) *v.t. irreg.* **(yo tengo)** to have
tener algo en la punta de la lengua *loc.* to have something on the tip of one's tongue
tener calor to be hot
tener cuidado to be careful
tener dolor to have a pain
tener dolor de... to have a(n) ...ache
tener en cuenta to keep in mind
tener éxito to be successful
tener fama de to be well-known for, to have a reputation for
tener buena/mala fama to have a good/bad reputation
tener fiebre to have a fever

tener frío to be cold
tener ganas de (+ *inf.*) to feel like (*doing something*); would like to **Tengo ganas de visitar Diamantina.** I would like to visit Diamantina.
tener hambre to be hungry
tener malas pulgas *idiom* to be bad tempered
tener miedo de to be afraid of, to be scared of
tener miedo (de) que to be afraid that
tener planes to have plans
tener prisa to be in a hurry
tener razón to be right
tener sed to be thirsty
tener sueño to be sleepy
tener suerte to be lucky
tener tiempo to have time
tener una cita to have a date; to have an appointment
tener... años to be . . . years old
Tengo... años. I'm . . . years old.
tener (e:ie) *v.aux. irreg.* **(yo tengo)** to have
tener que (+ *inf.*) to have to (*do something*) **Tengo que irme.** I have to go.
tener que ver con *loc.* to have to do with **La carta no tiene nada que ver con el problema.** The letter doesn't have anything to do with the problem.
tenis *m.* tennis(sport); tennis(sneakers)
tenista *m., f.* tennis player
tenor *m.* tenor
tensión *f.* tension
tentáculo *m.* tentacle
teñir (e:i) *v.t.* to dye
teoría *f.* theory
teorizar (sobre algo) *v.i.* to theorize (about something)
terapeútico/a *adj.* therapeutic
terapia *f.* therapy
tercer, tercero/a *adj.* third
en tercer lugar *adv.* thirdly
tercio *m.* third
terciopelo *m.* velvet
terminar *v.t.* to end; to finish
terminar de (+*inf.*) *v.i.* to finish (*doing something*)
¿Has terminado de leer el libro? Have you finished reading the book?
termostato *m.* thermostat
ternera *f.* veal
terraza *f.* terrace
terremoto *m.* earthquake
terreno *m.* plot of land, lot; terrain
terrible *adj.* terrible
Es terrible (que...) It's terrible (that...)
Es terrible que diga eso. It's terrible that he says that.
terrorista *adj./m., f.* terrorist
tertulia *f.* gathering (*to discuss literature, politics, etc.*)
tesis *f.* thesis
tesoro *m.* treasure
testarudo/a *adj.* stubborn
testigo *m., f.* witness; *m.* (*relay race*) baton
tetera *f.* teapot
ti *obj. of prep., fam.* you

tiburón *m.* shark
tiempo *m.* time; weather; occasion
a tiempo on time
tiempo completo/parcial full-time, part-time
tiempo libre free/spare time
tienda *f.* shop, store
tienda de campaña tent
tierno/a *adj.* tender; (*person*) affectionate
tierra *f.* land; ground; soil; Earth
tigre *m.* tiger
tijeras *f., pl.* scissors
timbre *m.* doorbell
tímido/a *adj.* timid, shy
timón *m.* (*ship*) rudder
tina *f.* (*L.A.*) bathtub
tinta *f.* ink
tinto *m.* red (wine)
tío/a *m.* uncle; *f.* aunt
tíos *m. pl.* aunts and uncles
típico/a *adj.* typical, traditional
tipo *m.* type, kind, sort; (*person*) figure
No es mi tipo. He's not my type.
¿Qué tipo de música te gusta? What kind of music do you like?
Tiene muy buen tipo. She has a lovely figure.
tirantes *m., pl.* suspenders
tirar *v.t.* to throw
tiro *m.* shot
tiro al blanco target shooting
tiro al plato trapshooting
tiro con arco archery
título *m.* title
tiza *f.* chalk
toalla *f.* towel
toallero *m.* towel bar
tobillo *m.* ankle
tobogán *m.* (*child's toy*) slide
tocadiscos compacto *m., sing.* compact disc player
tocar *v.t.* to touch
tocar (un instrumento musical) to play (a musical instrument)
todavía *adv.* yet; still; already
todo *m.* everything
Todo está bajo control. Everything is under control.
todo/a *adj.* whole, entire; all
del todo *adv.* entirely **No está del todo equivocada.** She is not entirely mistaken.
por todo el mundo all over the world
todo el mundo the whole world
todos los días every day
todos *m., pl.* all of us; everybody; everyone
tolerancia *f.* tolerance
tolerante *adj.* tolerant
tolerar *v.t.* to tolerate
tomar *v.t.* to take; to drink
algo de tomar something to drink
tomar clases to take classes
tomar el sol to sunbathe
tomar en cuenta take into account
tomar fotos to take photos
tomar la temperatura to take someone's temperature
tomarle el pelo a alguien *idiom* to pull someone's leg, to kid someone

tomate *m.* tomato
tomillo *m.* thyme
tonto/a *adj.* silly; foolish; dumb
torcer (o:ue) (c:z) *v.t.* to twist
torcerse (o:ue) (c:z) (el tobillo) *v. pron.* to sprain (one's ankle)
torcido/a *adj.* twisted; sprained
torero/a *m., f.* bullfighter
tormenta *f.* storm
tornado *m.* tornado
tornillo *m.* screw
toro *m.* bull
toronja *f.* (*L.A.*) grapefruit
torpe *adj.* clumsy, awkward
torre *f.* tower
  torre de control control tower
tortilla *f.* (*egg*) omelet; (*corn*) kind of flat bread
  tortilla de maíz flat bread made of corn flour
  tortilla de patatas potato omelet
tortuga *f.* turtle
tos *f., sing.* cough
toser *v.i.* to cough
tostado/a *adj.* toasted
tostadora *f.* toaster
trabajador(a) *m., f.* hard-working person
trabajar *v.i.* to work
trabajo *m.* job; work; (*paper*) written work
tradición *f.* tradition
traducción *f.* translation
traducir (c:zc) *v.t.* to translate
traductor(a) *m., f.* translator
traer *v.t. irreg.* **(yo traigo)** to bring; to take
traficante *m., f.* (*arms, drugs*) dealer
traficar (en/con) *v.i.* to traffic in
tráfico *m.* traffic
tragaluz *m.* skylight
tragaperras *f., sing.* slot machine
tragar *v.t.* to swallow
tragedia *f.* tragedy
trágico/a *adj.* tragic
traición *f.* treason, betrayal, treachery
traicionar (algo o a alguien) *v.t.* to betray (something or someone)
traicionero/a adj. treacherous
traído *p.p. of* **traer** brought
traje *m.* suit
  traje de baño bathing/swimming suit
traidor(a) *m., f.* traitor; *adj.* treacherous
tramar *v.t.* to plot, to scheme
trampa *f.* trap; trick; catch
  ¿Cuál es la trampa? What's the catch?
  hacer trampa(s) to cheat
trampolín *m.* diving board
tranquilidad *f.* calm, tranquility
tranquilizar *v.t.* to calm down
tranquilizarse *v. pron.* to calm down
tranquilo/a *adj.* (*person*) easygoing; quiet; calm
  ¡Tranquilo! Stay calm!
transatlántico *m.* ocean liner
transbordador *m.* ferry; (*space*) shuttle
transeúnte *m., f.* passer-by; non-resident

transferencia *f.* transfer
transfusión *f.* transfusion
transmitir *v.t.* to broadcast
transparente *adj.* transparent; see-through
transpiración *f.* perspiration
transpirar *v.i.* to perspire
transplante *m.* transplant
transportar *v.t.* to transport; to carry
transporte *m.* transportation
trapeador *m.* (*L.A.*) mop
trapear *v.t.* (*L.A.*) to mop
trapo *m.* dishcloth
trasnochar *v.i.* to stay up all night
trastorno *m.* (*medicine*) disorder
  trastorno estomacal stomach disorder
  trastorno mental mental disorder
trasvasar *v.t.* (*computer*) to download
tratar *v.i.* to try
  tratar de (+ *inf.*) to try (*to do something*)
  Trata de resolverlo. Try to solve it.
trato *m.* deal
  Trato hecho. It's a deal.
travesura *f.* prank; mischief
travieso/a *adj.* naughty, mischievous
trayectoria *f.* (*rocket, ball*) path, trajectory
trece thirteen
treinta thirty
tren *m.* train
  tren de alta velocidad high-speed train
trenza *f.* braid
tres three
trescientos/as three hundred
triángulo *m.* triangle
tribunal *m.* (*Spain*) court
  Tribunal Supremo (*Spain*) Supreme Court
triciclo *m.* tricycle
trigo *m.* wheat
trigonometría *f.* trigonometry
trimestre *m.* trimester; quarter
  El año tiene cuatro trimestres. The year has four quarters.
trípode *m.* tripod
triste *adj.* sad
  Es triste (que...) It's sad (that...)
  Es triste que esté tan enfermo. It's sad that he's so sick.
tristeza *f.* sadness
triturar *v.t.* to crush
  triturador de basura garbage disposal
triunfar *v.t.* to succeed; to win
trivialidad *f.* triviality
trivializar *v.t.* to trivialize
tronco *m.* (*living tree*) trunk; (*lumber*) log
  dormir como un tronco *idiom.* to sleep like a log
tropezar (e:ie) *v.i.* to stumble
tropezarse (e:ie) (con alguien) *v. pron.* to run/bump into (*somebody*)
trozo *m.* piece, bit, slice
trucha *f.* trout
trueno *m.* thunder

tú *pron. fam.* you
Tú eres... You are . . .
tu(s) *poss. fam.* your
tuberculosis *f.* tuberculosis
tubería *f.* pipe
tubo *m.* tube
tubo de ensayo test tube
tubo de escape exhaust pipe
tulipán *m.* tulip
tumbarse *v. pron.* to lie down
tumbarse al sol lie down in the sun, sunbathe
tumbona *f.* lounge chair, deck chair
túnel *m.* tunnel
turbina *f.* turbine
turismo *m.* tourism
turista *m., f.* tourist
turístico/a *adj.* touristic
turno *m.* turn; (*work*) shift
turquesa *f.* turquoise
tuyo/a(s) *poss. fam.* your; (of) yours

U

Ud. *pron. form. sing.* you
Uds. *pron. form. pl.* you
últimamente *adv.* lately
último/a *adj.* last
por último *adv.* finally
un, uno/a *indef. art.* a; one
uno/a *m., f., sing. pron.* one
a la una at one o'clock
único/a *adj.* only
...y ese es el único problema ...and that's the only problem
unido/a *adj.* close
una familia muy unida a close family
universidad *f.* university; college
universo *m.* universe
unos/as *m., f., pl., indef. art.* some
unos/as *pron.* some
untar *v.t.* to spread (*butter, honey*)
untar pan con mantequilla to butter a piece of bread
uña *f.* (*finger, toe*) nail
urbanización *f.* (*housing*) development
urgente *adj.* urgent
(No) Es urgente (que...) It's (not) urgent (that...)
Es urgente que termines. It's urgent that you finish.
usar *v.t.* to use; to wear
Esta camisa está sin usar. This shirt hasn't been worn.
usted *pron. form. sing.* you
ustedes *pron. form. pl.* you
utensilio *m.* utensil
útero *m.* womb, uterus
útil *adj.* useful
uva *f.* grape

V

vaca *f.* cow
vacaciones *f., pl.* vacation
de vacaciones on vacation
vacío/a *adj.* empty
vainilla *f.* vanilla
vajilla *f.* dishes, crockery, china
vale *interj.* (*Spain*) okay
Ven a la una, ¿vale? Come at one o'clock, okay?
¡Sí, vale! Yes, sure!

valentía *f.* bravery, courage
valer *v.t. irreg.* **(yo valgo)** to be worth, to cost
No vale la pena. It's not worth the trouble.
valiente *adj.* brave
valla *f.* fence
vallas *f., pl.* (*sport*) hurdles
valle *m.* valley
valor *m.* value; courage
valorar *v.t.* to value
vapor *m.* vapor, steam
vaquero/a *m.* cowboy; *f.* cowgirl
(una película) de vaqueros a western (movie)
variación *f.* variation
variado/a *adj.* varied, diverse
variar *v.t./v.i.* **(yo varío)** to vary
varios/as *pron.* several; various
Irán varios de ustedes. Several of you will go.
vaso *m.* glass
veces *f., pl.* times
a veces *adv.* sometimes
vecino/a *m., f.* neighbor
vegetación *f.* vegetation
vehículo *m.* vehicle
vehículos pesados heavy vehicles
veinte twenty
veinticinco twenty-five
veinticuatro twenty-four
veintidós twenty-two
veintinueve twenty-nine
veintiocho twenty-eight
veintiséis twenty-six
veintisiete twenty-seven
veintitrés twenty-three
veintiún, veintiuno/a twenty-one
vejez *f.* old age
vejiga *f.* bladder
vela *f.* (*ship*) sail; (*sport*) sailing; candle
velero *m.* sailboat
velocidad *f.* speed
velocidad máxima speed limit
velódromo *m.* velodrome
vena *f.* vein
venda *f.* bandage
vendaje *m.* dressing
vendar *v.t.* to bandage
vendedor(a) *m., f.* salesperson
vender *v.t.* to sell
venido *p.p. of* **venir** come; arrived
venir (e:ie) *v.i. irreg.* **(yo vengo)** to come
venir al mundo to be born; to come into the world
ventaja *f.* advantage
ventana *f.* window
ventilador *m.* fan
ver *v.t./v.i. irreg.* **(yo veo)** to see; to watch
¡A ver! Let's see!
ver películas to see movies
veraneante *m., f.* summer vacationer
veranear *v.i.* to spend the summer
Veraneo en las montañas. I summer in the mountains.
verano *m.* summer
veras: de veras *loc.* really
verbena *f.* festival; open-air dance

verbo *m.* verb
verdad *f.* truth
Es cierto, ¿verdad? It's true, right?
(No) Es verdad que (+ *ind.*) It's (not) true that… **¿Es verdad que eres millonario?** Is it true that you're a millionaire?
verdadero/a *adj.* true
verde *adj./m.* green
verde claro light green
verde oscuro dark green
verduras *f., pl.* vegetables
vergonzoso/a *adj.* disgraceful; shameful
vergüenza *f.* embarrassment; shame
verosímil *adj.* credible; realistic, true-to-life
Sus personajes no son verosímiles. His characters aren't realistic.
verruga *f.* wart
versátil *adj.* versatile
vértebra *f.* vertebra
vertebrado/a *adj./m.* vertebrate
vertedero *m.* garbage dump
vesícula (biliar) *f.* gall bladder
vestido *m.* dress
vestirse (e:i) *v. pron.* to get dressed
vestuario *m.* locker room
veterinaria *f.* veterinary science
veterinario/a *m., f.* veterinarian
vez *f.* time
a veces sometimes
dos veces twice
en vez de instead of
tres veces three times
una vez once; one time
una vez más one more time
vía *f.* (railroad) track
Vía Láctea Milky Way
viajar *v.i.* to travel
viaje *m.* trip
viajero/a *m., f.* traveler
vibración *f.* vibration
vibrar *v.i.* to vibrate
vicio *m.* vice
El trabajo es su único vicio. Work is his only vice.
vicioso/a *m., f.* dissolute person
vid *f.* (grape) vine
vida *f.* life
de mi vida of my life
video(casete) *m.* video (cassette)
videocasetera *f.* VCR
videoconferencia *f.* videoconference; teleconference
vidrio *m.* glass
de vidrio (*made*) of glass
vieira *f.* scallop
viejo/a *adj.* old
viento *m.* wind
viernes *m., sing.* Friday
villancicos *m., pl.* carols
vinagre *m.* vinegar
vínculo *m.* tie, bond
vino *m.* wine
vino blanco white wine
vino tinto red wine
violencia *f.* violence
viruela *f.* smallpox
visera *f.* eyeshade
visitante *m., f.* visitor

visitar *v.t.* to visit
visitar monumentos to visit monuments
vista *f.* (*senses*) sight; view
amor a primera vista love at first sight
habitación con vistas a room with a view
Hasta la vista. See you.
Tener vista de águila. To have eyes like a hawk.
Tierra a la vista. Land ho!
visto/a *p.p. of* **ver** seen
por lo visto *adv.* apparently
vitamina *f.* vitamin
vitrina *f.* (*L.A.*) shop window
viudo/a *m.* widower; *f.* widow; widowed
víveres *m., pl.* provisions, supplies
vivienda *f.* housing
vivir *v.i.* to live
vivo/a *adj.* bright; lively; living
volante *m.* steering wheel
volar (o:ue) *v.i.* to fly
volcán *m.* volcano
vóleibol *m.* volleyball
voltear *v.t.* (*L.A.*) to turn (over)
volumen *m.* volume
voluntario *adj.* voluntary; *m., f.* volunteer
volver (o:ue) *v.i.* to return; to come back
volver a ver(te, lo, la) to see (you/him/her) again
¿Cuándo te volveré a ver? When will I see you again?
vomitar *v.t./v.i.* to vomit
vos (*Argentina*) *pron.* you
vosotros/as *pron. fam. pl.* you
votar *v.t./v.i.* to vote
voto *m.* vote
voz *f.* voice
vuelta *f.* lap
vuelta *f.* return trip; (*sports*) lap; turn
de vuelta back
Estará de vuelta a la una. She will be back at one.
vuelto *p.p. of* **volver** returned
vuestro/a(s) *poss. fam.* your

W

walkman *m.* Walkman

X

xenofobia *f.* xenophobia
xenófobo/a *adj.* xenophobic; *m., f.* xenophobe

Y

y *conj.* and
y cuarto quarter after/past (time)
y media half-past (time)
y quince quarter after/past (time)
y treinta thirty (minutes past the hour)
¿Y Ud.? *form.* And you?
¿Y tú? *fam.* And you?
ya *adv.* already; still
Ya fui. I already went.
yerno *m.* son-in-law
yeso *f.* (*L.A.*) plaster cast
yo *pron.* I
Yo soy... I'm . . .
yoga *m.* yoga
yogur *m.* yogurt

Z

zanahoria *f.* carrot
zapatería *f.* shoe store
zapatilla *f.* slipper
  zapatillas de deporte tennis shoes; sneakers
zapato *m.* shoe
  zapato de tacón alto high-heeled shoe
  zapatos de tenis tennis shoes; sneakers
zona *f.* area
  zona verde green space
zoológico *m.* zoo
zoólogo/a *m., f.* zoologist
zorro *m.* fox
zueco *m.* clog
zumo *m.* (*Spain*) juice

English-Spanish
Inglés-Español

A

@ (symbol) arroba *f.*
a un, uno/a *m., f., sing., indef. art.*
A.M. en la mañana, de la mañana
abbey *n.* abadía *f.*
abbreviate *v.t.* abreviar
abbreviation *n.* abreviatura *f.*
able: be able to poder (o:ue)
abnormal *adj.* anormal
aboard *adv.* a bordo
  All aboard! ¡Todos a bordo!
abortion *n.* aborto *m.* provocado
  have an abortion abortar de manera provocada
abroad *adv.* en el extranjero
absence *n.* ausencia *f.*
absent *adj.* ausente
absorb *v.t.* absorber
absorbent *adj.* absorbente
absurd *adj.* absurdo/a
accelerate *v.t.* acelerar
accelerator (pedal) *n.* acelerador *m.*
accept *v.t.* aceptar
accessory *n.* accesorio *m.*
accident *n.* accidente *m.*
  industrial accident accidente laboral
accommodation: provide accommodation hospedar
accompany *v.t.* acompañar
according to *prep.* de acuerdo a; según
account *n.* cuenta *f.*
  checking account cuenta corriente
  take into account tomar en cuenta
accountant *n.* contador(a) *m., f.*
accounting *n.* contabilidad *f.*
accustomed *adj.* acostumbrado/a
  be accustomed to acostumbrarse (a)
ache *n.* dolor *m.*
achieve *v.t.* lograr
achievement *n.* logro *m.*
acid *n.* ácido *m.;* ácido/a *adj.*
  acid rain lluvia *f.* ácida
acquainted: be acquainted with conocer
acquire *v.t.* adquirir
acquisition *n.* adquisición *f.*
acrobat *n.* acróbata *m., f.*
acrobatics *n.* acrobacia *f.*
across from *prep.* enfrente
action *n.* acción *f.*; ...de acción
activate *v.t.* activar
active *adj.* activo/a
activity *n.* actividad *f.*
actor *n.* actor *m.*, actriz *f.*
adapt *v.i.* adaptarse
adaptation *n.* adaptación *f.*
addict *n.* adicto/a *m., f.*
  drug addict drogadicto/a
addicted *adj.* adicto/a
  drug-addicted drogadicto/a
addiction *n.* adicción *f.*
additional *adj.* adicional
additive *n.* aditivo *m.*
address *n.* dirección *f.*
adhesive bandage *n.* curita *f.*

adjective *n.* adjetivo *m.*
adjust *v.t. (temperature, etc.)* graduar; *v.i.* adaptarse
administration *n.* administración *f.*
adolescence *n.* adolescencia *f.*
adolescent *n.* adolescente *m., f.*
advance *n.* avance *m.*
advance *v.i.* avanzar
advanced *adj.* avanzado/a
advantage *n.* ventaja *f.*
adventure *n.* aventura *f.*; ...de aventuras
adventurer *n.* aventurero/a *m., f.*
adventurous *adj.* aventurero/a
advertise *v.t.* anunciar
advertisement *n.* anuncio *m.*
advice *n.* consejo *m.*
give advice dar un consejo
advisable *adj.* aconsejable, recomendable
advise *v.t.* aconsejar; recomendar
advisor *n.* consejero/a *m., f.*
aerobic *adj.* aeróbico/a
aerobic exercise *n.,* ejercicios *m., pl.* aeróbicos
do aerobics hacer ejercicios aeróbicos
aerobics class *n.* clase *f.* de ejercicios aeróbicos
affected *adj.* afectado/a
be affected (by) estar afectado/a (por)
affectionate *adj.* cariñoso/a, tierno/a
affirmative *adj.* afirmativo/a
afraid: be afraid (of) tener miedo (de); **be afraid that** tener miedo (de) que
African *n., adj.* africano/a *m., f.*
after *prep.* después de; después de que
afternoon *n.* tarde *f.*
in the afternoon de la tarde; por la tarde
afterwards *adv.* después (de); luego
again *adv.* otra vez
age *n.* edad *f.*
age *v.i.* envejecer
agility *n.* soltura *f.*
aging *n.* envejecimiento *m.*
agree (about) *v.* concordar (con), estar de acuerdo (sobre)
agreement *n.* acuerdo *m.*
be in agreement with estar de acuerdo (con)
reach an agreement llegar a un acuerdo
agricultural *adj.* agrícola
agriculture *n.* agricultura *f.*
AIDS (Acquired Immune Deficiency Syndrome) *n.* SIDA *m.* (Síndrome de Inmunodeficiencia Adquirida)
aim *n.* objetivo *m.*, meta *f.*
air *n.* aire *m.*
air-conditioned *adj.* climatizado/a
air conditioning *n.* aire acondicionado
air freshener *n.* ambientador *m.*
aircraft carrier *n.* portaaviones *m., sing.*

airline *n.* aerolínea *f.*
airplane *n.* aeroplano *m.*; avión *m.*
by plane en avión
go by plane ir en avión
airport *n.* aeropuerto *m.*
airtight *adj.* hermético/a
alarm *n.* alarma *f.*
alarming *adj.* alarmante
alcohol *n.* alcohol *m.*
alcoholic *adj.* alcohólico/a
alcoholic beverage bebida *f.* alcohólica
all *adj.* todo/a
all of a sudden de repente
all of us *n.* todos *m., pl.*
all over the world en todo el mundo
all-boys/girls school *n.* escuela *f.* de niños/as
allergic *adj.* alérgico/a
be allergic (to) ser alérgico/a (a)
alleviate *v.t.* aliviar
alley *n.* callejón *m.*
allow *v.* dejar
almond *n.* almendra *f.*
almond tree *n.* almendro *m.*
almost *adv.* casi
alms *n.* limosna *f.*
alone *adj.* solo/a
along *prep.* por
alphabet *n.* alfabeto *m.*, abecedario *m.*
already *adv.* ya; todavía
also *adv.* también
alternating current: AC corriente *f.* alterna
alternative *n.* alternativa *f.*
alternator *n.* alternador *m.*
although *conj.* aunque
aluminum *n.* aluminio *m.*
made of aluminum de aluminio
always *adv.* siempre
amazing *adj.* asombroso/a
ambition *n.* ambición *f.*
ambitious *adj.* ambicioso/a
ambulance *n.* ambulancia *f.*
American *n., adj.* norteamericano/a, *m., f.*; estadounidense *m., f.*
among *prep.* entre
amount *n.* cantidad *f.*
amuse oneself *v.* entretenerse
amusement *n.* diversión *f.*
amusement park *n.* parque *m.* de atracciones *(Spain)*; parque de diversiones *(L.A.)*
amusing *adj.* chistoso/a, gracioso/a, divertido/a
analyst *n.* analista *m., f.*
anarchic *adj.* anárquico/a
anarchy *n.* anarquía *f.*
anatomy *n.* anatomía *f.*
ancestor *n.* antepasado/a *m., f.*
anchovy *n.* anchoa *f.*
and *conj.* y *(e before words beginning with* i *or* hi)
and so forth y así sucesivamente
And you? ¿Y tú? *fam.*; ¿Y usted? *form.*
anesthesia *n.* anestesia *f.*
anesthesiologist *n.* anestesiólogo/a *m., f.*
anesthetize *v.t.* anestesiar
angle *n.* ángulo *m.*
Anglo-Saxon *n,. adj.* anglosajón *m.*, anglosajona *f.*

angry *adj.* enojado/a
get angry (with) enojarse (con)
animal *n.* animal *m.*
ankle *n.* tobillo *m.*
anniversary *n.* aniversario *m.; (wedding)* aniversario de bodas
announce *v.t.* anunciar
announcer *n. (TV/radio)* locutor(a) *m., f.*
annoy *v.t.* molestar
The noise is annoying me. Me molesta el ruido.
another *adj.* otro/a
answer *n.* respuesta *f.*
answer *v.t.* contestar
ant *n.* hormiga *f.*
anthology *n.* antología *f.*
antibiotic *n.* antibiótico *m.*
anticipation *n.* expectativa *f.*
antidote *n.* antídoto *m.*
antiques *n., pl.* antigüedades *f., pl.*
antiquities *n., pl.* antigüedades *f., pl.*
any *adj.* algún, alguno/a(s)
anybody *pron.* nadie
anyone *pron.* alguien
anything *pron.* algo; *n.* nada *f.*
apartment *n.* apartamento *m.*
apartment building *n.* edificio *m.* de apartamentos
apologize *v.i.* disculparse
apology *n.* disculpa *f.*
apparently *adv.* por lo visto
appear *v.i. (come into view)* aparecer; *(seem)* parecer
appearance *n.* *(looks)* aspecto *m.*
appetizers *n., pl.* aperitivos *m., pl.;* entremeses *(Spain) m., pl.*
applaud *v.t./v.i.* aplaudir
applause *n.* aplauso *m.*
apple *n.* manzana *f.*
appliance *n.* aparato *m.*
electric appliance *n.* electrodoméstico *m.*
household appliance aparato doméstico
applicant *n.* aspirante *m., f.*
application *n.* solicitud *f.*
job application solicitud de trabajo
apply *v.t.* *(for a job)* solicitar *(empleo)*; *(for a loan)* pedir un préstamo; *(oneself)* aplicarse
appointment *n.* cita *f.*
have an appointment tener una cita
appreciate *v.t.* apreciar
approach *n.* enfoque *m.*
apricot *n.* albaricoque *m.*
April *n.* abril *m.*
apron *n.* delantal *m.*
aptitude test *n.* prueba *f.* de aptitud
aquarium *n.* acuario *m.*
aquatic *adj.* acuático/a
Arab *n.* árabe *m., f.; (language)* árabe
Arabic *adj.* árabe
archaeologist *n.* arqueólogo/a *m., f.*
archery *n.* tiro *m.* con arco
archipelago *n.* archipiélago *m.*
architect *n.* arquitecto/a *m., f.*
area *n.* región *f.*; zona *f.*

argue *v.t.* discutir; argumentar
argument *n. (reasoning)* argumento *m.; (dispute)* discusión *f.*
aristocracy *n.* aristocracia *f.*
aristocrat *n.* aristócrata *m., f.*
arm *n.* (*limb*) brazo *m.; (weapon)* arma (el) *f.*
armchair *n.* sillón *m.*
armpit *n.* axila *f.*
army *n.* ejército *m.*
around *prep.* alrededor (de)
There is a wall around the old city. Hay una muralla alrededor de la ciudad vieja.
adv. alrededor **a table with four chairs around it** una mesa con cuatro sillas alrededor
around here por aquí
arrange *v.t.* colocar; organizar; arreglar **arranged marriage** *n.* boda *f.* concertada
arrangement *n. (position)* colocación *f.*
arrest *n.* detención *f.*, arresto *m.*
arrest *v.t.* arrestar
under arrest detenido/a; arrestado/a
be under arrest estar arrestado; estar detenido
arrested *p.p.* arrestado (*of* arrestar)
arrival *n.* llegada *f.*
arrive *v.i.* llegar
arrogant *adj.* arrogante
arrow *n.* flecha *f.*
art *n.* arte *m.*; las artes *f., pl.*
art exhibition *n.* exhibición *f.* de arte
artery *n.* arteria *f.*
artichoke *n.* alcachofa *f.*
article *n.* artículo *m.*
artist *n.* artista *m., f.*
artistic *adj.* artístico/a
arts *n., pl.* artes *f., pl.*
as como
as . . . as tan... como
as a child de niño/a
as many . . . as tantos/as... como
as much . . . as tanto... como
as soon as en cuanto; tan pronto como
ascent *n.* (*hill, mountain*) escalada *f.*
ash *n.* ceniza *f.*
ashamed: be ashamed avergonzarse
ashtray *n.* cenicero *m.*
Asian *n., adj.* asiático/a *m., f.*
ask *v.t.* (*a question*) preguntar
ask (for) pedir (e:i)
ask oneself *v.ref.* preguntarse; cuestionarse; **We have to ask ourselves if the conclusion is valid.** Tenemos que cuestionarnos si es válida la conclusión.
asparagus *n.* espárrago *m.*
asphalt *n.* asfalto *m.*
aspire (to) *v.i.* ambicionar
aspirin *n.* aspirina *f.*
assassin *n.* asesino/a *m., f.*
assassination *n.* asesinato *m.*
assemble (a puzzle) *v.t.* armar (un rompecabezas)
assess *v.t.* evaluar
assessment *n.* evaluación *f.*
assistance *n.* asistencia *f.*

association *n.* asociación *f.*
assortment *n.* surtido *m.*
assume *v.t.* asumir; suponer
assure *v.t.* asegurar
astonishing *adj.* asombroso/a
astrologist *n.* astrólogo/a *m., f.*
astrology *n.* astrología *f.*
astronaut *n.* astronauta *m., f.*
astronomer *n.* astrónomo/a *m., f.*
astronomy *n.* astronomía *f.*
at *prep.* a
  at + *time* a la(s) + ***time***
  At what time . . . ? ¿A qué hora...?
  At your service. A sus órdenes.
atheism *n.* ateísmo *m.*
atheist *n.* ateo/a *m., f.*
atheistic *adj.* ateo/a
athlete *n.* atleta *m., f.*
athletic *adj.* atlético/a
ATM *n.* cajero *m.* automático
atmosphere *n.* (*created by people, decoration*) ambiente *m.* *(metheorology)* atmósfera *f.*
atrocious *adj.* atroz
attack *n.* ataque *m.*
attack *v.t.* atacar
attempt *n.* intento *m.*
  assassination attempt atentado *m.* terrorista
attempt to assassinate *v.t.* atentar (contra)
attend *v.t.* asistir (a)
attention *n.* atención *f.*
attic *n.* altillo *m.*
attract *v.t.* atraer
attraction *n.* atracción *f.*
attractive *adj.* atractivo/a
audience *n.* público *m.*
audiotape *n.* cinta *f.*
audition *n.* *(try-out)* audición *f.*
auditorium *n.* auditorio *m.;* salón *m.* de actos
August *n.* agosto *m.*
aunt *n.* tía *f.*
aunts and uncles *n., pl.* tíos *m., pl.*
Australian *n., adj.* australiano/a *m., f.*
author *n.* autor(a) *m., f.*
authoritarian *adj.* autoritario/a
authoritarianism *n.* autoritarismo *m.*
autograph *n.* autógrafo *m.*
automatic *adj.* automático/a
  automatic teller machine *n.* **(ATM)** cajero *m.* automático
automobile *n.* automóvil *m.;* carro *m.*; coche *m.*
  auto racing *n.* automovilismo *m.*
autonomous *adj.* autónomo/a
autonomy *n.* autonomía *f.*
autumn *n.* otoño *m.*
availability *n.* disponibilidad *f.*
available *adj.* disponible
avarice *n.* avaricia *f.*
avaricious *adj.* avaricioso/a
avenue *n.* avenida *f.*
average *n.* promedio *m.*
aversion *n.* aversión *f.*
avocado *n.* aguacate *m.*
avoid *v.t.* evitar; *(danger, problem)* evadir
award *n.* premio *m.;* galardón *m.*
award *v.t.* galardonar; premiar
award-winner *n.* galardonado/a *m., f.*

aware: become aware of darse cuenta de
awful *adj.* atroz, horrible
awkward *adj.* torpe
ax *n.* hacha (el) *f.*

B

baby *n.* bebé *m., f.*
baby-sitter *n.* niñero/a *m., f.*
back *n.* espalda *f.*
back *v.t.* respaldar
be back estar de vuelta
backpack *n.* mochila *f.*
backseat *n.* asiento *m.* trasero
backstroke *n.* estilo *m.* espalda
backyard *n.* jardín *m.*
bad *adj. adv.* mal, malo/a
It's (not) bad that... (No) Es malo que...
It's not at all bad. No está nada mal.
bad-mannered *adj.* maleducado/a
bad-tempered: be bad-tempered *idiom* tener malas pulgas
bag *n.* bolsa *f.*
bail *n.* fianza *f.*
bake *v.t.* hornear
bakery *n.* panadería *f.*
baking soda *n.* bicarbonato *m.*
balanced *adj.* equilibrado/a
balcony *n.* balcón *m.*
bald *adj.* calvo/a
ball *n.* pelota *f.;* bola *f.*
ballet *n.* ballet *m.*
balloon *n.* globo *m.*
banana *n.* banana *f.;* plátano *m.*
band *n.* banda *f.*
bandage *n.* venda *f.*
bandage *v.t.* vendar
bank *n.* banco *m.*
bank draft *n.* giro *m.* bancario
banker *n.* banquero/a *m., f.*
banister *n.* pasamanos *m., sing.*
baptism *n.* bautizo *m.*
baptize *v.t.* bautizar
barbecue *n.* asador *m.*
barber *n.* barbero *m.*
bargain *n.* ganga *f.*
bargain *v.i.* regatear
bark *n.* ladrido *m.*
bark *v.i.* ladrar
barn *n.* granero *m.*
baroque *adj.* barroco/a
baseball *n. (sport)* béisbol *m.; (ball)* pelota *f.*
basement *n.* sótano *m.*
basil *n.* albahaca *f.*
basketball *n. (sport)* baloncesto *m.*
bat *n. (sport)* bate *m.; (animal)* murciélago *m.*
bath *n.* baño *m.*
take a bath bañarse
bathe *v.i.* bañarse
bathing suit *n.* traje *m.* de baño
bathrobe *n.* bata *f.* de baño
bathroom *n.* baño *m.;* cuarto *m.* de baño
bathtub *n.* bañera *f.;* tina *(L.A.) f.*
baton *n. (sport)* testigo *m.*
bay *n.* bahía *f.*
be *v.* ser; estar
be at/in/on estar en
be that as it may *loc.* sea lo que sea

He/She/It is from . . . Es de...
I'm from... Soy de...
beach *n.* playa *f.*
beach umbrella *n.* sombrilla *f.*
beak *n.* pico *m.*
bean *n. (coffee)* grano *m.;* frijol *m.*
bear *n.* oso/a *m., f.*
beard *n.* barba *f.*
bearded *adj.* barbudo/a
beat *n. (music)* compás *m.*
beat *v.t.* batir; *(an opponent)* derrotar; *(heart)* latir
beautician *n.* esteticista *m., f.*
beautiful *adj.* hermoso/a
beauty *n.* belleza *f.*
beauty salon *n.* peluquería *f.;* salón *m.* de belleza
because *conj.* porque
because of *prep.* debido a
become *v.i.* hacerse **He became famous.** Se hizo famoso.; llegar a ser **She wants to become president.** Ella quiere llegar a ser presidente.; ponerse (+ *adj.*) **He becomes sad sometimes.** A veces él se pone triste.; convertirse (en) **The church became a museum.** La iglesia se convirtió en museo.
bed *n.* cama *f.*
go to bed acostarse (o:ue)
make the bed hacer la cama
bedroom *n.* alcoba *f.;* recámara *f.;* cuarto *m.;* dormitorio
bee *n.* abeja *f.*
beef *n.* carne *f.* de res
been *p.p.* sido (*of* ser)
beer *n.* cerveza *f.*
beet *n.* remolacha *f.;* betabel *(Mexico.) f.*
before *adv., conj., prep.* antes; antes (de) que; antes de
beg *v.t.* rogar (o:ue)
beggar *n.* mendigo/a *m., f.*
begin *v.t.* comenzar (e:ie); empezar (e:ie)
behalf: on behalf of de parte de; en nombre de
behave (oneself) *v.* portarse (bien), comportarse
behave well/badly portarse bien/mal
behavior *n.* comportamiento *m.,* conducta *f.*
behind *prep.* detrás de; atrás
being *n.* ser *m.*
belch *v.i.* eructar
belch *n.* eructo *m.*
believe (in) *v.t.* creer (en)
be hard to believe parecer mentira **It's hard to believe, but he's only ten.** Aunque parezca mentira, tiene sólo diez años.
not to believe no creer
bellhop *n.* botones *m., sing.*
belly *n.* barriga *f.,* vientre *m.*
belong to *v.t.* pertenecer (a)
belongings *n., pl.* pertenencias *f., pl.*
beloved *adj.* querido/a; enamorado/a
below *adv., prep.* abajo; debajo de
belt *n.* correa *f.;* cinturón *m.*
bench *n.* banco *m.*

bend *n.* curva *f.*
beneficial *adj.* beneficioso/a
benefit *n.* beneficio *m.*
fringe benefits *n.* prestaciones *f., pl*
benefit *v.i.* beneficiarse
benign *adj.* benigno
beret *n.* boina *f.*
beside *prep.* al lado de
besides *adv.* además (de)
best *adj.* mejor
  the best *n.* el/la mejor *m., f.; (neuter)* lo mejor
betray *v.t.* traicionar
betrayal *n.* traición *f.*
better *adj.* mejor
  better than *adj.* mejor que
  It's better that . . . Es mejor que...
  get better mejorarse*; (health)* aliviarse
better (oneself) *v.t.* superarse
  Better late than never. *loc.* Más vale tarde que nunca.
between *prep.* entre
bib *n.* babero *m.*
bicycle *n.* bicicleta *f.*
  ride a bicycle pasear/montar en bicicleta
big *adj.* gran, grande
Big Dipper *n.* Osa *f.* Mayor
big shot *n.* pez *m.* gordo
bikini *n.* bikini *m.*
bill *n.* cuenta *f.;* factura *f.*
billion *n.* mil *m.* millones (de)
biodiversity *n.* biodiversidad *f.*
biographical *adj.* biográfico/a
biography *n.* biografía *f.*
biologist *n.* biólogo/a *m., f.*
biology *n.* biología *f.*
biosphere *n.* biosfera *f.*
bird *n.* ave (el) *f.,* pájaro *m.*
birth *n.* nacimiento *m.*
birth control *n.* control *m.* de natalidad
birthday *n.* cumpleaños *m., sing.*
  birthday cake pastel *m.* de cumpleaños
  birthday song *n.* mañanitas *f., pl.*
  Happy birthday! ¡Feliz cumpleaños!
  have a birthday cumplir años
  birthrate *n.* (índice *m.* de) natalidad *f.*
bite *n.* mordisco *m.*
bite *v.t.* morder
bitter *adj.* amargo/a
bittersweet *adj.* agridulce
black *n., adj.* negro/a
blackberry *n.* mora *f.*
blackboard *n.* pizarra *f.; m.* pizarrón
blackout *n.* apagón *m.*
bladder *n.* vejiga *f.*
bland *adj.* insípido/a; soso/a
blanket *n.* cobija *(L.A.) f.;* frazada *(L.A.) f.;* manta *f.*
bleach *n.* lejía *f.*
blend *v.t.* licuar
blender *n.* licuadora *(L.A.) f.;* batidora *(Spain) f.*
bless *v.t.* bendecir
blind *adj.* ciego/a
blind *n.* persiana *f.*
block *n. (city)* cuadra *(L.A.) f.;* manzana *(Spain)*
blond(e) *adj.* rubio/a
blood *n.* sangre *f.*

blood circulation *n.* circulación *f.* (sanguínea)
blood pressure *n.* presión *f.* sanguínea
blouse *n.* blusa *f.*
blue *n., adj.* azul
blueprint *n.* plano *m.*
bluish *adj.* azulado/a
blush *v.i.* ponerse rojo/a, sonrojarse
board *n. (organizational)* junta *f.;* tablero *m.*
board *v.i. (ship)* embarcar
board games *n., pl.* juegos *m., pl.* de mesa
board of directors *n.* junta *f.* directiva
boardinghouse *n.* pensión *f.*
boast (about) *v.t.* alardear (de) *(Spain)*
He was boasting about having won. Alardeaba de haber ganado.
boat *n.* barco *m.*
go by boat ir en barco
body *n.* cuerpo *m.*
boil *v.t.* hervir
boiled *adj.* hervido/a
bolt *n.* (*lock*) cerrojo *m.*
bolt (the door) *v.t.* correr el cerrojo
bomb *n.* bomba *f.*
bond *n.* vínculo *m.*
bone *n.* hueso *m.;* (*fish*) espina *f.*
bonfire *n.* hoguera *f.*
book *n.* libro *m.*
book *v.t.* hacer una reservación
bookcase *n.* estantería *f.;* estante *m.*
bookshelf, bookshelves *n.* estante *m.*
bookstore *n.* librería *f.*
bookworm *n.* ratón *m.* de biblioteca
boot *n.* bota *f.*
rubber boot bota de agua
bore *v.t.* aburrir
bored *adj.* aburrido/a
be bored estar aburrido/a
get bored aburrirse
boring *adj.* aburrido/a; soso/a
born: be born nacer
borrow *v.t.* pedir prestado
borrowed *adj.* prestado/a
boss *n.* jefe *m.,* jefa *f.*
botanical *adj.* botánico/a
botanist *n.* botánico/a *m., f.*
botany *n.* botánica *f.*
bother *v.t.* molestar **Does the music bother you?** ¿Te molesta la música?
bottle *n.* botella *f.*
bottle opener *n.* abrebotellas *m., sing.*
bottom *n.* fondo *m.*
boulevard *n.* bulevar *m.*
bow *n.* lazo *m.; (sport)* arco *m.*
bowl *n.* tazón *m.*
bowling *n.* boliche *m.*
box *v.i.* boxear
boxer *n.* boxeador(a) *m., f.*
boxer shorts *n., pl.* calzoncillos *m., pl.*
boxing *n.* boxeo *m.*
boy *n.* chico *m.;* muchacho *m.;* niño *m.*
boyfriend *n.* novio *m.*
bra *n.* sostén *m.;* sujetador *(Spain) m.;* brasier *(L.A.) m.*

braid *n.* trenza *f.*
brain *n.* cerebro *m.*
brake *v.i.* frenar
brake *n.* freno *m.*
brake pedal *n.* pedal *m.* del freno
branch *n.* rama *f.*
brand (name) *n.* marca *f.*
It's a well-known brand. Es una marca de prestigio.
brat *n.* niño/a *m., f.* mimado/a
brave *adj.* valiente
bravery *n.* valentía *f.*
bread *n.* pan *m.*
freshly-baked bread pan recién horneado
break *v.t.* romper **She breaks the glass.** Ella rompe el vaso.; romperse **He broke his leg.** Se rompió la pierna.
break a world record batir un récord mundial
break down *v.i. (auto)* descomponerse *(L.A.)*, dañarse *(L.A.)*; averiarse *(Spain)*; estropearse, sufrir una avería
The . . . broke down on us. Se nos dañó el/la…
break the ice *loc.* romper el hielo
break up (with) *v.i.* romper (con)
breakdown *n. (mechanical)* avería *(Spain) f.*
breakfast *n.* desayuno *m.*
have breakfast desayunar
breakwater *n.* rompeolas *m., sing.*
breast *n.* pecho *m.*
chicken breast pechuga *f.* (de pollo)
breaststroke *n.* estilo *m.* braza *(Spain)*; estilo *m.* pecho *(L.A.)*
breath *n.* aliento *m.*
breathe *v.i.* respirar
breathing *n.* respiración *f.*
breeze *n.* brisa *f.*
brick *n.* ladrillo *m.*
bricklayer *n.* albañil *m.*
bricklaying *n.* albañilería *f.*
bridge *n.* puente *m.*
bright *adj. (color)* vivo/a
bring *v.t.* traer
bring up *v.t. (children)* criar
broadcast *v.t.* transmitir; emitir
broccoli *n.* brócoli *m.*
brochure *n.* folleto *m.*
broiled *adj.* a la parrilla
broken *adj.* roto/a
be broken estar roto/a
broken down *adj.* averiado/a (*Spain*)
bronze *n.* bronce *m.*
brook *n.* riachuelo *m.*
broom *n.* escoba *f.*
broth *n.* caldo *m.*
brother *n.* hermano *m*
brothers and sisters *n., pl.* hermanos *m., pl.*
younger brother *n.* hermano *m.* menor
brother-in-law *n.* cuñado *m.*
brought *p.p.* traído (*of* traer)
brown *n., adj.* (*color*) café; marrón; *(eyes, hair)* castaño/a
brunet(te) *adj.* moreno/a
brush *n.* cepillo *m.*
brush *v.t.* cepillar

brush one's hair cepillarse el pelo
brush one's teeth cepillarse/lavarse los dientes
bubble *n.* burbuja *f.*
Buddhist *n., adj.* budista *m., f.*
build *v.t.* construir
builder *n.* albañil *m.*; constructor(a) *m., f.* (de obras)
building *n.* edificio *m.*; (*profession*) albañilería *f.*
apartment building casa *f.* de apartamentos/edificio *m.* de apartamentos
building contractor *n.* constructor(a) *m., f.* (de obras)
bull *n.* toro *m.*
bulletin *n.* boletín *m.*
bulletin board *n.* tablero *m.* de anuncios
bullfight *n.* corrida *f.* de toros
bullfighter *n.* torero/a *m., f.*
bullfighting *n.* tauromaquia *f.*
bullring *n.* plaza *f.* de toros
bump into *v. (meet accidentally)* darse con
bumper *n.* parachoques *m., sing.*
burglar *n.* ladrón *m.*, ladrona *f.*
burial *n.* entierro *m.*
burn *v.t.* quemar
burned (out) *adj.* quemado/a
burp *n.* eructo *m.*
burp *v.i.* eructar
bus *n.* autobús *m.*; camión *m. (Mexico)*
go by bus ir en autobús
bus station *n.* estación *f.* de autobuses
bush *n.* arbusto *m.*
business *n.* negocios *m., pl.*; empresa *f.*
business administration *n.* administración *f.* de empresas
businessman *n.* hombre *m.* de negocios
business-related *adj.* comercial
businesswoman *n.* mujer *f.* de negocios
busy *adj.* ocupado/a
but *conj.* pero; (*in negative sentences*) sino
butcher shop *n.* carnicería *f.*
butler *n.* mayordomo *m.*
butter *n.* mantequilla *f.*
butter a piece of toast untar una tostada con mantequilla
butterfly *n.* mariposa *f.*
butterfly stroke *n.* estilo *m.* mariposa
button *n.* botón *m.*
buy *v.t.* comprar
by *prep.* por
by the way a propósito, por cierto
bye *fam.* chau; adiós

C

cabbage *n.* col *(Spain) f.*; repollo *(L.A.) m.*
cabin *n.* cabaña *f.*
cable *n.* cable *m.*
cable television *n.* televisión *f.* por cable
café *n.* café *m.*
cafeteria *n.* cafetería *f.*

caffeine *n.* cafeína *f.*
cake *n.* pastel *m.*
calculate *v.t.* calcular
calculation *n.* cálculo *m.*
calculator *n.* calculadora *f.*
calendar *n.* calendario *m.*
calf *n. (anat.)* pantorrilla *f.*
call *v.t.* llamar
be called llamarse
be on call estar de guardia
call on the phone llamar por teléfono
calm *n., adj.* tranquilidad *f.;* tranquilo/a
Stay calm! ¡Tranquilo/a!
calm down *v.* tranquilizarse
calorie *n.* caloría *f.*
camaraderie *n.* compañerismo *m.*
camel *n.* camello *m.*
camera *n.* cámara *f.*
camp *n.* acampada *f.*
camp *v.i.* acampar
go camping ir de acampada/campamento
can *n.* (*tin*) lata *f.*
can opener *n.* abrelatas *m., sing.*
can *v.aux.* poder (o:ue)
I can't take it any more! *loc.* ¡No puedo más!/¡No soporto más!
Canadian *n., adj.* canadiense *m., f.*
canary *n.* canario *m.*
cancel *v.t.* cancelar; anular; *(performance)* suspender
candidate *n.* aspirante *m., f.;* candidato/a *m., f.*
candle *n.* vela *f.*
candy *n.* dulces *m., pl.*
cane *n.* caña *f.*
canoe *n.* piragua *f.*
canoeing *n.* piragüismo *m.*
canoeist *n.* piragüista *m., f.*
canvas *n.* lona *f.*
cap *n. (with a visor)* gorra *f.; (without a visor)* gorro *m.*
capital *n.* capital *f.*
capital letter *n.* mayúscula *f.*
capsule *n.* cápsula *f.*
capture *v.t.* capturar
car *n.* carro (*L.A.*) *m.;* coche (*Spain*) *m.;* automóvil *m.*
go by car ir en auto(móvil)
car accident *n.* (*crash*) choque *m.*
carbohydrate *n.* carbohidrato *m.*
carburator *n.* carburador *m.*
card *n.* tarjeta *f.; (playing)* carta *f.,* naipe *m.*
card table *n.* tapete (verde) *m.*
cardiology *n.* cardiología *f.*
care *n.* cuidado *m.,* atención *f.*
take care of cuidar
take care of oneself cuidarse
careful: be careful tener cuidado; ¡Cuidado!
career *n.* carrera *f.*
caretaker *n.* el ama *(m., f.)* de casa
Caribbean *adj.* caribeño/a
carnation *n.* clavel *m.*
carnivore *n.* carnívoro/a *m., f.*
carnivorous *adj.* carnívoro/a
carols *n.* villancicos *m., pl.*
carpenter *n.* carpintero/a *m., f.*
carpet *n.* alfombra *f.*

carrot *n.* zanahoria *f.*
carry *v.t.* llevar; transportar
cart *n.* carro *(Spain) m.*
cartoons *n., pl. (animated)* dibujos *m., pl.* animados; *(political)* caricaturas *f., pl.* (políticas)
carve *v.t.* tallar
case *n.* caso *m.*
in case of en caso de que
in case (that) en caso (de) que
cash *n.* (en) efectivo m.
cash (a check) *v.t.* cobrar
cash register *n.* caja *f.*
cashier *n.* cajero/a *m., f.*
casserole *n.* cazuela *f.*
cast *n.* yeso *(L.A.) m.;* escayola *(Spain) f.*
castle *n.* castillo *m.*
casual *adj.* informal
cat *n.* gato/a *m., f.*
catastrophe *n.* catástrofe *f.*
catastrophic *adj.* catastrófico/a
catch *v.t. (illness)* pegar
category *n.* categoría *f.*
cathedral *n.* catedral *f.*
Catholic *n., adj.* católico/a *m., f.*
cattle *n.* ganado *m.*
cattle farmer *n.* ganadero/a *m., f.*
cattle raising *n.* ganadería *f.*
cause *v.t.* causar; provocar
cavern *n.* caverna *f.*
CD-ROM *n.* cederrón *m.*
cedar *n.* cedro *m.*
celebrate *v.t.* celebrar; festejar
celebration *n.* festejo *m.*
celery *n.* apio *m.*
cell *n.* célula *f.*
cellar *n.* sótano *m.; (wine)* bodega *f.*
cellular *adj.* celular
cement *n.* cemento *m.*
cemetery *n.* cementerio *m.*
censor *v.t.* censurar
censorship *n.* censura *f.*
censure *n.* censura *f.*
censure *v.t.* censurar
census *n.* censo *m.*
century *n.* siglo *m.*
cereal *n.* cereales *m., pl.*
certain *adj.* cierto/a; seguro/a
it's (not) certain (no) es cierto/seguro
certainty *n.* certeza *f.*
chain *n.* cadena *f.*
chair *n.* silla *f.*
chalk *n.* tiza *f.*
challenge *n.* reto *m.;* desafío *m.*
challenge *v.t.* desafiar; retar
champagne *n.* champán *m.*
champion *n.* campeón *m.,* campeona *f.*
championship *n.* campeonato *m.*
chance *n.* azar *m.*
chandelier *n.* araña *f.* (de luces)
change *v.t.* cambiar (de/en); renovar
change *n.* cambio *m.*
change purse *n.* monedero *m.*
channel *n. (TV, radio)* canal *m.;* cadena *f.*
Chanukah *n.* Januká *m.*
chapel *n.* capilla *f.;* ermita *f.*
character *n.* carácter *m.; (fictional)* personaje *m.*

main character personaje principal
charisma *n.* carisma *m.*
charity *n.* caridad *f.; (money)* limosna *f.; (organization)* sociedad *f.* benéfica
charm *n.* encanto *m.*
charming *adj.* encantador(a)
chase *v.t.* perseguir
chat *v.* conversar
chatterbox *n.* charlatán *m.*, charlatana *f.*
chauffeur *n.* conductor(a) *m., f.*
cheap *adj.* barato/a
cheat *v.i.* hacer trampa(s); *(money)* engañar
cheat on *v.t. (relationship)* engañar
check *n. (bank)* cheque *m.*
check *v.t.* comprobar; revisar; averiguar
check the oil revisar el aceite
checkers *n., pl. (game)* damas (chinas) *f., pl.*
checkup *n.* revisión *(Spain) f.;* chequeo (médico) *(L.A.) m.*
cheek *n.* mejilla *f.*
cheeky *adj.* caradura
cheeky person *n.* caradura *m., f.*
cheer up *v.* animar(se)
cheese *n.* queso *m.*
chef *n.* cocinero/a *m., f.*
chemical *adj.* químico/a
chemist *n.* químico/a *m., f.*
chemistry *n.* química *f.*
cherry *n.* cereza *f.*
cherry tree *n.* cerezo *m.*
chess *n.* ajedrez *m.*
chess player *n.* ajedrecista *m., f.*
chest *n. (anatomy)* pecho
chest of drawers *n.* cómoda *f.*
chew *v.t.* masticar
chicken *n.* pollo *m.*
chickpea *n.* garbanzo *m.*
child *n.* niño/a *m., f. (son, daughter)* hijo/a *m., f.*
only child hijo/a único/a
childhood *n.* niñez *f.*
children *n., pl. (sons and daughters)* hijos *m., pl.*
chill *v.t.* enfríar
chilled *adj.* frío/a
chimney *n.* chimenea *f.*
china *n. (fine)* porcelana *f.*
Chinese *n., adj.* chino/a *m., f.; (language)* chino
chlorine *n.* cloro *m.*
chlorophyll *n.* clorofila *f.*
chocolate *n.* chocolate *m.*
chocolate cake *n.* pastel *m.* de chocolate
choir *n.* coro *m.*
choke *v.i.* atragantarse
cholesterol *n.* colesterol *m.*
choose *v.t.* escoger
chop *n. (meat)* chuleta *f.*
chop *v.t.* cortar
chores *n., pl.* quehaceres *m., pl.*
household chores quehaceres domésticos
do household chores hacer quehaceres domésticos
chorus *n.* coro *m.*
Christian *n., adj.* cristiano/a *m., f.*
Christmas *n.* Navidad *f.*

Christmas card *n.* tarjeta *f.* de Navidad
church *n.* iglesia *f.*
cider *n.* sidra *f.*
cinnamon *n.* canela *f.*
circle *n.* círculo *m.*
circuit *n. (electric)* circuito *m.*
circus *n.* circo *m.*
citizen *n.* ciudadano/a *m., f.*
citrus *adj.* cítrico/a
city *n.* ciudad *f.*
city hall *n.* ayuntamiento *m.*
clam *n.* almeja *f.*
clap *v.t./v.i.* aplaudir
clash *n.* enfrentamiento *m.*
class *n.* clase *f.*
take classes tomar clases
classical *adj.* clásico/a
classmate *n.* compañero/a *m., f.* de clase
classroom *n.* aula *f.;* salón *m.*
clavicle *n.* clavícula *f.*
clay *n.* arcilla *f.*
clean *adj.* limpio/a
clean *v.t.* limpiar
clean the house limpiar la casa
clear *adj.* claro/a; *(weather)* despejado/a
It's (very) clear. *(weather)* Está (muy) despejado.
clear *v.t. (pipes)* desatascar
clear the table quitar/recoger la mesa
clerk *n.* dependiente/a *m., f.*
cliff *n.* acantilado *m.*
climate *n.* clima *m.*
climatology *n.* climatología *f.*
climb *n. (mountain)* escalada *f.*
climb *v.t.* escalar
climb mountains escalar montañas
climb trees *v.* subirse a los árboles
climber *n. (mountain)* alpinista *m., f.,* escalador(a) *m., f.*
climbing *n. (mountain)* alpinismo *m.*
clinic *n.* clínica *f.*
clock *n.* reloj *m.*
alarm clock despertador *m.*
clog *n.* zueco *m.*
close *adj. (relative)* cercano/a; *(people)* unido/a
get close (to someone) intimar (con alguien)
close *v.t.* cerrar (e:ie)
closed *adj.* cerrado/a
closet *n.* armario *m.;* clóset *m.*
closing *n.* clausura *f.*
clothes *n., pl.* ropa *f.*
What pretty clothes! ¡Qué ropa más bonita!
clothes dryer *n.* secadora *f.*
clothesline *n.* tendedero *m.*
clothing *n.* ropa *f.*
cloud *n.* nube *f.*
have one's head in the clouds estar en las nubes
cloudy *adj.* nublado/a
It's (very) cloudy. Está (muy) nublado.
clown *n.* payaso/a *m., f.*
clue *n.* pista *f.*
Give me a clue. Dame una pista.
clumsy *adj.* torpe
clutch *n.* embrague *m.*
clutch pedal *n.* pedal *m.* del embrague

coach *n.* entrenador(a) *m., f.*
coaching *n.* entrenamiento *m.*
coal *n.* carbón *m.*
coast *n.* costa *f.*
coastal *adj.* costero/a
coastline *n.* costa *f.*
coat *n.* abrigo *m.*
  coat hanger *n.* perchero *m.*
cockroach *n.* cucaracha *f.*
coconut *n.* coco *m.*
cod *n.* bacalao *m.*
coffee *n.* café *m.*
  coffee maker *n.* cafetera *f.*
coffin *n.* ataúd *m.*
coincide *v.i.* coincidir
coincidence *n.* azar *m.;* coincidencia *f.*
colander *n.* colador *m.*
cold *n. (temperature)* frío *m.; (illness)* catarro *m.*, resfriado *m.*
  be cold *(thing)* estar frío/a
  be (feel) cold tener frío
  It's (very) cold. *(weather)* Hace (mucho) frío.
collaborate *v.i.* colaborar
  collaborate (with) *v. pron.* asociarse (con)
collaboration *n.* colaboración *f.*
collect *v.t.* coleccionar
collecting *n.* coleccionismo *m.*
collector *n.* coleccionista *m., f.*
college *n.* universidad *f.*
collision *n.* choque *m.*
cologne *n.* colonia *f.*
colonist *n.* colono *m.*
colonization *n.* colonización *f.*
colonize *v.t.* colonizar
colony *n.* colonia *f.*
color *n.* color *m.*
color *v.t.* colorear
column *n.* columna *f.*
comb *n.* peine *m.*
comb one's hair *v. refl.* peinarse
come *v.i.* venir
come back *v.* volver; regresar
comedy *n.* comedia *f.*
comfort *n.* confort *m.*
comfortable *adj.* confortable; cómodo/a
comic strip *n.* tira *f.* cómica, historieta *f.*
commemorate *v.t.* conmemorar
commemoration *n.* conmemoración *f.*
commerce *n.* negocios *m., pl.*
commercial *adj.* comercial
committee *n.* junta *f.*
common *adj.* común
communicate *v.t.* comunicar; *(speak with)* comunicarse (con)
communication *n.* comunicación *f.*
community *n.* comunidad *f.*
compact disc (CD) *n.* disco *m.* compacto
compact disc player *n.* tocadiscos *m., sing.* compacto
companion *n.* compañero/a *m., f.*
company *n.* compañía *f.;* empresa *f.*
comparison *n.* comparación *f.*
compete *v.i.* competir
competence *n.* aptitud *f.*
competent *adj.* competente

competition *n.* competencia *(L.A.) f.;* competición *(Spain) f.*
competitive *adj.* competitivo/a
competitor *n.* competidor(a) *m., f.;* participante *m., f.*
complain *v.i.* quejarse
complaint *n.* queja *f.*
completely *adv.* completamente; a fondo
complex *adj.* complejo
complexion *n.* cutis *m.*
complicate *v.t.* complicar
composer *n.* compositor(a) *m., f.*
computer *n.* computadora *f.*
computer disk *n.* disco *m.*
computer monitor *n.* monitor *m.*
computer programmer *n.* programador(a) *m., f.*
computer science *n.* computación *f.*
con artist *n.* estafador(a) *m., f.*
conceal *v.t.* disimular
conceited *adj.* engreído/a
concert *n.* concierto *m.*
concrete *n.* concreto *(L.A.) m.;* hormigón *(Spain) m.*
condense *v.t.* condensar
conditioned *adj.* acondicionado/a
conduct *n.* conducta *f.*
conductor *n. (musical)* director(a) *m., f.*
conference *n.* congreso *m.*
confirm *v.t.* confirmar
confirm a reservation confirmar una reservación
confirmation *n.* confirmación *f.*
confront *v.t.* enfrentar; enfrentarse (con)
The army will confront the enemy. El ejército se enfrentará con el enemigo.
confuse *v.t.* confundir
confused *adj.* confundido/a
confusion *n.* confusión *f.*
congested *adj.* congestionado/a
congratulate *v.t.* felicitar
Congratulations! *(for an event such as a birthday or anniversary)* ¡Felicidades! *f., pl.; (for an event such as an engagement or a good grade on a test)* ¡Felicitaciones! *f., pl.*
conquer *v.t.* conquistar
conqueror *n.* conquistador(a) *m., f.*
conquest *n.* conquista *f.*
conscience *n.* conciencia *f.*
consensus *n.* consenso *m.*
consent *n.* consentimiento *m.*
consent to *v.* consentir
conservation *n.* conservación *f.*
conservative *n., adj.* conservador(a) *m., f.*
conserve *v.t.* conservar
considerate *adj.* considerado/a
constellation *n.* constelación *f.*
constipated *adj.* estreñido/a
constipation *n.* estreñimiento *m.*
constitution *n.* constitución *f.*
consume *v.t.* consumir
consume alcohol consumir alcohol

consumer *n.* consumidor(a) *m., f.*
consumption *n.* consumo *m.*
contact lenses *n., pl.* lentes *m., pl.* de contacto
contagion *n.* contagio *m.*
contagious *adj.* contagioso/a
container *n.* recipiente *m.*; envase *m.*
contamination *n.* contaminación *f.*
content *adj.* contento/a
contest *n.* competencia *(L.A.) f.*; concurso *m.*
continue *v.t.* seguir (e:i)
contraceptive *n.* anticonceptivo *m.*
contract *n.* contrato *m.*
contradict *v.t.* contradecir
contradiction *n.* contradicción *f.*
contrast *v.t.* contraponer
control *n.* control *m.*
  control panel *n.* tablero *m.* de control
  control tower *n.* torre *f.* de control
control *v.t.* controlar
  be under control estar bajo control
control oneself *v.* dominarse
controversial *adj.* polémico/a
controversy *n.* polémica *f.*
convent *n.* convento *m.*
conversation *n.* conversación *f.*
converse *v.* conversar
convertible *n., adj. (car)* descapotable *m.*
convict *n.* presidiario/a *m., f.*
conviction *n.* convicción *f.*
convince *v.t.* convencer
convincing *adj.* convincente
cook *n.* cocinero/a *m., f.*
cook *v.t./v.i.* cocinar
cookie *n.* galleta *f.*
cool *adj.* fresco/a; *(slang)* chévere
  It's cool. (*weather*) Hace fresco.
copper *n.* cobre *m.*
copy *v.t.* copiar
cork *n.* corcho *m.*
corkscrew *n.* sacacorchos *m, sing.*
corn *n.* maíz *m.*
corner *n.* esquina *m.*
corpse *n.* cadáver *m.*
correct *v.t.* corregir
correction *n.* corrección *f.*
correctness *n.* corrección *f.*
cost *v.t.* costar (o:ue)
  cost an arm and a leg *idiom.* costar un ojo de la cara
costume *n.* disfraz *m.*
cotton *n.* algodón *m.*
  made of cotton de algoldón
couch *n.* sofá *m.*
  couch potato *n.* teleadicto/a *m., f.*
cough *n.* tos *f.*
cough syrup *n.* jarabe *m.* para la tos
cough *v.i.* toser
counselor *n.* consejero/a *m., f.*
count (o:ue) *v.t.* contar
counter *n. (game)* ficha *f.*
country *n. (nation)* país *m.*; *(rural)* campo *m.*
  developed country país desarrollado

developing country país en vías de desarrollo
countryside *n.* campo *m.;* paisaje *m.*
couple, (married) *n.* pareja *f.*
a couple of days un par de días
courage *n.* valentía *f.;* valor *m.*
course *n.* curso *m.;* materia *f.*
court *n. (of law)* corte *(L.A.) f.,* tribunal *(Spain) m.; (sport)* cancha *f.*
clay court pista *f.* de tierra batida
grass court pista *f.* de hierba
courtesy *n.* cortesía *f.*
cousin *n.* primo/a *m., f.*
cover *v.t.* cubrir; *(container, pan)* tapar
covered *p.p.* cubierto (*of* cubrir)
cow *n.* vaca *f.*
coward *adj.* cobarde
cowardice *n.* cobardía *f.*
cowboy *n.* vaquero *m.*
cowgirl *n.* vaquera *f.*
cozy *adj.* acogedor(a)
crab *n.* cangrejo *m.*
cracker *n.* galleta *f.* (salada)
cradle *n.* cuna *f.*
crafts *n.* artesanía *f.*
craftsmanship *n.* artesanía *f.*
crane *n. (machinery)* grúa *f.*
crash (into sthg.) *v.i.* chocar (contra algo)
crash a party colarse en una fiesta
crater *n.* cráter *m.*
crave *v.t.* ansiar
crawl *v.i.* arrastrarse (por el suelo)
crazy *adj.* loco/a
cream *n.* crema *f.; (dairy)* nata *f.*
anti-wrinkle cream crema antiarrugas
creamy *adj.* cremoso/a
create *v.t.* crear
creative *adj.* creativo/a
creator *n.* creador(a) *m., f.*
credible *adj.* verosímil
credit *n.* crédito *m.*
credit card *n.* tarjeta *f.* de crédito
cricket *n.* grillo *m.*
crime *n.* crimen *m.;* delincuencia *f.*
criminal *n.* delincuente *m., f.*
crisis *n.* crisis *f.*
mid-life crisis crisis de los cuarenta
critic *n.* detractor(a) *m., f.*
crockery *n.* vajilla *f.*
cross *v.t.* cruzar; atravesar
cross section *n. (Tech.)* corte *m.* transversal
crossroads *n., pl.* cruce *m.*
crosswalk *n.* paso *m.* de peatones
crossword (puzzle) *n.* crucigrama *m.*
cruise *n.* crucero *m.*
crunchy *adj.* crujiente
crusty *adj. (bread)* crujiente
cry *v.i.* llorar
crybaby *n.* llorón *m.,* llorona *f.*
crystal *n.* cristal *m.*
cucumber *n.* pepino *m.*
culture *n.* cultura *f.*
cup *n.* taza *f.*

cure *n.* cura *f.*
cure *v.t.* curar
currency exchange *n.* cambio *m.* de moneda
current *n.* corriente *f.*
alternating current (AC) corriente alterna
direct current (CD) corriente continua
current events *n., pl.* actualidades *f., pl.*
curriculum vitae *n.* currículum *m.*
curtain *n.* cortina *f.*
curve *n.* curva *f.*
cushion *n.* cojín *m.*
custard *n. (baked)* flan *m.;* natillas *f., pl.*
baked caramel custard flan de caramelo
custom *n.* costumbre *f.*
customer *n.* cliente/a *m., f.*
customs *n.* aduana *f.*
go through customs pasar por la aduana
customs inspector *n.* inspector(a) *m., f.* de aduanas
cut *n.* corte *f.*
cut *v.t.* cortar; partir (un pastel)
cut class *idiom* irse de pinta *(Mexico);* hacer novillos *(Spain)*
cutlery *n.* cubertería *f.*
cybercafé *n.* cibercafé *m.*
cycling *n.* ciclismo *m.*
cycling race *n.* carrera *f.* ciclista
cyclist *n.* ciclista *m., f.*
cylinder *n.* cilindro *m.*
cypress *n.* ciprés *m.*

D

dad *n.* papá *m.*
daily *adj.* diario/a
daily routine *n.* rutina *f.* diaria
dairy *n.* productos *m., pl.* lácteos
daisy *n.* margarita *f.*
dam *n.* represa *f.*
damage *v.t.* dañar; estropear
damp *adj.* húmedo/a
dance *n.* baile *m.;* danza *f.*
dance *v.t.* bailar
dance floor *n.* pista *f.* de baile
dancer *n.* bailarín *m.*, bailarina *f.*
danger *n.* peligro *m.*
dangerous *adj.* peligroso/a
dare (to + *inf.*) *v.t.* atreverse (a + *inf.*)
daring *adj.* atrevido/a
dark-skinned *adj.* moreno/a
darken *v.t.* (*sky, clouds*) ennegrecerse
darts *n., pl.* (*game*) dardos *m., pl.*
date (someone) *v.t.* salir con (alguien)
date *n. (appointment)* cita *f.; (calendar)* fecha *f.*
have a date tener una cita
What is the date (today)? ¿Cuál es la fecha (de hoy)?
What is today's date? ¿Cuál es la fecha de hoy?
daughter *n.* hija *f.*
daughter-in-law *n.* nuera *f.*
dawn *n.* amanecer *m.*
dawn *v.i.* amanecer

day *n.* día *m.*
What day is it? ¿Qué día es hoy?
day before yesterday *adv.* anteayer
day-care center *n.* guardería *f.*
daydream *v.i.* soñar despierto
dazed *adj.* atontado/a
dead-end street *n.* callejón *m.* sin salida
deaf *adj.* sordo/a
deal *n.* trato *m.*
It's a deal. Trato hecho.
It's no big deal. No es para tanto.
dealer *n. (arms, drugs)* traficante *m., f.*
dean *n. (university)* decano/a *m., f.*
death *n.* muerte *f.;* defunción *f.;* fallecimiento *m.*
debate *n.* debate *m.*
debate *v.t.* debatir
debut *v.t. (movie, play)* estrenar
decadence *n.* decadencia *f.*
decaffeinated *adj.* descafeinado/a
deceased *n., adj.* fallecido/a *m., f.,* difunto/a *m., f.*
deceive *v.t.* engañar
December *n.* diciembre *m.*
deception *n.* engaño *m.*
decide *v.t.* decidir (+ inf.)
decided *adj.* decidido/a
decipher *v.t.* descifrar
decision *n.* decisión *f.*
make a decision tomar una decisión
deck (of cards) *n.* baraja *f.* (de cartas/naipes)
deck chair *n.* tumbona *f.*
declare *v.t.* declarar
decline *n.* descenso *m.;* decadencia *f.*
decode *v.t.* descifrar
decorate *v.t.* decorar; adornar
decorate the tree poner el árbol
decrease *n.* descenso *m.;* disminución *f.*
decrease *v.t.* disminuir
dedicate *v.t.* dedicar
dedication *n.* dedicación; dedicatoria *f.*
deer *n.* ciervo *m.*
defeat *n.* derrota *f.*
defeat *v.t.* derrotar
deficiency *n.* deficiencia *f.*
deficit *n.* déficit *m.*
define *v.t.* definir
definition *n.* definición *f.*
deforestation *n.* deforestación *f.*
defraud *v.t.* estafar
defuse *v.t.* desactivar
dejected *adj.* abatido/a
delay *n.* retraso *m.,* atraso *m.*
delicious *adj.* delicioso/a, rico/a, sabroso/a
be delicious *loc.* estar para chuparse los dedos
delight *n.* deleite *m.,* placer *m.*
delighted *adj.* encantado/a
delineate *v.t.* delinear
delinquency *n.* delincuencia *f.*
democracy *n.* democracia *f.*
democrat *n.* demócrata *m., f.*
democratic *adj.* democrático/a
demonstrate *v.i.* manifestarse

demonstration *n.* manifestación *f.*
demonstrator *n.* manifestante *m., f.*
density *n.* densidad *f.*
dental floss *n.* hilo *m.* dental
dentist *n.* dentista *m., f.*
deny *v.t.* negar (e:ie)
not to deny no negar
deodorant *n.* desodorante *m.*
department *n.* departamento *m.*
department head *n.* catedrático/a *m., f.*
department store *n.* almacén *m.*
departure *n.* partida *f.*; salida *f.*
deposit *v.t.* depositar
depressed *adj.* deprimido/a
depression *n.* depresión *f.*
depth *n.* profundidad *f.*
derail *v.t.* descarrilar
derailment *n.* descarrilamiento *m.*
dermatologist *n.* dermatólogo/a *m., f.*
descend *v.i.* descender
descendant *n.* descendiente *m., f.*
descent *n.* descenso *m.*
describe *v.t.* describir
described *pp.* descrito (*of describir*)
desert *n., adj.* desierto *m.*; desértico/a
deserve *v.t.* merecer
design *n.* diseño *m.*
designer *n.* diseñador(a) *m., f.*
desire *n.* deseo *m.*
desire *v.t.* desear
desk *n.* escritorio *m.*
despair *n.* desesperanza *f.*
despair *v.i.* desesperar(se); perder las esperanzas
desperate *adj.* desesperado/a
desperation *n.* desesperación *f.*
dessert *n.* postre *m.*
destroy *v.t.* destruir
destruction *n.* destrucción *f.*
detail *n.* detalle *m.*
detained *adj.* detenido/a
deteriorate *v.* decaer
determined *adj.* condicionado/a
detoxification *n.* desintoxicación *f.*
detoxify *v.t.* desintoxicar
detractor *n.* detractor(a) *m., f.*
develop *v.t.* desarrollar
development *n.* desarrollo *m.*; *(housing)* urbanización *f.*
dew *n.* rocío *m.*
diabetes *n.* diabetes *f.*
diabetic *n., adj.* diabético/a *m., f.*
diagnose *v.t.* diagnosticar
diagnostic *n.* diagnóstico *m.*
dial (the number) *v.t.* marcar (el número)
dialogue *n.* diálogo *m.*
diamond *n.* diamante *m.*
diarrhea *n.* diarrea *f.*
diary *n.* diario *m.*
dice *n., pl.* dados *m., pl.*
dictator *n.* dictador(a) *m., f.*
dictatorship *n.* dictadura *f.*
dictionary *n.* diccionario *m.*
die out *v.t.* extinguirse
die *v.i.* morir (o:ue)

died *p.p.* muerto (*of* morir)
diet *n.* dieta *f.*; alimentación *f.*
eat a balanced diet comer una dieta equilibrada
be on a diet estar a dieta
differ *v.i.* divergir
difference *n.* diferencia *f.*, divergencia *f.*
different *adj.* diferente
differing *adj. (opinions)* divergente
difficult *adj.* difícil
make difficult dificultar; complicar
difficulty *n.* dificultad *f.*
dig *v.t.* excavar
digital camera cámara digital
dine *v.i.* cenar
dining room *n.* comedor *m.*
dinner *n.* cena *f.*
have dinner cenar
dinosaur *n.* dinosaurio *m.*
diplomat *n.* diplomático/a *m., f.*
diplomatic *adj.* diplomático/a
direct *v.t.* dirigir
directions *n., pl.* direcciones *f., pl.* indicaciones *(Spain) f., pl.*
give directions dar direcciones
director *n.* director(a) *m., f.*
dirty *adj.* sucio/a
dirty *v.t.* ensuciar
get (something) dirty ensuciar
disabled *adj. (person)* inválido/a
disadvantage *n.* desventaja *f.*
disagree *v.i.* no estar de acuerdo
disappear *v.i.* desaparecer
disappearance *n.* desaparición *f.*
disappointed *adj.* decepcionado/a; desilusionado/a
be disappointed decepcionarse
disaster *n.* desastre *m.*
natural disaster desastre natural
disastrous *adj.* desastroso/a
discipline *n.* disciplina *f.*
discoteque *n.* discoteca *f.*
discount *n.* descuento *m.*
discount *v.t.* descontar
give a discount descontar
discover *v.t.* descubrir
discovered *p.p.* descubierto (*of* descubrir)
discovery *n.* descubrimiento *m.*; hallazgo *m.*
discreet *adj.* discreto/a
discrete *adj.* discreto/a
discrimination *n.* discriminación *f.*
discuss *v.t.* discutir
discus throw *n.* lanzamiento *m.* de disco
disgraceful *adj.* vergonzoso/a
disgusting *adj.* asqueroso/a
dish *n.* plato *m.*; platillo
main dish plato principal
serving dish fuente *f.*
dishcloth *n.* trapo *m.*
dishes (set) *n., pl.* vajilla *f.*
disheveled *adj.* despeinado/a
dishonest *adj.* deshonesto/a
dishwasher *n.* lavaplatos *m., sing.*
disinfect *v.t.* desinfectar

disinfectant *n., adj.* desinfectante
disk *n.* disco *m.*
dislike *n.* antipatía *f.;* aversión *f.*
dislike *v.i.* chocar
disobey *v.t.* desobedecer
disorder *n.* desorden *m.; (medical)* trastorno *m.*
disorderly *adj.* desordenado/a
disposable *adj.* desechable
disqualification *n. (sport)* descalificación *f.*
disqualify *v.t. (sports)* descalificar
disseminate *v.t.* propagar
distant *adj.* lejano/a
distinction *n. (grade)* matrícula *f.* de honor
distinguish *v.t.* distinguir
distinguished *adj.* distinguido/a
distribute *v.t.* distribuir
distribution *n.* distribución *f.*
distrustful *adj.* receloso/a
dive *n.* salto *m.;* clavado *(L.A.) m.*
dive, (scuba) *v.i. (underwater)* bucear
diving board *n.* trampolín *m.*
diver *n. (scuba)* buceador(a) *m., f.*
diverse *adj.* variado/a
divorce *n.* divorcio *m.*
divorced *adj.* divorciado/a
  get divorced (from) divorciarse (de)
dizzy *adj.* mareado/a
  feel dizzy marearse
do *v.t.* hacer
  do the dishes lavar los platos
do oneself up *v.* arreglarse
doctor *n.* doctor(a) *m., f.;* médico/a *m., f.*
  doctor on call/duty médico/a de guardia
doctorate *n.* doctorado *m.*
document *n.* documento *m.*
document *v.t.* documentar
documentary *n.* documental *m.*
dodge ball *n.* quemados *m., pl.*
dog *n.* perro/a *m., f.*
doll *n.* muñeco/a *m., f.*
dolphin *n.* delfín *m.*
domestic *adj.* doméstico/a
  domestic appliance electrodoméstico *m.*
dominate *v.t.* dominar
domino *n.* dominó *m.*
done *p.p.* hecho (*of* hacer)
donor *n.* donante *m., f.*
donut *n.* dona *f.*
door *n.* puerta *f.*
  back door puerta trasera
  front door puerta principal
doorbell *n.* timbre *m.*
doorman *n.* portero/a *m., f.*
dormitory *n.* residencia *f.* estudiantil
double *adj.* doble
doubt *n.* duda *f.*
  There is no doubt that . . . No cabe duda (de) que… ; No hay duda (de) que…
  without a doubt sin duda
doubt *v.t.* dudar
  not to doubt no dudar
dough *n.* masa *f.*
dove *n.* paloma *f.*
down *adv.* abajo, debajo (de)

Down with...! ¡Abajo el/la...!
downhearted *adj.* desanimado/a
download *v.t. (computer)* descargar
downtown *n.* centro *m.*
draftsman *n.* delineante *m.*
draftswoman *n.* delineante *f.*
drag *v.t.* arrastrar
drain *v.t.* colar *(L.A.)*; *(the dishes)* escurrir (los platos)
drainpipe *n.* desagüe *m.*
drama *n.* drama *m.*
dramatic *adj.* dramático/a
draw *v.t.* dibujar
drawback *n.* inconveniente *m.*
drawing *n.* dibujo *m.*
dream *v.i.* soñar
dress *n.* vestido *m.*
dress *v.t.* vestirse (e:i); (*salad*) aderezar; aliñar
get dressed vestirse (e:i)
dress up *v.* ponerse elegante
You have dressed up tonight. Te has puesto muy elegante esta noche.
dresser *n.* cómoda *f.*
dressing *n. (culinary)* aderezo *m.*, aliño *m.*; *(medical)* vendaje *m.*
dressing room *n.* probador *m.*
dressmaker *n.* modista *f.*
drill *n. (tool)* perforadora *f.*
drill *v.t.* perforar
drink *n.* bebida *f.*
drink *v.t.* beber; tomar
Do you want something to drink? ¿Quieres algo de tomar?
drive *v.t.* conducir *(Spain)*; manejar *(L.A.)*
driver *n.* conductor(a) *m., f.*
driveway *n.* entrada *f.*
drop *n.* gota *f.*; *(temperature, price)* descenso *m.*
drop off *v.t.* dejar
drought *n.* sequía *f.*
drown *v.t.* ahogar **Ahoga sus penas cantando.** She drowns her sorrows by singing. *v.i.* ahogarse **Te ahogas en un vaso de agua.** You get worked up about nothing.
drowned *adj.* ahogado/a
drug *n.* droga *f.*
drug addict *n., adj.* drogadicto/a *m., f.*
drunk *adj.* borracho/a; ebrio/a; embriagado/a
dry *adj.* seco/a
dry (oneself) *v. pron.* secarse
due to *prep.* debido a; por
due to the fact that debido a
dull *adj.* sin brillo; *(person)* aburrido/a, soso/a
dumb *adj.* tonto/a
dune *n.* duna *f.*
during *prep.* durante; por
dusk *n.* atardecer *m.*
dust *n.* polvo *m.*
dust *v.t.* sacudir
dust the furniture sacudir los muebles
duty: be on duty estar de guardia
DVD player reproductor de DVD
dye *v.t.* teñir
dying *adj.* moribundo/a
I'm dying to/for . . . Me muero por (+ *inf.*)/*n.* . . .

dynamite *n.* dinamita *f.*
dynamite *v.t.* dinamitar
dynasty *n.* dinastía *f.*
dysfunction *n.* disfunción *f.*

E

each *adj.* cada
eagle *n.* águila (el) *f.*
ear, (outer) *n.* oreja *f.*
  inner ear *n.* oído *m.*
early *adj., adv.* temprano/a
  early morning *n.* madrugada *f.*
earn *v.t.* ganar
  earn one's living *idiom* ganarse la vida
earring *n.* arete *(L.A) m.;* pendiente *m. (Spain)*
earth *n.* tierra *f.*
earthquake *n.* terremoto *m.*
earthworm *n.* lombriz *f.*
ease *n.* soltura *f.*
ease *v.t.* aliviar
east *n.* este *m.*
  to the east al este
easy *adj.* fácil
  make easier facilitar
  Easier said than done. *idiom* Del dicho al hecho hay gran trecho.
easygoing *adj.* tranquilo/a
eat *v.t.* comer
eclipse *n.* eclipse *m.*
ecological *adj.* ecológico/a
ecologist *n.* ecologista *m., f.*
ecology *n.* ecología *f.*
economics *n.* economía *f.*
ecosystem *n.* ecosistema *m.*
ecotourism *n.* ecoturismo *m.*
Ecuadorian *n., adj.* ecuatoriano/a *m., f.*
edible *adj.* comestible
educator *n.* educador(a) m., f.
eel *n.* anguila *f.*
effective *adj.* eficaz
effectiveness *n.* eficacia *f.*
efficiency *n.* eficiencia *f.*
efficient *adj.* eficiente, eficaz
effort *n.* esfuerzo *m.*
egg *n.* huevo *m.*
eggplant *n.* berenjena *f.*
eight ocho
eight hundred ochocientos/as
eighteen dieciocho
eighth octavo *m.; adj.* octavo/a
eighty ochenta
either . . . or *conj.* o… o
elastic *adj.* elástico/a
elbow *n.* codo *m.*
elderly *adj.* anciano/a
eldest el/la mayor
elect *v.t.* elegir
election *n.* elección *f.,* elecciones *f., pl.*
electorate *n.* electorado *m.*
electric *adj.* eléctrico/a
electric current *n.* corriente *f.* eléctrica
electric shock *n.* descarga *f.* eléctrica
electrician *n.* electricista *m., f.*
electricity *n.* electricidad *f.;* luz *f.*
electrocuted: be electrocuted electrocutarse
electrolysis *n.* electrólisis *f.*
electronics *n.* electrónica *f.*
elegant *adj.* elegante
elementary *adj.* elemental; *(school)* primario/a

elephant *n.* elefante *m.*
elevator *n.* ascensor *m.*
eleven once
eliminate *v.t.* eliminar
elimination *n.* eliminación *f.*
eloquence *n.* elocuencia *f.*
eloquent *adj.* elocuente
e-mail *n.* correo *m.* electrónico
  e-mail address dirección electrónica
  e-mail message *n.* mensaje *m.* electrónico
embarrass *v.t.* avergonzar
embarrassed *adj.* avergonzado/a
embarrassment *n.* vergüenza *f.*
embrace *v.t.* abrazar; *(each other)* abrazarse
embroider *v.t.* bordar
emerald *n.* esmeralda *f.*
emergency *n.* emergencia *f.*
emergency room *n.* sala *f.* de emergencia
emigrant *n.* emigrante *m., f.*
emigrate *v.i.* emigrar
emigration *n.* emigración *f.*
emphasis *n.* énfasis *m.*
emphasize *v.t.* destacar; enfatizar
empire *n.* imperio *m.*
employee *n.* empleado/a *m., f.*
employment *n.* empleo *m.*
enchant *v.t.* encantar
encourage *v.t.* dar aliento; animar
end *n.* fin *m.*
  at the end (of) *(physical location)* al fondo (de); *(month, century)* a fines de
end *v.t.* terminar
end table *n.* mesita *f.*
endangered species *n., pl.* especie(s) *f. (pl.)* en peligro de extinción
endurance *n.* resistencia *f.*; aguante *m.;*
endure *v.t.* soportar; aguantar
energy *n.* energía *f.*
  (nuclear/solar) energy energía (nuclear/solar)
engaged: get engaged (to) comprometerse (con)
engagement *n.* compromiso *m.,* noviazgo *m.*
engagement ring *n.* anillo *m.* de compromiso
engineer *n.* ingeniero/a *m., f.*
English *adj., n.* inglés *m.,* inglesa *f.*; *(language)* inglés
enigma *n.* enigma *m.*
enigmatic *adj.* enigmático/a
enjoy *v.t.* disfrutar (de)
enjoyable *adj.* agradable; divertido/a
enough *adj.* bastante
enrich *v.t.* enriquecer
enroll *v.i.* matricularse; inscribirse
enrollment *n.* inscripción *f.*
enter *v.* entrar
entertaining *adj.* entretenido/a
entertainment *n.* diversión *f.*
enthusiasm *n.* entusiasmo *m.*
enthusiastic *adj.* entusiasmado/a
entirely *adv.* totalmente; del todo **He is not entirely mistaken.** No está del todo equivocado.
entrance *n.* entrada *f.*

entrance hall *n. (residence)* recibidor *m.*
entrepreneur *n.* empresario/a *m., f.*
envelope *n.* sobre *m.*
envious *adj.* envidioso/a
environment *n.* medio ambiente *m.; (natural)* ambiente *m.*
environmentalist *n.* ecologista *m., f.*
equality *n.* igualdad *f.*
equestrian sports *n., pl.* hípica *f.*
equipped *adj.* equipado/a
equivalence *n.* equivalencia *f.*
equivalent: be equivalent to equivaler
erase *v.t.* borrar
eraser *n.* borrador *m.; (pencil)* goma *f.*
errand *n.* diligencia *f.*
do/run errands hacer diligencias
erupt *v.i.* (*volcano*) hacer erupción
eruption *n.* erupción *f.*
escalator *n.* escalera *f.* mecánica
escape *n.* evasión *f.;* huida *f.; (prison)* fuga *f.*
escape *v.i.* huir; fugarse; evadirse **Luis escaped responsibility.** Luis se evadió de la responsabilidad.
esophagus *n.* esófago *m.*
establish *v.t.* establecer
esteem *n.* aprecio *m.*
estimate *n.* cálculo *m.*
ethical *adj.* ético/a
ethics *n.* ética *f.*
euphoria *n.* euforia *f.*
euphoric *adj.* eufórico/a
European *n., adj.* europeo/a *m., f.*
evade *v.t.* evadir
evening *n.* tarde *f.;* noche *f.*
in the evening de la noche; por la noche
event *n.* acontecimiento *m.*
ever alguna vez
every *adj.* cada
every day cada día, todos los días
everybody *n.* todos *m., pl.*
everything *n.* todo *m.*
Everything is under control. Todo está bajo control.
evidence *n.* indicio *m.;* pruebas *f., pl.*
lack of evidence falta *f.* de pruebas
evolution *n.* evolución *f.*
evolve *v.i.* evolucionar
exactly *adv.* exactamente; (*time*) en punto
exaggerate *v.t.* exagerar
exaggeration *n.* exageración *f.*
exam *n.* examen *m.*
example: for example por ejemplo
exasperate *v.t.* desesperar
The slowness of the train exasperated him. La lentitud del tren le desesperó.
excavate *v.t.* excavar
excavator *n.* excavadora *f.*
exceed *v.t.* superar
excel *v.i.* sobresalir

excellent *adj.* excelente; *(grade)* sobresaliente
exceptional *adj.* prodigioso/a
excess *n.* exceso *m.*
in excess en exceso
exchange *n.* intercambio *m.*
in exchange for a cambio de; por
exchange *v.t.* intercambiar
excited *adj.* emocionado/a
exciting *adj.* emocionante
excursion *n.* excursión *f.*
excuse *v.t.* disculpar
Excuse me. *(May I?)* Con permiso.; *(Pardon me.)* Perdón.; *(interrupting)* Disculpe. **Excuse me, can you tell me...** Disculpe, puede decirme...
exercise *n.* ejercicio *m.*
exercise *v.i.* hacer ejercicio
do stretching exercises hacer ejercicios de estiramiento
exhaust pipe *n.* tubo *m.* de escape
exhausted *adj.* agotado/a
exhaustion *n.* agotamiento *m.*
exhibit *v.t.* *(paintings, goods)* exponer; *(skill)* demostrar
exhibition *n.* exposición *f.*
exit *n.* salida *f.*
exodus *n.* éxodo *m.*
expect *v.t.* esperar
expel *v.t.* expulsar
expense *n.* gasto *m.*
expensive *adj.* caro/a
experience *n.* experiencia *f.*
experiment *v.i.* experimentar
expiration *n.* expiración *f.*
expiration date *n.* fecha *f.* de caducidad
expire *v.i.* expirar
explain *v.t.* explicar
explore *v.t.* explorar
explore a city/town explorar una ciudad/un pueblo
explosive *adj.* explosivo/a
export *v.t.* exportar
exportation *n.* exportación *f.*
expression *n.* expresión *f.*
expressive *adj.* expresivo/a
expressway *n.* autopista *f.*
expulsion *n.* expulsión *m.*
extinction *n.* extinción *f.*
become extinct extinguirse
extinguish *v.t.* extinguir
extremely *adv.* sumamente
extremities *n., pl.* extremidades *f., pl.*
extroverted *adj.* extrovertido/a
eye *n.* ojo *m.*
eyebrow *n.* ceja *f.*
eyelash *n.* pestaña *f.*
eyelid *n.* párpado *m.*

F

fabric *n.* tela *f.*
fabulous *adj.* fabuloso/a
façade *n.* fachada *f.*
face *n.* cara *f.*
face *v.t.* enfrentar **It's necessary to face the problem immediately.** Hay que enfrentar el problema en seguida.
facedown *adv.* boca abajo
faceup *adv.* boca arriba
facilitate *v.t.* facilitar
facing *prep.* enfrente de

fact *n.* hecho *m.*
in fact de hecho; en efecto
factory *n.* fábrica *f.*
fail *v.t. (exam)* suspender; fracasar
fail *n. (grade)* suspenso *m.*
failed *adj.* fracasado/a
failure *n.* fracaso *m.*
fair *adj.* justo/a
fairy *n.* hada (el) *f.*
fairy godmother *n.* hada madrina
faithful *adj.* fiel
fall *n.* **(season)** otoño *m.*
faithfulness *n.* fidelidad *f.*
fall *v.i.* caer; *(down)* caerse
fall asleep *v.* dormirse (o:ue)
fallen *p.p.* caído (*of* caer)
familiar *adj.* conocido/a
family *n., adj.* familia *f.;* familiar
family doctor *n.* médico/a *m., f.* de cabecera; médico/a de familia
family tree *n.* árbol *m.* genealógico
famine *n.* hambre *m.*
famous *adj.* famoso/a
fan *n., adj.* aficionado/a *m., f.;* ventilador *m.*
be a fan of ser aficionado/a a
fang *n.* colmillo *m.*
far from *adv.* lejos de
farewell *n.* despedida *f.*
farmer *n.* agricultor(a) *m., f.*
farming *n.* agricultura *f.*
far-off *adj.* lejano/a
fascinate *v.t.* fascinar
be fascinated by fascinar
fashion *n.* moda *f.*
be in fashion estar de moda
be fashionably dressed ir a la moda
fast *adj.* rápido/a
fast *n.* ayuno *m.*
fast *v.i.* ayunar
fast *adj.* rápido/a, veloz
fast food *n.* comida *f.* rápida
fat *adj.* gordo/a
fat *n.* grasa *f.*
father *n.* padre *m.*
father-in-law *n.* suegro *m.*
fatigue *n.* cansancio *m.*
fatten *v.t.* engordar
faucet *n.* grifo *m.*
fault *n.* culpa *f.*
favorable *adj.* favorable
favorite *adj.* favorito/a
fax (machine) *n.* fax *m.*
fear *n.* miedo *m.*
fear *v.t.* temer
February *n.* febrero *m.*
feed *v.t.* alimentar, dar de comer
get fed up hartarse
feel *v.t.* sentir, sentirse
feel like (doing something) tener ganas de (+ *inf.*)
feeling sorry *adj.* arrepentido/a
female *n.* hembra *f.*
fence *n.* valla *f.*
fencer *n.* esgrimidor(a) *m., f.*
fencing *n. (sport)* esgrima *f.*
fender *n.* guardabarros *m., sing.*
ferry *n.* transbordador *m.*
fertile *adj.* fértil
fertility *n.* fertilidad *f.*
fertilization *n.* fecundación *f.*
fertilize *v.t.* fecundar; *(the soil)* abonar (la tierra)

fertilizer *n.* abono *m.;* fertilizante *m.*
festival *n.* festival *m.;* verbena *f.*
fever *n.* fiebre *f.*
  have a fever tener fiebre
few *adj.* pocos/as
  fewer than menos de (+ *number*)
fidelity *n.* fidelidad *f.*
field *n.* campo *m.; (sport)* cancha *f.*
  major field of study *n.* especialización *f.*
field hockey *n.* hockey *m.* sobre césped *(L.A.);* hockey sobre hierba *(Spain)*
fifteen quince
fifth quinto *m.; adj.* quinto/a
fifty cincuenta
fig *n.* higo *m.*
fig tree *n.* higuera *f.*
fight *n.* pelea *f.;* lucha *f.*
fight *v.i.* luchar (por/contra); pelear; pelearse
figure *n.* figura *f.; (number) n.* cifra *f.*
figure skating *n.* patinaje *m.* artístico
file *n.* archivo *m.; (tool)* lima *f.*
file *v.t.* archivar
fill *v.t.* llenar
  fill the tank llenar el tanque
fill out *v.t. (document)* rellenar *(Spain);* llenar *(L.A.)*
  fill out a form llenar un formulario
film *v.t.* rodar
film *n.* película
film library *n.* filmoteca *f.*
filming *n.* rodaje *m.*
filmmaker *n.* cineasta *m., f.*
fin *n.* aleta *f.*
finally *adv.* finalmente; por último; por fin
finance *v.t.* financiar
find *n.* hallazgo *m.* **That restaurant was a real find.** Ese restaurante fue un verdadero hallazgo.
find *v.t.* encontrar (o:ue); *(each other)* encontrarse
  I can't find my shoe. No encuentro el zapato.
  Finally, they found each other. Al fin se encontraron.
find out *v.t.* averiguar
fine *n.* multa *f.*
fine *adj.* bien
  That's fine. Está bien.
fine arts *n., pl.* bellas artes *f., pl.*
finger *n.* dedo *m.* (de la mano)
fingerprint *n.* huella *f.* dactilar
finish *v.t.* terminar; *(doing something)* terminar de (+ *inf.)*
fir tree *n.* abeto *m.*
fire *n.* fuego *m.;* incendio *m.*
  fire engine *n.* carro *m.* de bomberos
  fire escape *n.* escalera *f.* de incendios
fire *v.* despedir (e:i)
firefighter *n.* bombero/a *m., f.*
fireplace *n.* chimenea *f.*
firewood *n.* leña *f.*
fireworks *n., pl.* fuegos *m., pl.* artificiales
firm *n.* compañía *f.;* empresa *f.*

first *adj.* primer, primero/a
first of all *adv.* en primer lugar
first name *n.* nombre *m.* de pila
first-aid kit *n.* botiquín *m.* de primeros auxilios
firstborn *n.* primogénito/a *m., f.*
fish *n. (food)* pescado *m.; (live)* pez *m.*
marinated fish *n.* ceviche *m.*
fish *v.t.* pescar
fish market *n.* pescadería *f.*
fisherman *n.* pescador *m.*
fisherwoman *n.* pescadora *f.*
fishing *n.* pesca *f.*
go fishing ir de pesca
fit *adj. (suitable)* apto/a **He's not fit to practice psychology.** No es apto para ejercer la psicología.; *(physically)* en forma
fit *v.i. (clothing)* quedar
Does it fit me? ¿Me queda bien?
five cinco
five hundred quinientos/as
fix *v.t. (put in working order)* arreglar
fixed *adj. (set)* fijo/a
fixed price *n.* precio *m.* fijo
fixed schedule horario fijo
flag *n.* bandera *f.*
flamboyant *adj.* extravagante
flank steak *n.* lomo *m.*
flashlight *n.* linterna *f.;* foco *m.*
flat: go flat *v.t.* ponchar *(Mexico);* pinchar **We got a flat tire.** Se nos ponchó/pinchó una llanta.
flatter *v.t.* adular
flatter someone *idiom* echarle flores a alguien
flatterer *n.* adulador(a) *m., f.*
flattery *n.* adulación *f.*
flavor *n.* sabor *m.*
flee *v.i.* fugarse; huir
flex *v.t.* flexionar
flexible *adj.* flexible
flexible schedule horario flexible
flight *n.* vuelo *m.; (escape)* huida *f.*
flipper *n.* aleta *f.*
flirt *n.* coqueta *f.*
flirt *v.i.* coquetear
float *n.* carroza *f.*
float *v.i.* flotar
flood *n.* inundación *f.*
flood *v.t.* inundar
floor *n. (story in a building)* piso *m.; (ground)* suelo *(Spain) m., piso (L.A.) m.*
ground floor planta *f.* baja
top floor planta alta
florist *n.* florista *(Spain) m., f.;* florero/a *(L.A.) m., f.*
flour *n.* harina *f.*
flow *v.i.* fluir
flower *n.* flor *f.*
flower pot *n.* maceta *f.*
flower shop *n.* florería *(L.A.) f.;* floristería *(Spain) f.*
flu *n.* gripe *f.*
fluffy *adj. (fabric, baked goods)* esponjoso/a
fly *n.* mosca *f.*
foam *n.* espuma *f.*
focus on *v.t.* enfocar
fog *n.* niebla *f.*

It's (very) foggy. Hay (mucha) niebla.
fold *v.t.* plegar
folder *n.* carpeta *f.*
folding *adj.* plegable
folic acid *n.* ácido *m.* fólico
folk *adj.* folklórico/a
follow *v.t.* seguir (e:i)
food *n.* comida *f.;* alimento *m.*
foolish *adj.* tonto/a
foot *n.* pie *m.*
football *n.* fútbol *m.* americano
footprint *n.* huella *f.*
foot race *n.* carrera *f.* pedestre
for *prep.* para; por
for me para mí
forbid *v.t.* prohibir
forehead *n.* frente *f.*
foreign *adj.* extranjero/a
forensic scientist *n.* forense *m., f.*
forest *n.* bosque *m.*
tropical forest bosque tropical
forget *v.t.* olvidar
forgive *v.t.* perdonar
forgiveness *n.* perdón *m.*
fork *n.* tenedor *m.*
forklift *n.* montacargas *m., sing.*
form *n. (shape)* forma *f.; (document)* formulario *m.*
formal *adj.* formal
fortnight *n.* quincena *f.*
fortress *n.* fortaleza *f.*
forty cuarenta
forward *adv.* hacia adelante; en marcha
fossil *n.* fósil *m.*
fossilize *v.i.* fosilizarse
become fossilized fosilizarse
foundation *n. (building)* cimientos *m., pl.*
fountain *n.* fuente *f.*
four cuatro
four hundred cuatrocientos/as
fourteen catorce
fourth cuarto *m.; adj.* cuarto/a
fox *n.* zorro *m.*
fraud *n.* estafador(a) *m., f.*
freckle *n.* peca *f.*
freckled *adj.* pecoso/a
free *adj.* libre; *(price)* gratis
be free of charge ser gratis
free fall *n.* caída *f.* libre
free time *n.* tiempo *m.* libre; ratos *m., pl.* libres
free *v.t.* liberar
freedom *n.* libertad *f.*
freedom of speech *n.* libertad de expresión
freelancer *n.* [trabajador(a)] autónomo/a *m., f.*
freestyle *n.* estilo *m.* libre
freeway *n.* autopista *f.*
freezer *n.* congelador *m.*
French *n., adj.* francés *m.,* francesa *f.; (language)* francés
French fries *n., pl.* papas *f., pl.* fritas; patatas *f., pl.* fritas
frequently *adv.* frecuentemente; con frecuencia; a menudo
fresh *adj.* fresco/a
Friday *n.* viernes *m., sing.*
fried *adj.* frito/a
fried food *n.* fritada *f.*
fried potatoes *n., pl.* papas (L.A.) *f., pl.* fritas; patatas

(Spain) f., pl. fritas
friend *n.* amigo/a *m., f.*
make friends hacer amigos
friendly *adj.* amable; amistoso/a
friendship *n.* amistad *f.*
frog *n.* rana *f.*
from *prep.* de; desde
from the United States estadounidense
from time to time *adv.* de vez en cuando
front desk *n.* recepción *f.*
front door *n.* puerta *f.* principal
front seat *n.* asiento *m.* delantero
frost *n.* escarcha *f.*
frugal *adj.* ahorrador(a)
fruit *n.* fruta *f.*
fruit juice jugo *m.* de fruta
fruit store *n.* frutería *f.*
fruit tree *n.* árbol *m.* frutal
fuchsia *adj.* fucsia
fuel *n.* combustible *m.*
fugitive *n.* fugitivo/a *m., f.*
full *adj.* lleno/a
fun *adj.* divertido/a
have fun divertirse (e:ie)
fun activity *n.* diversión *f.*
function *v.i.* funcionar
funds *n., pl. (money)* fondos *m., pl.*
funeral *n.* funeral *m.*
funnel *n.* embudo *m.*
funny *adj.* chistoso/a; gracioso/a
furious *adj.* furioso/a
furnish *v.t.* amueblar
furnished *adj.* amueblado/a
furniture *n.* muebles *m., pl.*
furthermore *adv.* además (de)
fuse *n.* fusible *m.*
future *n., adj.* futuro/a; futuro *m.;* porvenir *m.*
in the (near) future en el futuro (cercano)

G

gain *v.t.* ganar; obtener
gain weight aumentar de peso; engordar
galaxy *n.* galaxia *f.*
gallbladder *n.* vesícula *f.* (biliar)
gallery *n.* galería *f.*
art gallery pinacoteca *f.*
gambler *n.* jugador(a) *m., f.*
gambling *n.* juegos *m., pl.* de azar
game *n.* juego *m.; (match)* partido *m.*
game piece *n.* ficha *f.*
game show *n.* concurso *m.*
gang *n.* pandilla *f.*
gang member *n.* pandillero/a *m., f.*
garage *n.* garaje *m.*
garbage *n.* basura *f.*
garbage can *n.* basurero *m.*
garbage collector *n.* basurero/a *m., f.*
garbage disposal *n.* triturador *m.* de basura
garbage dump *n.* basurero *m.;* vertedero *m.*
garden *n.* jardín *m.;* huerto *m.*
large garden *n.* huerta *f.*
gardener *n.* jardinero/a *m., f.*
gardenia *n.* gardenia *f.*
gardening *n.* jardinería *f.*

garlic *n.* ajo *m.*
garment *n.* prenda *f.*
garnish *v.t.* decorar; adornar
gas pedal *n.* pedal *m.* del acelerador
gas station *n.* gasolinera *f.*
gas tank *n.* depósito *m.* de gasolina
gasoline *n.* gasolina *f.*
gastronomy *n.* gastronomía *f.*
gathering *n. (to discuss politics, literature, etc.)* tertulia *f.*
gaze at *v.* contemplar
gazelle *n.* gacela *f.*
gearshift *n. (car)* cambio *m.* de marchas/velocidades
gelatin *n.* gelatina *f.*
generous *adj.* generoso/a
genetic *adj.* genético/a
genetic engineering *n.* biogenética *f.*
genetics *n.* genética *f.*
geography *n.* geografía *f.*
geologist *n.* geólogo/a *m., f.*
geometric(al) *adj.* geométrico/a
geometry *n.* geometría *f.*
geranium *n.* geranio *m.*
German *n., adj.* alemán *m.,* alemana *f.; (language)* alemán
get *v.t.* conseguir (e:i); obtener
  get along well/badly with llevarse bien/mal con
  get good grades *v.* sacar buenas notas
  get hurt *v. pron.* lastimarse
  get into trouble *v.* hacer travesuras
  get pregnant *v.* quedar embarazada
  get together *v. pron.* juntarse
get off (at) *v.* salirse (en)
get off of (a vehicle) *v.* bajar(se) de
get on/in to (a vehicle) *v.* subir(se) a
get up *v.* levantarse
  get up early madrugar
getaway *n.* escapada *f.*
geyser *n.* géiser *m.*
gift *n.* regalo *m.*
giraffe *n.* jirafa *f.*
girl *n.* chica *f.;* muchacha *f.;* niña
girlfriend *n.* novia *f.*
give *v.t.* dar; *(gift)* regalar
give in *v.* ceder
give up (doing something) *v.* dejar de (+ *inf.*)
give up hope *v.* desesperarse
give way *v.* ceder (el paso)
glass *n. (drinking)* vaso *m., (material)* vidrio *m.,* cristal *m.*
  made of glass de vidrio
glasses *n., pl.* gafas *f., pl.*
glassware *n.* cristalería *f.*
gloves *n.* guantes *m.*
glue *v.t.* pegar
gluttonous *adj.* glotón *m.,* glotona *f.*
go *v.i.* ir
  go on rides *v.* subirse a los juegos
  go on the swings *v.* subirse a los columpios
  go shopping ir de compras
  Let's go. Vamos.
go away *v.* irse; ausentarse

go beyond *v.* superar
go by *v.* pasar por
go by the bank pasar por el banco
go down *v.* bajar(se)
go off *v. (alarm)* sonar
go out (with) *v.* salir (con)
go out and have a snack in a bar ir de tapas *(Spain)*
go overboard *loc.* echar la casa por la ventana
go up *v.* subir
go with *v.* acompañar
goal *n.* meta *f.;* objetivo *m.*
goblet *n.* copa *f.*
God *n.* Dios *m.*
god *n. (deity)* dios
goddaughter *n.* ahijada *f.*
godfather *n.* padrino *m.*
godmother *n.* madrina *f.*
godson *n.* ahijado *m.*
going to: be going to *(do something)* ir a (+ *inf.)*
gold *adj.* dorado/a
gold *n.* oro *m.*
golden *adj.* dorado/a
golf *n.* golf *m.*
golf club *n.* palo *m.* de golf
golf course *n.* campo *m.* de golf
golfer *n.* golfista *m., f.*
good *adj.* buen, bueno/a
Good afternoon. Buenas tardes.
Good evening. Buenas noches.
Good morning. Buenos días.
Good night. Buenas noches.
I'm good, thanks. Bien, gracias.
in good spirits *adj.* animado/a
It's good that... Es bueno que...
good sense *n.* sensatez *f.*
good-bye *n.* adiós *m.;* despedida *f.*
say good-bye despedirse
good-looking *adj.* guapo/a
goods *n.* artículos *m., pl.*
gossip *n.* chismes *m., pl.;* cotilleo *(Spain) m.*
gossip *v.i.* cotillear *(Spain);* chismear
Gothic *adj.* gótico/a
govern *v.t.* gobernar
government *n.* gobierno *m.*
grade *n.* calificación *f.;* nota *f.*
grade *v.t.* calificar
graduate (from, in) *v.i.* graduarse (de), recibirse
graduation *n.* graduación *f.*
graffiti *n.* pintada *f.*
There was gang graffiti on the wall. Había pintadas de pandillas en la pared.
grain *n.* grano *m.*
grains *n., pl.* cereales *m., pl.*
grammar school *n.* primaria *f.*
grandchildren *n., pl.* nietos *m., pl.*
granddaughter *n.* nieta *f.*
grandfather *n.* abuelo *m.*
grandmother *n.* abuela *f.*
grandparents *n., pl.* abuelos *m., pl.*
grandson *n.* nieto *m.*
grant *n.* beca *f.*
grape *n.* uva *f.*
grapefruit *n.* pomelo

(Argentina, Spain) m.; toronja *(L.A.) f.*

grass *n.* césped *m.;* hierba *f.;* pasto *(L.A.) m.*

grateful *adj.* agradecido/a

grater *n.* rallador *m.*

grave *n.* tumba *f.*

grave *adj.* grave

gravity *n.* gravedad *f.*

gray *n., adj.* gris *m.*

gray hair *n.* cana *f.*

great *adj.* fenomenal

great-grandchildren *n., pl.* bisnietos *m., pl.*

great-granddaughter *n.* bisnieta *f.*

great-grandfather *n.* bisabuelo *m.*

great-grandmother *n.* bisabuela *f.*

great-grandparents *n., pl.* bisabuelos *m., pl.*

great-grandson *n.* bisnieto *m.*

great-great-grandfather *n.* tatarabuelo *m.*

great-great-grandmother *n.* tatarabuela *f.*

great-great-grandparents *n., pl.* tatarabuelos *m., pl.*

greedy *adj.* avaricioso/a

Greek *n., adj.* griego/a *m., f.; (language)* griego

green *n., adj.* verde *m.*

dark green verde oscuro

green space *n.* zona *f.* verde

greet *v.t.* saludar **He greets his friend.** Él saluda a su amigo.; *(each other)* saludarse **They greet each other.** Ellos se saludan.

greeting *n.* saludo *m.*

Greetings to . . . Saludos a...

grenade *n. (military)* granada *f.*

grill *n.* parrilla *f.;* plancha *f.*

grilled *adj. (food)* a la plancha; a la parrilla **grilled flank steak** lomo a la plancha

groceries *n., pl.* comestibles *m., pl.*

group *n.* grupo *m.*

group *v.t.* agrupar

get into groups agruparse

grove *n.* arboleda *f.*

grow *v.t.* cultivar; *v.i.* crecer

growing *adj.* creciente

growth *n.* crecimiento *m.*

grudge *n.* rencor *m.*

guarantee *n.* garantía *f.*

guarantee *v.t.* garantizar; asegurar

guard *v.t.* custodiar

guess *v.t.* adivinar

guest *n. (at a house/hotel)* huésped *m., f.; (at a function)* invitado/a *m., f.*

guide *n.* guía *m., f.*

guitar *n.* guitarra *f.*

gum *n. (chewing)* chicle *m.; (anat.)* encía *f.*

gunshot *n.* disparo *m.*

gymnasium *n.* gimnasio *m.*

gymnast *n.* gimnasta *m., f.*

gymnastics *n.* gimnasia *f.*

rhythmic gymnastics gimnasia rítmica

gynecologist *n.* ginecólogo/a *m., f.*

H

hair *n.* pelo *m.;* cabello *m.*

hairbrush *n.* cepillo *m.* de pelo
hairdo *n.* peinado *m.* **Her new hairdo suits/suited her.** Su nuevo peinado le sienta/le sentaba bien.
hairdresser *n.* peluquero/a *m., f.*
hairdryer *n.* secador *m.*
hairstyle *n.* peinado *m.*
hairy *adj.* peludo/a
hake *n.* merluza *f.*
half *n., adj.* medio *m.;* medio/a
half-brother *n.* medio hermano *m.*
half-past . . . ...y media
half-sister *n.* media hermana *f.*
hall *n.* salón *m.*
hallway *n.* pasillo *m.*
ham *n.* jamón *m.*
hamburger *n.* hamburguesa *f.*
hammer *n.* martillo *m.*
hammock *n.* hamaca *f.*
hand *n.* mano *f.*
Hands up! ¡Manos arriba!
handball *n.* balonmano *m.*
handbrake *n.* freno *m.* de mano
handkerchief *n.* pañuelo *m.*
handle *n.* asa *m.*
handlebars *n., pl.* manillar *(Spain) m.;* manubrio *(L.A.) m.*
handrail *n.* pasamanos *m., sing.*
handsome *adj.* guapo/a
handy *adj.* práctico/a
hang *v.t.* colgar
hang clothes on the line colgar la ropa en el tendedero
hang glider *n.* ala (el) *f.* delta
hang gliding *v.* practicar el ala delta
hang out (clothes) *v.* tender (ropa)
hanger *n.* percha *f.*
hangover *n.* resaca *(Spain) f.;* cruda *(Mexico) f.*
have a hangover tener cruda; tener resaca
happen *v.t.* ocurrir
What happened? ¿Qué pasó?
What's happening? ¿Qué pasa?
happiness *n.* alegría *f.*
happy *adj.* alegre; contento/a; feliz
be happy alegrarse (de)
be happy (with) contentarse (con)
harbor *n.* puerto *m.*
hard *adj.* difícil; duro/a
hard to believe *idiom* parece mentira
hard feelings *n., pl.* rencor *m.*
hardly *adv.* apenas
hardship *n.* dificultad *f.*
hard-working *adj.* trabajador(a)
harmful *adj.* dañino/a
harvest *n.* cosecha *f.*
harvest *v.t.* cosechar
haste *n.* prisa *f.*
hat *n.* sombrero *m.*
hate *v.i.* odiar
have *v.t.* tener
have a(n) ...ache tener dolor de...
have a good/bad time pasarlo bien/mal
have a flat tire poncharse una llanta

have a picnic hacer un picnic
have an unfinished (matter) tener (un asunto) pendiente
have just done something acabar de (+ inf.)
have something on the tip of one's tongue *loc.* tener algo en la punta de la lengua
have to (do something) tener que (+ *inf.*); deber (+ *inf.*)
have to do with *loc.* tener que ver con **The letter doesn't have anything to do with the problem.** La carta no tiene nada que ver con el problema.
haze (someone) *v.t.* hacer una novatada (a alguien)
hazel tree *n.* avellano *m.*
hazelnut *n.* avellana *f.*
head *n.* cabeza *f.*
headache *n.* dolor *m.* de cabeza
headlight *n.* faro *m.*
headphone *n.* auricular *m.*
health *n.* salud *f.*
health care *n.* asistencia *f.* médica
health center *n.* enfermería *f.*
healthful *adj.* saludable
healthy *adj.* sano/a, saludable
hear *v.t.* oír
heard *p.p.* oído (*of* oír)
have heard *idiom* oír decir que
I've heard that Mapi and Kiko are getting married. He oído decir que Mapi y Kiko se van a casar.
hearing: (sense of) hearing *n.* oído *m.*
heart *n.* corazón *m.*
by heart de memoria **He knows the poem by heart.** Se sabe el poema de memoria.
heart attack *n.* infarto *m.*; ataque *m.* al corazón; ataque cardíaco
heartbeat *n.* latido *m.*
heat *n.* calor *m.*
heat *v.t.* calentar
heater *n.* calentador *m.*
heating *n.* calefacción *f.*
heaven *n.* cielo *m.*
Heaven forbid! *loc.* ¡Dios me libre!
heavy vehicles *n., pl.* vehículos *m., pl.* pesados
Hebrew *n., adj.* hebreo/a *m., f.*; *(language)* hebreo
hedge *n.* seto *m.*
heel *n.* talón *m.*
hefty *adj.* corpulento/a
height *n.* altura *f.*
heir *n.* heredero *m.*
heiress *n.* heredera *f.*
helicopter *n.* helicóptero *m.*
hello *interj.* hola; *(on the telephone)* ¿Aló?, ¿Bueno?, ¿Diga?
helmet *n.* casco *m.*
help (to) *v.t.* ayudar (a); servir (e:i); (*each other*) ayudarse (a)
Help! *interj.* ¡Auxilio!; ¡Socorro!
hemisphere *n.* hemisferio *m.*
hemorrhage *n.* hemorragia *f.*
her *poss. adj.* su(s)

herbivore *n.* herbívoro/a *m., f.*
herbivorous *adj.* herbívoro/a
herbs *n., pl.* hierbas *f., pl.*
here *adv.* aquí
Here it is. Aquí está.
Here we are in . . . Aquí estamos en…
hereditary *adj.* hereditario/a
heritage *n.* patrimonio *m.*
hermit *n.* ermitaño/a *m., f.*
hero *n.* héroe *m.*
heroine *n.* heroína *f.*
hers *poss. pron.* suyo(s)/suya(s)
hi *interj.* hola
hiccups *n., pl.* hipo *m.*
hide *v.t.* esconder; disimular
hide-and-seek *n.* escondidillas *f.;* al escondite *m.*
hierarchical *adj.* jerárquico/a; jerarquizado/a
hierarchy *n.* jerarquía *f.*
high *adj.* alto/a
high jump *n.* salto *m.* alto *(L.A.);* salto *m.* de altura *(Spain)*
high school *n.* escuela *f.* secundaria; preparatoria *f.*
highway *n.* autopista *f.;* carretera *f.*
hijack *n.* secuestro *m.*
hijack *v.t (aircraft)* secuestrar
hike *n.* excursión *f.*
go for a hike (in the mountains) ir de excursión (a las montañas)
go hiking ir de excursión
go on a hike hacer una excursión
hiker *n.* excursionista *m., f.*
hillside *n.* ladera *f.*
Hindu *n., adj.* hindú *m., f*
hint *n.* consejo *m.;* indicación *f.*
hip *n.* cadera *f.*
hippodrome *n.* hipódromo *m.*
hire *v.* contratar
his su(s) poss. *adj.;* suyo(s)/suya(s) *poss. pron.*
Hispanic *n., adj.* hispano/a *m., f.*
historian *n.* historiador(a) *m., f.*
history *n.* historia *f.*
hit *n.* golpe *m.*
hit *v.i.* pegar
hit (a car) *v.i.* chocar
hitchhike *v.i.* hacer auto(e)stop
hitchhiker *n.* auto(e)stopista *m., f.*
hobby *n.* afición *f.;* pasatiempo *m.*
hockey *n.* hockey *m.*
hold *v.t.* aguantar *(Spain)*
hold up *v.t. (bank)* atracar
holdup *n.* atraco *m.*
hole *n.* agujero *m.;* hueco *m.; (in the ground)* hoyo
make holes in agujerear
holiday *n.* día *m.* de fiesta
Holy Week *n.* Semana *f.* Santa
homage *n.* homenaje *m.*
pay homage to homenajear
home *n.* casa *f.;* hogar *m.*
at home en casa
home for the elderly *n.* residencia *f.* de ancianos
homemade *adj.* casero/a
home-maker *n.* el ama (*m., f.*) de casa
home page *n.* página *f.* principal

home run *n.* cuadrilátero *m.*
home style *adj.* casero/a
home team *n. (sports)* equipo *m.* local
hometown *n.* ciudad *f.* natal; *(my...)* mi pueblo *m.,* mi ciudad *f.*
homework *n.* deberes *m., pl.;* asignación *f.;* tarea *f.*
honest *adj.* honesto/a
honey *n.* miel *f.*
honeymoon *n.* luna *f.* de miel
hood *n. (car)* capó *m.,* cofre *m.* *(jacket)* capucha *f.*
hope *n.* esperanza *f.*
hope *v.t.* esperar
I hope (that) *interj.* Ojalá (que)
hopefully ojalá que...
horizon *n.* horizonte *m.*
hormone *n.* hormona *f.*
horn *n.* cuerno *m.; (car)* bocina *f.*
horror *n.* horror *m.;* ...de horror
hors d'oeuvres *n., pl.* entremeses *m., pl.*
horse *n.* caballo *m.*
ride a horse montar a caballo
horse race *n.* carrera *f.* de caballos
horseback riding *n.* equitación *f.*
horticulturalist *n.* horticultor(a) *m., f.*
horticulture *n.* horticultura *f.*
hose *n.* manguera *f.*
hospitable *adj.* hospitalario/a
hospital *n.* hospital *m.*
hospitality *n.* hospitalidad *f.*
host *n.* anfitrión *m.*
hostel *n.* albergue *m.;* hostal *m.*
hostess *n.* anfitriona *f.*
hot *adj.* caliente
be hot *(weather)* hacer calor; *(feel)* tener calor; *(thing)* estar caliente
It's (very) hot. *(weather)* Hace (mucho) calor.
hotel *n.* hotel *m.*
hour *n.* hora *f.*
house *n.* casa *f.*
housekeeper *n.* el ama (*m., f.*) de casa
housewife *n.* ama *f.* de casa
housing *n.* vivienda *f.*
how? *adv.* ¿cómo?
How are you? *fam.* ¿Cómo estás?; ¿Qué tal? *form.* ¿Cómo está usted?
How did it go for you . . .? ¿Cómo le/les fue...?
How is it going? ¿Qué tal?
How is/are . . . ? ¿Qué tal...?
How many? ¿Cuánto/a(s)?
How may I help you? ¿En qué puedo servirle(s)?
how much? *adv.* ¿cuanto/a?
How much does it cost? ¿Cuánto cuesta...?
How...! ¡Qué...!
How big! ¡Qué grande!
How nice to see you. *loc.* Dichosos los ojos (que te ven).
however *conj.* sin embargo
hug *v.t.* abrazar; (*each other*) abrazarse

human *adj.* humano/a
human being *n.* ser *m.* humano
humanism *n.* humanismo *m.*
humanist *n.* humanista *m., f.*
humanities *n., pl.* humanidades *f., pl.*
humble *adj.* humilde
humid *adj.* húmedo/a
humidity *n.* humedad *f.*
humiliated *adj.* humillado/a
humming bird *n.* colibrí *m.*
hump *n.* joroba *f.*
hunchbacked *adj.* jorobado/a
hunger *n.* hambre *f.*
be hungry tener hambre
hungry *adj.* hambriento/a
hunt *v.t.* cazar
hunter *n.* cazador(a) *m., f.*
hunting *n.* caza *f.*
hurdles *n., pl. (sport)* vallas *f., pl.*
hurricane *n.* huracán *m.*
hurry *v.i.* apurarse; darse prisa; apresurarse
be in a hurry tener prisa
hurt *v.t.* doler (o:ue); lastimar
hurt oneself hacerse daño
It hurts me a lot . Me duele mucho.
husband *n.* esposo *m.;* marido *m.*
hydrangea *n.* hortensia *f.*
hydraulic *adj.* hidráulico/a
hyperbole *n.* hipérbole *f.*
hypothesis *n.* hipótesis *f.*
hypothetical *adj.* hipotético/a

I

I am... Yo soy...
ice *n.* hielo *m.*
ice cream *n.* helado *m.*
ice cream shop *n.* heladería *f.*
ice hockey *n.* hockey *m.* sobre hielo
ice rink *n.* pista *f.* de hielo
ice skate patinar en hielo
ice skating *n.* patinaje *m.* sobre hielo
iceberg *n.* iceberg *m.*
iced *adj.* helado/a
iced tea *n.* té *m.* helado
idea *n.* idea *f.*
idealist *adj.* idealista
idle *adj.* ocioso/a
if *conj.* si
ignorance *n.* ignorancia *f.*
ignorant *adj.* ignorante
ill *adv.* mal
illiterate (person) *n., adj.* analfabeto/a *m., f.*
ill-mannered *adj.* grosero/a; maleducado/a
illness *n.* enfermedad *f.*
imagine *v.t.* imaginar
imitate *v.t.* imitar
imitation *n.* imitación *f.*
immediately *adv.* inmediatamente; en el acto
immigrant *n., adj.* inmigrante *m., f.*
immigrate *v.i.* inmigrar
immigration *n.* inmigración *f.*
immune system *n.* sistema *m.* inmunológico
immunize *v.t.* inmunizar
immunological *adj.* inmunológico/a
impatience *n.* impaciencia *f.*
impatient *adj.* impaciente
get impatient impacientarse

She got impatient over the delay. Se impacientó con el atraso.

impetuous *adj. (person)* lanzado/a, impulsivo/a

impolite *adj.* grosero/a

import *v.t.* importar

important *adj.* importante

be important (to) *v.i.* importar

It's (not) important that... (No) Es importante que...

importation *n.* importación *f.*

impossible *adj.* imposible

it's impossible es imposible

impostor *n.* impostor(a) *m., f.*

impoverish *v.t.* empobrecer

impression *n.* impresión *f.*

make a good/bad impression causar una buena/mala impresión

imprison *v.t.* encarcelar

improbable *adj.* improbable; inverosímil

it's improbable es improbable

improve *v.t.* mejorar

improvement *n.* mejora *f.*

impulsive *adj.* lanzado/a

in *prep.* en

in a jiffy *idiom* en un dos por tres; en un santiamén

in front of *prep.* delante de; enfrente

inaugurate *v.t.* inaugurar

inauguration *n.* inauguración *f.*

incomprehensible *adj.* incomprensible

inconceivable *adj.* inconcebible

inconvenience *n.* molestia *f.*

increase *n.* aumento *m.*; incremento *m.*

be on the increase estar en auge

increasing *adj.* creciente

incredible *adj.* increíble

independent *adj.* independiente

become independent independizarse

indescribable *adj.* inefable

indigenous *adj.* indígena

indigo *n., adj.* añil *m.*

individual *n., adj.* individuo *m.* *(may be pejorative:* **Who's that guy?** ¿Quién es ese individuo?); individual

individuality *n.* individualidad *f.*

inebriated *adj.* ebrio/a; embriagado/a

inequality *n.* desigualdad *f.*

inexperienced *adj.* novato/a

inexplicable *adj.* inexplicable

infection *n.* infección *f.*

influence *v.t.* influir en; influenciar

Darío's poems influenced other poets. Los poemas de Darío influyeron en otros poetas.

inform *v.t.* informar

inform oneself informarse

information *n.* información *f.*

ingest *v.t.* ingerir

ingestion *n.* ingestión *f.*

inherit *v.t.* heredar

inheritance *n.* herencia *f.*

inject *v.t.* inyectar

injection *n.* inyección *f.*

give an injection poner una inyección
injure *v.t. (oneself)* lastimarse
injure one's (foot) lastimarse el (pie)
injured *n., adj.* herido/a *m., f.*
inn *n.* hostal *m.*
innovate *v.i.* innovar
innovation *n.* innovación *f.*
innovative *adj.* innovador(a)
innovator *n.* innovador(a) *m., f.*
insect *n.* insecto *m.*
inside *adv.* (a)dentro
insipid *adj.* insípido/a
insist (on + *gerund*) insistir (en + *inf.*)
He insists on going. Insiste en ir.
insistence *n.* insistencia *f.*
insomnia *n.* insomnio *m.*
inspire *v.t.* inspirar
install *v.t. (equipment)* instalar
install oneself instalarse
installment *n. (payment)* plazo *m. (monthly payment)* mensualidad *f.*
pay in installments pagar a plazos
institution *n.* institución *f.*
instrument *n.* instrumento *m.*
insulate *v.t.* aislar
insulation *n.* aislante *m.*
insulin *n.* insulina *f.*
insult *n.* insulto *m.*; ofensa *f.*
insurance *n.* seguro *m.*
intake *n.* consumo *m.*
intelligent *adj.* inteligente
intend (*to do something*) *v.* pensar (+ *inf.*)
intentionally *adv.* intencionalmente, adrede, a propósito
interest *n.* interés *m.*
interest *v.t.* interesar
take an interest (in) interesarse (en) **He's only interested in the results.** Sólo se interesa en los resultados.
be interested interesar
interesting *adj.* interesante
be interesting to interesar
intermediate *adj.* intermedio/a
international *adj.* internacional
Internet *n.* Internet *m.*; red *f.*
interpreter *n.* intérprete *m., f.*
interpreting *n.* interpretación *f.*
interrupt *v.t.* interrumpir
intersection *n.* intersección *f.*
intervention *n.* intervención *f.*
interview *n.* entrevista *f.*
interview *v.t.* entrevistar
interviewer *n.* entrevistador(a) *m., f.*
intestine *n.* intestino *m.*
intolerant *adj.* intolerante
intrigue *n.* intriga *f.*
intrigued *adj.* intrigado/a
introduction *n.* presentación *f.*
invertebrate *n., adj.* invertebrado *m.*; invertebrado/a
invest *v.t.* invertir (e:ie)
investigator *n.* investigador(a) *m., f.*
invitation *n.* invitación *f.*
invite *v.t.* invitar
involuntary *adj.* involuntario/a
iron *n. (metal)* hierro *m.*; *(clothes)* plancha *f.*

iron *v.t.* planchar (la ropa)
ironic *adj.* irónico/a
irony *n.* ironía *f.*
irresponsible *adj.* irresponsable
irritating *adj.* antipático/a
isolate *v.t.* aislar
  isolate oneself aislarse
issue *n.* cuestión *f.*
Italian *n., adj.* italiano/a *m., f.; (language)* italiano
item *n.* artículo *m.*
itinerary *n.* itinerario *m.*
its su(s) *poss. adj.*; suyo(s)/suya(s) *poss. pron.*
ivy *n.* hiedra *f.*

J

jack *n. (playing cards)* jota *f.*
jacket *n.* chaqueta *f.*; abrigo; saco
jackknife *n.* navaja *f.*
jail *n.* cárcel *f.*
jail *v.t.* encarcelar
jam *n.* mermelada *f.*
January *n.* enero *m.*
Japanese *n., adj.* japonés *m.*, japonesa *f.; (language)* japonés
javelin throw *n.* lanzamiento *m.* de jabalina
jealous *adj.* celoso/a; envidioso/a
jealousy *n.* celos *m., pl.*
jeans *n.* (blue)jeans *(L.A.) m., pl.*; vaqueros, tejanos *(Spain) m., pl.*
jellyfish *n.* medusa *f.*
jest: in jest en broma
jetty *n.* embarcadero *m.*
Jew *n.* judío/a *m., f.*
jeweler *n.* joyero/a *m., f.*
jewelry box *n.* joyero *m.*
jewelry store *n.* joyería *f.*
jewel *n.* joya *f.*
Jewish *adj.* judío/a
job *n.* empleo *m.;* puesto *m.;* trabajo *m.*
job application *n.* solicitud *f.* de trabajo
jog *v.i.* correr
joint *n. (anatomy)* articulación *f.*
joke *n.* broma *f.*
  as a joke en broma
  make jokes hacer bromas
  practical joke broma pesada; novatada *f.*
joker *n.* bromista *m., f.*
journalism *n.* periodismo *m.*
journalist *n.* periodista *m., f.;* reportero/a *m., f.*
joy *n.* alegría *f.*
  give joy dar alegría
joyful *adj.* alegre
jubilation *n.* algarabía *f.*
judge *n.* juez *m., f.*
judge *v.t.* juzgar
judgment *n.* juicio *m.*
juice *n.* jugo *(L.A.) m.;* zumo *(Spain) m.*
  fruit juice jugo/zumo de fruta
juicer *n.* exprimidor *m.*
juicy *adj.* jugoso/a
July *n.* julio *m.*
jump *n.* salto *m.*
jump *v.i.* saltar, brincar
June *n.* junio *m.*
jungle *n.* selva *f.*, jungla *f.*
jury *n.* jurado *m.*

just *adv.* apenas
justice *n.* justicia *f.*

K

kangaroo *n.* canguro *m.*
key *n.* llave *f.*
key chain *n.* llavero *m.*
keyboard *n.* teclado *m.*
kid *n.* niño/a *m., f.*
kid *v.i.* bromear
kid someone *idiom* tomarle el pelo a alguien
kidnap *v.t. (people)* secuestrar
kidnapping *n.* secuestro *m.*
kidney *n.* riñón *m.*
kill *v.t.* matar (a alguien)
kill two birds with one stone *loc.* matar dos pájaros de un tiro
kilometer *n.* kilómetro *m.*
kind *adj.* amable
That's very kind of you. (Eres/Es usted) Muy amable.
kingdom *n.* reino *m.*
kiss *n.* beso *m.*
give a kiss dar un beso
kiss *v.t.* besar; *(each other)* besarse
kitchen *n.* cocina *f.*
kitchenware *n.* artículos *m., pl.* de cocina
knee *n.* rodilla *f.*
knife *n.* cuchillo *m.*
knit *v.i.* hacer punto
knitted *adj.* de punto
knitwear *n.* artículos *m., pl.* de punto
know *v.t.* saber; conocer
know how (to) saber
know-it-all *n., adj.* sabihondo/a *m., f.*
known *adj.* conocido/a

L

laboratory *n.* laboratorio *m.*
lack *n.* falta *f.;* carencia *f.*
lack *v.t.* faltar
lack of understanding *n.* incomprensión *f.*
ladle *n.* cucharón *m.*
lake *n.* lago *m.*
lamb *n.* cordero *m.*
lame *adj.* cojo/a
lamp *n.* lámpara *f.*
land *n.* tierra *f.; (parcel)* terreno *m.*
land *v.t.* aterrizar
landing *n.* aterrizaje *m.*
landing strip *n.* pista *f.* de aterrizaje
landlord *n.* dueño/a *m., f.*
landscape *n.* paisaje *m.*
lane *n. (highway)* carril *m.*
language *n.* lengua *f.;* idioma *m.*
foreign languages *n., pl.* lenguas *f., pl.* extranjeras
lap *n. (sports)* vuelta *f.*
laptop (computer) *n.* computadora *f.* portátil
large *n., adj. (clothing size)* talla *m.* grande; grande, *(quantity)* elevado/a **You notice a large quantity of fat in the food.** Se nota una cantidad elevada de grasa en la comida.
large intestine *n.* intestino *m.* grueso
larva *n.* larva *f.*

larynx *n.* laringe *f.*
last *adj.* pasado/a; último/a
last *v.i.* durar
last week la semana pasada
last year el año pasado
last night *adv.* anoche
lasting *adj.* duradero/a
late *adv.* tarde
be late llegar tarde; retrasarse **be late (in)** tardar en **The bus was late (in arriving).** El autobús tardó en llegar.
lately *adv.* últimamente
later *adv.* más tarde
at the very latest a más tardar **Bring it to me on Thursday at the very latest.** Tráemelo el jueves a más tardar.
Latin *n., adj.* latino/a *m., f.*; *(language)* latín *m.*
laugh *v.i.* reír, reírse (e:i)
laughed *p.p.* reído (*of* reír)
launch *n.* lanzamiento *m.*
launch *v.t.* lanzar **NASA launched a rocket to Saturn.** La NASA lanzó un cohete a Saturno.
laundromat *n.* lavandería *f.*
law *n.* ley *f.*
lawn *n.* pasto *m.*
lawn mower *n.* cortacésped *f.*
lawyer *n.* abogado/a *m., f.*
laziness *n.* pereza *f.*
lazy *adj.* perezoso/a; flojo/a
lead *n.* plomo *m.* **a lead pipe** un tubo de plomo
lead *v.t.* liderar
leader *n.* líder *m., f.*
leadership *n.* liderazgo *m.*
leaf *n.* hoja *f.*
leak *n. (gas, water)* fuga *f.*
learn *v.t.* aprender (a + *inf.*)
learned *adj.* sabio/a
learning *n.* enseñanza *f.*
lease *n.* contrato *m.*
least: at least por lo menos
leather *n.* piel
made of leather de piel
leather goods *n., pl.* artículos *m., pl.* de piel
leave *v.i.* salir; irse; partir; dejar
leave a message dejar un mensaje/recado
leave alone dejar
leave (behind) dejar
leave for *(a place)* salir para...
leave from salir de
lecture *n.* conferencia *f.*
lecture hall *n.* aula (el) *f.*
main lecture hall aula magna
left *adj., n.* izquierdo/a *m., f.*
be left over quedar, sobrar
to the left (of) a la izquierda (de)
leftovers *n., pl.* restos *m., pl.*; sobras *f., pl.*
leg *n.* pierna *f.*
legacy *n.* legado *m.*
legal *adj.* legal
legalize *v.t.* legalizar
legend *n.* leyenda *f.*
leisure time *n.* ocio *m.*
lemon *n.* limón *m.*
lemon tree *n.* limonero *m.*
lemonade *n.* limonada *f.*

lend *v.t.* prestar
lengthwise section *n. (Tech.)* corte *m.* longitudinal
lentil *n.* lenteja *f.*
leopard *n.* leopardo *m.*
less *adv.* menos
less . . . than menos... que
less than + *(number)* menos de + *(number)*
lesson *n.* lección *f.*
let *v.t.* dejar
let go soltar
let up *(pain)* aliviarse
letter *n.* carta *f.; (alphabet)* letra *f.*
put a letter in the mailbox echar una carta al buzón
lettuce *n.* lechuga *f.*
level *n.* nivel *m.*
lever *n.* palanca *f.*
liar *n.* mentiroso/a *m., f.*
liberal *n., adj.* liberal *m., f.*
liberation *n.* liberación *f.*
liberty *n.* libertad *f.*
librarian *n.* bibliotecario/a *m., f.*
library *n.* biblioteca *f.*
license *n. (driver's)* licencia *f.* de manejar/conducir
license plate *n.* (placa *f.* de) matrícula *f.*
lid *n.* tapa *f.*
lie *n.* mentira *f.*
lie *v.i.* mentir
lie down (in the sun) *v.* tumbarse (al sol)
life *n.* vida *f.*
in my life en mi vida
life expectancy *n.* esperanza *f.* de vida
life imprisonment *n.* cadena *f.* perpétua
life jacket *n.* salvavidas *m., sing.*
life sentence *n.* cadena *f.* perpétua
lifeguard *n.* salvavidas *m., f., sing.*
lifestyle: lead a healthy lifestyle llevar una vida sana
lift *v.t.* levantar
lift weights levantar pesas
light *n., adj.* luz *f.;* liviano/a; ligero/a
light aircraft *n.* avioneta *f.*
light green *n., adj.* verde *m.* claro
lighter *n.* encendedor *m.*
lightning bolt *n.* rayo *m.;* relámpago *m.*
lightning rod *n.* pararrayos *m., sing.*
like *prep.* como
What's . . . like? ¿Cómo es...?
like *v.t.* gustar
Do you like . . . ? ¿Te gusta(n)...?
I like . . . very much. Me encanta...
I would like to introduce... to you. Te presento a...
would like to tener ganas de (+ *inf.*) **I would like to visit Diamantina.** Tengo ganas de visitar Diamantina.
Would you like to? ¿Te gustaría?
Like father, like son. *loc.* De tal palo, tal astilla.
like this *adv.* así

likeable *adj.* simpático/a
likely: be likely that *(something will happen)* ser probable que (+ *subj.)* **It's likely that they won't arrive on time.** Es probable que no lleguen a tiempo.
likewise *adv.* igualmente
lily *n.* lirio *m.*
limb *n. (body)* miembro *m.*
limit *v.t.* limitar
limousine *n.* limusina *f.*
line *n.* línea *f.;* cola *f.* **There is a long line at the cinema.** Hay una larga cola en el cine.
stand in/on line hacer cola
line up hacer cola
linen *adj.* de hilo
linguist *n.* lingüista *m., f.*
linguistic *adj.* lingüístico/a
linguistics *n.* lingüística *f.*
lion *n.* león *m.*
lipstick *n.* lápiz *m.* labial; pintalabios *m., sing.*
liqueur *n.* licor *m.*
liquid *n., adj.* líquido *m.;* líquido/a
listen (to) *v.t.* escuchar
listen to music escuchar música
listen to the radio escuchar la radio
Listen! *(command)* ¡Oye! *fam., sing.;* ¡Oigan! *form., pl.*
listener *n.* oyente *m., f.; (radio)* radioyente *m., f.*
literature *n.* literatura *f.*
little *adj.* pequeño/a; *adv.* poco/a
little bit *n.* pizca *f.*
Little Dipper *n.* Osa *f.* Menor
live *v.i.* vivir; residir
live by begging vivir de limosnas
lively *adj.* vivo/a
liver *n.* hígado *m.*
living being *n.* ser *m.* vivo
living room *n.* sala *f.*
lizard *n.* lagarto *f.*
loaf (of bread) *n.* barra *f.* (de pan) *(Spain)*
loan *n.* préstamo *m.*
loan *v.* prestar
lobster *n.* langosta *f.*
located *adj.* situado/a
be located quedar
locker room *n.* vestuario *m.*
locomotive *n.* locomotora *f.*
lodge *v.t.* alojar
lodging *n.* alojamiento *m.;* parador *m.*
log *n. (wood)* tronco *m.,* leño *m.*
long *adj.* (*length*) largo/a
long-distance race *n.* carrera *f.* de fondo
long jump *n.* salto *m.* de longitud *(Spain);* salto *m.* largo *(L.A.)*
long for *v.* ansiar
long for (someone) añorar (a alguien)
longevity *n.* longevidad *f.*
longing *n.* ansia *f.*
look after oneself *v.* cuidarse
look at *v.* mirar*; (a topic)* enfocar **The program looks at the problem of homelessness.** El programa

enfoca el problema de la falta de vivienda.
look for *v.* buscar
look good *v.* lucir
look in *v. (reference)* consultar
I'll look in the dictionary. Consultaré el diccionario.
look up *v. (word)* buscar (en el diccionario)
lose *v.t.* perder (e:ie)
lose weight adelgazar
lost *adj.* perdido/a
be lost estar perdido/a
lot *n.* terreno *m.*
lot (of), a *adj.* mucho/a
a lot *n.* sinfín *m.* **She still has a lot of things to do.** Todavía tiene un sinfín de cosas que hacer.
a lot *adv.* muchas veces
loud *adj.* escandaloso/a
loudspeaker *n.* altavoz *m.*
lounge chair *n.* tumbona *f.*
love *n.* amor *m.*
in love (with) *adj.* enamorado/a (de)
fall in love (with) enamorarse (de)
love *v.t. (another person)* querer (e:ie); *(things)* encantar; fascinar
loyal *adj.* fiel
luck *n.* suerte *f.*
be lucky tener suerte
luggage *n.* equipaje *m.*
lunch *n.* almuerzo *m.*
have lunch almorzar (o:ue); comer
lung *n.* pulmón *m.*
luxurious *adj.* lujoso/a
luxury *n.* lujo *m.*
lying *adj.* mentiroso/a

M

ma'am *n.* señora *f.* (Sra.)
machine *n.* máquina *f.*
answering machine contestadora *f.*
mad *adj.* enojado/a
be hopping mad *idiom* echar chispas
madness *n.* locura *f.*
magazine *n.* revista *f.*
magic *n.* magia *f.*
magical *adj.* mágico/a
magician *n.* mago/a *m., f.*
magma *n.* magma *m.*
magna cum laude *(grade)* matrícula de honor
magnesium *n.* magnesio *m.*
magnet *n.* imán *m.*
magnificent *adj.* magnífico/a
magnifying glass *n.* lupa *f.*
mail carrier *n.* cartero/a *m., f.*
mail *n.* correo *m.* **I sent it in the mail.** Lo mandé por correo.; correspondencia *f.* **You got a lot of mail.** Recibiste mucha correspondencia.
mail carrier cartero *m.*
mail *v.t.* enviar, mandar (por correo); echar una carta al buzón
mailbox *n.* buzón *m.*
main *adj.* principal
maintain *v.t.* mantener
major *n.* especialización *f.*
majority *n.* mayoría *f.*
make *v.t.* hacer; *(coffee)* colar

make a living *idiom* ganarse la vida **Mario makes his living writing soap opera scripts.** Mario se gana la vida escribiendo guiones de telenovela.
make a long story short *loc.* en resumidas cuentas
make one's mouth water *idiom.* hacérsele agua la boca **It smells good. It makes my mouth water.** ¡Qué bien huele! Se me hace agua la boca.
make sure *v.* asegurarse
make up *v.* maquillar
make up one's mind *v.* decidirse
makeup *n.* maquillaje *m.*
put on makeup *v.* maquillarse; pintarse
makeup artist *n.* maquillador(a) *m., f.*
male *n.* macho *m.*
malignant *adj.* maligno/a
mall *n.* centro *m.* comercial
mammal *n.* mamífero *m.*
man *n.* hombre *m.*
manage *v.t. (business)* administrar
management *n.* administración *f.*
manager *n.* gerente *m., f.*
manicure *n.* manicura *f.*
mannequin *n.* maniquí *m.*
manufacture *n.* fabricación *f.*
manufacture *v.t.* fabricar
manufacturer *n.* fabricante *m., f.*
manure *n.* estiércol *m.*
many *adj.* muchos/as
a great many *n.* sinfín *m.*
map *n.* mapa *m.*
city map *n.* plano *m.*
road map mapa *m.* de carreteras
marathon *n.* maratón *m.*
marble *n.* mármol *m.*
March *n.* marzo *m.*
margarine *n.* margarina *f.*
marital status *n.* estado *m.* civil
mark *n.* marca *f.; (imprint)* huella *f.; (grade)* nota *f.*
market *n.* mercado *m.*; supermercado *m.*
open-air market mercado al aire libre
street market *n.* mercadillo *m.*
marriage *n.* matrimonio *m.*
married *adj.* casado/a
marrow *n.* médula *f.*
marry: get married (to) *v.* casarse (con)
marsh *n.* pantano *m.*
martial arts *n., pl.* artes *f., pl.* marciales
marvelous *adj.* maravilloso/a
marvelously *adv.* maravillosamente
mask *n.* máscara *f.;* mascarilla *f.;* antifaz *m.*
mass produce *v.t.* fabricar en serie
mass production *n.* fabricación *f.* en serie
massage *n.* masaje *m.*
masseur *n.* masajista *m.*
masseuse *n.* masajista *f.*
master *v.t.* dominar

I am far from mastering Spanish. Estoy lejos de dominar el español.

Master's degree *n.* maestría *(L.A.) f.*

pursue a Master's degree hacer una maestría

masterpiece *n.* obra *f.* maestra

match *n.* cerilla *f.;* fósforo *m.; (sports)* partido *m.*

match (with) *v.t.* hacer juego (con)

match up *v.i.* coincidir

mate n. compañero/a *m., f.*

materialistic *adj.* materialista

maternal *adj. (relative)* materno/a

mathematician *n.* matemático/a *m., f.*

mathematics *n.* matemáticas *f., pl.*

matriculation *n.* matrícula *f.*

matter *n.* cuestión *f.* **She's an expert in matters of medieval history.** Es una experta en cuestiones de historia medieval.

matter *v.t.* importar

mattress *n.* colchón *m.*

foam mattress colchón de espuma

sprung mattress colchón de muelles

mature *adj.* maduro/a

maturity *n.* madurez *f.*

maximum *n., adj.* máximo *m.;* máximo/a

May *n.* mayo *m.*

maybe *adv.* tal vez; quizás

mayonnaise *n.* mayonesa *f.*

mayor *n.* alcalde *m.,* alcaldesa *f.*

mayor's office *n.* alcaldía *f.*

me: It's me./That's me. Soy yo.

meal *n.* comida *f.*

mean *adj. (person)* malo/a

means of communication *n., pl.* medios *m., pl.* de comunicación

means: by no means de ninguna manera, de ningún modo

measles *n.* sarampión *m.*

measure *v.t.* medir

measurement *n.* medición *f.;* medida *f.*

meat *n.* carne *f.*

mechanic *n.* mecánico/a *m., f.*

mechanic's workshop *n.* taller *m.* de mecánica

mechanic's repair shop taller mecánico

mechanism *n.* mecanismo *m.*

medal *n.* medalla *f.*

media *n.* medios *m., pl.* de comunicación

medical *adj.* médico/a

medical insurance *n.* seguro *m.* médico

medication *n.* medicamento *m.*

medicine *n.* medicina *f.*

medicine cabinet *n.* botiquín *m.*

mediocre *adj.* mediocre

meditate *v.i.* meditar

meditation *n.* meditación *f.*

medium *adj.* mediano/a

meet *v.t.* encontrar; conocer; *(each other)* encontrarse; conocerse

Where shall we meet? ¿Dónde nos encontramos? **They met in Paris.** Se conocieron en París.

meeting *n.* reunión *f.; (political) n.* mitin *m.*

megaphone *n.* megáfono *m.*

melon *n.* melón *m.*

melt *v.t.* derretir **The heat will melt the butter.** El calor derritirá la mantequilla.; *v.i.* derretirse **The ice cream melted.** El helado se derritió.

member *n.* miembro *m.*

membrane *n.* membrana *f.*

memorize *v.t.* memorizar

memory *n.* memoria *f.*

menopause *n.* menopausia *f.*

mental disorder *n.* trastorno *m.* mental

mental hospital *n.* manicomio *m.*

mentality *n.* mentalidad *f.*

menu *n.* menú *m.*

mercury *n.* mercurio *m.*

merit *n.* mérito *m.*

mess around: Don't mess around on the way to school. No te entretengas camino a la escuela.

message *n.* mensaje *m.; (telephone)* recado *m.*

messy *adj.* desarreglado/a

metabolism *n.* metabolismo *m.*

metabolize *v.t.* metabolizar

metal *n.* metal *m.*

metamorphosis *n.* metamorfosis *f.*

metaphor *n.* metáfora *f.*

metaphoric *adj.* metafórico/a

meteorite *n.* meteorito *m.*

meteorologist *n.* meteorólogo/a *m., f.*

meteorology *n.* metereología *f.*

method *n.* método *m.*

methodical *adj.* metódico/a

Mexican *n., adj.* mexicano/a *m., f.*

Mexico *n.* México *m.*

microphone *n.* micrófono *m.*

microscope *n.* microscopio *m.*

microwave *n.* microonda *f.*

microwave oven *n.* horno *m.* de microondas

middle age *n.* madurez *f.*

middle school *n.* escuela *f.* secundaria

midnight *n.* medianoche *f.*

mild *adj. (taste)* suave

mile *n.* milla *f.*

milk *n.* leche *f.*

Milky Way *n.* Vía Láctea *f.*

mill *n.* molino *m.*

million (of) *n.* millón (de) *m.*

mind *n.* mente
keep in mind tener en cuenta

mine *n.* mina *f.*

mine mío(s)/mía(s) *poss. pron.*

miner *n.* minero/a *m., f.*

mineral *n.* mineral *m.*

mining industry *n.* minería *f.*

miniskirt *n.* minifalda *f.*

minister *n. (government)* ministro/a *m., f.*

minority *n.* minoría *f.*

mint *n.* menta *f.*

minute *adj.* minúsculo/a

minute *n.* minuto *m.*

minute *adj. (object)* diminuto/a

mirror *n.* espejo *m.*
misbehave *v.* portarse mal
miscarriage *n.* aborto *m.* espontáneo
  have a miscarriage abortar
mischief *n.* travesura *f.*
mischievous *adj.* travieso/a
miser *n.* avaro/a *m., f.*
misfortune *n.* desgracia *f.*
Miss *n.* señorita *f.* (Srta.)
miss *v.* perder (e:ie)
  miss someone *v.t.* añorar a alguien
missile *n.* misil *m.;* proyectil *m.*
missing *adj.* desaparecido/a
mistake *n.* equivocación *f.*
  make a mistake equivocarse
mistaken *adj.* equivocado/a
  be mistaken equivocarse
  You are mistaken in thinking that. Te equivocas si piensas eso.
mister *n.* señor *m.*
mix *v.t.* mezclar
mixer *n.* batidora *(Spain) f.*
mobile *adj.* móvil
mobility *n.* movilidad *f.*
modem *n.* módem *m.*
modern *adj.* moderno/a
modernize *v.t.* modernizar
modest *adj. (person)* modesto/a; *(simple)* sencillo/a
modify *v.t.* modificar
moisturizer *n.* crema *n.* hidratante; humectante *m.*
molar *n.* muela *f.*
mold *n.* moho *m.*
mom *n.* mamá *f.,* mami *f.*
moment *n.* momento *m.*
monarch *n.* monarca *m., f.*
monarchy *n.* monarquía *f.*
monastery *n.* monasterio *m.*
Monday *n.* lunes *m., sing.*
money *n.* dinero *m.*
  paper money billete *m.*
money order *n.* giro *m.* postal
monitor *n.* monitor *m.*
monk *n.* monje *m.*
monkey *n.* mono *m.*
monologue *n.* monólogo *m.*
month *n.* mes *m.*
monument *n.* monumento *m.*
mood: in a good/bad mood de buen/mal humor
moon *n.* luna *f.*
mop *n.* fregona *(Spain) f.;* trapeador (*L.A.*) *m.*
mop (the floor) *v.t.* trapear (el piso) *(L.A.);* fregar (el suelo) *(Spain)*
moral *n.* moral *f.*
morality *n.* moralidad *f.*
more *adj., adv.* más
  more . . . than más... que
  more than (+ *number*) más de (+ *number*)
moribund *adj.* moribundo/a
morning *n.* mañana *f.*
  in the morning de la mañana; por la mañana
morphology *n.* morfología *f.*
mortality *n.* mortalidad *f.*
mortality rate *n.* índice *m.* de mortalidad
mortgage *n.* hipoteca *f.*
mortgage *v.t.* hipotecar
mosque *n.* mezquita *f.*
mosquito net *n.* mosquitero *m.*
mother *n.* madre *f.*

mother-in-law *n.* suegra *f.*
motor *n.* motor *m.*
motorboat *n.* lancha *f.*
motorcycle *n.* moto *f.;* motocicleta *f.*
go by motorcycle ir en motocicleta
motorcycling *n.* motociclismo *m.*
motorcyclist *n.* motociclista *m., f.*
motorist *n.* automovilista *m., f.*
mountain *n.* montaña *f.*
mountain range *n.* cordillera *f.* (montañosa)
mountainside *n.* ladera *f.*
mouse *n.* ratón *m.*
moustache *n.* bigote(s) *m. (pl.)*
mouth *n.* boca *f.; (river)* desembocadura *f.*
mouth-to-mouth resuscitation *n.* respiración *f.* boca a boca
move *n.* mudanza *f.*
move *v.i. (from one house to another)* mudarse*; (from one place to another)* desplazarse
move forward *v.i.* avanzar
movement *n.* desplazamiento *m.*
movie *n.* película *f.*
see movies ver películas
moviemaker *n.* cineasta *m., f.*
movie star *n.* estrella *m., f.* de cine
movie theater *n.* cine *m.*
movies *n.* cine *m.*
mow the lawn *v.t.* cortar el pasto
Mr. *n.* señor *m.* (Sr.), don
Mrs. *n.* señora *f.* (Sra.)
much *adj., adv.* mucho/a
mud *n.* barro *m.;* fango *m.*
muffler *n. (car)* silenciador *m.*
mug *n.* taza *f.*
mug *v.t.* atracar
municipal *n.* municipal *m.*
murder *n.* asesinato *m.*; crimen *m.*
murderer *n.* asesino/a *m., f.*
muscle *n.* músculo *m.*
muscular *adj.* musculoso/a
museum *n.* museo *m.*
mushroom *n.* champiñón *m.*
music *n.* música *f.*
play loud music poner la música muy alta
musical *adj.* musical
musician *n.* músico/a *m., f*
Muslim *n., adj.* musulmán *m.,* musulmana *f.*
mussel *n.* mejillón *m.*
must deber (+ *inf.*)
It must be… Debe ser…
mustard *n.* mostaza *f.*
mute *adj.* mudo/a
my mi(s) *poss. adj.*
myopia *n.* miopía *f.*
myopic *adj.* miope
mysterious *adj.* enigmático/a; misterioso/a
mystery *n.* misterio *m.*; enigma *m.*
a mystery novel una novela de misterio

N

nail *n.* clavo *m.; (finger, toe)* uña *f.*
hit the nail on the head

idiom dar en el clavo
nail file *n.* lima *f.*
name *n.* nombre *m.*
be named llamarse
in the name of a nombre de
last name apellido *m.*
My name is . . . Me llamo…
What's your name? *fam.* ¿Cómo te llamas (tú)?, *form.* ¿Cómo se llama usted?
name *v.t.* ponerle nombre a
nap *n. (afternoon)* siesta *f.*
napkin *n.* servilleta *f.*
narrator *n.* narrador(a) *m., f.*
nasty *adj.* antipático/a
national *adj.* nacional
nationalism *n.* nacionalismo *m.*
nationalist *adj.* nacionalista
nationality *n.* nacionalidad *f.*
native *adj.* indígena
natural *adj.* natural
nature *n.* naturaleza *f.*
nature reserve *n.* parque *m.* natural
naughty *adj.* travieso/a
nausea *n.* náusea *f.*
nauseate *v.t.* asquear, repugnar, dar asco
nauseated *adj.* mareado/a
nauseating *adj.* asqueroso/a, repugnante
navel *n.* ombligo *m.*
navy blue *n., adj.* azul *m.* marino
near *prep.* cerca de
neaten *v.* arreglar
necessary *adj.* necesario/a
It's (not) necessary that… (No) Es necesario que…
necessity *n.* necesidad *f.*
neck *n.* cuello *m.*
necklace *n.* collar *m.*
nectarine *n.* nectarina *f.*
need *v.t.* faltar; necesitar
needle *n.* aguja *f.*
negative *adj.* negativo/a
neighbor *n.* vecino/a *m., f.*
neighborhood *n.* barrio *m.*
neither *adv.* tampoco
neither . . . nor *conj.* ni… ni
I eat neither meat nor fish. No como ni carne ni pescado.
nephew *n.* sobrino *m.*
nerve *n.* nervio *m.;* atrevimiento *m.*
You've got some nerve! ¡Qué cara más dura tienes!
nervous *adj.* nervioso/a
nervous breakdown *n.* crisis *f.* nerviosa
network *n.* red *f.*
neuron *n.* neurona *f.*
never *adv.* nunca; jamás
new *adj.* nuevo/a; novato/a
What's new? ¿Qué hay de nuevo?
newlywed *n.* recién casado/a *m., f.*
news *n.* noticias *f., pl.;* actualidades *f., pl.*
newscast *n.* noticiero *m.*
newsletter *n.* boletín *m.* informativo
newspaper *n.* periódico *m.;* diario *m.*
next *adj.* próximo/a
next to *prep.* al lado de
nice *adj.* simpático/a; amable; agradable

nice person *idiom* buena gente
Nice to meet you. Mucho gusto.
nickname *n.* apodo *m.*
niece *n.* sobrina *f.*
nieces and nephews *n., pl.* sobrinos *m., pl.*
night *n.* noche *f.*
at night *adv.* por la noche
night stand *n.* mesita *f.* de noche
night table mesa de noche
nightmare *n.* pesadilla *f.*
nine nueve
nine hundred novecientos/as
nineteen diecinueve
ninety noventa
ninth noveno *m.; adj.* noveno/a
nitrogen *n.* nitrógeno *m.*
no *adj.* ningún, ninguno/a(s)
no one *pron.* nadie
no *adv.* no; ningún, ninguno/a(s) *adj.*
no entry (*sign*) prohibido el paso
no one *pron.* nadie
no problem ningún problema
no way de ninguna manera
nobody *pron.* nadie
noise *n.* ruido *m.*
noisy *adj.* ruidoso/a
none *adj.* ningún, ninguno/a(s)
non-fattening *adj.* que no engorda
non-resident *n.* transeúnte *m., f.*
noon *n.* mediodía *m.*
nor *conj.* ni
Nordic *adj.* nórdico/a
north *n.* norte *m.*
to the north al norte
Northern European *n.* nórdico/a *m., f.*
nose *n.* nariz *f.*
not *adv.* no
not any *adj.* ningún, ninguno/a(s)
not anyone *pron.* nadie
not anything *pron.* nada
not bad at all nada mal
not either *adv.* tampoco
not ever *adv.* nunca; jamás
Not very well. No muy bien.
note *n.* nota *f.*
notebook *n.* cuaderno *m.*
nothing *pron.* nada
I've nothing to say. No tengo nada que decir.
nothingness *n.* nada *f.*
notice *v.t.* notar; advertir
noun *n.* sustantivo *m.*
November *n.* noviembre *m.*
now *adv.* ahora
nowadays *adv.* hoy día
nowhere a ninguna parte
nuclear *adj.* nuclear
nucleus *n.* núcleo *m.*
number *n.* número *m.; (figure)* cifra *f.*
nun *n.* monja *f.*
nunnery *n.* convento *m.*
nurse *n.* enfermero/a *m., f.*
nursery school *n.* guardería *f.*
nutcracker *n.* cascanueces *m., sing.*
nutrition *n.* nutrición *f.*
nutritionist *n.* nutricionista *m., f.*

O

o'clock: It's . . . o'clock. Son las...
It's one o'clock. Es la una.
oak tree *n.* roble *m.*
oar *n.* remo *m.*
obese *adj.* obeso/a
obesity *n.* obesidad *f.*
obey *v.t.* obedecer (c:zc)
objective *adj.* objetivo/a
objective *n.* meta *f.,* objetivo *m.*
obligation *n.* deber *m.*
observant *adj.* observador(a)
observation *n.* observación *f.*
observatory *n.* observatorio *m.*
observe *v.t.* observar
obstacle course carrera de obstáculos
obtain *v.t.* conseguir (e:i); obtener (e:ie)
obvious *adj.* obvio
it's obvious es obvio
occasion *n.* tiempo *m.*
occupation *n.* ocupación *f.*
occur *v.i. (happen)* ocurrir, suceder, pasar, realizarse; *(come to mind)* ocurrir
ocean *n.* mar *m., f.;* océano *m.*
ocean liner *n.* transatlántico *m.*
ocher *n.* ocre *m.*
October *n.* octubre *m.*
octopus *n.* pulpo *m.*
odor *n.* olor *m.*
of *prep.* de
of course claro que sí; por supuesto; *(idiom)* desde luego
offend *v.t.* ofender
offer *n.* oferta *f.*
offer *v.t.* ofrecer (c:zc)
offering *n.* ofrenda *f.*
office *n.* oficina *f.; (medical)* consultorio *m.*
often *adv.* a menudo
Oh! *interj.* ¡Ay!
oil *n.* aceite *m.;* petróleo *m.*
OK! *interj.* ¡Vale! *(Spain);* de acuerdo
okay *adj.* regular
It's okay. Está bien.
old *adj.* viejo/a; antiguo/a
be . . . years old tener... años
How old are you? ¿Cuántos años tienes?
become old hacerse viejo/a
grow old envejecer
old age *n.* vejez *f.*
older *adj.* mayor
older brother/sister *n.* hermano/a mayor *m., f.*
oldest *adj.* el/la mayor
old-fashioned *adj.* anticuado/a
olive *n.* aceituna *f.*
Olympic *adj.* olímpico/a
Olympic Games *n., pl.* Juegos *m., pl.* Olímpicos
omelet *n.* tortilla (de huevo) *(Spain) f.*
on *prep.* en; sobre
on the dot en punto
on (the) one hand. . . on the other hand. . . por un lado... por otro lado...
on the other hand en cambio
on top of *prep.* encima de
once *adv.* una vez
oncologist *n.* oncólogo/a *m., f.*

one un, uno/a *m., f., sing. pron.*
one of these days un día de estos
one hundred cien(to)
our nuestro(s)/nuestra(s) *poss. adj.; poss. pron.*
one thousand mil
one-way *n. (travel)* ida *f.*
onion *n.* cebolla *f.*
only *adj.* único/a
only *adv.* sólo, solamente
opaque *adj.* opaco/a
open *adj.* abierto/a
open *v.t.* abrir
in the open air al aire libre
open-air dance *n.* verbena *f.*
opened *p.p.* abierto (*of* abrir)
opener *n.* abridor *m.*
opera *n.* ópera *f.*
operating room *n.* quirófano *m.*
operation *n.* operación *f.;* intervención *f.* quirúrgica
ophthalmologist *n.* oftalmólogo/a *m., f.*
opinion *n.* opinión *f.*
express an opinion opinar
in my opinion en mi opinión
opponent *n.* contrincante *m., f.*
opposite *prep.* en frente de
optimist *n.* optimista *m., f.*
optimistic *adj.* optimista
or *conj.* o
orange *adj.* anaranjado/a
orange *n.* naranja *f.*
orange tree *n.* naranjo *m.*
orchard *n.* huerta *f.*
orchestra *n.* orquesta *f.*
order *n.* orden *m.;* (commercial) encargo *m.*
in order to (+ *inf.*) *prep.* para (+ *inf.*) ; a fin de (+ *inf.*)
out of order descompuesto/a *(L.A.);* averiado/a *(Spain); (sign)* no funciona
order *v.t.* mandar; *(food)* pedir (e:i); encargar
orderly *adj.* ordenado/a
ordinal *adj.* ordinal
oregano *n.* orégano *m.*
organ *n.* órgano *m.*
organic *adj.* orgánico/a; *(food)* ecológico/a
organization *n.* organización *f.*
organize *v.t.* organizar
original *adj.* original
originality *n.* originalidad *f.*
ostrich *n.* avestruz *m.*
other *adj.* otro/a
ounce *n.* onza *f.*
our nuestro(s)/nuestra(s) *poss. adj.; poss pron.*
out *adv.* fuera, afuera
out of stock *adj.* agotado/a
outline *v.t.* delinear
outrageous *adj.* escandaloso/a
outside *adv.* (a)fuera
outskirts *n., pl.* afueras *f., pl.;* alrededores *m., pl.* **on the outskirts of Barcelona** en los alrededores de Barcelona
outstanding *adj.* sobresaliente, extraordinario, excepcional
oven *n.* horno *m.*
over *prep.* sobre
overcome *v.t.* superar
oversleep *v.i.* quedarse dormido
owl *n.* búho *m.*
own *adj.* propio/a
own *v.t.* poseer

owner *n.* dueño/a *m., f.*
oxygen *n.* oxígeno *m.*
oyster *n.* ostra *f.*

P

p.m. en la tarde, de la tarde
pacemaker *n.* marcapasos *m., sing.*
pacifist *n., adj.* pacifista *m., f.*
pack (one's suitcases) *v.t.* hacer las maletas; empacar
package *n.* paquete *m.*
padded *adj.* acolchado/a
page *n.* página *f.*
pain *n.* dolor *m.*
  have a pain in the (knee) tener dolor de (rodilla)
  What pain! ¡Qué dolor!
paint *v.t.* pintar
painter *n.* pintor(a) *m., f.*
painting *n.* pintura *f.*
pair *n.* par *m.*
  a pair of shoes un par de zapatos
pajamas *n., pl.* pijama *(Spain) m.*; piyama *(L.A.) m.*
palace *n.* palacio *m.*
palate *n.* paladar *m.*
paleontologist *n.* paleontólogo/a *m., f.*
paleontology *n.* paleontología *f.*
palm tree *n.* palmera *f.*
pan *n. (frying)* sartén *f.*
pancreas *n.* páncreas *m.*
panic attack *n.* ataque *m.* de nervios
panties *n., pl.* bragas *(Spain.) f., pl.*; pantaletas *(Venezuela) f., pl.*; calzones *(L.A.) m., pl.*
pantry *n.* despensa *f.*
pants *n., pl.* pantalones *m., pl.*
pantyhose *n., pl.* medias *f., pl.*
paper *n.* papel *m.; (report)* informe *m.*; *(school essay)* trabajo *m.*
paperback *n.* libro *m.* de bolsillo
parachute *n.* paracaídas *m.*
parachuting *n.* paracaidismo *m.*
parachutist *n.* paracaidista *m., f.*
parade *n.* desfile *m.*
paragraph *n.* párrafo *m.*
parakeet *n.* perico *m.*; periquito *m.*
Paralympics *n., pl.* Juegos *m., pl.* Paralímpicos
parasite *n.* parásito *m.*
Pardon me. Perdón.; *(May I?)* Con permiso.
parents *n., pl.* padres *m., pl.*; papás *m., pl.*
park *n.* parque *m.*
park *v.t.* estacionar(se)
parking lot *n.* estacionamiento *m.*
parking *n.* estacionamiento *m.*
parking space *n.* estacionamiento *m.*
parole *n.* libertad *f.* condicional
parrot *n.* loro *m.*
parsley *n.* perejil *m.*
participate *v.i.* participar; *(contest)* concursar
participation *n.* participación *f.*; intervención *f.*
partner *n.* compañero/a *m., f.; (business)* socio/a *m., f. (marriage, romance, sport)* pareja *f.*

partnership *n.* asociación *f.*
party *n.* fiesta *f.; (political)* partido *m.* (*político*)
throw a party hacer una fiesta
party pooper *n.* aguafiestas *m., f., sing.*
pass *v.t.* pasar; *(test)* aprobar
He passed the test. Aprobó el examen.
no passing (*traffic sign*) prohibido adelantar
pass (a vehicle) adelantar (a un vehículo)
pass away *v.* fallecer
pass on *v. (illness)* contagiar
passed *p.p.* pasado/a (*of* pasar)
passenger *n.* pasajero/a *m., f.*
passer-by *n.* transeúnte *m., f.*
passing grade *n.* aprobado *m.*
passport *n.* pasaporte *m.*
past *n., adj.* pasado *m.;* pasado/a
pastime *n.* pasatiempo *m.*
pastry shop *n.* pastelería *f.*
paternal *adj. (relative)* paterno/a
path *n.* camino *m.;* sendero *m.; (of an object)* trayectoria *f.*
patience *n.* paciencia *f.*
patient *n., adj.* paciente *m., f.*
patio *n.* patio *m.*
patterned *adj. (fabric)* estampado/a
pay *v.t.* pagar
pay attention atender; prestar atención
pay in cash pagar en efectivo; pagar al contado
pay in installments pagar a plazos
pay the bill pagar la cuenta
pea *n.* arveja *(L.A.) f.;* chícharo *(Mexico) m.;* guisante *(Spain) m.*
peace *n.* paz *f.*
peach *n.* durazno *(L.A.) m.;* melocotón *(Spain) m.*
peak *n.* (mountain) cumbre *m.,* cima *f.;* auge *m.*
pear *n.* pera *f.*
pedagogical *adj.* pedagógico/a
pedagogue *n.* pedagogo/a *m., f.*
pedagogy *n.* pedagogía *f.*
pedal *n.* pedal *m.*
pedantic *adj.* pedante
pedestrian *n.* peatón *m.*
pedicure *n.* pedicura *f.*
peel *v.t.* pelar
peeler *n.* pelapapas *m., sing.*
pen *n.* pluma *f.;* bolígrafo *m.*
pencil *n.* lápiz *m.*
penguin *n.* pingüino *m.*
penicillin *n.* penicilina *f.*
peninsula *n.* península *f.*
penitentiary *n.* penitenciaría *f.*
penknife *n.* navaja *f.*
pensioner *n.* pensionista *m., f.*
people *n., pl.* gente *f., sing.*
pepper *n. (black)* pimienta *f.; (bell)* pimiento *m.*
percent por ciento
percentage *n.* porcentaje *m.*
perfect *adj.* perfecto/a
perfectionist *adj.* perfeccionista; detallista
perforate *v.t.* perforar
perform *v.t.* interpretar

perfume *n.* perfume *m.*
perfume shop *n.* perfumería *f.*
perhaps *adv.* quizás; tal vez
perimeter *n.* perímetro *m.*
period *n.* periodo *m.; (limited time)* plazo *m., (punctuation)* punto *m.*
permission *n.* permiso *m.;* consentimiento *m.*
permit *v.t.* permitir; consentir
persecution *n.* persecución *f.*
He suffered persecution for his ideas. Sufrió persecuciones por sus creencias.
persist *v.i.* persistir
persistent *adj.* persistente
person *n.* persona *f.*
personality *n.* personalidad *f.*
perspiration *n.* transpiración *f.*
perspire *v.i.* transpirar
pessimist *n.* pesimista *m., f.*
pessimistic *adj.* pesimista
pesticide *n.* pesticida *m.*
petal *n.* pétalo *m.*
petrified *adj.* petrificado/a
Ph.D. *n.* doctorado *m.; (title)* Dr. *m.,* Dra. *f.*
pharmacy *n.* farmacia *f.*
pharynx *n.* faringe *f.*
pheasant *n.* faisán *m.*
phenomenal *adj.* espectacular, extraordinario; increíble; fenomenal
phenomenon *n.* fenómeno *m.*
philately *n.* filatelia *f.*
philologist *n.* filólogo/a *m., f.*
philology *n.* filología *f.*
philosopher *n.* filósofo/a *m., f.*
philosophize *v.i.* filosofar
philosophy *n.* filosofía *f.*
phonetics *n.* fonética *f.*
phonology *n.* fonología *f.*
photocopier *n.* fotocopiadora *f.*
photocopy *v.t.* fotocopiar
photograph *n.* foto(grafía) *f.*
take photos tomar/sacar fotos
photosynthesis *n.* fotosíntesis *f., sing.*
physical (exam) *n.* chequeo *m.* (médico), revisión f. médica; examen *m.* médico
physician *n.* doctor(a) *m., f.,* médico/a *m., f.*
physicist *n.* físico/a *m., f.*
physics *n.* física *f.*
physique *n.* tipo *m.*
pick up *v.t.* recoger
pick up boys/girls *v.i.* ligar
pickup truck *n.* camioneta *f.*
picture *n.* cuadro *m.;* pintura *f.*
picturesque *adj.* pintoresco/a
pie *n.* pastel *m.*
pig *n.* cerdo *m.;* puerco *m.*
pilgrim *n.* peregrino/a *m., f.*
pilgrimage *n.* peregrinación *f.*
pill *n.* pastilla *f.;* píldora *f.*
pillow *n.* almohada *f.*
pimple *n.* grano *m.*
pinch *n. (quantity)* pizca *f.*
pine forest *n.* pinar *m.*
pine tree *n.* pino *m.*
pineapple *n.* piña *f.*
pink *adj.* rosado/a
pipe *n.* tubo *m.,* caño *m.;* cañería *f.,* tubería *f.*
pit *n. (fruit)* hueso *m.*
pitcher *n.* jarra *f.*
pity *n.* lástima *f.*

place *n.* lugar *m.*
place *v.t.* poner; colocar
placing *n.* colocación *f.*
plagiarism *n.* plagio *m.*
plagiarize *v.t.* plagiar
plaid *adj.* de cuadros
plan (to do something) *v.* pensar *(+ inf.)*
plan *n.* plan *m.*
have plans tener planes
plane *n.* avión *m.*
planet *n.* planeta *m.*
planetarium *n.* planetario *m.*
plant *n.* planta *f.*
climbing plant enredadera *f.*
plantain *n.* plátano *m.*
plastic *n.* plástico *m.*
made of plastic de plástico
plate *n.* plato *m.*
license plate placa *f.*
plateau *n.* meseta *f.*
platter *n.* fuente *f.*
platter of fried food *n.* fuente de fritada
play *n.* drama *m.;* comedia *f.*
play *v.t.* jugar (u:ue);
play (a musical instrument) tocar (un instrumento musical)
play hooky hacer novillos *(Spain)*
play sports practicar deportes
play the role (of) hacer el papel (de)
player *n.* jugador(a) *m., f.*
playwright *n.* dramaturgo/a *m., f.*
plead *v.i.* rogar (o:ue), suplicar
pleasant *adj.* agradable
please *interj.* por favor
be pleased (with) contentarse (con)
Pleased to meet you. Mucho gusto.; Encantado/a (de conocerle).
pleasing: be pleasing to gustar
pleasure *n.* gusto *m.;* placer *m.*
It's a pleasure to . . . Gusto de *(+ inf.)*
It's been a pleasure. Ha sido un placer.
The pleasure is mine. El gusto es mío.
What a pleasure to . . . ! ¡Qué gusto (+ *inf.*)...
plot *n. (story)* argumento *m.; (land)* terreno *m.*
plot *v.t.* tramar
pluck *v. (eyebrows)* depilarse
plum *n.* ciruela *f.*
plumber *n.* fontanero/a *(Spain) m., f.;* plomero/a *(L.A.) m., f.*
plumbing *n.* fontanería *(Spain) f.;* plomería *(L.A.) f.*
pluralism *n.* pluralismo *m.*
plurality *n.* pluralidad *f.*
pocket *n.* bolsillo *m.*
podium *n.* podio *m.*
poem *n.* poema *m.*
poet *n.* poeta *m., f.*
poetry *n.* poesía *f.*
point *n.* punto *m.*
polemical *adj.* polémico/a
police *n. (force)* policía *f.*
police officer *n.* policía *m.,* mujer *f.* policía
police station *n.* comisaría *f.* (de policía)
polish *n. (shoe)* brillo *m.* (para

zapatos); *(floor)* abrillantador *m.* (para pisos/suelos)
polish *v.t.* abrillantar; encerar
polite *adj.* educado/a
political *adj.* político/a
politician *n.* político/a *m., f.*
politics *n.* política *f.*
polka dot *n.* lunar *m.*
polka-doted *adj.* de lunares
poll *n.* encuesta *f.*
pollen *n.* polen *m.*
pollinate *v.t.* polinizar
pollute *v.t.* contaminar
polluted *adj.* contaminado/a
be polluted estar contaminado/a
pollution *n.* contaminación *f.*
air/water pollution contaminación del aire/del agua
pomegranate *n.* granada *f.*
pond *n. (man-made)* estanque *m.; (natural)* charca *f.*
pony tail *n.* cola *f.* de caballo
pool: swimming pool *n.* piscina *f.;* alberca *(Mexico) f.*
indoor pool piscina climatizada
poor *adj.* pobre
become poor empobrecerse
make poor empobrecer
poppy *n.* amapola *f.*
populate *v.t.* poblar
population *n.* población *f.*
porch *n.* porche *m.*
pork *n.* cerdo *m.*
pork chop *n.* chuleta *f.* de cerdo
port *n.* puerto *m.*
portable *adj.* portátil
portable computer *n.* computadora *f.* portátil
porter *n.* portero/a *m., f.*
position *n. (job)* puesto *m.*
possession *n.* posesión *f.*
possessive *adj.* posesivo/a
possible *adj.* posible
it's (not) possible (no) es posible
post office *n.* correo *m.;* correos *(Spain) m., pl.*
postcard *n.* postal *f.;* tarjeta *f.* postal
poster *n.* cartel *m.*
postpone *v.t.* aplazar
postponement *n.* aplazamiento *m.*
pot *n. (cooking)* olla *f.*
potato *n.* papa *(L.A.) f.;* patata *(Spain) f.*
potato omelet *n.* tortilla *f.* de patatas
potter *n.* ceramista *m., f.*
pottery *n.* cerámica *f.*
pound *n.* libra *f.*
pour *v.i.* llover a cántaros
poverty *n.* pobreza *f.*
power *n.* poder *m.;* potencia *f.*
power failure *n.* apagón *m.*
power steering *n.* dirección *f.* asistida
powerful *adj.* poderoso/a
practice *n.* práctica *f.*
practice *v.t.* practicar; entrenarse
prairie *n.* llanura *f.*
praise *n.* elogio *m.*
praise *v.t.* elogiar
prank *n.* travesura *f.*
prawn *n.* langostino *m.*

pray *v.i.* rezar
predator *n.* depredador *m.*
predatory *adj.* depredador(a)
prefabricate *v.t.* prefabricar
prefabricated *adj.* prefabricado/a
prefer *v.t.* preferir (e:ie)
pregnant *adj.* embarazada
premiere *n. (film, play)* estreno *m.*
preparations *n., pl.* preparativos *m., pl.*
prepare *v.t.* preparar
preposition *n.* preposición *f.*
prescribe *v.t.* recetar
prescription *n.* receta *f.*
present *n. (gift)* regalo *m.; (time)* presente *m.*
present *v.t.* presentar
presenter *n.* presentador(a) *m., f.*
press *n.* prensa *f.*
pressure *n.* presión *f.*
be under (a lot of) pressure sufrir (muchas) presiones
pressure cooker *n.* olla *f.* a presión
pretend *v.t./v.i.* fingir; disimular
pretentious *adj.* pretencioso/a
pretty *adj.* bonito/a; bastante *adv.*
prevent *v.t.* prevenir; impedir; evitar
prevention *n.* prevención *f.*
prey *n.* presa *f.*
price *n.* precio *m.*
What is the price? ¿Qué precio tiene?
pride *n.* orgullo *m.*
priest *n.* padre *m.*
primitive *adj.* primitivo/a
print *adj.* estampado
print *v.t.* imprimir
printer *n. (machine)* impresora *f.*
prison *n.* prisión *f.;* cárcel *f.*
prisoner *n.* preso/a *m., f.*
privacy *n.* intimidad *f.*
private *adj.* privado/a; particular; individual
prize *n.* premio *m.;* galardón *m.*
probable *adj.* probable
it's (not) probable (no) es probable
problem *n.* problema *m.*
prodigy *n.* prodigio/a *m., f.*
produce *n.* frutas *f., pl.* y verduras *f., pl.*
produce *v.t.* fabricar
product *n.* producto *m.*
profession *n.* profesión *f.*
professor *n.* profesor(a) *m., f.;* catedrático/a *m., f.*
program *n.* programa *m.*
programmer *n.* programador(a) *m., f.*
prohibit *v.t.* prohibir
prohibited *p.p.* prohibido (*of* prohibir)
project *v.t.* proyectar
projection *n.* proyección *f.*
prolific *adj.* prolífico/a
promise *v.* prometer
promote *v.i. (work)* ascender
promotion *n. (career)* ascenso *m.*
prone to *adj.* propenso/a a
pronoun *n.* pronombre *m.*
proof *n.* demostración *f.*
proposal *n.* propuesta *f.*

propose *v.t.* proponer
protect *v.t.* proteger
protection *n.* protección *f.*
protein *n.* proteína *f.*
protest *n.* protesta *f.*
protest *v.t.* protestar
Protestant *n., adj.* protestante *m., f.*
proud *adj.* orgulloso/a
prove *v.t.* demostrar
provided (that) *conj.* con tal (de) que
provisions *n., pl.* provisiones *f., pl.;* víveres *m., pl.*
provocation *n.* provocación *f.*
provocative *adj. (dress)* atrevido/a
provoke *v.t.* provocar
psychiatrist *n.* (p)siquiatra *m., f.*
psychiatry *n.* (p)siquiatría *f.*
psychologist *n.* (p)sicólogo/a *m., f.*
psychology *n.* (p)sicología *f.*
puberty *n.* pubertad *f.*
public school *n.* escuela *f.* pública
publish *v.t.* publicar
Puerto Rican *n., adj.* puertorriqueño/a *m., f.*
Puerto Rico *n.* Puerto Rico *m.*
pull *v.t.* halar *(L.A.),* jalar *(L.A.);* tirar *(Spain)*
pull an all-nighter *idiom* quemarse las pestañas
pull out all the stops *loc.* echar la casa por la ventana
pull someone's leg *idiom* tomarle el pelo a alguien
pumpkin *n.* calabaza *f.*
punchbowl *n.* ponchera *f.*
punctual *adj.* puntual
punish *v.t.* castigar
punishment *n.* castigo *m.*
pupil *n. (eye)* pupila *f.; (student)* pupilo/a *m., f.;* alumno/a *m., f.*
purchase *n.* compra *f.,* adquisición *f.*
purchase *v.t.* comprar, adquirir
pure *adj.* puro/a
purple *n., adj.* morado *m.;* morado/a
purpose *n.* propósito *m.*
on purpose *adv.* adrede; a propósito
purse *n.* bolsa *f.*
pursue *v.t.* perseguir
pursuit *n.* persecución *f.* **The police took off in pursuit of the fugitive.** La policía salió en persecución del fugitivo.; búsqueda *f.* **the pursuit of truth** la búsqueda de la verdad
push *v.t.* empujar
put *v.t.* poner; colocar
put in a cast escayolar *(Spain);* enyesar *(L.A.)*
put *p.p.* puesto (*of* poner)
put off *v.* aplazar
put on *v. (a performance)* presentar; *(clothing)* ponerse
put out *v.t.* sofocar; extinguir **The firefighters put out the blaze.** Los bomberos extinguieron el incendio.
put something over (on somebody) *idiom* dar gato por liebre

put up *v.t. (give lodging)* alojar
put up with *v.* aguantar
puzzle, (jigsaw) *n.* rompecabezas *m., sing.*
pyramid *n.* pirámide *f.*

Q

quail *n.* codorniz *f.*
qualify *v.t./v.i.* calificarse
quality *n.* calidad *f.*
quarrel *n.* pelea *f.*
quarrel *v.i.* pelearse; discutir
They always quarrel over money. Siempre se pelean por el dinero.
quarter *n.* trimestre *m.;* cuarto *m.*
quarter after *(time)* y cuarto; y quince **It's quarter after three.** Son las tres y cuarto/quince.
quarter to menos cuarto; menos quince **It's quarter to five.** Son las cinco menos cuarto/quince.
queen *n.* reina *f.*
question *v.t.* cuestionar
question *n.* pregunta *f.*
quickly *adv.* rápido
quiet *adj.* tranquilo/a; callado/a
quit (doing something) *v.t. (habit)* dejar de (+ *inf.*); dejar
quiz *n.* prueba *f.*

R

rabbi *n.* rabino/a *m., f.*
rabbit *n.* conejo *m.*
race *n. (sport)* carrera *f.; (people)* raza *f.*
racecar *n.* carro *m.* de carreras
racism *n.* racismo *m.*
racist *adj.* racista
racket *n. (sport)* raqueta *f.*
radio *n. (medium)* radio *f.; (set receiver)* radio *m.*
radish *n.* rábano *m.*
railroad *n.* ferrocarril *m.*
railroad crossing *n.* paso *m.* a nivel
rain *n.* lluvia *f.*
rain *v.imp.* llover (o:ue)
It's raining. Llueve.
rain cats and dogs *idiom* llover a cántaros
rain forest *n.* bosque *m.* tropical
rainbow *n.* arco *m.* iris
raincoat *n.* impermeable *m.*
raise *n. (salary)* aumento *m.* de sueldo
raise *v.t. (children, animals)* criar; *(money)* recaudar (fondos)
raisin *n.* pasa *f.*
rake *n.* rastrillo *m.*
rancher *n.* ganadero/a *m., f.*
ranching *n.* ganadería *f.*
randomly *adv.* al azar
at random *adv.* al azar
ranger *n.* guarda *m., f.* forestal
raspberry *n.* frambuesa *f.*
rate *n.* índice *m.*
rather *adv.* bastante
rattlesnake *n.* serpiente *f.* de cascabel
raw *adj. (food)* crudo/a
razor *n.* máquina *f.* de afeitar; rasuradora *f.*
reach *n.* alcance

within arm's reach al alcance de la mano

reach *v.t.* alcanzar; llegar a; contactar, ponerse en contacto con
reach a conclusion llegar a una conclusión
reach an agreement llegar a un acuerdo
How can I reach you? ¿Cómo puedo ponerme en contacto contigo?

react *v.i.* reaccionar

reaction *n.* reacción *f.*

read *v.t.* leer
read e-mail/a newspaper/a magazine leer correo electrónico/un periódico/una revista

read *p.p.* leído (*of* leer)

reader *n.* lector(a) *m., f.*

ready *adj.* listo/a
be ready estar listo/a
get ready prepararse; arreglarse **He takes forever getting ready.** Tarda mucho en arreglarse.

real *adj.* auténtico/a

real estate *n.* bienes raíces *m., pl.*

realistic *adj.* verosímil **His characters aren't realistic.** Sus personajes no son verosímiles.

realize *v.t.* darse cuenta de (que) **Gustavo realized he was alone.** Gustavo se dio cuenta de que estaba solo.

reap the benefits (of) *v.t.* disfrutar (de)

rearview mirror *n.* retrovisor *m.*

reason *n.* razón *f.*

reason *v.i.* razonar

rebellious *adj.* rebelde

receive *v.t.* recibir

receptionist *n.* recepcionista *m., f.; (hotel)* conserje *m., f.*

recess *n.* recreo *m.*

recipe *n.* receta *f.*

recital *n.* recital *m.*

recognition *n.* reconocimiento *m.*

recognize *v.t.* reconocer

recommend *v.t.* recomendar (e:ie)

record *n. (sport)* marca *f.;* récord *m.*

record *v.t.* grabar

recreation *n.* diversión *f.*

rectangle *n.* rectángulo *m.*

rectify *v.t.* rectificar

recycle *v.t.* reciclar

recycling *n.* reciclaje *m.*

red *n., adj.* rojo *m.;* rojo/a

Red Cross *n.* Cruz *f.* Roja

reddish *adj.* rojizo/a

red-hair *adj.* pelirrojo/a

red-headed *adj.* pelirrojo/a

reduce *v.t.* reducir
reduce stress/tension aliviar el estrés/la tensión

reduced *adj.* de rebaja

reef *n.* arrecife *m.*

referee *n.* árbitro/a *m., f.*

reference book *n.* libro *m.* de consulta

reflect *v.t. (light) reflejar; v.i.* **(on something)** reflexionar (sobre algo)

reform *n.* reforma *f.*

reform *v.t.* reformar
refreshing *adj.* refrescante
refrigerate *v.t.* refrigerar
refrigerator *n.* refrigerador *m.*
refund *n.* devolución *f.*
refusal *n.* negación *f.*
refuse *v.i.* negarse; *v.t.* negarse a (+ *inf.*)
He refused to answer. Se negó a contestar.
regarding to (con) respecto a
regards *n., pl.* recuerdos *m., pl.;* saludos *m., pl.*
Lila sends her regards. Lila manda saludos.
region *n.* región *f.*
register *v.i. (school)* matricularse; inscribirse **She intends to register for the astronomy class.** Pretende inscribirse en la clase de astronomía.
registration *n.* inscripción *f.; (education)* matrícula *f.*
registration number *n. (car)* matrícula *f.*
regret *v.t.* arrepentirse (de) (e:ie); lamentar; sentir (e:ie)
regular (customer) *n.* asiduo/a *m., f.*
regularization *n.* regularización *f.*
regulate *v.t.* regular; *(temperature, etc.)* graduar
rehearsal *n.* ensayo *m.*
rehearse *v.t.* ensayar
reign *v.i.* reinar
reinforce *v.t.* reforzar
reinforcement *n.* refuerzo *m.*
reject *v.t.* rechazar
rejection *n.* rechazo *m.*
rejoicing *n.* algarabía *f.*
rejuvenate *v.i.* rejuvenecer
rejuvenation *n.* rejuvenecimiento *m.*
relationship *n.* relación *f.*
relative *adj., n.* relativo/a; pariente *m., f.*
relatives *n.* familiares *m., pl.;* parientes *m., pl.*
relax *v.i.* relajarse
relaxation *n.* relajación *f.*
relay race *n.* carrera *f.* de relevos
release *v.t.* liberar; soltar; poner en libertad
relief *n.* alivio *m.*
relieve *v.t. (pain)* aliviar
religion *n.* religión *f.*
religious *adj.* religioso/a
remain *v.i.* quedarse
remember *v.t./v.i.* recordar (o:ue); acordarse (de) (o:ue)
remembrance *n.* conmemoración *f.*
remote *adj.* alejado/a; lejano/a
remote control *m.* control *m.* remoto
Renaissance *adj.* renacimento *m.*
Renaissance artist *n.* renacentista *m., f.*
renew *v.t.* renovar
renewal *n.* renovación *f.*
rent *n.* (*payment*) alquiler *m.*
rent *v.t.* alquilar
repeat *v.t.* repetir (e:i)
repellent *n.* repelente *m.*
replace *v.t.* reemplazar; sustituir **They replaced the**

sugar with honey. Sustituyeron el azúcar por la miel.

report *n.* informe *m.;* reportaje *m.;* boletín *m.;* denuncia *f.*

report *v.t. (crime)* denunciar

reporter *n.* reportero/a *m., f.*

representative *n.* representante *m., f.*

repress *v.t.* reprimir

repression *n.* represión *f.*

reprimand *v.t.* regañar

reproduce *v.t.* reproducir **It's difficult to reproduce the results.** Es difícil reproducir los resultados.; *(biology)* reproducirse **Rabbits reproduce quickly.** Los conejos se reproducen rápidamente.

reptile *n.* reptil *m.*

reputation *n.* reputación *f.;* fama *f.*
have a good/bad reputation tener buena/mala fama
have a reputation for tener fama de

request *v.t.* pedir (e:i); solicitar

rescue *n.* rescate *m.;* salvamento *m.*

rescue *v.t.* rescatar

research *v.t.* investigar
do research documentarse

researcher *n.* investigador(a) *m., f.*

resentful *adj.* rencoroso/a

resentment *n.* rencor *m.*

reservation *n.* reservación *f.*

reserved *adj.* reservado/a

reservoir *n.* embalse *m.;* pantano *m.*

reside *v.i.* residir

residence *n.* residencia *f.*

resident *n., adj.* residente *m., f.*

resign (from) *v.i.* renunciar (a)

resign *v.i.* dimitir

resignation *n.* dimisión *f.*

resist *v.t.* resistir

resistance *n.* resistencia *f.*

resolve *v.t.* resolver (o:ue)

resolved *p.p.* resuelto (*of* resolver)

resort *n. (coastal)* balneario *m.*

resource *n.* recurso *m.*
natural resource recurso natural

respect *n.* respeto *m.*

respect *v.t.* respetar

respiration *n.* respiración *f.*

respiratory failure *n.* crisis *f.* respiratoria

responsibility *n.* responsabilidad *f.* ; deber *m.*

responsible *adj.* responsable

rest *n.* reposo *m.;* descanso *m.*

rest *v.i.* descansar; reposar **He had to rest for several weeks after the operation.** Tuvo que reposar por varias semanas después de la operación.
the rest *n.* lo/los/las demás

restaurant *n.* restaurante *m.*

restore *v.t.* restaurar

restrain oneself *v.refl.* dominarse

result *n.* resultado *m.*

résumé *n.* currículum *m.* (vitae); hoja *f.* de vida *(Colombia)*

retire (from work) *v.i.* jubilarse
retired person *n.* pensionista *m., f.;* jubilado/a *m., f.*
retirement pension *n.* pensión *f.*
return *n. (object)* devolución *f.*
return *v.i.* regresar; volver (o:ue); *v.t.* (*object*) devolver (o:ue)
return trip *n.* vuelta *f.*
returned *p.p.* vuelto (*of* volver)
rewind *v.t.* rebobinar
rewind button *n.* botón *m.* de rebobinado
  push the rewind button apriete el botón de rebobinado
rhetoric *n.* retórica *f.*
rhetorical *adj.* retórico/a
rheumatism *n.* reumatismo *m.*
rhinoceros *n.* rinoceronte *m.*
rhythm *n.* ritmo *m.*; compás *m.*
rib *n.* costilla *f.*
ribbon *n.* cinta *f.*
rice *n.* arroz *m.*
rich *adj.* rico/a
  get rich enriquecerse
  make rich enriquecer
riddle *n.* adivinanza *f.*
ride *v.* pasear
ride bikes/a bike *v.i.* andar/pasear en bicicleta
ridiculous *adj.* ridículo/a
  It's ridiculous (that...) Es ridículo (que...)
right *n., adj. (direction)* derecha *f.;* derecho *m.;* derecho/a; correcto/a
  be right tener razón
  right? *interj.* ¿no?; ¿verdad?
  right away *adv.* enseguida; en el acto
  right here/there aquí/allí mismo
  right now ahora mismo
  to the right (of) a la derecha de
rights *n., pl.* derechos *m., pl*
  human rights derechos humanos
ring *n.* anillo *m.;* sortija *f.; (boxing)* cuadrilátero *m.*
  wedding ring anillo de bodas
ring *v.t. (bell)* sonar (o:ue)
rise *n. (advance)* ascenso *m.*
rise *v.i.* ascender
river *n.* río *m.*
road *n.* camino *m.*
roar *n.* rugido *m.*
roar *v.i.* rugir
roast *n.* asado *m.*
  roast chicken *n.* pollo *m.* asado
  roast lamb *n.* asado de cordero
roasted *p.p.* asado/a (*of* asar)
rob *v.t.* robar
robber *n.* ladrón *m.*, ladrona *f.*
robbery *n.* atraco *m.;* robo *m.*
robe *n.* bata *f.*
rock *n.* roca *f.*, piedra *f.*
rock *v.t.* mecer
rocket *n.* cohete *m.*
rocking chair *n.* mecedora *f.*
role *n. (movie, theater)* papel *m.*
  leading role papel principal
  supporting role papel secundario
roller skating *n.* patinaje *m.*

sobre ruedas
rollerblade *v.* patinar en línea
Roman *n., adj.* romano/a *m., f.*
Romanesque *adj.* románico/a
romantic *n., adj.* romántico/a *m., f.*
Romanticism *n.* romanticismo *m.*
room *n.* cuarto *m.;* habitación *f.;* sala *f.*
double room habitación doble
single room habitación individual
roommate *n.* compañero/a *m., f.* de cuarto
rooster *n.* gallo *m.*
root *n.* raíz *f.*
rope *n.* cuerda *f.*
rose *n.* rosa *f.*
rosebush *n.* rosal *m.*
rosemary *n.* romero *m.*
rough *adj. (surface, skin)* áspero/a; (*person*) grosero/a
roulette *n.* ruleta *f.*
roundtrip *n., adj.* de ida y vuelta
roundtrip ticket *n.* pasaje *m.* de ida y vuelta
route *n.* ruta *f.*
routine *n.* rutina *f.*
row *n.* hilera *f.;* fila *f.*
row *v.i.* remar
rower *n.* remero/a *m., f.*
royal *adj.* real
royalty *n.* realeza *f.*
rubber *adj.* de goma
ruby *n.* rubí *m.*
rude *adj.* maleducado/a; grosero/a
rug *n.* alfombra *f.*
rugged *adj. (terrain)* accidentado/a
rule *v.t.* gobernar
rum *n.* ron *m.*
rumor *n.* rumor *m.*
run *v.t.* correr; *v.i. (business)* administrar
run a red light *v. pron.* pasarse (el alto/el semáforo en rojo)
run away *v.* fugarse
run into *v. (have an accident)* chocar (con); *(meet accidentally)* darse con; (*each other*) encontrarse (o:ue)
run out *v. (supplies)* agotar(se)
run over *v.* derramarse
run over (someone with a vehicle) *v.* atropellar (a alguien con un vehículo)
rural *adj.* rural; campestre
rush *v.i.* apurarse; darse prisa
rust *n.* óxido *m.*
rust *v.i.* oxidarse

S

sacred *adj.* sagrado/a
sad *adj.* triste
It's sad (that...) Es triste (que...)
sadness *n.* tristeza *f.*
safe *n.* seguro *m.*
safe *adj.* seguro/a
saffron *n.* azafrán *m.*
saga *n.* saga *f.*
sage *n. (herb)* salvia *f.*
said *p.p.* dicho (*of* decir)
sail *n.* vela *f.*

sailboat *n.* velero *m.*
sailing *n.* vela *f.*
sake: for the sake of por
for the sake of love por amor
salad *n.* ensalada *f.*
salad bowl *n.* ensaladera *f.*
salary *n.* salario *m.;* sueldo *m.*
sale *n.* rebaja *f.*
salesperson *n.* vendedor(a) *m., f.*
salmon *n.* salmón *m.*
salt *n.* sal *f.*
salt shaker *n.* salero *m.*
salty *adj.* salado/a
same *adj.* mismo/a; igual
be all the same dar lo mismo
It's all the same to me if she comes or not. Me da lo mismo si viene o no.
sand *n.* arena *f.*
sandal *n.* sandalia *f.*
sandwich *n.* sándwich *m.*
sap *n.* savia *f.*
sardine *n.* sardina *f.*
Saturday *n.* sábado *m.*
sauce *n.* salsa *f.*
sauna *n.* sauna *f.*
sausage *n.* salchicha *f.*
sauté *v.t.* saltear, sofreír
save *v.t. (on a computer)* guardar; *(money)* ahorrar (dinero); salvar
savings *n.* ahorros *m., pl.*
savings account *n.* cuenta *f.* de ahorros
saw *n.* sierra *f.*
saw *v.t.* serrar
say *v.t.* decir (e:i); declarar
You don't say! ¡No me diga(s)!
say good-bye (to) despedirse (de) (e:i)
saying *n.* dicho *m.;* refrán *m.*
scale *n.* balanza *f.;* báscula *f.*
scallop *n.* vieira *f.*
scalpel *n.* bisturí *m.*
scapula *n.* omoplato *m.*
scar *v.i.* cicatrizar
scarcely *adv.* apenas
He can scarcely talk. Apenas sabe hablar.
scared: be scared (of) tener miedo (de)
scarf *n.* bufanda *f.*
scent *n.* aroma *m.*
schedule *n.* horario *m.*
scheme *v.i.* tramar
scholarship *n.* beca *f.*
school *n.* escuela *f.*
school report *n.* boletín *m.* de notas
science *n.* ciencia *f.*
science-fiction *n.* ciencia *f.* ficción; ...de ciencia ficción
scientist *n.* científico/a *m., f.*
scissors *n.* tijeras *f., pl.*
scold *v.t.* regañar
scoreboard *n.* marcador *m.*
scorpion *n.* escorpión *m.*
scream *v.i.* gritar
screen *n.* pantalla *f.*
screenplay *n.* guión *m.*
screenwriter *n.* guionista *m., f.*
screw *n.* tornillo *m.*
screwdriver *n.* destornillador *m.*
script *n.* guión *m.*
scriptwriter *n.* guionista *m., f.*
scuba dive *v.* bucear
sculpt *v.t./v.i.* esculpir

sculptor *n.* escultor(a) *m., f.*
sculpture *n.* escultura *f.*
sea *n.* mar *m.*; océano *m.*
seafood *n.* mariscos *m., pl.*
  assorted seafood mariscada *f.*
seal *n.* foca *f.*
seaquake *n.* maremoto *m.*
search *n.* búsqueda *f.*
season *n.* estación *f.*; temporada *f.*
season *v.t. (salad)* aderezar, aliñar
seasoning *n.* aderezo *m.*; aliño *m.*
seat *n.* silla *f.*; asiento *m.*
seat belt *n.* cinturón *n.* de seguridad
seaweed *n.* alga (el) *f.*
second *n., adj.* segundo *m.*; segundo/a
secretary *n.* secretario/a *m., f.*
security guard *n.* guardia *m., f.* de seguridad
sedentary *adj.* sedentario/a
sediment *n.* sedimento *m.*
sedimentation *n.* sedimentación *f.*
seduce *v.t.* seducir
seducer *n.* seductor(a) *m., f.*
seductive *adj.* seductor(a)
seductress *n.* seductor(a) *m., f.*
see *v.t.* ver; mirar
  let's see a ver; veamos
  See you. Nos vemos.
  see (you) again volver a ver(te/lo/la)
  See you later. Hasta la vista.; Hasta luego.
  See you soon. Hasta pronto.
  See you tomorrow. Hasta mañana.
see-through *adj.* transparente
seed *n.* semilla *f.*; grano *m.*
seem *v.i.* parecer
seen *p.p.* visto/a (*of* ver)
select *adj.* selecto/a
select *v.t.* seleccionar
self-employed worker *n.* autónomo/a *m., f.*
self-portrait *n.* autorretrato *m.*
self-taught *adj.* autodidacta
selfish *adj.* egoísta
selfishness *n.* egoísmo *m.*
sell *v.t.* vender
semantics *n.* semántica *f.*
semester *n.* semestre *m.*
seminar *n.* seminario *m.*
senate *n.* senado *m.*
send *v.t.* enviar, mandar
sense *n.* sentido *m.*
  common sense sentido común
sense of order *n.* sentido *m.* del orden
sensible *adj.* sensato/a
sensitive *adj.* sensible
sensitivity *n.* sensibilidad *f.*
sensory organs *n., pl.* órganos *m., pl.* de los sentidos
sentimental *adj.* sentimental
separate (from) *v.* separarse (de)
separated *adj.* separado/a
September *n.* septiembre *m.*
sequence *n.* secuencia *f.*
series circuit *n.* circuito *m.* en serie
serious *adj.* serio/a; *(illness, wound)* grave

serve *v.t./v.i.* servir (e:i)
service *n.* servicio *m.*
serving *n.* porción *f.*
set *adj. (price)* fijo/a
set *n. (theater)* decorado *m.*
set *v.t.* poner, colocar
set the table poner la mesa
set (a world record) *v.* establecer (una marca mundial)
settle *v.i.* instalarse **He settled in front of the TV and didn't budge.** Se instaló ante la tele y no se movió.
settlement *n.* colonización *f.; (agreement)* resolución *f.*
settler *n.* colono/a *m., f.*
seven siete
seven hundred setecientos/as
seventeen diecisiete
seventh séptimo *m.; adj.* séptimo/a
seventy setenta
sew *v.t./v.i.* coser
sewer *n.* cloaca *f.*
sewing machine *n.* máquina *f.* de coser
sexism *n.* sexismo *m.*
shame *n.* lástima *f.;* vergüenza *f.*
It's a shame (that...) Es una lástima (que...)
shame *v.t.* avergonzar
shameful *adj.* vergonzoso/a
shampoo *n.* champú *m.*
shape *n.* forma *f.*
be in good shape estar en buena forma
stay in shape mantenerse en forma
share *v.t.* compartir
shark *n.* tiburón *m.*
sharp *adv. (time)* en punto **It starts at 4:00 sharp.** Empieza a las cuatro en punto.
sharp curve *n.* curva *f.* peligrosa
shave *v.i.* afeitarse*; (legs)* depilarse
shaving cream *n.* crema *f.* de afeitar
shawl *n.* chal *m.*
shed *n.* cobertizo *m.*
sheep *n.* oveja *f.*
sheet *n.* sábana *f.; (paper)* hoja *f.*
shellfish *n.* mariscos *m. pl.*
sherry *n.* jerez *m.*
shift *n. (work)* turno *m.*
shift gears *v.t.* cambiar de marcha
shine *v.i.* brillar
ship *n.* barco *m.*
go by ship ir en barco
shirt *n.* camisa *f.*
shiver *n.* escalofrío *m.*
shiver *v.i.* temblar; tener escalofríos
shock *n.* choque *m.,* impacto *m.*
shock absorber *n.* amortiguador *m.*
electric shock *n.* descarga *f.* (eléctrica)
shoe *n.* zapato *m.*
put one's shoes on calzarse
shoe size *n.* número *m.*
take (wear) a shoe size calzar
shoe store *n.* zapatería *f.*

shoelace *n.* cordón *m.*
shoes *n.* calzado *m.*
shoot *v.t.* disparar; *(movies)* rodar
shooting *n.* rodaje *m.*
shooting star *n.* estrella *f.* fugaz
shop *n.* tienda *f.*
shop window *n.* escaparate *(Spain) m.;* vitrina *(L.A.) f.*
shopping mall/center *n.* centro *m.* comercial
shore *n.* orilla *f.* **The house is on the seashore.** La casa está a orillas del mar.
short *adj. (height)* bajo/a; *(length)* corto/a
in short *loc.* en resumidas cuentas
short circuit *n.* cortocircuito *m.*
short cut *n.* atajo *m.*
short story *n.* cuento *m.*
shortage *n.* carencia *f.*
shortcoming *n.* deficiencia *f.*
shorts *n., pl.* pantalones *m., pl.* cortos
shot *n.* disparo *m.;* tiro *m.*
shotput *n. (sport)* lanzamiento *m.* de bala *(L.A.);* lanzamiento *m.* de peso *(Spain)*
should ***(do something)*** deber (+ *inf.)*
shoulder *n.* hombro *m.*
shoulder bag *n.* bolso *m.*
shovel *n.* pala *f.*
show *n.* espectáculo *m.*
show *v.t.* mostrar (o:ue); enseñar
shower *n.* ducha *f.*
shower *v.i.* ducharse, *v.t.* bañarse
shrewd *adj.* astuto/a
shrimp *n.* camarón *(L.A.)m.;* gamba *(Spain)* f.
marinated shrimp ceviche *m.* de camarón *m.*
shrub *n.* arbusto *m.*
shy *adj.* tímido/a
sick *adj.* enfermo/a
be sick estar enfermo/a
get sick enfermarse
side *n.* lado *m.*
sideburn *n.* patilla *f.*
sight *n. (senses)* vista *f.*
sight *v.t.* divisar
sightseeing: go sightseeing hacer turismo
sign *n. (board)* letrero *m.;* señal *f.*
sign *v.t.* firmar
signature *n.* firma *f.*
silence *n.* silencio *m.*
silk *n., adj.* seda *f.;* de seda
silky *adj.* sedoso/a
silly *adj.* tonto/a
silver *n., adj.* plata *f.;* plateado/a
silverware *n.* cubiertos *m., pl.*
similar *adj.* similar; semejante
simmer *v.t.* cocer a fuego lento
simple *adj.* sencillo/a, simple
sinagogue *n.* sinagoga *f.*
since *prep.* desde
sing *v.t.* cantar
singer *n.* cantante *m., f.*
single *adj. (unmarried)* soltero/a
single room *n.* habitación *f.* individual
singles *n. (sports)* individual *m.*

sink *n. (bathroom)* lavabo *m.;* lavamanos *m.; (kitchen)* fregadero (de la cocina) *m.*
sip *n.* sorbo *m.*
sir *n.* señor *m.* (Sr.); don
sister *n.* hermana *f.*
younger sister hermana menor
sister-in-law *n.* cuñada *f.*
sit down *v.* sentarse (e:ie)
sitting: related to sitting sedentario/a *adj.*
six seis
six hundred seiscientos/as
sixteen dieciséis
sixth sexto *m.; adj.* sexto/a
sixty sesenta
size *n.* talla *f.*
What size do you take? ¿Qué talla lleva/usa?
skate *v.i.* patinar
skate in-line patinar en línea
skateboard *v.t.* andar en patineta
skating *n.* patinaje *m.*
skating rink *n.* pista *f.* de patinaje
skeleton *n.* esqueleto *m.*
ski *v.i.* esquiar
ski cap *n.* gorro *m.* de lana
ski slope *n.* pista *f.* de esquí
skier *n.* esquiador(a) *m., f.*
skiing *n.* esquí *m.*
skill *n.* habilidad *f.*
skillful *adj.* hábil
skimmed *adj. (dairy products)* descremado/a; desnatado/a
skin *n.* cutis *m.;* piel *f.; (on boiled milk)* nata *f.*
skinny *adj.* flaco/a
skirt *n.* falda *f.*
skull *n.* calavera *f.;* cráneo *m.*
sky *n.* cielo *m.*
sky blue *n., adj. (color)* azul *m.* celeste
skylight *n.* tragaluz *m.*
skyscraper *n.* rascacielos *m., sing.*
sleep *n.* sueño *m.*
sleep *v.i.* dormir (o:ue)
fall asleep dormirse (o:ue)
I couldn't fall asleep last night. No pude dormirme anoche.
go to sleep dormirse (o:ue)
sleepy: be sleepy tener sueño
sleeping bag *n.* saco *m.* de dormir
sleeve *n.* manga *f.*
slender *adj. (person)* delgado/a, esbelto/a
slice *n.* trozo *m.;* rebanada *f.* **a slice of bread** una rebanada de pan; rodaja *f.* **sliced onions** rodajas de cebolla
slice *v.t.* cortar
slide *n. (photo.)* diapositiva *f.*
slim down *v.* adelgazar
slippers *n., pl.* pantuflas *f., pl.*
slope *n.* ladera *f.* **The group ascended the northern slope.** El equipo subió por la ladera norte.
slot machine *n.* tragaperras *(Spain) f., sing.;* tragamonedas *(L.A.) f., sing.*
sloth *n.* perezoso *m.*
slow *adj.* lento/a; *adv.* despacio
slowly *adv.* despacio

small *adj.* pequeño/a
small intestine *n.* intestino *m.* delgado
smallpox *n.* viruela *f.*
smart *adj.* listo/a
smell *n. (sense)* olfato *m.;* olor *m.* **The smell of gasoline makes me sick.** El olor a gasolina me da asco.
smell (like) *v.i.* oler (a) **It smells like smoke here.** Huele a humo aquí.
smile *n.* sonrisa *f.*
smile *v.i.* sonreír (e:i)
smiled *p.p.* sonreído (*of* sonreír)
smoggy: It's (very) smoggy. Hay (mucha) contaminación.
smoke *n.* humo *m.*
smoke *v.t./v.i.* fumar
smoking section *n.* sección *f.* de fumar
non smoking section sección de no fumar
not to smoke no fumar
smother *v.t. (fire)* sofocar
snack *n. (in the afternoon)* merienda *f.; (at a bar)* tapa *f.*
snack *v.i.* merendar
have an afternoon snack merendar
snail *n.* caracol *m.*
snake *n.* serpiente *f.;* culebra *f.;* víbora *f.*
sneakers *n., pl.* zapatos *m., pl.* de tenis
sneeze *v.i.* estornudar
snob *n.* esnob *m., f.*
snobbery *n.* esnobismo *m.*
snobby *adj.* esnob
snore *n.* ronquido *m.*
snore *v.i.* roncar
snorkel *n.* esnórkel *m.*
snow *n.* nieve *f.*
snow *v.imp.* nevar (e:ie) **It's snowing.** Nieva.
so *adv.* tan; *(in such a way)* así **It's so big.** Es tan grande.
and so on y así sucesivamente
so much *adv.* tanto
so so *adv.* así así; regular; más o menos
so that *conj.* para que
soap *n.* jabón *m.*
soap dish *n.* jabonera *f.*
soap opera *n.* telenovela *f.*
sob *n.* sollozo *m.*
sob *v.i.* sollozar
sober *adj.* sobrio/a
sobriety test *n.* prueba *f.* de la alcoholemia
soccer *n.* fútbol *m.*
soccer field *n.* campo *m.* de fútbol
soccer player *n.* futbolista *m., f.*
sociable *adj.* sociable
socialize *v.i.* socializar
society *n.* sociedad *f.*
sociologist *n.* sociólogo/a *m., f*
sociology *n.* sociología *f.*
sock *n.* calcetín *m.*
soda *n.* refresco *m.*
sodium *n.* sodio *m.*
sofa *n.* sofá *m.*
soft *adj. (to the touch)* suave; esponjoso/a
soft drink *n.* refresco *m.*
software *n.* programa *m.* de computación

soil *n.* tierra *f.*
solar *adj.* solar
solarium *n.* solario *m.*
soldier *n.* soldado *m., f.*
solution *n. (to a problem)* resolución *f.; solución f.*
solve *v.t.* resolver (o:ue); solucionar
some *pron., adj.* algún, alguno/a(s); unos/as, *m., f., pl., indef. art.*
somebody *pron.* alguien
someone *pron.* alguien
somersault *n.* salto *m.* mortal; voltereta *f.*
something *pron.* algo
  something like that algo por el estilo
sometimes *adv.* a veces
son *n.* hijo *m.*
son-in-law *n.* yerno *m.*
song *n.* canción *f.*
soon *adv.* pronto
  as soon as en cuanto; tan pronto como
  as soon as possible lo antes posible
soprano *n.* soprano *m., f.*
sorbet *n.* sorbete *m.*
sore *adj.* adolorido/a
sorry: be sorry sentir(se) (e:ie); arrepentirse
  I'm extremely sorry. Mil perdones.
  I'm sorry. Lo siento.
soul *n.* alma (el) *f.*
soup *n.* sopa *f.; (broth)* caldo *m.*
  beef soup caldo de patas
sour *adj.* agrio/a
south *n.* sur *m.*
  to the south al sur
South American *n., adj.* sudamericano/a *m., f.*
souvenir *n.* recuerdo *m.*
spa *n.* balneario *m.*
space shuttle *n.* transbordador *m.*
spaghetti *n.* espagueti *m.*
Spain *n.* España *f.*
Spaniard *n.* español(a) *m., f.*
Spanish *n., adj.* español(a) *m., f.; (language)* español
spare time *n.* ratos *m., pl.* libres; tiempo *m.* libre
spare tire *n.* rueda *f.* de recambio/repuesto
spark plug *n.* bujía *f.*
sparkling wine *n.* cava *m.*
sparrow *n.* gorrión *m.*
spatula *n.* espátula *f.*
speak *v.i.* hablar
Special Olympics *n., pl.* Olimpiadas *f., pl.* Especiales
specialist *n.* especialista *m., f.*
specialization *n.* especialización *f.*
specialize (in something) *v.i.* especializarse (en algo)
species *n.* especie *f.*
  protected species *n.* especie *f.* protegida
spectacular *adj.* espectacular
spectator *n.* espectador(a) *m., f.*
speech *n.* discurso *m.*
speed *n.* velocidad *f.*
  speed limit *n.* velocidad *f.* máxima
speed *v.* ir a exceso de velocidad

spelling *n., adj.* ortografía *f.;* ortográfico/a
spend *v.t. (money)* gastar
spend time pasar tiempo
sphere *n.* esfera *f.*
spicy *adj.* picante
spider *n.* araña *f.*
spiderweb *n.* telaraña *f.*
spill *v.t.* derramar
spill over *v.* derramarse
spinach *n.* espinaca *f.*
spinal column *n.* columna *f.* vertebral
spine *n.* columna *f.* vertebral
spleen *n.* bazo *m.*
spoiled (child) *n.* (*niño/a*) *m., f.* mimado/a/consentido/a
spokesperson *n.* portavoz *m., f.*
sponge *n.* esponja *f.*
spongy *adj.* esponjoso/a
sponsor *n.* patrocinador(a) *m., f.*
sponsor *v.t.* patrocinar
spontaneous *adj.* espontáneo/a
spoon *n.* (*table or large*) cuchara *f.*
sport *n.* deporte *m.*
sports-loving *adj.* deportivo/a
sports-related *adj.* deportivo/a
sporting *adj.* deportista
sporting goods *n., pl.* artículos *m., pl.* de deporte
sports car *n.* carro *m.* deportivo
sports center *n.* polideportivo *m.*
sports facilities *n., pl.* instalaciones *f., pl.* deportivas
sports-loving *adj.* deportivo/a
sportswear *n.* ropa *f.* deportiva
spouse *n.* esposo/a *m., f.*
sprain *n.* esguince
sprain (an ankle) *v.t.* torcerse (el tobillo)
sprained *adj.* torcido/a
be sprained estar torcido/a
spread *v.t. (information)* divulgar; propagar **Some papers spread rumors.** Algunos periódicos propagan rumores.; propagarse **The rumor was spreading rapidly.** El rumor se propagaba rápidamente.; *(butter, etc.)* untar
spreading *n. (news, ideas)* divulgación *f.*
spring *n. (season)* primavera *f.; (coil)* muelle *m.,* resorte *m.; (water)* manantial *m.*
sprinkle *v.t. (sugar, etc.)* espolvorear
square *n.* cuadrado *m.*
square: city or town square *n.* plaza *f.*
squat *v.i.* agacharse
squid *n.* calamar *m.*
squirrel *n.* ardilla *f.*
stable *n.* establo *m.*
stack *v.t.* apilar
stadium *n.* estadio *m.*
stage *n.* etapa *f.; (theater)* escenario *m.*
the stages of life las etapas de la vida
stained-glass window *n.* vidriera *f.* (de colores)

stainless steel *n.* acero *m.* inoxidable
stair *n.* escalón *m.;* peldaño *m.*
stairs *n.* escalera *f.*
stairway *n.* escalera *f.*
stammer *v.i.* tartamudear
stamp *n.* estampilla *(L.A.) f.;* sello *(Spain) m.*
stamp collecting *n.* filatelia *f.*
stand *v.i. (person)* estar parado *(L.A.);* estar de pie
stand in line *v.* hacer cola
stand out *v.* sobresalir
stand somebody up *v.* dejar a alguien plantado/a
star *n.* estrella *f.*
starry *adj.* estrellado/a
start *v.t. (vehicle)* arrancar; *(begin)* empezar (e:ie), comenzar (e:ie)
state *n.* estado *m.*
station *n. (train, bus)* estación *f.*
statue *n.* estatua *f.*
status: marital status estado *m.* civil
stay *n.* estancia *f.* **Our stay in La Coruña was magnificent.** Nuestra estancia en La Coruña fue magnífica.
stay *v.i.* quedarse*; (hotel)* alojarse
stay up all night *v.* trasnochar
steady *adj.* fijo/a
steak *n.* bistec *m.*
steal *v.t.* robar
steam *n.* vapor *m.*
steel *n.* acero *m.*
steering wheel *n.* volante *m.*
step *n.* etapa *f.;* paso *m.; (stair)* escalón *m.,* peldaño *m.*
stepbrother *n.* hermanastro *m.*
stepdaughter *n.* hijastra *f.*
stepfather *n.* padrastro *m.*
stepmother *n.* madrastra *f.*
stepsister *n.* hermanastra *f.*
stepson *n.* hijastro *m.*
stereo *n.* estéreo *m.*
sterile *adj.* estéril
sterilize *v.t.* esterilizar
stethoscope *n.* estetoscopio *m.*
stew *n.* guiso *m.*
stick *v.t.* pegar
stifling *adj. (heat)* sofocante, agobiante **The heat is stifling.** Este calor es agobiante.
still *adv.* todavía, aún, ya
stingy *adj.* tacaño/a
stir *v.t.* remover
stockbroker *n.* bolsista *m., f.;* corredor(a) *m., f.* de bolsa
stockings *n.* medias *f., pl.*
stomach *n.* estómago *m. f.* **get an upset stomach** empacharse
stomach disorder *n.* trastorno *m.* estomacal
stone *n.* piedra *f.*
stool *n.* taburete *m.*
stop *v.i.* parar(se)
stop *(doing something)* *v.* dejar de (+ *inf.)*
stop sign *n.* señal *m.* de alto
storage *n.* almacenamiento *m.*
store *n.* tienda *f.*
store *v.t.* almacenar
stork *n.* cigüeña *f.*
storm *n.* tormenta *f.*
story *n.* cuento *m.;* historia *f.*

stove *n.* estufa *f.;* cocina *(Spain) f.*
straight *adj.* derecho/a; recto/a; *(hair)* lacio/a
straight *adv.* derecho
straight ahead (todo) derecho
straighten up *v.* arreglar
strain *v.t.* colar
strange *adj.* extraño/a
It's strange (that...) Es extraño (que...)
straw *n.* paja *f.; (drinking)* pajita *f.,* popote *m.*
That's the last straw! *loc.* ¡Esto es el colmo!
strawberry *n.* fresa *f.,* frutilla *(Ecuador) f.*
stream *n.* riachuelo *m.*
streamer *n.* serpentina *f.*
street *n.* calle *m.*
street light *n.* semáforo *m.*
stress *n.* estrés *m.;* tensión *f.*
under stress *adj.* estresado/a
stress *v.t.* destacar, enfatizar, recalcar
stressful *adj.* estresante
stretch *v.t.* estirar
stretcher *n.* camilla *f.*
stretching *n.* estiramiento *m.*
do stretching exercises hacer ejercicios *m., pl.* de estiramiento
strike *n. (labor)* huelga *f.*
striker *n.* huelguista *m., f.*
stripe *n.* raya *f.*
striped *adj.* de rayas
stroke *n. (swimming)* estilo *m.*
stroll *v.i.* pasear
strong *adj.* fuerte
struggle (for/against; to + *inf.*) *v.* luchar (por/contra; para + *inf.*)
stubborn *adj.* testarudo/a
student *n., adj.* estudiante *m., f.;* estudiantil
student desk *n.* pupitre *m.*
studious *adj.* estudioso/a
study *v.t./v.i.* estudiar
stuff *v.t. (culinary)* rellenar
stuff oneself *v.* hartarse
stuffed *adj.* relleno/a
I love stuffed chilies. Adoro los chiles rellenos.
stuffed-up *adj.* congestionado/a
stuffing *n.* relleno *m.*
stunned *adj.* atontado/a
stupendous *adj.* estupendo/a
stutter *v.i.* tartamudear
style *n.* estilo *m.*
subject matter *n.* temática *f.*
subject *n. (university)* disciplina *f.;* tema *m.*
subjective *adj.* subjetivo/a
submarine *n.* submarino *m.*
substance *n.* sustancia *f.*
substitute *n.* sustituto/a *m., f.*
substitute *v.t.* sustituir
He substituted coffe for tea. Sustituyó el café por el té.
subterranean *adj.* subterráneo/a
suburbs *n.* afueras *f., pl.*
subway *n.* metro *m.*
go by subway ir en metro
subway station *n.* estación *f.* del metro
succeed *v.i.* triunfar
success *n.* éxito *m.*

be successful tener éxito
successively *adv.* sucesivamente
such as [tal(es)] como
She used words such as justice and freedom. Usó palabras (tales) como justicia y libertad.
suddenly *adv.* de repente
suffer *v.t.* sufrir
suffer an illness sufrir una enfermedad
suffer from *v. (disease)* padecer de **He suffers from heart problems.** Padece del corazón.
suffering *n.* padecimiento *m.*
sufficient *adj.* bastante
suffocation *n.* sofoco *m.*
sugar *n.* azúcar *m.*
sugar bowl *n.* azucarero *m.*
suggest *v.t.* sugerir (e:ie)
suggestion *n.* sugerencia *f.*
suicide *n.* suicidio *m.*
commit suicide suicidarse
suit *n.* traje *m.*
suit *v.t. (clothes)* sentar
That jacket suits you. Esa chaqueta te sienta bien.
suitable *adj.* apto/a
suitcase *n.* maleta *f.*
summer *n.* verano *m.*
summer *v.i.* veranear
She summers in the mountains. Veranea en las montañas.
summit *n.* cima *f.*
sumptuous *adj.* suntuoso/a
sun *n.* sol *m.*
sunbathe *v.i.* tomar el sol; tumbarse al sol
Sunday *n.* domingo *m.*
sunflower *n.* girasol *m.*
sunglasses *n., pl.* lentes *m., pl.* de sol; gafas *f., pl.* oscuras/negras/de sol
sunny *adj.* soleado/a
It's (very) sunny. Hace (mucho) sol.
sunrise *n.* salida *f.* del sol
sunset *n.* puesta *f.* de(l) sol
sunshade *n.* sombrilla *f.*
suntan lotion *n.* bronceador *m.*
sun-tanned *adj.* bronceado/a
supermarket *n.* supermercado *m.*
superstition *n.* superstición *f.*
superstitious *adj.* supersticioso/a
supervise *v.t.* supervisar
supper *n.* cena *f.*
supplier *n.* suministrador(a) *m., f.*
supplies *n., pl.* provisiones *f., pl.;* víveres *m., pl.*
supply *n.* suministro *m.*
supply *v.t.* suministrar
support *v.t.* apoyar; sostener; soportar; respaldar
suppose *v.t.* suponer
Supreme Court *n.* Corte *f.* Suprema *(L.A.);* Tribunal *m.* Supremo *(Spain)*
sure *adj.* seguro/a
be sure estar seguro/a
surf (the Internet) *v.i.* navegar (en Internet)
surgeon *n.* cirujano/a *m., f.*
surgery *n.* cirugía *f.*
surprise *n.* sorpresa *f.*

What a surprise! ¡Qué sorpresa!
surprise *v.t.* sorprender
be surprised sorprenderse
He was surprised to see me. Se sorprendió al verme.
surrounding area *n.* alrededores *m., pl.*
survey *n.* encuesta *f.*
survival *n.* supervivencia *f.*
survivor *n.* superviviente *m., f.*
suspect *v.t.* sospechar
suspenders *n., pl.* tirantes *m., pl.*
suspense: in suspense *adj.* intrigado/a
suspension bridge *n.* puente *f.* colgante
suspicion *n.* sospecha *f.*
suspicious *adj.* sospechoso/a
swallow *v.t./v.i.* tragar
swamp *n.* pantano *m.;* ciénaga *f.*
swan *n.* cisne *m.*
swear *v.t.* jurar
sweat *v.i.* sudar
sweater *n.* suéter *m.*
sweaty *adj.* sudado/a
sweep (the floor) *v.t.* barrer (el piso/suelo)
sweet *adj.* dulce
sweets *n., pl.* dulces *m., pl.*
swim *v.i.* nadar
swimmer *n.* nadador(a) *m., f.*
swimming *n.* natación *f.*
synchronized swimming natación sincronizada
swimming pool *n.* piscina *f.;* alberca *(Mexico) f.*
swimming suit *n.* traje *m.* de baño
symbiosis *n.* simbiosis *f.*
symbolize *v.t.* simbolizar
symphonic *adj.* sinfónico/a
symphony *n.* sinfonía *f.*
symphony orchestra *n.* sinfónica *f.*
symptom *n.* síntoma *m.*
synonym *n.* sinónimo *m.*
synonymous *adj.* sinónimo/a
syntax *n.* sintaxis *f.*
syringe *n.* jeringa *f.*
syrup *n.* almíbar *m.*
system *n.* sistema *f.*

T

table *n.* mesa *f.*
tablecloth *n.* mantel *m.*
tablespoon *n.* cuchara *f.*
tablet *n. (pill)* pastilla *f.*
tactful *adj.* diplomático/a
tactless *adj.* indiscreto/a
tail *n.* cola *f.*
tailor *n.* sastre *m.*
take *v.t.* llevar; tomar; traer
take a bath *v. pron.* bañarse
take a shower *v. pron.* ducharse
take a trip *v.* hacer un viaje
take someone somewhere llevar
take advantage of *v.* aprovecharse de
take back *v.t.* devolver
take care of cuidar
take care of oneself cuidarse
take care of clients *v.i.* atender a los clientes
take off *v. (clothes)* quitarse; *(airplane, rocket)* despegar

take off one's shoes descalzarse
take-off *n.* despegue *m.*
take offense *v.* ofenderse
take out (the trash) *v.* sacar (la basura)
take out (walk) the dog sacar al perro a pasear
take the risk *v.* arriesgarse
take up *v. (hobby)* aficionarse
talented *adj.* talentoso/a
talk *v.i.* hablar; conversar
talk show *n.* programa *m.* de entrevistas
talkative *adj. (person)* hablador(a); charlatán, charlatana
tall *adj.* alto/a
tan *v.t.* broncear; *v.i.* broncearse
tangerine *n.* mandarina *f.*
tangy *adj.* ácido/a
tank *n.* depósito *m.;* tanque *m.*
tanned *adj.* moreno/a
tantrum *n.* berrinche *m.*
throw tantrums hacer berrinches
tape *n.* cinta *f.*
tape recorder *n.* grabadora *f.*
tapestry *n.* tapiz *m.*
target shooting *n.* tiro *m.* al blanco
tart *adj.* ácido/a
taste *n. (senses)* gusto *m.*
taste *v.t.* probar (o:ue)
tasteless *adj.* soso/a
tasty *adj.* rico/a, sabroso/a
tax *n.* impuesto *m.*
taxi(cab) *n.* taxi *m.*
go by taxi ir en taxi
tea *n.* té *m.*
herbal tea *n.* infusión *f.* (de hierbas)
teabag *n.* bolsita *f.* de té
teach *v.t.* enseñar
teacher *n.* profesor(a) *m., f.; (elementary school)* maestro/a *m., f.*
team *n.* equipo *m.*
technical team equipo de técnicos
teapot *n.* tetera *f.*
tear *n.* lágrima *f.*
tear gas *n.* gas *m.* lacrimógeno
technician *n.* técnico/a *m., f.*
teddy bear *n.* osito *m.* de peluche
telecommuting *n.* teletrabajo *m.*
teleconference *n.* videoconferencia *f.*
telephone *n.* teléfono *m.*
cellular telephone teléfono celular
by phone por teléfono
telescope *n.* telescopio *m.*
television *n.* televisión *f.; (set)* televisor *m.*
tell *v.* decir; contar
temperament *n.* temperamento *m.*
temperature *n.* temperatura *f.*
take (someone's) temperature tomar la temperatura (a alguien)
temple *n.* templo *m.*
ten diez
tendency *n.* tendencia *f.*
tender *adj. (meat; loving)* tierno/a
tendon *n.* tendón *m.*

tennis *n. (sport)* tenis *m.; (sneakers)* tenis *m.*
tennis court *n.* pista *f.* de tenis
tennis player *n.* tenista *m., f.*
tennis shoes *n.* zapatillas *f., pl.* de deporte; zapatos *m., pl.* de tenis
tenor *n.* tenor *m.*
tension *n.* tensión *f.*
tent *n.* tienda *f.* (de campaña)
tenth décimo *m.; adj.* décimo/a
terrace *n.* terraza *f.*
terrible *adj.* terrible
It's terrible (that...) Es terrible (que...)
terrific *adj.* genial, fantástico, estupendo, chévere
terrorist *n., adj.* terrorista *m., f.*
terrorist attack *n.* atentado *m.* terrorista
test *n.* examen *m.;* prueba *f.;* evaluación *f.*
placement test prueba de nivel
aptitude test prueba de aptitud
test *v.t.* evaluar
thanks *interj.* gracias
Thank you. Gracias.
Thank you very much. Muchas gracias.
Thank you very, very much. Muchísimas gracias.
Thanks (a lot). (Muchas) gracias.
Thanks again. Gracias una vez más.
Thanks for everything. Gracias por todo.
that (one) ése, esa, eso *pron.;* ese, esa *adj.*
that (over there) aquél, aquélla, aquello *pron.;* aquel, aquella *adj.*
that *conj.* que
that which *conj.* lo que
that's why por eso
theater *n.* teatro *m.;* auditorio
theft *n.* robo *m.*
their su(s) *poss. adj.;* suyo(s)/suya(s) *poss. pron.*
thematic *adj.* temático/a
theme *n.* tema *m.*
then *adv. (afterward)* después (de); *(as a result)* entonces; *(next)* luego, pues
theorize *v.i.* teorizar
theory *n.* teoría *f.*
therapeutic *adj.* terapeútico/a
therapy *n.* terapia *f.*
there *adv.* allí
There is/are... Hay...
There is/are not... No hay...
therefore *adv.* por eso; por lo tanto
thermostat *m.* termostato
these estos, estas *adj.;* éstos, éstas *pron.*
thesis *f.* tesis
thief *n.* ladrón *m.,* ladrona *f.*
thigh *n.* muslo *m.*
thin *adj.* delgado/a
thing *n.* cosa *f.*
think *v.t.* pensar (e:ie); *(believe)* creer
What do you think? *form.* ¿Qué le/les parece?
think about *v.* pensar en
third tercio *m.; adj.* tercer, tercero/a

third-world country *n.* país *m.* tercermundista
thirst *n.* sed *f.*
be thirsty tener sed
thirsty *adj.* sediento/a
thirteen trece
thirty treinta; *(minutes past the hour)* y treinta, y media
It's six thirty. Son las seis y treinta/media.
this este, esta *adj.*; éste, ésta, esto *pron.*
This is he/she. *(on the phone)* Con él/ella habla.
thorn *n.* espina *f.*
those esos, esas *adj.*; ésos, ésas pron.
thread *n.* hilo *m.*
threat *n.* amenaza *f.*
threaten *v.t.* amenazar
three tres
three hundred trescientos/as
thrilled *adj.* ilusionado/a
throat *n.* garganta *f.*
through *prep.* por; a través de
throw *n.* lanzamiento *m.*
throw *v.t.* echar; tirar; lanzar
throw away *v.t. (leftovers)* desechar, tirar
thunder *n.* trueno *m.*
Thursday *n.* jueves *m., sing.*
thus *adv.* así
thyme *n.* tomillo *m.*
ticket *n. (show)* boleto *(L.A.) m.*; entrada *(Spain) f.; (trip)* pasaje; (*fine*) multa *f.*
tidal wave *n.* maremoto *m.*
tidy *adj.* arreglado/a
tie *n. (clothing)* corbata *f.; (sports)* empate *m.; (bond)* lazo *m.*, vínculo *m*
family ties lazos familiares
tie *v.t.* atar; *(sports)* empatar
tiger *n.* tigre *m.*
tile *n. (ceramic)* azulejo *m.; (floor)* baldosa *f.; (roof)* teja *f.*
time *n.* tiempo *m.; (occasion)* vez *f.*
We have time. Tenemos tiempo.
We had a great time. Lo pasamos de película/super bien.
What time is it? ¿Qué hora es?
ahead of time con anticipación
full-time tiempo completo
many times muchas veces
on time a tiempo
one more time una vez más
one time una vez
part-time tiempo parcial
time trial *n.* carrera *n.* contra reloj
timid *adj.* tímido/a
tinfoil *n.* papel *m.* de aluminio
tiny *adj.* minúsculo/a
tip *n.* propina *f.*
leave a tip dejar una propina
tire *n.* llanta *f.*; neumático *m.*
tire oneself out *v.* cansarse
tired *adj.* cansado/a
be tired estar cansado/a
tissue *n. (anat.)* tejido *m.*; pañuelo *m.* de papel
title *n.* título *m.*
to *prep.* a
toad *n.* sapo *m.*
toast *n.* pan *m.* tostado;

tostada *f.; (drinking)* brindis *m.*
toast *v.t.* tostar; *(drinking)* brindar (por)
toasted *adj.* tostado/a
toasted bread pan tostado
toaster *n.* tostadora *f.*
today *adv.* hoy
Today is... Hoy es...
toe *n.* dedo *m.* (del pie)
together *adj.* juntos/as
toilet *n.* inodoro *m.*
toiletry kit *n.* neceser *m.*
toilet paper *n.* papel *m.* higiénico
tolerance *n.* tolerancia *f.*
tolerant *adj.* tolerante
tolerate *v.t.* tolerar
tomato *n.* tomate *m.*
tomorrow *adv.* mañana
tongs *n., pl.* tenazas *f., pl.*
tonight *adv.* esta noche
tonsil *n.* amígdala *f.*
too *adv.* también
too much *adv.* demasiado; en exceso
tool *n.* herramienta *f.*
tooth *n.* diente *m.; (back)* muela *f.*
pull a tooth sacar una muela
I had a tooth pulled. Me sacaron una muela.
toothbrush *n.* cepillo *m.* de dientes
toothpaste *n.* pasta *f.* de dientes
toothpick *n.* mondadientes *m., sing.;* palillo *m.* (de dientes)
top *n.* cima *f.*
torch *n.* antorcha *f.*
tornado *n.* tornado *m.*
tortilla *n.* tortilla *f.*
toss *v.t.* tirar; mezclar
touch *n. (sense)* tacto *m.*
touch *v.t.* tocar
tour *n.* visita *f.* turística; viaje *m.*
go on a tour hacer una excursión
tour around an area excursión *f.*
tourism *n.* turismo *m.*
tourist *adj.* turístico/a
tourist *n.* turista *m., f.*
toward *prep.* hacia
towel *n.* toalla *f.*
towel bar *n.* toallero *m.*
tower *n.* torre *f.*
town *n.* pueblo *m.*
town square *n.* plaza *f.* mayor
toy *n.* juguete *m.*
toy store *n.* juguetería *f.*
track *n.* pista *f.; (sport)* pista de atletismo; *(railroad)* vía *f.*
indoor track *n.* pista *f.* cubierta
track and field *n.* atletismo *m.*
trade *n.* oficio *m.*
tradition *n.* tradición *f.*
traffic *n.* circulación *f.;* tráfico *m.*
traffic (in) *v.t.* traficar (en)
traffic jam *n.* atasco *m.;* embotellamiento *m.* (de tráfico) *(Spain)*
traffic sign *n.* señal *f.* de tráfico
traffic signal *n.* semáforo *m.*
tragedy *n.* tragedia *f.*
tragic *adj.* trágico/a

trail *n.* sendero *m.*
trailer *n.* caravana *f.*
trailhead *n.* sendero *m.*
train *n.* tren *m.*
go by train ir en tren
train station estación *f.* de tren
train *v.i.* entrenarse
trainer *n.* entrenador(a) *m., f.;* monitor(a) *m., f.*
training *n.* entrenamiento *m.;* capacitación *f.*
traitor *n.* traidor(a) *m., f.*
trajectory *n.* trayectoria *f.*
transfer *n.* transferencia *f.*
transfusion *n.* transfusión *f.*
translate *v.t.* traducir
translation *n.* traducción *f.*
translator *n.* traductor(a) *m., f.*
transparent *adj.* transparente
transplant *n.* transplante *m.*
transport *v.t.* transportar
transportation *n.* transporte *m.*
trapshooting *n.* tiro *m.* al plato
trash *n.* basura *f.*
travel *v.i.* viajar; desplazarse
travel agency *n.* agencia *f.* de viajes
travel agent *n.* agente *m., f.* de viajes
travel document *n.* documento *m.* de viaje
traveler *n.* viajero/a *m., f.*
traveler's check *n.* cheque *m.* de viajero
treacherous *adj.* traicionero/a, traidor(a); peligroso/a
treachery *n.* traición *f.*
treadmill cinta caminadora
treason *n.* traición *f.*
treasure *n.* tesoro *m.*
tree *n.* árbol *m.*
trendy: be trendy ir a la moda
trial *n.* juicio *m.*
triangle *n.* triángulo *m.*
tribute *n.* homenaje *m.*
tricycle *n.* triciclo *m.*
trigger *n. (firearm)* gatillo *m.*
trigonometry *n.* trigonometría *f.*
trimester *n.* trimestre *m.*
trip *n.* viaje *m.;* desplazamiento *m.*
go on/take a trip hacer un viaje
tripod *n.* trípode *m.*
triviality *n.* trivialidad *f.*
trivialize *v.t.* trivializar
trout *n.* trucha *f.*
truck *n.* camión *m.*
truck driver *n.* camionero/a *m., f.*
true *adj.* verdadero/a; cierto
it's (not) true (no) es verdad
true-to-life *adj.* verosímil
trunk *n.* baúl *m.; (car)* maletero *(Spain) m.; (live tree)* tronco *m.*
truth *n.* verdad *f.*
try *n.* intento *m.*
try *v.t.* intentar; probar (o:ue)*; (to do something)* tratar de (+ *inf.)*
try hard *v.* esforzarse
try on *v. (clothes)* probarse (o:ue)
try out *v.t./v.i.* experimentar
t-shirt *n.* camiseta *f.*
tube *n.* tubo *m.*
tuberculosis *n.* tuberculosis *f.*
Tuesday *n.* martes *m., sing.*
tulip *n.* tulipán *m.*

tuna *n.* atún *m.*
tune up *v.t.* afinar
  out of tune *adj.* desafinado/a
tunnel *n.* túnel *m.*
turbine *n.* turbina *f.*
turkey *n.* pavo *m.*
turn *n.* giro *m.;* turno *m.;* vuelta *f.*
turn *v.t./v.i.* doblar; girar; dar(se) la vuelta **Turn left at the next corner.** Gira a la izquierda en la próxima esquina.
turn off *v.t. (electricity/appliance)* apagar
turn on *v.t. (electricity/appliance)* poner, encender; prender
turn over *v.t. (tortilla, cup)* voltear *(L.A.)*
turn signal *n. (car)* intermitente *m*
turquoise *n.* turquesa *f.*
turtle *n.* tortuga *f.*
tutor *n.* profesor(a) *m., f.* particular
tweezers *n., pl.* pinzas *f., pl.* (para depilar)
twelve doce
twenty veinte
twenty-eight veintiocho
twenty-five veinticinco
twenty-four veinticuatro
twenty-nine veintinueve
twenty-one veintiún, veintiuno/a
twenty-seven veintisiete
twenty-six veintiséis
twenty-three veintitrés
twenty-two veintidós
twice *adv.* dos veces
twin *n.* gemelo/a *m., f.;* mellizo/a *m., f.*
twisted *adj.* torcido/a
  be twisted estar torcido/a
two dos
  two times dos veces
two hundred doscientos/as
two weeks *n., pl.* quincena *f.*
type *n.* especie *f.*
type *v.i.* escribir a máquina; teclear
typewriter *n.* máquina *f.* de escribir
typist *n.* mecanógrafo/a *m., f.*

U

UFO (Unidentified Flying Object) *n.* OVNI *m.* (Objeto Volador No Identificado)
ugly *adj.* feo/a
umbrella *n.* paraguas *m.*
umbrella stand *n.* paragüero *m.*
umpire *n.* árbitro/a *m.*
unbearable *adj.* insoportable
unblock *v.t.* desatascar
uncertainty *n.* incertidumbre *f.*
uncle *n.* tío *m.*
under *adv.* bajo, debajo (de)
undergo *v.t. (test, examination)* someterse a
underground *adj.* subterráneo/a
underlined *adj.* subrayado/a
understand *v.t.* comprender; entender (e:ie)
understanding *n.* comprensión *f.*
underwear *n.* ropa *f.* interior
  long underwear *n.* calzoncillos *m., pl.* largos

undress *v.i.* desvestirse
unemployment *n.* desempleo *m.*
unexpected *adj.* inesperado/a
unfair *adj.* injusto/a
unfavorable *adj.* desfavorable
unforgettable *adj.* inolvidable
unfortunate *adj.* desgraciado/a
unfortunately *adv.* desafortunadamente; desgraciadamente
unfriendly *adj.* antipático/a; arisco/a
ungrateful *adj.* desagradecido/a
unhappy *adj.* infeliz; desgraciado/a
United States *n., pl.* Estados *m., pl.* Unidos
universe *n.* universo *m.*
university *n.* universidad *f.*
unkempt *adj. (appearance)* desarreglado/a
unless *adv.* a menos que
unlikely *adj.* improbable, poco probable
be unlikely that *(something will happen)* ser poco probable que (+ *subj.)* **It's unlikely that they will arrive on time.** Es poco probable que lleguen a tiempo.
unmarried *adj.* soltero/a
unnoticed *adj.* inadvertido/a
unpack *v.t.* desempacar
unpleasant *adj.* desagradable; *(person)* antipático/a
unresolved *adj.* pendiente
unsociable *adj.* insociable
unsuccessful *adj.* fracasado/a
unthinkable *adj.* impensable
until *adv.* hasta (que)
until *prep.* hasta
until now hasta ahora
unusual *adj.* inusual, poco corriente; insólito/a
unwillingly *adv.* de mala gana
up *adv.* arriba
up to date al día, al corriente
bring someone up to date *idiom* poner a uno al día/al corriente
upset enojado/a; molesto/a
urgent *adj.* urgente
It's (not) urgent that... (No) Es urgente que...
urinate *v.i.* orinar
urine *n.* orina *f.*
use *v.t.* usar
make good use of aprovechar
useful *adj.* útil; práctico/a
usually *adv.* soler (o:ue) +*inf.*
I usually study at night. Suelo estudiar por la noche.
utensil *n.* utensilio *m.*
uterus *n.* útero *m.*

V

vacation *n.* vacaciones *f., pl.*
be on vacation estar de vacaciones
go on vacation ir(se) de vacaciones
vacationer *n. (summer)* veraneante *m., f.*
vacuum *v.i.* pasar la aspiradora
vacuum cleaner *n.* aspiradora *f.*
vain *adj.* presumido/a

valley *n.* valle *m.*
value *n.* valor *m.*
value *v.t.* valorar
vanilla *n.* vainilla *f.*
vapor *n.* vapor *m.*
variation *n.* variación *f.*
varied *adj.* variado/a
variety *n.* surtido *m.*
various *adj.* varios/as
vary *v.i.* variar
vase *n.* florero *m.;* jarrón *m.*
VCR *n.* videocasetera *f.*
veal *n.* ternera *f.*
vegetables *n., pl.* verduras *f., pl.*
vegetation *n.* vegetación *f.*
vehicle *n.* vehículo *m.*
vein *n.* vena *f.*
velodrome *n.* velódromo *m.*
velvet *n.* terciopelo *m.*
verb *n.* verbo *m.*
verisimilitude *n.* verosimilitud *f.*
vermillion *n.* bermellón *m.*
vermouth *n.* vermut *m.*
versatile *adj.* versátil
vertebra *n.* vértebra *f.*
vertebrate *n., adj.* vertebrado *m.;* vertebrado/a
very *adv.* muy
Very good, thank you. Muy bien, gracias.
very well *adv.* muy bien
very much *adv.* muchísimo/a
vest *n.* chaleco *m.*
veterinarian *n.* veterinario/a *m., f.*
veterinary science *n.* veterinaria *f.*
vibrate *v.i.* vibrar
vibration *n.* vibración *f.*
video *n.* video *(L.A.) m.;* vídeo *(Spain) m.*
video(cassette) *n.* video(casete) *m.*
video camera *n.* cámara *f.* de video
videoconference *n.* videoconferencia *f.*
visor n. visera f.
view *n.* vista *f.*
village *n.* aldea *f.*
vinegar *n.* vinagre *m.*
violence *n.* violencia *f.*
visit *v.t.* visitar
visit monuments visitar monumentos
visiting team *n. (sports)* equipo *m.* visitante
visitor *n.* visitante *m., f.*
visor *n.* visera *f.*
vitamin *n.* vitamina *f.*
vocational training *n.* formación *f.* profesional
volcano *n.* volcán *m.*
volleyball *n.* vóleibol *m.*
volume *n.* volumen *m.*
voluntary *adj.* voluntario
volunteer *n.* voluntario/a *m., f.*
vomit *v.i.* vomitar
vote *n.* voto *m.*
vote *v.i.* votar
vulture *n.* buitre *m.*

W

wage *n.* sueldo *m.*
waist *n.* cintura *f.*
wait (for) *v.i.* esperar
be waiting estar pendiente

I'm waiting for Woody to call me. Estoy pendiente de que Woody me llame.
waiter *n.* camarero *m.;* mesero *m.;* mozo *m. (L.A.)*
waitress *n.* camarera *f.;* mesera *f.;* moza *f. (L.A.)*
wake up *v.i.* despertarse (e:ie)
walk *v.i.* caminar
go for a walk dar un paseo
take a walk pasear
walk around the city/the town pasear por la ciudad/el pueblo
walking stick *n.* bastón *m.*
Walkman *n.* walkman *m.*
wall *n.* pared *f.;* muro *m.*
wallet *n.* cartera *f.*
walnut *n.* nuez *f.*
walnut tree *n.* nogal *m.*
want *v.t.* querer (e:ie)
I don't want to. No quiero.
war *n.* guerra *f.*
wardrobe *n.* ropero *m.;* vestuario *m.*
warm (oneself) up *v.* calentarse (e:ie)
warranty *n.* garantía *f.*
wart *n.* verruga *f.*
wash *v.t.* lavar*; v.ref. (oneself)* lavarse
wash one's face/hands lavarse la cara/las manos
wash the floor lavar el piso
washing machine *n.* lavadora *f.*
wasp *n.* avispa *f.*
waste *v.t.* malgastar
wastebasket *n.* papelera *f.*
watch *n.* reloj *m.*
watch *v.t./v.i.* mirar; ver
watch television mirar (la) televisión
watch out *interj.* cuidado
water *n.* agua (el) *f.*
drinking water agua potable
fresh water agua dulce
holy water agua bendita
mineral water agua mineral
salt water agua salada
water *v.t. (plants)* regar
water park *n.* parque *m.* acuático
water skiing *n.* esquí *m.* acuático
waterfall *n.* catarata *f.*
watering can *n.* regadera *f.*
watermelon *n.* sandía *f.*
waterproof *adj.* impermeable
waterskiing *n.* esquí *m.* acuático
wave *n. (water)* ola *f.; (physics, radio)* onda *f.*
wax *n.* cera *f.*
wax *v.t.* encerar*; (legs)* depilarse
way *n.* manera *f.;* camino *m.*
weak *adj.* débil
weapon *n.* arma (el) *f.*
wear *v.t.* llevar*;* usar; ponerse
wear a costume disfrazarse de
wear for the first time estrenar
wear oneself out *v.* fatigarse
weary *adj.* fatigado/a
weather *n.* tiempo *m.*
It's nice/bad weather. Hace buen/mal tiempo.
What's the weather like?

¿Qué tiempo hace?
weaving *n.* tejido *m.*
Web *n.* red *f.*
website *n.* sitio *m.* web
wedding *n.* boda *f.*
wedding ring *n.* anillo *m.* de bodas
Wednesday *n.* miércoles *m., sing.*
week *n.* semana *f.*
next week semana entrante, semana que viene
weekdays, (on) entre semana
weekend *n.* fin *m.* de semana
weigh oneself *v.* pesarse
weight *n.* pesa *f.;* peso *m.*
weightless *adj.* ingrávido/a
weightlifting *n. (sport)* halterofilia *f.*
welcome *adj.* bienvenido/a(s)
You're welcome. *(responding to thanks)* De nada; No hay de qué
weld *v.t.* soldar
welding *n.* soldadura *f.*
well *adv.* bien; pues; bueno
well *n.* pozo *m.*
well-being *n.* bienestar *m.*
well-known *adj.* conocido/a
be well-known for tener fama de
well-mannered *adj.* educado/a
well-organized *adj.* ordenado/a
west *n.* oeste *m.*
to the west al oeste
western *adj. (genre)* ...de vaqueros
a western una (película) de vaqueros
wet *adj.* mojado/a
wet *v.t.* mojar
get wet mojarse
whale *n.* ballena *f.*
wharf *n.* embarcadero *m.*
what *rel. pron.* lo que
what? *adj., pron.* ¿qué?
What did you say? ¿Cómo?
What's going on? ¿Qué pasa?
What a . . . ! ¡Qué...!
What a drag! *loc.* ¡Qué lata!
wheat *n.* trigo *m.*
wheel *n.* rueda *f.*
wheel chair *n.* silla *f.* de ruedas
wheelbarrow *n.* carretilla *f.*
when *adv., conj.* cuando
when? *adv.* ¿cuándo?
when all's said and done *loc.* a fin de cuentas
where *prep.* donde
where? *adv. (destination)* ¿adónde?; *(location)* ¿dónde?
Where are you from? *(fam.)* ¿De dónde eres?; *(form.)* ¿De dónde es Ud.?
Where is . . .? ¿Dónde está...?
which? *adj., pron.* ¿cuál(es)?; ¿qué?
which one(s)? ¿cuál(es)?
while *adv.* mientras
whim *n.* antojo *m.;* capricho *m.*
whine *v.i.* lloriquear
whisk *v.t.* batir
whisk *n.* batidor *m.*
whistle *n.* silbato *m.*
whistle *v.i.* silbar
white *n., adj.* blanco *m.;*

blanco/a
who *pron.* que **Is there anyone who speaks English?** ¿Hay alguien que hable inglés?; quien(es)
who? *pron.* ¿quién(es)?
Who is . . . ? ¿Quién es...?
Who is calling? *(on telephone)* ¿De parte de quién?
Who is speaking? *(on telephone)* ¿Quién habla?
whole *adj.* todo/a
whole-wheat bread *n.* pan *m.* integral
whose? *adj., pron.* ¿de quién(es)?
why? *adv.* ¿por qué?
wicker *n.* mimbre *m.*
widow *adj.* viuda
widowed *adj.* viudo/a
widower *adj.* viudo
wife *n.* esposa *f.*
wig *n.* peluca *f.*
wild *adj. (animal)* salvaje; *(plant)* silvestre
willingly *adv.* de buena gana
win *v.t.* ganar; vencer
wind *n.* viento *m.*
It's (very) windy. Hace (mucho) viento.
window *n.* ventana *f.;* cristal *m.*
windshield *n.* parabrisas *m., sing.*
windshield wiper *n.* limpiaparabrisas *m., sing.*
wine *n.* vino *m.*
bottle of wine *n.* botella *f.* de vino
red/white wine vino tinto/blanco
wine cellar *n.* bodega *f.*
wineglass *n.* copa *f.*
wink (one's eye) *v.t.* guiñar(le) (el ojo) (a alguien)
winter *n.* invierno *m.*
wire netting *n.* tela *f.* metálica
wisdom *n.* sabiduría *f.*
wisdom tooth *n.* muela *f.* del juicio
wise *adj.* sabio/a
wise person *n.* sabio/a *m., f.*
wish *n.* deseo *m.*
wish *v.t.* desear; esperar
I wish (that) *interj.* Ojalá (que)
with *prep.* con
with me conmigo
with you *fam.* contigo
with regard to con respecto a
withdrawn *adj. (person)* retraído/a
within *prep.* dentro de
without *conj.* sin que
without *prep.* sin
withstand *v.t.* soportar, resistir, aguantar
witness *n.* testigo *m., f.*
wolf *n.* lobo *m.*
woman *n.* mujer *f.*
womanizer *n.* donjuán *m.;* mujeriego *m.*
womb *n.* útero *m.*
wool *n.* lana *f.*
made of wool de lana
wool cap *n.* gorro *m.* de lana
word *n.* palabra *f.*
work *n.* trabajo *m.; (of art,*

literature, music, etc.) obra *f.*
work *v.i.* trabajar; funcionar
not working *adj.* descompuesto/a
work out *v.i.* hacer gimnasia
workshop *n.* taller *m.; (mechanic's)* taller de mecánica
world *n.* mundo *m.*
worldwide *adj.* mundial
worm *n.* gusano *m.*
worried (about) *adj.* preocupado/a (por); inquieto/a
worry (about) *v.* preocuparse (por); inquietar(se)
Don't worry. No se/te preocupe/s.
worrysome *adj.* inquietante
worse *adj.* peor
worse than *adv.* peor que
worst *adj.* el/la peor, lo peor
the worst *n.* el/la peor *m., f.* lo peor
worth *n.* valor
be worth the trouble valer la pena
wound *n.* herida *f.*
wrap *v.t.* envolver
wretch *n.* desgraciado/a *m., f.*
wrist *n.* muñeca *f.*
write *v.t.* escribir
write a letter/postcard/e-mail message escribir una carta/una (tarjeta) postal/un mensaje electrónico
writer *n.* escritor(a) *m., f.*
written *p.p.* escrito/a (*of* escribir)
wrong *adj.* equivocado/a
be wrong no tener razón
What's wrong? ¿Qué pasa?

X

X-ray *n.* radiografía *f.*

Y

yam *n.* ñame *m.*
yard *n.* jardín *m.;* patio *m.*
year *n.* año *m.*
yearning *n.* añoranza *f.*
yeast *n.* levadura *f.*
yellow *n., adj.* amarillo *m.;* amarillo/a
yellowish *adj.* amarillento/a
yes *interj.* sí
Yes, sure! ¡Sí, vale!
yesterday *adv.* ayer
yet *adv.* todavía
yield (the right of way) *v.* ceder el paso
yoga *n.* yoga *m.*
yogurt *n.* yogur *m.*
young *adj.* joven
young person *n.* joven *m., f.;* chico/a *m., f.*
younger *adj.* menor
youngest *n.* el/la menor *m., f.*
your su(s) *poss. adj. form.;* tu(s) *poss. adj. fam. sing.;* vuestro(s)/vuestra(s) *poss. adj. form. pl.;* suyo(s)/suya(s) *poss. pron. form.;* tuyo(s)/tuya(s) *poss. fam. sing.*
youth *n.* juventud *f.;* joven *m., f.*
youth hostel *n.* albergue *m.* juvenil
youthful *adj.* juvenil

Z

zebra *n.* cebra *f.*
zero *n.* cero *m.*
zipper *n.* cremallera *f.*
zoo *n.* zoológico *m.*
zoologist *n.* zoólogo/a *m., f.*

Useful Expressions

The *Useful Expressions* section of the **Vista Higher Learning Introductory Spanish Pocket Dictionary & Language Guide** puts at your fingertips a great variety of useful language organized according to situations similar to those in your textbook. This section of the dictionary provides numerous models of natural and expressive Spanish and covers all the conversational situations likely to come up as you progress through your book.

To use *Useful Expressions* for your class work, look for situations similar to those in the lesson you are studying, read through the section, copy out sentences and expressions that interest you, review them several times, and write new sentences modeled on them. Before you know it, you will find that you have acquired the new vocabulary, expressions, and language structures. This section can not only help you make yourself understood, it can help you express yourself, your opinions, and your personality in fluent and natural Spanish.

SALUDOS, PRESENTACIONES Y DESPEDIDAS	GREETINGS, INTRODUCTIONS, AND FAREWELLS
Buenos días.	Good morning.
¿Hay alguien?	Is anyone there?
¿Se puede pasar?	May I come in?
Pues claro, adelante.	Of course, come in.
Pasa./Pase./Pasen.	Come in.
Es (todo) un placer conocerle.	It's a (great) pleasure to meet you.
El placer es mío.	The pleasure is mine.
(Muchísimas) Gracias.	Thank you (very much).
Quiero presentarle a la Sra. Paredes.	I would like you to meet Mrs. Paredes.
ENCUENTROS	UPON MEETING
¡Cuánto tiempo sin verte/verlo/verla/verlos/verlas!	Long time no see!
¡Qué alegría volver a verte!	How nice to see you again!
¿Qué (te) cuentas?	What's going on?/What's up?
Ha pasado mucho tiempo.	What a long time it's been.
¡Cómo vuela el tiempo!	How time flies!
¿Cómo va la vida?	How's life?
Bien, muy bien.	Good, very good.
Todo va sobre ruedas.	Everything's going smoothly.
Y tú, ¿qué tal?	How are things with you?
No me puedo quejar.	I can't complain.
Me alegro de volver a verte.	I'm so glad to see you again.
Es estupendo verte otra vez.	It's great to see you again.

Igualmente.	Likewise./The same to you.
Lo mismo digo.	Same here.

EXPRESIONES CORTESES Y SERVICIALES	EXPRESSIONS OF COURTESY AND HELPFULNESS
Con permiso.	Excuse me.
Permítame.	Allow me.
¡A la orden!	At your service.
No hay de qué.	Don't mention it./You're welcome.
Con gusto.	With pleasure.
¡Para servirle!	At your service./You're welcome.
Perdone.	Pardon me./Excuse me.
Perdóneme.	Pardon me./Excuse me.
Sin falta.	By all means.
Ahora mismo.	Right away.
Al minuto.	Right away.
No faltaba más.	Of course./No problem.
¿Cómo no?	But of course./Sure.
Enseguida.	Right away.

EXPRESIONES DE TIEMPO	EXPRESSIONS OF TIME
¿A cuántos estamos? A doce de agosto.	What's the date? The twelfth of August.
¿A qué día estamos hoy? A seis.	What's the date today? The sixth.
¿Qué día es hoy? Miércoles veinticuatro.	What day is it? Wednesday, the twenty-fourth.
¡Uy, qué tarde es!	Oh, it's so late!
Se me ha hecho tarde.	I'm late.
¡Ya es mediodía!	It's already noon!

Tengo mucha prisa.	I'm in a big hurry.
¡Qué contratiempo! No tengo reloj.	What a nuisance! I don't have a watch.
¡Qué inconveniente!	How inconvenient!
Son las dos de la tarde.	It's two in the afternoon.
Son las tres de la madrugada.	It's three in the morning.
Es la una de la noche.	It's one in the morning.
Son las siete de la tarde.	It's seven in the evening.
¿Tiene (Ud.) hora, por favor?	Do you have the time, please?
¿Qué hora tiene?	What time do you have?
¿Me dice la hora?	Can you tell me the time?
¿Podría Ud. decirme qué hora es?	Could you please tell me what time it is?
Pasan diez minutos de las once.	It's ten minutes past eleven.
Llego justito.	I'm just in the nick of time.
Falta (un) cuarto para las dos.	It's (a) quarter to two.
Tengo tiempo de tomar un café.	I have time for a cup of coffee.
Es la una y media.	It's one thirty.
Aún es temprano.	It's still early.
Son las tres en punto.	It's three on the dot.
Aún falta una hora.	There's still an hour to go.
Son las seis menos cuarto.	It's a quarter to six.
No llego, no llego.	I'll never make it.
Se me/nos ha ido el día en tonterías.	I/We have fiddled away the entire day.
Son las cinco cuarenta y cinco.	It's five forty-five.
Ya llego tarde.	I'm already late.

¡Cómo vuela/pasa el tiempo!	How time flies!
El tiempo vuela.	Time flies.
¿Te das cuenta de lo rápido que pasa el tiempo?	Do you realize how fast time goes by?
¡Qué de prisa/despacio pasan las horas!	The hours pass so quickly/slowly!
Vamos, date prisa/apresúrate que llegamos tarde.	Let's go! Hurry up or we'll be late.
Siempre de prisa./Siempre con prisas.	Always in a hurry./Always in a rush.

DE VIAJE	TRAVELING
¡Por fin (nos) vamos de viaje!	At last we're going on a trip!
Nos vamos.	We're leaving.
Es hora de irse/partir.	It's time to leave.
¡Todos a bordo!	All aboard!
Vamos de excursión.	We're going on a field trip/day trip.
¡Vámonos!	Let's go!
Estamos listos.	We're ready.
Buen viaje.	Have a good trip!/Bon voyage!
¡Que (te/le/les) vaya bien!	Have a nice time!/Hope it goes well!
¡Que lo pases/pasen bien!	Have a nice time!/Hope it goes well!
¡Que disfrutes/disfrute/disfruten!	Enjoy yourself/yourselves!
Nada de despedidas.	No goodbyes.
Feliz viaje y hasta la vuelta.	Have a nice trip. See you when you get back.

Nos vemos a la vuelta.	We'll see each other when you/we/I return.
¡Que se divierta/diviertan!	Have fun!
No olviden mandar una postal.	Don't forget to send a postcard.
A ver si nos escribes unas líneas.	Drop a line.

DE REGRESO	BACK HOME
¡Estamos de vuelta!	We're back!
Aquí estamos, sanos y salvos.	Here we are, safe and sound.
Bienvenidos.	Welcome.
¡Qué alegría!	Great!/Wonderful!
¿Qué tal el viaje?	How was your trip?
Indescriptible. Inolvidable.	Indescribable. Unforgettable.
¿Cómo (te/le/les) fue?	How was it?
Lo pasé/pasamos en grande.	I/We had a great time.
Lo pasé/pasamos super bien.	I/We had a terrific time.
No hay nada como volver a casa.	There's no place like home./It's great to be home.
Me alegro de que estés/esté/estén de vuelta.	I'm glad you're back.
Me alegra volver a verte/verlo/verlos.	It's nice to see you again.
Ya te/los echaba de menos./Ya te/los extrañaba.	I missed you.
¿Me/Nos echaste de menos?/¿Me/Nos extrañaste?	Did you miss me/us?
Te/Los eché muchísimo de menos./Te/Los extrañé muchísimo.	I missed you a lot.

Pues claro que te/los extrané.	Of course I missed you.
Estamos impacientes por ver las fotos.	We can't wait to see the pictures.
Hogar, dulce hogar.	Home sweet home.

EN CLASE	IN CLASS
Buenos días, clase.	Good morning, class.
Ahora voy a pasar lista.	Now I'll take the roll/attendance.
A ver… ¿Adams?	Let's see, Adams?
Presente.	Present./Here.
Ahora, presten atención.	Now pay attention.
Fíjense bien.	Pay attention.
¡Qué profe tan estupendo/a!	What a terrific professor!
La profesora de historia del arte es buenísima.	The art history professor is great.
Sabe muchísimo y además explica muy bien.	She knows a lot and explains everything so well.
Sus clases son muy interesantes, y aprendo mucho.	Her classes are really interesting, and I learn a lot.
¡Qué profe tan pesado/a!	That professor is a pain in the neck!
Siempre habla de lo mismo.	He/She says the same thing over and over again.
¡Qué clase más/tan aburrida!	What a boring class!
El próximo semestre (no) voy a tomar geografía.	Next semester I'm (not) going to take geography.
Las fechas no son mi fuerte.	I don't have a head for dates.
Tengo ganas de que se acabe/termine el curso.	I can't wait until this course is over.

Yo también tengo ganas de ir de vacaciones.	I also want a vacation.
Tranquilo, hombre. Sólo faltan los exámenes finales.	Take it easy, man. Just the final exams are left.
Uf, no quiero ni pensarlo.	Ugh, I don't even want to think about it.
Tengo que presentar un trabajo el próximo martes.	I have to hand in a paper next Tuesday.
Es sobre la sociología de las masas.	It's on the sociology of the masses.
Tengo tanto/tantísimo trabajo.	I have so much work.
No sé por dónde empezar.	I don't know where to begin.
No te preocupes.	Don't worry.
Vas a sacar unas notas de fábula, como siempre.	You're going to get excellent grades, as always.
Ya lo verás.	You'll see.
Tú siempre apruebas todos los exámenes.	You always pass all your exams.
Y además con buena nota.	And with a good grade to boot.
DESPUÉS DE CLASE	*AFTER CLASS*
Ay, dormilón/dormilona, ¿de dónde sales?	Hey, sleepyhead, where have you been?
¿Dónde estabas esta mañana?	Where were you this morning?
¿Se te pegaron las sábanas?	Couldn't you drag yourself out of bed?
La clase de historia estuvo muy interesante; como siempre.	History class was very interesting, as always.
Anoche no pegué ojo.	I didn't sleep a wink last night.
Estoy/Voy atrasado/a en álgebra.	I'm behind in algebra.
Soy fatal para las matemáticas.	I'm lousy in math.

A mí se me dan muy bien las ciencias en general.	I do very well in science, in general.
Si necesitas ayuda, te hecho una mano.	If you need help, I'll give you a hand.
Laura es una sabihonda, ¡se cree que lo sabe todo!	Laura is a know-it-all; she thinks she knows everything!
Su nombre de pila es Eduardo; su apodo es Dudu.	His given name is Eduardo; his nickname is Dudu.
¿Por qué estudia tanto ese individuo?	Why does that guy study so much?
Quiere (llegar a) ser presidente.	He/she wants to be president (some day).
Tiene fama de ambicioso.	He/she has a reputation for being ambitious.
No me digas. ¿En serio? ¿Me tomas el pelo?	You don't say. Seriously? Are you pulling my leg?
¿Cómo te fue en el examen de química?... Fatal./Estupendo.	How was the chemistry exam?... Terrible./Great.
El examen fue pan comido.	The exam was a piece of cake.
Tengo que ponerme al día en biología.	I need to catch up in biology.
No quiero suspender otra vez.	I don't want to flunk again.
Los exámenes finales ya están cerca.	Final exams are getting close.
Sí, están a la vuelta de la esquina.	Yes, they're just around the corner.
No sé qué me pasa.	I don't know what's happening to me.
No me puedo concentrar.	I can't concentrate.
Estoy lleno/a de dudas.	I'm full of doubts.

No me gusta nada la computación.	I don't like computer science at all.
A mí tampoco.	Neither do I.
A mí se me dan muy bien los idiomas.	I do very well with languages.
¡Qué casualidad! A mí también.	What a coincidence! Me too.
¡Qué coincidencia! Compartimos el mismo interés por las lenguas.	What a coincidence! We share an interest for languages.
Tengo mucho interés en las lenguas clásicas.	I'm very interested in classical languages.
¡Genial! A mí me interesa muchísimo el latín.	Great! I'm really interested in Latin.
El único inconveniente es que no tengo con quién practicarlo.	The only drawback is that I don't have anyone to practice with.
¿Te importa dejarme tus apuntes de literatura?	Would you mind lending me your literature notes?
En absoluto./Pues claro que no./Aquí los tienes./Aquí están.	Not at all. /Of course not./Here you go./Here they are.
Espero que entiendas mi letra.	I hope you can read my writing.
Tengo una letra horrible/ilegible.	My handwriting is terrible/illegible.
Pero están muy completos.	But they're very complete.

LA FAMILIA — YOUR FAMILY

¿Todos bien?	Is everyone well?
Sí, todos bien, gracias a Dios.	Yes, everyone's well, thank goodness.
¿Tienes muchos hermanos/parientes/sobrinos?	Do you have a lot of brothers and sisters/relatives/nieces and nephews?
¿Dónde viven tus padres?	Where do your parents live?

¿Visitas muy a menudo a tus familiares/parientes?	Do you visit your family/relatives often?
¿Son tus padres muy mayores?	Are your parents very old?
¿Vives con tus padres?	Do you live with your parents?
¿Quién es mayor, tu padre o tu madre?	Who is older, your father or your mother?
¿A qué se dedica tu padre/madre?	What does your father/mother do for a living?
¿Qué estudia tu hermano mayor?	What does your older brother study?
¿Tienen bisnietos tus abuelos?	Do your grandparents have great-grandchildren?
¿Conoces a todos tus primos?	Do you know all your cousins?
¿Son tus padres de la misma nacionalidad?	Are your parents of the same nationality?
¿Hablan tus padres español?	Do your parents speak Spanish?
¿Te llevas bien con tus hermanos?	Do you get along well with your brothers and sisters?
¿Dónde se conocieron tus padres?	Where did your parents meet?
¿Tienes familiares en el extranjero?	Do you have relatives abroad?
¿Dónde nacieron tus padres?	Where were your parents born?
¡Qué dicha ver a toda la familia junta!	What good fortune to see the whole family together!
Con una familia tan grande, siempre hay de qué/con quién hablar.	With such a big family, there is always something to talk about/someone to talk to.

EL OCIO	LEISURE
¿Dónde vas a ir este sábado?	Where are you going this Saturday?
¿Vas a hacer algo especial el domingo?	Are you going to do anything special on Sunday?
¿Tienes algún pasatiempo favorito/preferido?	Do you have a favorite pastime?
¿Cuál es tu pasatiempo favorito/preferido?	What is your favorite pastime?
¿Qué vas a hacer después de clase?	What are you doing after class?
¿Qué vas a hacer este fin de semana?	What are you doing this weekend?
Creo que voy a ir al zoológico.	I think I'll go to the zoo.
La entrada es gratuita los fines de semana.	Admission is free on weekends.
¿Puedes creerlo?	Can you believe it?
Y tú, ¿qué? ¿Vas a ir al cine este fin de semana?	What about you? Are you going to go to the movies this weekend?
Bah, ya estoy harto/a de ir al cine.	I'm tired/sick of going to the movies.
No hay ninguna película interesante.	There aren't any interesting movies.
¿Ves mucho la televisión?	Do you watch a lot of television?
¡Que va! Es terrible. Siempre hacen lo mismo.	No way! It's awful. It's always the same thing.
Me gusta divertirme sin gastar mucho dinero.	I like to have fun without spending too much money.
Me gustan las actividades que no cuestan dinero.	I like activities that don't cost money.

Oye, ¿por qué no vienes conmigo al zoológico?	Hey, why don't you come to the zoo with me?
Estupendo. ¡Decidido, pues!	Great. It's decided, then!
El domingo vamos los dos al zoológico. ¡Y no se hable más!	On Sunday the two of us will go to the zoo. That's settled!
A partir de ahora voy a comprar la guía del ocio todas las semanas.	From now on I'm going to buy the city entertainment guide every week.
Quiero estar informado de todas las actividades que tienen lugar en la ciudad.	I want to know about all the activities that take place in the city.
No quiero perderme nada, sobre todo si es gratis.	I don't want to miss anything, especially if it's free.
Nos vemos en el zoológico.	We'll see each other at the zoo.
¡Que se diviertan en el zoológico!	Have a good time at the zoo!

EXPRESIONES DEL TIEMPO / WEATHER EXPRESSIONS

¡Qué buen día hace hoy!	What a nice day it is today!
Hoy hace un día espléndido.	It's a beautiful day today.
El cielo está totalmente despejado.	The sky is perfectly clear.
No hay ni una nube.	There's not a cloud in the sky.
El hombre del tiempo pronosticó lluvia para el fin de semana.	The weatherman predicted rain for the weekend.
Afortunadamente, ¡se equivocó!	Fortunately, he was wrong!
Me pregunto qué tiempo va a hacer mañana.	I wonder what the weather will be like tomorrow.
¡Últimamente el tiempo es tan variable!	The weather has been so variable lately!
Sí, es imprevisible. No es fácil adivinar/predecir.	Yes, it's unpredictable. It's not easy to predict.

Mañana (dicen que) va a caer un aguacero.	Tomorrow (they say that) there will be a downpour.
Llueve a cántaros.	It's raining cats and dogs.
Y yo sin paraguas. ¡Qué contratiempo!	And me without an umbrella. How annoying!
No salgas sin paraguas.	Don't leave/go out without an umbrella.
Si llueve y hace sol, va a salir el arco iris.	If it rains and the sun comes out, there will be a rainbow.
¡Qué emoción! Me fascinan los arco iris.	Cool! I love rainbows.
A ver si vemos uno bien grande.	Maybe we'll see a nice big one.
¡Qué lunes tan horrible!	What a horrible Monday!
Hace viento y hace frío.	It's windy and it's cold.
¡Qué día tan feo! Es feo con ganas.	What an awful day! It's awful and then some.
Hay mucha niebla y no se ve nada.	There's a lot of fog and you can't see anything.
Hoy hace un día para no salir de casa/para quedarse en casa.	Today is a nice day to stay home.
¡Que pase/tenga un buen día!	Have a nice day!
Igualmente.	Same to you.

EN LA AGENCIA DE VIAJES	AT THE TRAVEL AGENCY
Bueno, ¡menos mal! Parece que hoy está abierto.	Okay, great! It looks like it's open today.
Quisiéramos dos pasajes para Octopulco, ida y vuelta.	We'd like two round-trip tickets to Octopulco.
En primera clase, por supuesto.	In first class, of course.
Cómo no.	But of course.

¿Para qué día?	For what day?
¿Cuándo quieren regresar?	When would you like to return?
Queremos hospedarnos en un hotel de cinco estrellas/hotel barato.	We'd like to stay in a five-star hotel/an inexpensive hotel.
¿Cuántos días van a quedarse?	How many days will you stay?
Nos vamos a quedar quince días.	We're going to stay two weeks.
¿Quieren alquilar un auto?	Do you want to rent a car?
No, no hace falta.	No, we don't need one.
La isla es pequeña. Podemos ir en bicicleta.	The island is small. We can get around by bike.
Aquí tienen sus pasajes.	Here are your tickets.

EN EL AEROPUERTO	AT THE AIRPORT
¿Dónde está la aerolínea Gavilán?	Where is Gavilán Airlines?
Vuelo 8778	Flight 8778
Destino Octopulco	Destination: Octopulco
¿Cancelado?... No, retrasado.	Canceled? . . . No, delayed.
Bueno, pues a esperar.	Okay, then we'll wait.
¡Estoy cansado/a de esperar en los aeropuertos!	I'm tired of waiting in airports!
¿Debemos facturar el equipaje ahora?	Should we check our luggage now?
Me olvidé el itinerario.	I forgot the itinerary.
Al menos es un vuelo directo, sin escalas.	At least it's a direct flight, without any stopovers.
¿Dónde está la tienda libre de impuestos?	Where is the duty-free shop?

Da igual. No tenemos tiempo. Ya vamos a embarcar.	It doesn't matter. We don't have time. We're going to board now.
Esta maleta pesa demasiado/es demasiado pesada.	This suitcase weighs too much/is too heavy.
Voy a buscar un carrito.	I'm going to look for a cart.
Yo prefiero viajar ligero de equipaje.	I prefer to travel light.
A la vuelta debemos pasar por la aduana.	On the way back we have to go through customs.
¿Algo que declarar?	Anything to declare?
No, nada.	No, nothing.

EN EL HOTEL	AT THE HOTEL
Bienvenidos al hotel Miramar.	Welcome to the Hotel Miramar.
Por fin llegamos.	Finally we're here.
¿Tuvieron un vuelo agradable?	Did you have a good flight?
¡Qué vuelo tan largo!	What a long flight!
Lo sentimos, pero el ascensor/el elevador no funciona hoy.	We're sorry, but the elevator is out of order today.
Deben subir por las escaleras.	You need to take the stairs.
Por suerte están Uds. en el primer piso.	Luckily you're on the second floor.
Ésta es la mejor habitación con vista(s) al mar.	This is the best room with an ocean view.
Esperamos que todo sea de su agrado.	We hope that everything will be to your liking.
Cualquier cosa que necesiten, llamen a recepción.	If you need anything, call the front desk.
Gracias por hospedarse en/elegir nuestro hotel.	Thank you for staying in/choosing our hotel.

Esperamos que tengan una estancia agradable.	We hope you have an enjoyable stay.
¡Que tengan una feliz estancia!	Have a nice stay!

EN LA PLAYA	AT THE BEACH
¡Qué belleza de paisaje!	What beautiful scenery!
Pues, espera a ver el atardecer.	Wait until you see the sunset.
Dicen que es de película.	They say it's fantastic.
¡Qué paz!	What peace!
¡Qué aire tan puro y fresco!	What pure, fresh air!
No hay nada como la brisa del mar.	There's nothing like a sea breeze.
¡Qué calor!	It's so hot!
Este verano no quiero quemarme.	This summer I don't want to get sunburned.
¡Cuánta gente!	What a lot of people!
Pensaba que veníamos a una isla desierta.	I though we were going to a desert island.
¡Qué tonto/a! Me olvidé el traje de baño.	How stupid! I forgot my bathing suit.
Hoy no me apetece hacer nada.	Today I'm not in the mood to do anything.
Voy a contemplar el paisaje y pasear por la orilla.	I'm going to contemplate the scenery and take a walk along the shore.

¿QUÉ ME PONGO PARA LA FIESTA DEL SÁBADO?	WHAT SHOULD I WEAR TO THE PARTY SATURDAY?
¡Qué problema!	What a problem!
No tengo nada que ponerme.	I don't have anything to wear.
Necesito renovar mi vestuario.	I need a new wardrobe.

No tengo nada que me guste.	I don't have anything that I like.
Estoy harta de ponerme siempre la misma ropa.	I'm tired of always wearing the same clothes.
Lo que necesitas es un cambio de imagen.	You need a new image.
Sí, tienes razón.	Yes, you're right.
Es justo lo que necesito.	It's just what I need.
¿Quieres ser mi asesor de imagen?	Would you like to be my image consultant?
Esta misma tarde voy a ir al centro (comercial) a ver qué encuentro.	This afternoon I'm going to the mall/downtown to see what I can find.
Esta semana hay unas rebajas espectaculares.	This week there are some great discounts.
No me gustan los mercados; odio regatear.	I don't like markets; I hate to haggle.

EN LA TIENDA DE ROPA PARA DAMAS

IN THE WOMEN'S CLOTHING STORE

¡Cuánta variedad! ¡Cuánto colorido!	What variety! So many colors!
Va a ser difícil decidir.	It's going to be hard to decide.
Quiero un vestido bien llamativo.	I want an attractive dress.
Señorita, ¿podría probarme este vestido?	Miss, may I try on this dress?
Naturalmente. El probador está al fondo a la derecha.	Of course. The fitting room is in the back to the right.
Uy, me queda un poco justo.	Aw, it's a little too small.
Necesito una talla más grande.	I need a bigger size.
¿Qué talla quiere?	What size do you want?
La mediana, por favor.	Medium, please.

Sí, éste me sienta bien/mejor.	Yes, this one fits me well/better.
¿Cuál te gusta más, el rojo o el negro?	Which do you like better, the red or the black?
El negro te va como anillo al dedo.	The black one suits you to a "T."
El color negro te favorece.	You look good in black.
Te ves más delgada.	It makes you look thinner.
Sí, el rojo no me sienta tan bien.	Yes, the red one doesn't fit me as well.
Te ves muy atractiva con ese vestido.	You look very attractive in that dress.
¡Y qué suave es!	And it's so soft!
¡Buena compra!	A good buy!
Ahora necesitas otro bolso.	Now you need another purse.
Ese bolso no va (bien) con el vestido.	This purse doesn't go (well) with this dress.
Y también unos zapatos a juego.	And also shoes to match.
Espérame, voy a pagar el vestido y nos vamos a una zapatería.	Wait, I'll pay for the dress, then we'll go to a shoe store.
¿Cuánto vale?	How much does it cost?
Uy, baratísimo.	Oh, really inexpensive/cheap.
¡Hoy es mi día de suerte!/¡Hoy estoy de suerte!	Today is my lucky day!
¿Vamos a la zapatería?	Shall we go to the shoe store?

EN LA TIENDA DE ROPA PARA CABALLEROS

IN THE MEN'S CLOTHING STORE

Necesito un traje bien elegante.	I need an elegant suit.
¿De qué color lo quiere?	What color would you like?

No sé... ¿Qué me sugiere Ud.?	I don't know . . . What would you suggest?
Un color oscuro le quedará/sentará bien.	You'd look good in a dark color.
Venga por aquí, joven.	Come over hear, young man.
¿Qué talla usa?	What size do you wear?
No sé, es mi primer traje.	I don't know. It's my first suit.
Bueno, Ud. debe usar la talla 52 para la chaqueta... y la talla 32 para los pantalones.	Well, you should wear a size 52 jacket . . . and size 32 pants.
A ver, pruébese este traje azul marino... ¿Qué tal?	Let's see. Try on this dark blue suit. What do you think?
Le queda perfecto.	It fits you perfectly.
Parece hecho a su medida.	It looks like it was made for you.
Ahora necesita una bonita camisa.	Now you need a nice shirt.
¿La prefiere blanca o azul?	Would you like white or blue?
¿Blanca?	White?
Muy bien. Tenga, pruébese ésta.	Okay. Here you are. Try on this one.
Es la talla 16.	It's size 16.
Sí, me gusta...¡Qué tela más fina!	Yes, I like it. . . . What nice material!
Ahora sólo falta el último toque... ¡la corbata!	Now all you need is the last touch . . .a tie!
¿Qué tal esta roja?	How about this red one?
Ni hablar... demasiado llamativa.	Don't even suggest it . . . too flashy.
Necesitamos un color más suave.	We need a more muted color.

Azul celeste... Confíe en mí.	Light blue . . . trust me.
Mire, pruébese ésta... Es de seda italiana.	Look, try this one on. It's Italian silk.
Está Ud. impecable.	You are impeccable.
Pues sí, parezco otra persona.	Yes, I look like another person.
No sabía que era tan guapo.	I didn't know I was so handsome.
Muchísimas gracias por su ayuda.	Thanks so much for your help.
¿Cuánto le debo?	How much do I owe you?

LA RUTINA DIARIA / DAILY ROUTINE

¿Necesitas simplificar tu vida?	Do you need to simplify your life?
¿A qué hora te levantas?	What time do you get up?
¿Qué es lo primero que haces al levantarte?	What's the first thing you do when you get up?
¿Desayunas en casa?	Do you have/eat breakfast at home?
¿Qué desayunas? ¿Tostadas con mantequilla?	What do you have/eat for breakfast? Toast with butter?
¿Desayunas lo mismo todos los días?	Do you have/eat the same thing for breakfast every day?
¿Te vistes antes de desayunar o desayunas primero y luego te vistes?	Do you get dressed before breakfast or do you eat breakfast first and then get dressed?
¿A qué hora sales de casa?	What time do you leave the house?
¿Cuánto tiempo necesitas para prepararte por la mañana?	How much time do you need to get ready in the morning?
¿Te gusta ir de prisa o te tomas las cosas con calma?	Do you like to be quick or do you take your time?
¿A qué hora almuerzas?	What time do you eat lunch?

¿Dónde? ¿Con quién?	Where? With whom?
¿Te gusta almorzar solo o acompañado/a?	Do you like to eat lunch alone or with other people?
¿Estudias, trabajas o haces las dos cosas?	Are you studying, working, or both?
¿Qué haces de las 3 a las 5 de la tarde?	What do you do from 3:00 to 5:00 in the afternoon?
¿Qué haces después de las clases/después del trabajo?	What do you do after class/after work?
¿A qué hora regresas a casa?	What time do you get home?
¿Llegas muy tarde a casa por la noche?	Do you get home very late at night?
¿Qué es lo primero que haces al llegar a casa?	What's the first thing you do when you get home?
¿A qué hora cenas?	What time do you eat/have dinner?
¿Qué haces después de cenar?	What do you do after dinner?
¿Cuántas veces al día te lavas los dientes?	How many times a day do you brush your teeth?
¿A qué hora te vas a dormir/te acuestas?	What time do you go to sleep/to bed?
¿Qué es lo último que haces antes de acostarte?	What is the last thing you do before going to bed?
¿Cuántas horas duermes?	How many hours do you sleep?
¿Crees que duermes pocas horas?	Do you think you don't get enough sleep?
¿Es necesaria la rutina?	Is routine necessary?
¿Estás contento/a con tu rutina?	Are you happy with your routine?
¿Pierdes mucho tiempo por las mañanas?	Do you waste a lot of time in the morning?

¿Cuál es tu secreto para ganar tiempo libre?	What is your secret for finding free time?

EN EL RESTAURANTE	AT THE RESTAURANT
¿Mesa para dos?	Table for two?
¡Qué ambiente más selecto!	What an exclusive place!
Este lugar es muy acogedor.	This place is very cozy.
Está decorado con mucho gusto.	This place is decorated in very good taste.
Sin duda es el restaurante más caro de la ciudad.	Without a doubt, this is the most expensive restaurant in the city.
Tiene fama de ser excelente... y de ser carísimo.	It is supposed to be excellent . . . and very expensive.
Todo el mundo habla muy bien de este sitio.	Everyone speaks very well of this place.
Los cubiertos son de plata.	The silverware is real silver.
A ver el menú.	Let's look at the menu.
Aquí tienen el menú.	Here's the menu.
Mmm, se me hace la boca agua.	Mmm, it makes my mouth water.
No sé qué pedir.	I don't know what to order.
¿Qué nos sugiere?	What do you suggest?
Pidan lo que más les guste.	Order whatever you like the best.
Todo es exquisito, sin excepción.	Everything is superb, without exception.
Esta carne está en su punto.	This meat is just right.
¡Qué ensalada más original!	What an original salad!
Sí, combina frutas y verduras.	Yes, it combines fruit and vegetables.
El aderezo/aliño es divino.	The dressing is divine.

¿Nos trae la carta de vinos, por favor?	Would you bring us the wine list, please?
No me gusta el vino tinto; prefiero el vino blanco.	I don't like red wine; I prefer white wine.
Yo no puedo tomar vino de ningún color; enseguida me emborracho.	I can't drink wine of any color; it goes right to my head.
Tenemos una selección de postres que les va a encantar.	You're going to love our dessert selection.
¡Qué carta de postres más creativa!	What a creative dessert menu!
Tiremos la casa por la ventana.	Let's go all out.
Probémoslos todos.	Let's try everything.
Camarero/a, nos trae la cuenta (cuando pueda), por favor.	Waiter, please bring us the check (when you can).
¿Cuánto se debe?	How much is it?
Quédese con el cambio.	Keep the change.
Nos quedamos sin plata/dinero.	We're broke.
¡Qué velada más/tan agradable!	What a pleasant evening!
¿A quién vamos a recomendar este restaurante?	To whom are we going to recommend this restaurant?

EL ALMUERZO — LUNCH

¡A comer!	Lunch is ready!
¿Qué hay para comer?	What is there/do we have to eat?
¡Qué hambre tengo!	I'm so hungry!
Estoy muerto/a de hambre./Me muero de hambre.	I'm starved.
Tengo un hambre feroz.	I'm famished./I could eat a horse.
Yo me lo como todo.	I'll eat anything.

Pues yo no. Estoy harto/a de lentejas.	Well, not me. I'm tired of lentils.
¿Otra vez lo mismo?	The same thing again?
No tengo (nada de) hambre.	I'm not hungry (at all).
¡Mmm, qué bien huele!	Mmm, it smells good!
Este estofado sabe a gloria.	This casserole tastes heavenly.
Esta sopa quema.	This soup is burning hot.
¡Pues sopla!	So blow on it!
Por favor, ¿me pasas la sal?	Please pass the salt.
¿Qué es esto rojo?	What's this red stuff?
Esta carne no me la como, está cruda.	I won't eat this meat, it's raw.
No me gusta este pescado, tiene muchas espinas.	I don't like this fish, it has lots of bones.
Esta salsa es demasiado picante/pica demasiado.	This sauce is too spicy.
¿Qué hay de postre?	What's for dessert?
Yo estoy lleno/a.	I'm full.
Claro, te comiste todo el pan.	Of course, you ate all the bread.
Voy a explotar.	I'm going to explode.
Mejor dejo el postre para la noche.	I'd better leave dessert until later tonight.
¡Coman, coman!	Eat up!
¡Buen provecho!/¡Que aproveche!	Enjoy your meal!

CELEBRACIONES / CELEBRATIONS

¡Estamos de fiesta!	Let's celebrate!
¿Qué se celebra?	What is being celebrated?

El nacimiento de nuestro hijo	*The birth of our son*
Mi esposa dio a luz a nuestro tercer hijo.	My wife gave birth to our third child/son.
¿Cuándo nació?	When was he born?
El 1º de enero.	January first.
¡Enhorabuena! ¡Felicidades!	Congratulations!
¡Es un niño precioso!	What a beautiful child!
El cumpleaños de mi hermano Jorge	*My brother Jorge's birthday*
¿Cuántos años cumple?	How old is he?
Dieciocho. Ya es mayor de edad.	Eighteen. He's of legal age now.
¡Cuántos amigos y amigas tiene tu hermano!	Your brother has so many friends!
En esta fiesta no cabe ni un alfiler.	This party is packed.
¡Muchísimas felicidades, Jorge!	Best wishes, Jorge!
¡Y que cumplas muchos más!	And may you have many more!
La graduación de Margarita	*Margarita's graduation*
Es nuestra hija más pequeña.	She's our youngest daughter.
Se acaba de graduar en geología.	She's just graduated with a degree in geology.
Estamos muy orgullosos de ella.	We're very proud of her.
¡Felicidades!	Congratulations!
¡Por un futuro brillante!	To a bright future!
El aniversario de bodas de mis padres	*My parents' anniversary*
¿Cuántos años hace que se casaron?	How many years have they been married?

Cincuenta. Celebran sus bodas de oro.	Fifty. They are celebrating their golden anniversary.
Y aún se quieren como cuando eran recién casados.	They still love each other as much as they did when they were newlyweds.
¡Qué maravilla!	How wonderful!
¡Feliz aniversario!	Happy anniversary!
¡Y que celebren muchos más!	May you have many more!

La boda de mi tía Carolina	*My aunt Carolina's wedding*
¡Qué dicha!	What good fortune!
¡Que sean muy felices!	May they be very happy!
¡Que se besen los novios!	A kiss!
Un brindis por los recién casados.	A toast to the newlyweds.
¡Vivan los novios!	Long live the newlyweds!

DAR EL PÉSAME — GIVING CONDOLENCES

Estamos de luto.	We're in mourning.
¡Qué desgracia!	How unfortunate!
Murió Roberto.	Roberto died.
¡Qué lastima!	What a shame!
Pobre Roberto, era tan joven.	Poor Roberto, he was so young.
Estamos todos muy apenados/tristes.	We're all very sad.
Le acompaño en el sentimiento.	My thoughts are with you.
Reciba nuestro más sincero pésame.	Our deepest sympathies.
No sé qué decir.	I don't know what to say.
Sólo puedo llorar.	I can only cry.

Lo vamos a echar mucho de menos.	We're going to miss him very much.

EN EL CONSULTORIO — IN THE DOCTOR'S OFFICE

¡Me duele todo el cuerpo!	My whole body aches!
¿Cuál es el problema?	What is the problem?
¿Qué le pasa?	What's the matter?
¿Dónde le duele?	Where does it hurt?
¿Qué síntomas tiene?	What are your symptoms?
¿Cuáles son sus síntomas?	What are your symptoms?
¿Cómo se encuentra hoy?	How are you feeling today?
Mejor./Peor.	Better./Worse.
Doctor, parece que no mejoro.	Doctor, it seems like I'm not getting better.
¿Se encuentra mejor hoy?	Are you feeling better today?
Al contrario, cada día estoy peor.	No, just the opposite, every day I'm worse.
¿Qué dicen los resultados de los análisis?	What do the test results show?
Tiene Ud. el colesterol muy alto/por las nubes.	Your cholesterol is very high/sky-high.
¿(Le) Duele?	Does it hurt?
Sólo va a notar un pinchazo.	You'll only feel a pinch.
¿Me va a doler, doctor?	Will it hurt, doctor?
Esto le va a doler un poco.	This will hurt a little.
Ay, creo que me voy a desmayar.	Oh, I think I'm going to faint.
Me aterran las agujas.	I'm afraid of needles.
No va a sentir ningún dolor.	You won't feel any pain.

Le vamos a operar con anestesia local/general.	We'll operate with local/general anesthesia.
¡Qué valiente es Vicente!	Vicente is so brave!
¿Hay que operar?	Do you have to operate?
¿Me quedará cicatriz?	Will I have/it leave a scar?
¿Podré volver a caminar/andar?	Will I be able to walk again?
¿Cuánto dura el tratamiento?	How long will the treatment last?
Doctor, ¿puede recetarme algo para el dolor?	Doctor, can you prescribe me something for the pain?
Inyecciones no, por favor.	Please, no shots.
¿No hay otra solución?	There's no other solution?
Le recomiendo que siga el tratamiento al pie de la letra.	I recommend that you follow the treatment to the letter.
¿Qué efectos secundarios tiene este medicamento?	What are the side effects of this medication?
Produce vómito y somnolencia.	It causes vomiting and drowsiness.
¿Qué opciones tengo?	What options do I have?
¿Va a tomarme la presión?	Are you going to take my blood pressure?
Tiene Ud. la presión/tensión muy alta/baja.	You have very high/low pressure.
¿Cuándo empezó a fumar?	When did you start smoking?
¿Cuántos años hace que fuma?	How many years have you been smoking?
Debe dejar de fumar YA.	You must stop smoking NOW.
Le aconsejo que deje de fumar cuanto antes.	I advise you to stop smoking immediately.
El tabaco perjudica la salud.	Tobacco jeopardizes your health.

Durante el embarazo no debe fumar ni consumir alcohol.	While you're pregnant, you shouldn't smoke or drink alcohol.
Debe Ud. ver a un especialista.	You need to see a specialist.
Es una enfermedad muy grave.	It's a very serious illness.
Conocemos los síntomas, pero no las causas.	We are familiar with the symptoms, but not the causes.
El pronóstico es grave/favorable.	The prognosis is serious/good.
Lo que yo necesito es reposo indefinido.	What I need is a prolonged rest.

LA COMUNICACIÓN TELEFÓNICA — TELEPHONING

¿Con quién hablo?	With whom am I speaking?
Soy el vecino de al lado…	I'm the next-door neighbor.
¿Quién es? ¿Quién?	Who is it? Who?
Hable más fuerte. No oigo./No oigo nada.	Please, speak up. I can't hear you/a thing.
Soy Juan, tu vecino.	It's Juan, your neighbor.
¿Te importaría bajar el volumen del radio, por favor?	Would you mind turning the radio down, please?
¿Podría hablar con el director?	May I speak with the director?
Por favor, me pone con el Sr. Ramos.	May I speak with Mr. Ramos, please?
¿De parte de quién? ¿Quién lo llama?	May I tell him/ask who's calling?
Dígale que lo llama Ruti, su primo.	Tell him that his cousin Ruti is calling.
Espere un momentito, ahora pongo.	Just a minute, here he is.
No cuelgue por favor, ahora paso.	Don't hang up, please; here he is.

Oiga, el Sr. Ramos salió a almorzar.	Oh, Mr. Ramos is out to lunch.
¿Quiere dejar un mensaje?	Would you like to leave a message?
No, yo vuelvo a llamar mañana.	No, I'll call back tomorrow.
Dígale que me llame, por favor.	Tell him to call me, please.
¿Quiere que le devuelva la llamada cuando regrese?	Would you like me to have him call you when he gets back?
Pues sí. Gracias.	Yes, thanks.
Mire, mi número es el 001-1100.	My number is 001-1100.
¿Es éste el 010-0110?	Is this 010-0110?
Lo siento, se ha equivocado de número.	I'm sorry, you have the wrong number.
Disculpe.	Oh, excuse me./I'm sorry.
Vuelva a marcar.	Try dialing again.
Estoy esperando una llamada importante.	I'm expecting an important call.
¡Ese teléfono no para de sonar!	That phone won't stop ringing/is ringing off the hook!
¿Quieres hacer el favor de contestar el teléfono?	Would you please answer the phone?
¿Cómo? ¿No tienes contestador automático?	What? You don't have an answering machine?
Señora, tiene una llamada a cobro revertido. ¿Acepta Ud. la llamada?	Ma'am, you have a collect call. Will you accept the call?
Hago un sinfín de llamadas de larga distancia e internacionales.	I make a ton of long distance and international calls.

La factura del teléfono me cuesta cada mes una fortuna/un dineral.	My phone bill costs a fortune each month.
Ring, riiiing,... riiiiiiing. No contestan.	Ring, ring, riiiing. No answer.
Parece que la línea está ocupada.	It seems that the line is busy.
Llama/e a la operadora.	Call the operator.
¿A qué número llama?	What number are you calling?
Ay, olvidé el número.	Oh, I forgot the number.
Llame a información. Marque el 003.	Call information. Dial 003.
Para más información, llame al 1-800-289-1948.	For more information, call 1-800-289-1948.
Las líneas están abiertas 24 horas al día, siete días a la semana.	The lines are open 24 hours a day, seven days a week.

LOS APARATOS / MECHANICAL DEVICES

¿Cómo funciona esto?	How does this thing work?
¿Y me preguntas a mí?	You're asking me?
¡Qué sé yo!	What do I know?
¿Y a mí me lo preguntas?	You're asking me?
No tengo ni (la más mínima) idea.	I have no idea./I haven't the foggiest idea.
Las máquinas me asustan.	Machines frighten me.
Las instrucciones me aburren.	Instructions bore me.
¿No hay una versión abreviada?	Isn't there a shorter version?
¿Cuándo viene el técnico a arreglar la antena?	When is the repair man coming to fix the antenna?

Hace semanas que no funciona el televisor.	It's been weeks since the television worked.
Me vuelvo loco/a sin la caja tonta.	I'm going crazy without the idiot box.
Creo que quiero una computadora portátil.	I think I want a laptop.
Están de moda.	They are in style.
Son prácticas, ¿no?	They're practical, aren't they?
¿Cómo se pone en marcha este trasto?	How do you get this thing/piece of junk to work?
Esta máquina de coser funciona a las mil maravillas.	This sewing machine works like a dream.
No sé qué haría sin ella.	I don't know what I would do without it.
En fin, ¿qué más?	So, what else?

LOS AUTOMÓVILES — CARS

¿Necesito carro?	Do I need a car?
A lo mejor me compro uno de segunda mano.	Maybe I should get a used one.
Cuanto más barato sea, mejor, ¿no?	The cheaper the better, no?
Total, ¿qué más da? Se va a estropear/descomponer igual.	Bah, what does it matter? It will break down just the same.
Al menos si me cuesta barato, no me preocupo tanto.	At least if it's cheap, I won't worry too much.
Un carro puede durar muchos años si lo cuidas bien.	A car can last many years if you take good care of it.
Creo que voy a vender mi carro viejo y me voy a comprar uno nuevo.	I think I'll sell my old car and buy a new one.

Pero no puedo tomar una decisión sin ton ni son.	But I can't make a decision willy nilly.
Esto es un asunto serio.	This is a serious matter.
Debo pensarlo bien.	I should think it over well.
A ver, ¿qué tipo de carro me conviene más?	Let's see, what kind of car is best for me?
¿Uno automático o uno de marchas?	An automatic or manual transmission?
¿Uno deportivo o uno familiar?	A sports car or a family car?
¿Uno de lujo o uno todo terreno?	A luxury car or an all-terrain vehicle?
¿Cuánto dinero me quiero gastar?	How much money do I want to spend?
¿Qué es lo más importante a la hora de comprar un carro?	What is the most important thing when it comes time to buy a car?
¿Cuál es mi máxima necesidad/prioridad?	What is my top priority?
¿Una carretera sin baches?	A road without potholes?
Pero pensándolo bien/mejor, ¿para qué necesito yo un carro?	But, on second thought, what do I need a car for?
¿Qué sé yo de mecánica?	What do I know about mechanics?

LAS AVERÍAS — BREAKDOWNS

Otra vez al mecánico.	To the mechanic again.
Este carro es un tremendo dolor de cabeza.	This car is a big headache.
Se estropea/descompone cada dos por tres.	It breaks down all the time.
Cuando no es una cosa es otra.	If it's not one thing, it's another.
El mes pasado eran los frenos.	Last month it was the brakes.

Hace dos meses, el cambio de marchas.	Two months ago, the gear shift.
Ayer, el intermitente delantero izquierdo.	Yesterday, the front left directional signal.
Ya te digo, me da más problemas que alegrías/satisfacciones.	I'm telling you, it's more trouble than it's worth.
Cada reparación me cuesta una fortuna/un ojo de la cara.	Every repair costs a fortune/an arm and a leg.
Además, es dificilísimo encontrar un buen mecánico en quien poder confiar.	And it's so hard to find a good, trustworthy mechanic.
Encontrar un buen mecánico es como buscar una aguja en un pajar.	Finding a good mechanic is like finding a needle in a haystack.
Ahora llevo el tubo de escape colgando y, cuando llueve, no hay quien lo ponga en marcha.	Now my exhaust pipe is hanging, and when it rains the car won't start.

EN LA CARRETERA / ON THE HIGHWAY

Iba yo conduciendo tan tranquilo/a y me paró la policía.	I was just driving along and the police pulled me over.
Me paró un policía de tráfico…	A traffic cop stopped me…
Aparentemente, por ir demasiado despacio.	Apparently, for driving too slowly.
La velocidad límite era de 65 millas por hora.	The speed limit was 65 miles per hour.
Yo iba a 15 millas por hora.	I was going 15 miles per hour.
Le dije que no tenía gasolina.	I told him that I didn't have gas.
El policía se hizo el sordo y me puso una multa.	The policeman didn't listen and gave me a fine.
Fue inútil discutir.	It was pointless to argue about it.

Me pregunto quién la va a pagar.	I'm wondering who is going to pay it.
¿Dónde hay una estación de servicio?	Where is there a service station?
Necesito llenar el tanque/el depósito.	I need to fill the tank.

UNA VIVIENDA DESASTROSA	A DISASTROUS HOUSE
¡Esta casa es un desastre!	This house is a disaster!
¡Qué casa, madre mía! Un frigorífico en invierno y un horno en verano.	What a house! A refrigerator in the winter and an oven in the summer.
Las luces se encienden y se apagan cuando les da la gana.	The lights turn on and off when they feel like it.
¿Electrodomésticos? ¿Para qué?	Appliances? For what?
Por la noche hay que tener las velas preparadas.	At night we have to have candles ready.
Siempre hay que estar prevenido (por lo que pueda pasar).	You always have to be prepared (for what may happen).
Ninguna puerta cierra bien; ninguna ventana abre bien.	None of the doors close tight; none of the windows open easily.
Las paredes son de papel.	The walls are paper thin.
No existe la intimidad.	There is no privacy.
El gato que tenía se ha mudado.	The cat I had has moved.
La ropa sale de la lavadora tal y como estaba.	The clothes come out of the washing machine the same as they went in.
Las goteras inundan el altillo.	The leaks flood the attic.
El día que llueve es todo un espectáculo.	When it rains, it's a show.

No queda pintura en la fachada.	There's no paint left on the outside.
Y esta escalera de caracol es una pesadilla a cualquier hora del día.	And this spiral staircase is a nightmare at any time of day.
Las sorpresas no faltan viviendo en tal casa.	We have no lack of surprises living in such a house.
¿Por qué no vienen Uds. mañana?	Why don't you come over tomorrow?

LA VIVIENDA PERFECTA / THE PERFECT HOUSE

¡Qué ilusión me hace tener una casa!	How I'd love to own a house!
Una casa bien grande, con jardín y con terraza.	A fairly large house, with a garden and a patio.
Siempre he querido ser ama de casa.	I have always wanted to be a housewife.
Limpiar, ordenar y lavar a todas horas del día.	Cleaning, straightening up, and washing at all hours of the day.
Cantar y cantar mientras preparo la comida.	Singing and singing while I prepare the meals.
Tener una cocina moderna y práctica a la vez.	I'd have a kitchen that was both modern and practical.
Tener electrodomésticos de todos los colores y tamaños.	I'd have appliances of all shapes and colors.
Pues no son sólo trastos; algunos te echan una mano.	They're not just pieces of junk; some help you out.
Y con un lavaplatos, todo está limpio y ordenado.	And with a dishwasher, all is clean and organized.
¡Qué maravilla! ¡Qué sueño de vida!	How wonderful! What a dream of a life!

MEDIO AMBIENTE Y ECOLOGÍA	ENVIRONMENT AND ECOLOGY
Parece que la contaminación del aire crece a un ritmo alarmante.	It seems that air pollution is growing at an alarming rate.
El dióxido de carbono es cada vez más abundante en la atmósfera.	There is more and more carbon dioxide in the atmosphere.
La sequía es un grave problema en muchos países de África.	Drought is a serious problem in many African countries.
Las aguas de los ríos, océanos y mares están cada vez más contaminadas.	Rivers, oceans, and seas are becoming more and more polluted.
El agujero de la capa de ozono sigue creciendo.	The hole in the ozone layer keeps growing.
Los incendios forestales y las inundaciones están a la orden del día.	Forest fires and floods are everyday events.

PREGUNTAS SOBRE ECOLOGÍA	ENVIRONMENTAL QUESTIONS
¿Está en peligro la vida en la Tierra?	Is life on earth in danger?
¿A quién afecta la destrucción del medio ambiente?	Who does the destruction of the environment affect?
¿Qué predicen los científicos para dentro de cincuenta años?	What do scientists predict for the next fifty years?
¿Qué consecuencias puede tener el calentamiento global de la Tierra?	What can the consequences of global warming be?
¿Es posible que se deshielen los casquetes polares?	Is it possible that the polar caps will melt?

¿Crees que hay solución a los problemas actuales de contaminación?	Do you think there's a solution to the current pollution problems?
¿Cuáles son las condiciones medioambientales óptimas que garantizan la existencia de los seres vivos en la Tierra?	What are the optimal environmental conditions that guarantee the existence of living beings on earth?
¿Qué medidas se pueden tomar para poner marcha atrás al problema de la contaminación atmosférica? ¿Y de la contaminación del agua?	What measures can be taken to reverse the problem of atmospheric pollution? And of water pollution?
¿Qué medidas generales se pueden adoptar para conservar la naturaleza?	What general measures can be adopted to conserve nature?
¿Qué países producen más basura? ¿Cuáles consumen más recursos naturales?	What countries produce the most garbage? Consume more natural resources?
¿Perteneces a alguna organización dedicada a la conservación del medio ambiente?	Do you belong to an organization dedicated to environmental conservation?
¿Crees que son exagerados los datos sobre el calentamiento global del planeta?	Do you think the global warming data is exaggerated?
¿Crees que es todo una farsa? ¿Una exageración de los Verdes?	Do you think it is all a farce? An exaggeration of the Green Party?
¿Cómo afecta la tala de árboles al ecosistema?	How does the cutting of trees affect the ecosystem?
¿Cuáles son en tu opinión las principales causas del creciente deterioro medioambiental?	In your opinion, what are the main causes of the increasing environmental degradation?
¿De qué modo colaboras tú en la conservación de la naturaleza?	In what way do you help in the conservation of nature?

¿Quién tiene la culpa del deterioro medioambiental? ¿Hay algún culpable?	Whose fault is environmental degradation? Is anyone at fault?

DAR Y PEDIR DIRECCIONES — GIVING AND ASKING FOR DIRECTIONS

¿Por dónde se va al centro?	How do I get downtown?
Sigan todo recto/derecho hasta el final de esta calle.	Keep going straight until you get to the end of this street.
Luego doblen/giren a la derecha.	Then turn right.
Sigan tres cuadras y ya están en pleno centro.	Go three blocks and you'll be right downtown.
Señor, ¿sabe cómo llegar al Museo Nacional de Arte Contemporáneo?	Sir, do you know how to get to the National Museum of Contemporary Art?
Está en la otra punta de la ciudad.	It's on the other side of the city.
Está demasiado lejos para ir caminando.	It's too far to walk.
Tienen que tomar el metro.	You need to take the subway.
Tomen la línea roja en dirección Colinas.	Take the red line towards Colinas.
Deben bajarse en la última parada.	You should get off at the last stop.
Luego deben tomar la línea amarilla en dirección Paseo Coral.	Then you need to take the yellow line towards Paseo Coral.
Y bajarse en la penúltima parada.	Get off at the next-to-last stop.
Todo el trayecto les tomará casi una hora y cuarto.	The whole trip should take you about an hour and a quarter.

Al salir del metro verán el Museo Nacional justo enfrente.	When you get out of the subway, you'll see the National Museum right in front of you.
Señora, ¿le importaría decirnos cómo llegar al Ayuntamiento?	Ma'am, would you mind telling us how to get to City Hall?
Es que somos turistas y queremos verlo todo.	We're tourists and we want to see everything.
Es mejor que no vayan caminando.	It's better not to walk.
Les recomiendo que tomen un taxi.	I recommend that you take a taxi.
¡Qué paciencia tiene con nosotros la gente de esta ciudad!	The people in this city are so patient with us!
Creo que debemos dejar de preguntar.	I think we should stop asking questions.
Esta ciudad es monstruosa, gigantesca y complicada.	This city is monstrous, gigantic, and complicated.
Y una de dos, o compramos un mapa o tomamos un autobús turístico.	One or the other: do we buy a map or take a tour bus?
Si es que queremos llegar a algún sitio.	If we want to get anywhere.
¿Qué opinas?	What do you think?
Me parece buena la idea del autobús turístico.	I think the tour bus idea is a good idea.

PREGUNTAS SOBRE NUTRICIÓN / QUESTIONS ABOUT NUTRITION

¿Cuántas calorías tiene este plato preparado?	How many calories does this prepared meal have?
¿Qué porcentaje de sodio tiene una lata de frijoles?	What percentage of sodium does a can of beans have?

¿Cuántos gramos de azúcar suele tener más o menos un jugo envasado?	How many grams of sugar, more ore less, does a container of juice have?
¿Qué alimentos son ricos en Vitamina A?	What foods are rich in Vitamin A?
¿Es verdad que el aceite de hígado de bacalao contiene Vitamina D?	Is it true that cod liver oil has Vitamin D?
¿Es verdad que la falta de hierro en la sangre causa anemia?	Is it true that a lack of iron in the blood causes anemia?
¿Para qué es importante la Vitamina C?	What is Vitamin C important for?
¿Por qué necesita el cuerpo vitaminas y minerales?	Why does the body need vitamins and minerals?
¿Es bueno ingerir fibra para evitar el estreñimiento?	Is it good to eat fiber to avoid constipation?
¿Por qué es mejor comer pan integral que pan blanco?	Why is it better to eat whole-wheat bread than white bread?
¿Qué alimentos son esenciales para llevar una dieta equilibrada?	What foods are essential to a balanced diet?
¿Qué alimentos deben ingerirse diariamente?	What foods should you eat daily?
¿Qué alimentos deben consumirse con moderación?	What foods should you eat in moderation?
¿Qué desventajas tiene la dieta vegetariana?	What drawbacks does a vegetarian diet have?
¿Qué ventajas tiene la dieta mediterránea?	What advantages does a Mediterranean diet have?
¿Qué alimentos constituyen la base de la dieta mediterránea?	What are the basic foods in a Mediterranean diet?
¿Qué dieta proporciona mayores ventajas para la salud?	What diet offers the most health advantages?

¿Qué es el colesterol?	What is cholesterol?
¿Qué alimentos son ricos en colesterol?	What foods are high in cholesterol?
¿Qué alimentos contienen elevados índices de colesterol?	What foods have high amounts of cholesterol?
¿Cuáles son los inconvenientes de la comida rápida?	What are the drawbacks of fast food?
¿Qué tipo de alimentación favorece el buen funcionamiento del organismo?	What kind of nutrition promotes the proper functioning of the body?
¿Qué sustancias son perjudiciales para la salud?	What substances are harmful to your health?
¿Qué comían nuestros antepasados?	What did our ancestors eat?
¿Cómo han evolucionado los hábitos alimenticios a lo largo de la historia?	How have nutritional habits evolved throughout history?

PREGUNTAS SOBRE LA FORMA FÍSICA Y MENTAL	QUESTIONS ABOUT PHYSICAL AND MENTAL WELL-BEING
¿Es el estar en forma una moda o un estilo de vida?	Is being in shape a fashion or a lifestyle?
¿Hasta qué punto es importante estar en forma?	How important is it to be in shape?
¿Qué es aconsejable hacer para mantenerse en forma?	What activities are advisable for staying in shape?
¿Qué es recomendable hacer para perder peso?	What is recommended for losing weight?
¿Hasta qué punto es importante mantener un peso adecuado?	How important is it to maintain an adecuete weight?
¿Por qué es aconsejable realizar algún tipo de actividad física?	Why is it advisable to keep up some kind of physical activity?

¿Es la obesidad una cuestión estética o un grave problema de salud?	Is obesity an issue of appearance or a serious health problem?
¿Qué inconvenientes presenta para la salud el estilo de vida de los países industrializados?	What disadvantages does the lifestyle of industrialized countries have to health?
¿Qué es el estrés?	What is stress?
¿Qué papel juega el estrés en la salud de la sociedad actual?	What role does stress play in the health of society today?
¿En qué medida puede afectar el medio ambiente a la salud?	To what extent can the environment affect health?
¿Qué condiciones medioambientales son perjudiciales para la salud?	What environmental conditions are hazardous to our health?
¿Debo preocuparme por lo que como/bebo?	Should I worry about what I eat/drink?
¿Qué puedo hacer para mantenerme en forma?	What can I do to stay in shape?
¿Debo vigilar mi peso?	Should I watch my weight?
¿Soy un fanático/una fanática de la nutrición?	Am I a nutrition fanatic?
¿Qué me preocupa más, el número de calorías que ingiero al día o el valor nutritivo de los alimentos que tomo?	What should I worry about more, the number of calories I take in every day or the nutritional value of the foods I eat?
¿Quiero vivir cien años? ¿Por qué?	Do I want to live a hundred years? Why?
PREGUNTAS SOBRE EL FUTURO LABORAL	QUESTIONS ABOUT YOUR FUTURE IN THE WORKPLACE
¿Qué piensas hacer cuando te gradúes?	What do you think you'll do after you graduate?

¿Piensas en el futuro o vives al día?	Do you think about the future, or do you live day to day?
¿Has pensado seriamente en tu futuro?	Have you thought seriously about your future?
¿De qué color lo ves?	And how do you see it?/What do you think it will be like?
¿Eres optimista o pesimista?	Are you an optimist or a pessimist?
¿Te gustan los retos?	Do you like challenges?
¿Te interesa correr riesgos?	Are you interested in taking risks?
¿Cuál es tu trabajo/profesión ideal?	What is your ideal job/ profession?
¿Qué buscas en un trabajo? ¿Y en un jefe o jefa?	What do you look for in a job? And in a boss?
¿Qué alicientes crees que ofrece el mundo del trabajo?	What incentives/attractions do you think the working world offers?
¿Quieres ganar mucho dinero?	Do you want to earn a lot of money?
¿Podrías vivir sin dinero?	Could you live without money?
¿Qué tipo de trabajo buscas?	What kind of job are you looking for?
¿En qué tipo de ambiente laboral piensas?	What kind of work atmosphere are you thinking about?
¿Estás impaciente por salir de la universidad e incorporarte al mundo laboral?	Are you eager to leave school and enter the working world?
¿Eres una persona responsable?	Are you a responsible person?
¿Crees que trabajar es más interesante que estudiar?	Do you think working is more interesting than studying?

¿Has asistido ya a alguna entrevista de trabajo?	Have you gone on a job interview yet?
¿Cuáles consideras tus puntos fuertes?	What do you consider your strong points to be?
¿Cuáles crees que son tus puntos débiles?	What do you think your weak points are?
¿Buscas un trabajo creativo, de atención al público o de dirección?	What kind of job are you looking for, a creative one, one where you have to work with the public, or a managerial one?
¿Buscas un trabajo vocacional o uno puramente lucrativo?	Are you looking for a job you love, or just one that will make a lot of money?
¿Para qué tipo de trabajo crees que estás mejor preparado?	For what type of job do you think you are best prepared?
¿Qué crees que puedes ofrecer?	What do you think you have to offer?
¿Qué esperas recibir a cambio?	What do expect to get in return?
¿Cuál es tu meta u objetivo principal?	What is your main goal or objective?
¿Hasta dónde quieres llegar?	How far do you want to go?
¿Qué estás dispuesto/a a arriesgar para conseguirlo?	What are you willing to risk to get there?
¿Qué precio estás dispuesto/a a pagar?	What price are you willing to pay?
¿Cuáles serían tus prioridades?	What would your priorities be?
¿Estarías interesado/a en trabajar horas extras?	Would you be interested in working extra hours?
En caso afirmativo, ¿esperarías algo a cambio?	If so, would you expect something in return?
¿Por qué cualidades te gustaría ser recordado?	For what qualities would you like to be remembered?

¿Cómo te gustaría pasar a la historia?	How would you like to go down in history?
¿O prefieres vivir tranquilo/a y pasar desapercibido/a?	Or do you prefer to live quietly and go unnoticed?

LAS ARTES / THE ARTS

¿Para qué sirve el arte?	What is art for?
¿Qué significa el término artista?	What does the term "artist" mean?
¿Para qué usa el arte el/la "artista"?	What does an artist use art for?
¿Cuál es la misión del/de la artista?	What is the artist's mission?
¿Son los artistas egocentristas?	Are artists egocentric/self-centered?
¿Son realistas los artistas?	Are artists realists?
¿Envidias la vida del/de la artista?	Do you envy the life of an artist?
¿Tienes tú madera de artista?	Do you have what it takes to be an artist?
¿Qué significa la expresión "trabajar por amor al arte"?	What does the expression "to work for the love of art" mean?
¿Por qué llaman al cine el séptimo arte?	Why do they call film the seventh art?
¿Crees que una imagen vale más que mil palabras?	Do you think a picture is worth a thousand words?
¿Te gusta ver películas extranjeras en versión original subtitulada?	Do you like to see foreign films in the original language with subtitles?
¿Cómo expresas lo que piensas, lo que sientes, lo que quieres, lo que te gusta?	How do you express what you think, feel, want, and like?

¿Eres aficionado/a a la pintura?	Are you a painting aficionado?
¿Estás familiarizado/a con el surrealismo? ¿Y con el cubismo?	Are you familiar with surrealism? With cubism?
¿Qué otras tendencias artísticas conoces? ¿Cuáles te interesan más? ¿Por qué?	What other artistic movements do you know about? Which ones interest you the most? Why?
¿Te gusta o te gustaría coleccionar objetos de arte?	Do you or would you like to collect works of art?
¿Pagarías cincuenta millones de dólares por un original de Picasso?	Would you pay fifty million dollars for a Picasso original?
¿Eres amante de la música?	Are you a music lover?
¿A qué sentidos seduce la música?	Which senses does music affect?
¿Qué se necesita para disfrutar del arte?	What do you need to enjoy art?
¿Hace falta un sexto sentido?	Do you need a sixth sense?
¿Sin cuál de los cinco sentidos no podrías vivir?	Which of the five senses could you not live without?
¿Qué tipo de música está de moda entre la juventud actual?	What kind of music is popular with today's youth?
Y por último, la pregunta del millón, ¿Beatles o Rolling Stones?	And finally, the million-dollar question, the Beatles or the Rolling Stones?

PREGUNTAS SOBRE LAS ACTUALIDADES	QUESTIONS ABOUT CURRENT EVENTS
¿Estás al día?	Are you up to date?
¿Qué dicen hoy los periódicos?	What do the newspapers say today?
¿Has leído las últimas noticias?	Have you read the latest news?

¿Te interesa la política? ¿Por qué?	Are you interested in politics? Why?
¿Estás al día de lo que pasa en tu país? ¿Y en el resto del mundo?	Are you up to date with what's happening in your country? And in the rest of the world?
¿Qué temas sociales y políticos te preocupan?	What social and political topics concern you?
Si fueras político/a, ¿qué medidas tomarías para solucionar los problemas actuales del medio ambiente?	If you were a politician, what measures would you take to solve the current environmental problems?
¿Sigues de cerca la actualidad (política)?	Do you follow current events (politics) closely?
¿Lees las noticias internacionales?	Do you read international news?
¿Te interesa la política exterior?	Does foreign politics interest you?
¿(Te) Crees todo lo que lees en los periódicos?	Do you believe everything you read in the newspapers?
¿Te consideras una persona bien informada?	Do you consider yourself well-informed?
¿Crees que estamos bien informados?	Do you think we are well-informed?
¿Cómo es posible digerir tanta información?	How can one take in so much information?
En tu opinión, ¿qué cualidades debe tener un buen político/una buena política?	In your opinion, what qualities should a good politician have?
¿Qué harías si fueras presidente de los Estados Unidos?	What would you do if you were president of the United States?
¿Cuáles crees que son las causas principales de la violencia?	What do you think the principal causes of violence are?

¿Qué opinas de las campañas electorales/publicitarias?	What do you think of electoral/publicity campaigns?
¿Crees que los políticos tienen demasiado poder?	Do you think politicians have too much power?
¿Crees que el poder corrompe?	Do you think that power corrupts?
¿Qué opinas de la sociedad actual?	What do you think about present-day society?
¿Cómo valoras los últimos avances de la tecnología?	What do you think of/How do you rate the latest technology advances?
¿Ha avanzado el ser humano al mismo ritmo que la tecnología?	Have human beings advanced at the same rate as technology?
¿Qué avances positivos se lograron a lo largo del siglo XX?	What positive advances were made over the course of the 20th century?
¿Qué cuestiones te gustaría ver resueltas en el siglo XXI?	What issues would you like to see resolved in the 21st century?
¿Confías en los líderes políticos de tu país?	Do you trust the political leaders of your country?
¿Qué papel crees que juega el dinero en la sociedad actual?	What role do you think money plays in present-day society?
¿Hasta qué punto crees que los medios de comunicación influyen en la visión que tenemos del mundo?	To what extent do you think that the media influence our world view?
¿Crees que está bien repartida la riqueza del planeta?	Do you think the wealth of the planet is well distributed?
¿Hay problemas de discriminación en tu ciudad y/o país?	Are there discrimination problems in your city and/or country?
¿Crees que vivimos en un mundo justo y solidario?	Do you think we live in a just and supportive world?

¿Qué medidas tomarías para que el mundo fuera un lugar mejor para todos?	What measures would you take so that the world would be a better place for everyone?
¿Quién tiene la última palabra?	Who has the last word?

Verb conjugation tables

The verb lists

The list of verbs below and the model-verb tables that start on page 270 show you how to conjugate every verb taught in **VISTAS, AVENTURAS,** and **INVITACIONES.** Each verb in the list is followed by a model verb that is conjugated according to the same pattern. The number in parentheses indicates where in the tables you can find the conjugated forms of the model verb. If you want to find out how to conjugate **divertirse,** for example, look up number 33, **sentir,** the model for verbs that follow the e:ie stem-change pattern.

abrazar (z:c) like cruzar (37)
abrir like vivir (3) *except* past participle is abierto
aburrir(se) like vivir (3)
acabar de like hablar (1)
acampar like hablar (1)
aceptar like hablar (1)
acompañar like hablar (1)
aconsejar like hablar (1)
acordarse (o:ue) like contar (24)
acostarse (o:ue) like contar (24)
adelgazar (z:c) like cruzar (37)
afeitarse like hablar (1)
ahorrar like hablar (1)
alegrarse like hablar (1)
aliviar like hablar (1)
almorzar (o:ue) like contar (24) *except* (z:c)
alquilar like hablar (1)
andar like hablar (1) *except* preterite stem is anduv-
anunciar like hablar (1)
apagar (g:gu) like llegar (41)
aplaudir like vivir (3)
apreciar like hablar (1)
aprender like comer (2)
apurarse like hablar (1)
armar like hablar (1)
arrancar (c:qu) like tocar (43)
arreglar like hablar (1)
asistir like vivir (3)
aumentar like hablar (1)
ayudar(se) like hablar (1)
bailar like hablar (1)
bajar(se) like hablar (1)
bañarse like hablar (1)
barrer like comer (2)
beber like comer (2)
besar(se) like hablar (1)
borrar like hablar (1)
brindar like hablar (1)
bucear like hablar (1)
buscar (c:qu) like tocar (43)
caber (4)
caer(se) (5)
calentarse (e:ie) like pensar (30)
calzar (z:c) like cruzar (37)
cambiar like hablar (1)
caminar like hablar (1)
cantar like hablar (1)
casarse like hablar (1)
castigar like hablar (1)
cazar (z:c) like cruzar (37)
celebrar like hablar (1)
cenar like hablar (1)

How to use the verb tables

In the tables you will find the infinitive, present and past participles, and all the simple forms of each model verb. The formation of the compound tenses of any verb can be inferred from the table of compound tenses, pages 270–271, either by combining the past participle of the verb with a conjugated form of **haber** or by combining the present participle with a conjugated form of **estar**.

cepillarse like hablar (1)
cerrar (e:ie) like pensar (30)
chocar (c:qu) like tocar (43)
cobrar like hablar (1)
cocinar like hablar (1)
colorear like hablar (1)
comenzar (e:ie) (z:c) like empezar (26)
comer (2)
compartir like vivir (3)
comprar like hablar (1)
comprender like comer (2)
comprometerse like comer (2)
comunicarse (c:qu) like tocar (43)
conducir (c:zc) (6)
confirmar like hablar (1)
conocer (c:zc) (35)
conseguir (e:i) like seguir (32)
conservar like hablar (1)
consumir like vivir (3)
contaminar like hablar (1)
contar (o:ue) (24)
controlar like hablar (1)
correr like comer (2)
cortar like hablar (1)
costar (o:ue) like contar (24)
creer (y) (36)
cruzar (z:c) (37)
cubrir like vivir (3) *except* past participle is cubierto
cuidar(se) like hablar (1)
cumplir like vivir (3)
dañar like hablar (1)
dar(se) (7)
deber like comer (2)
decidir like vivir (3)
decir (e:i) (8)
declarar like hablar (1)
dejar like hablar (1)
depositar like hablar (1)
desarrollar like hablar (1)
desayunar like hablar (1)
descansar like hablar (1)
descargar like hablar (1)
descomponer(se) like poner(se) (15)
describir like vivir (3) *except* past participle is descrito
descubrir like vivir (3) *except* past participle is descubierto
desear like hablar (1)
despedirse (e:i) like pedir (29)
despertarse (e:ie) like pensar (30)
destruir (y) (38)
dibujar like hablar (1)
dirigir (g:j) like vivir (3) *except* (g:j)
discutir like vivir (3)

disfrazar(se) like hablar (1)
disfrutar like hablar (1)
divertirse (e:ie) like sentir (33)
divorciarse like hablar (1)
doblar like hablar (1)
doler (o:ue) like volver (34) *except* past participle is regular
dormir(se) (o:ue) (25)
ducharse like hablar (1)
dudar like hablar (1)
durar like hablar (1)
echar like hablar (1)
elegir (e:i) like pedir (29) *except* (g:j)
embarazarse like hablar (1)
emitir like vivir (3)
empezar (e:ie) (z:c) (26)
empujar like hablar (1)
enamorarse like hablar (1)
encantar like hablar (1)
encontrar(se) (o:ue) like contar (24)
enfermarse like hablar (1)
engordar like hablar (1)
enojarse like hablar (1)
enseñar like hablar (1)
ensuciar like hablar (1)
entender (e:ie) (27)
entrar like hablar (1)
entregar like hablar (1) *except* (g:gu)
entrenarse like hablar (1)
entrevistar like hablar (1)
enviar (envío) (39)
escalar like hablar (1)
escoger (g:j) like proteger (42)
escribir like vivir (3) *except* past participle is escrito
escuchar like hablar (1)
esculpir like vivir (3)
esperar like hablar (1)
esquiar (esquío) like enviar (39)
establecer (c:zc) like conocer (35)
estacionar(se) like hablar (1)
estar (9)
estornudar like hablar (1)
estudiar like hablar (1)
evitar like hablar (1)
explicar (c:qu) like tocar (43)
explorar like hablar (1)
faltar like hablar (1)
fascinar like hablar (1)
firmar like hablar (1)
frenar like hablar (1)
fumar like hablar (1)
funcionar like hablar (1)
ganar like hablar (1)
gastar like hablar (1)
grabar like hablar (1)
graduarse (gradúo) (40)
guardar like hablar (1)
gustar like hablar (1)
haber (hay) (10)
hablar (1)
hacer (11)
iluminar like hablar (1)
importar like hablar (1)
imprimir like vivir (3)
informar like hablar (1)
insistir like vivir (3)
interesar like hablar (1)
invertir (e:ie) like sentir (33)
invitar like hablar (1)
ir(se) (12)
jubilarse like hablar (1)
jugar (u:ue) (g:gu) (28)
juntar(se) like hablar (1)
lastimarse like hablar (1)
lavar(se) like hablar (1)
leer (y) like creer (36)
levantar(se) like hablar (1)
limpiar like hablar (1)
llamar(se) like hablar (1)
llegar (g:gu) (41)
llenar like hablar (1)
llevar(se) like hablar (1)
llover (o:ue) like volver (34) *except* past participle is regular
luchar like hablar (1)
mandar like hablar (1)
manejar like hablar (1)
mantener(se) (e:ie) like tener (20)

maquillarse like hablar (1)
mejorar like hablar (1)
merendar (e:ie) like pensar (30)
mirar like hablar (1)
molestar like hablar (1)
montar like hablar (1)
morir (o:ue) like dominar (25) *except* past participle is muerto
mostrar (o:ue) like contar (24)
mudarse like hablar (1)
nacer (c:zc) like conocer (35)
nadar like hablar (1)
navegar (g:gu) like llegar (41)
necesitar like hablar (1)
negar (e:ie) like pensar (30) *except* (g:gu)
nevar (e:ie) like pensar (30)
obedecer (c:zc) like conocer (35)
obtener (e:ie) like tener (20)
ocurrir like vivir (3)
odiar like hablar (1)
ofrecer (c:zc) like conocer (35)
oír (13)
olvidar like hablar (1)
pagar (g:gu) like llegar (41)
parar(se) like hablar (1)
parecer (c:zc) like conocer (35)
pasar(se) like hablar (1)
pasear like hablar (1)
patinar like hablar (1)
pedir (e:i) (29)
pegar like hablar (1) *except* (g:gu)
peinarse like hablar (1)
pelearse like hablar (1)
pensar(se) (e:ie) (30)
perder (e:ie) like entender (27)
pescar (c:qu) like tocar (43)
pintar(se) like hablar (1)
planchar like hablar (1)
poder (o:ue) (14)
ponchar(se) like hablar (1)
poner(se) (15)
portar(se) like hablar (1)
practicar (c:qu) like tocar (43)
preferir (e:ie) like sentir (33)
preguntar like hablar (1)
preocuparse like hablar (1)
preparar like hablar (1)
presentar like hablar (1)
prestar like hablar (1)
probar(se) (o:ue) like contar (24)
prohibir like vivir (3)
prometer like comer (2)
proteger (g:j) (42)
publicar (c:qu) like tocar (43)
quedar(se) like hablar (1)
quemar like hablar (1)
querer (e:ie) (16)
quitar(se) like hablar (1)
rasurar(se) like hablar (1)
recetar like hablar (1)
recibir(se) like vivir (3)
reciclar like hablar (1)
recoger (g:j) like proteger (42)
recomendar (e:ie) like pensar (30)
recordar (o:ue) like contar (24)
reducir (c:zc) like conducir (6)
regalar like hablar (1)
regañar like hablar (1)
regatear like hablar (1)
regresar like hablar (1)
reír(se) (e:i) (31)
relajarse like hablar (1)
renunciar like hablar (1)
repetir (e:i) like pedir (29)
resolver (o:ue) like volver (34)
respirar like hablar (1)
revisar like hablar (1)
rogar (o:ue) like contar (24) *except* (g:gu)
romper(se) like comer (2) *except* past participle is roto
saber (17)
sacar (c:qu) like tocar (43)
sacudir like vivir (3)
salir(se) (18)
saltar like hablar (1)
saludar(se) like hablar (1)
secar(se) (c:q) like tocar (43)
seguir (e:i) (32)

sentarse (e:ie) like pensar (30)
sentir(se) (e:ie) (33)
separarse like hablar (1)
ser (19)
servir (e:i) like pedir (29)
solicitar like hablar (1)
sonar (o:ue) like contar (24)
sonreír (e:i) like reír(se) (31)
sorprender like comer (2)
subir(se) like vivir (3)
sudar like hablar (1)
sufrir like vivir (3)
sugerir (e:ie) like sentir (33)
suponer like poner (15)
temer like comer (2)
tener (e:ie) (20)
terminar like hablar (1)
tocar (c:qu) (43)

tomar like hablar (1)
torcerse (o:ue) like volver (34) *except* (c:z) and past participle is regular; e.g. yo me tuerzo
toser like comer (2)
trabajar like hablar (1)
traducir (c:zc) like conducir (6)
traer (21)
transmitir like vivir (3)
tratar like hablar (1)
usar like hablar (1)
vender like comer (2)
venir (e:ie) (22)
ver (23)
vestirse (e:i) (44)
viajar like hablar (1)
visitar like hablar (1)
vivir (3)
volver (o:ue) (34)
votar like hablar (1)

Regular verbs: simple tenses

		INDICATIVE			
	Infinitive	Present	Imperfect	Preterite	Future
1	hablar	hablo	hablaba	hablé	hablaré
		hablas	hablabas	hablaste	hablarás
	Participles:	habla	hablaba	habló	hablará
	hablando	hablamos	hablábamos	hablamos	hablaremos
	hablado	habláis	hablabais	hablasteis	hablaréis
		hablan	hablaban	hablaron	hablarán
2	comer	como	comía	comí	comeré
		comes	comías	comiste	comerás
	Participles:	come	comía	comió	comerá
	comiendo	comemos	comíamos	comimos	comeremos
	comido	coméis	comíais	comisteis	comeréis
		comen	comían	comieron	comerán
3	vivir	vivo	vivía	viví	viviré
		vives	vivías	viviste	vivirás
	Participles:	vive	vivía	vivió	vivirá
	viviendo	vivimos	vivíamos	vivimos	viviremos
	vivido	vivís	vivíais	vivisteis	viviréis
		viven	vivían	vivieron	vivirán

All verbs: compound tenses

PERFECT TENSES		
INDICATIVE		
Present Perfect	**Past Perfect**	**Future Perfect**
he has ha hemos habéis han } hablado / comido / vivido	había habías había habíamos habíais habían } hablado / comido / vivido	habré habrás habrá habremos habréis habrán } hablado / comido / vivido

INDICATIVE	SUBJUNCTIVE		IMPERATIVE
Conditional	**Present**	**Past**	
hablaría	hable	hablara	
hablarías	hables	hablaras	habla (no hables)
hablaría	hable	hablara	hable
hablaríamos	hablemos	habláramos	hablemos
hablaríais	habléis	hablarais	hablad (no habléis)
hablarían	hablen	hablaran	hablen
comería	coma	comiera	
comerías	comas	comieras	come (no comas)
comería	coma	comiera	coma
comeríamos	comamos	comiéramos	comamos
comeríais	comáis	comierais	comed (no comáis)
comerían	coman	comieran	coman
viviría	viva	viviera	
vivirías	vivas	vivieras	vive (no vivas)
viviría	viva	viviera	viva
viviríamos	vivamos	viviéramos	vivamos
viviríais	viváis	vivierais	vivid (no viváis)
vivirían	vivan	vivieran	vivan

PERFECT TENSES

INDICATIVE	SUBJUNCTIVE	
Conditional Perfect	**Present Perfect**	**Past Perfect**
habría habrías habría habríamos habríais habrían } hablado / comido / vivido	haya hayas haya hayamos hayáis hayan } hablado / comido / vivido	hubiera hubieras hubiera hubiéramos hubierais hubieran } hablado / comido / vivido

PROGRESSIVE TENSES		
INDICATIVE		
Present Progressive	**Past Progressive**	**Future Progressive**
estoy estás está estamos estáis estan } hablando comiendo viviendo	estaba estabas estaba estábamos estabais estaban } hablando comiendo viviendo	estaré estarás estará estaremos estaréis estarán } hablando comiendo viviendo

Irregular verbs

		INDICATIVE			
	Infinitive	**Present**	**Imperfect**	**Preterite**	**Future**
4	caber	**quepo**	cabía	**cupe**	**cabré**
		cabes	cabías	**cupiste**	**cabrás**
	Participles:	cabe	cabía	**cupo**	**cabrá**
	cabiendo	cabemos	cabíamos	**cupimos**	**cabremos**
	cabido	cabéis	cabíais	**cupisteis**	**cabréis**
		caben	cabían	**cupieron**	**cabrán**
5	caer(se)	**caigo**	**caía**	**caí**	caeré
		caes	**caías**	**caíste**	caerás
	Participles:	cae	**caía**	**cayó**	caerá
	cayendo	caemos	**caíamos**	**caímos**	caeremos
	caído	caéis	**caíais**	**caísteis**	caeréis
		caen	**caían**	**cayeron**	caerán
6	conducir	**conduzco**	conducía	**conduje**	conduciré
	(c:zc)	conduces	conducías	**condujiste**	conducirás
	Participles:	conduce	conducía	**condujo**	conducirá
	conduciendo	conducimos	conducíamos	**condujimos**	conduciremos
	conducido	conducís	conducíais	**condujisteis**	conduciréis
		conducen	conducían	**condujeron**	conducirán

PROGRESSIVE TENSES		
	SUBJUNCTIVE	
Conditional Progressive	Present Progressive	Past Progressive
estaría estarías estaría estaríamos estaríais estarían } hablando comiendo viviendo	esté estés esté estemos estéis estén } hablando comiendo viviendo	estuviera estuvieras estuviera estuviéramos estuvierais estuvieran } hablando comiendo viviendo

	SUBJUNCTIVE		IMPERATIVE
Conditional	Present	Past	
cabría	**quepa**	**cupiera**	
cabrías	**quepas**	**cupieras**	cabe (no **quepas**)
cabría	**quepa**	**cupiera**	**quepa**
cabríamos	**quepamos**	**cupiéramos**	**quepamos**
cabríais	**quepáis**	**cupierais**	cabed (no **quepáis**)
cabrían	**quepan**	**cupieran**	**quepan**
caería	**caiga**	**cayera**	
caerías	**caigas**	**cayeras**	cae (no **caigas**)
caería	**caiga**	**cayera**	**caiga**
caeríamos	**caigamos**	**cayéramos**	**caigamos**
caeríais	**caigáis**	**cayerais**	caed (no **caigáis**)
caerían	**caigan**	**cayeran**	**caigan**
conduciría	**conduzca**	**condujera**	
conducirías	**conduzcas**	**condujeras**	conduce **(no conduzcas)**
conduciría	**conduzca**	**condujera**	**conduzca**
conduciríamos	**conduzcamos**	**condujéramos**	**conduzcamos**
conduciríais	**conduzcáis**	**condujerais**	conducid (no **conduzcáis**)
conducirían	**conduzcan**	**condujeran**	**conduzcan**

	Infinitive	INDICATIVE			
		Present	Imperfect	Preterite	Future
7	dar	**doy**	daba	**di**	daré
		das	dabas	**diste**	darás
	Participles:	da	daba	**dio**	dará
	dando	damos	dábamos	**dimos**	daremos
	dado	dais	dabais	**disteis**	daréis
		dan	daban	**dieron**	darán
8	decir (e:i)	**digo**	decía	**dije**	**diré**
		dices	decías	**dijiste**	**dirás**
	Participles:	**dice**	decía	**dijo**	**dirá**
	diciendo	decimos	decíamos	**dijimos**	**diremos**
	dicho	decís	decíais	**dijisteis**	**diréis**
		dicen	decían	**dijeron**	**dirán**
9	estar	**estoy**	estaba	**estuve**	estaré
		estás	estabas	**estuviste**	estarás
	Participles:	está	estaba	**estuvo**	estará
	estando	estamos	estábamos	**estuvimos**	estaremos
	estado	estáis	estabais	**estuvisteis**	estaréis
		están	estaban	**estuvieron**	estarán
0	haber	**he**	había	**hube**	**habré**
		has	habías	**hubiste**	**habrás**
	Participles:	**ha**	había	**hubo**	**habrá**
	habiendo	**hemos**	habíamos	**hubimos**	**habremos**
	habido	habéis	habíais	**hubisteis**	**habréis**
		han	habían	**hubieron**	**habrán**
1	hacer	**hago**	hacía	**hice**	**haré**
		haces	hacías	**hiciste**	**harás**
	Participles:	hace	hacía	**hizo**	**hará**
	haciendo	hacemos	hacíamos	**hicimos**	**haremos**
	hecho	hacéis	hacíais	**hicisteis**	**haréis**
		hacen	hacían	**hicieron**	**harán**
2	ir	**voy**	**iba**	**fui**	iré
		vas	**ibas**	**fuiste**	irás
	Participles:	**va**	**iba**	**fue**	irá
	yendo	**vamos**	**íbamos**	**fuimos**	iremos
	ido	**vais**	**ibais**	**fuisteis**	iréis
		van	**iban**	**fueron**	irán
3	oír (y)	**oigo**	**oía**	**oí**	oiré
		oyes	**oías**	**oíste**	oirás
	Participles:	**oye**	**oía**	**oyó**	oirá
	oyendo	**oímos**	**oíamos**	**oímos**	oiremos
	oído	**oís**	**oíais**	**oísteis**	oiréis
		oyen	**oían**	**oyeron**	oirán

	SUBJUNCTIVE		IMPERATIVE
Conditional	**Present**	**Past**	
daría	**dé**	**diera**	
darías	**des**	**dieras**	da (no **des**)
daría	**dé**	**diera**	**dé**
daríamos	**demos**	**diéramos**	**demos**
daríais	**deis**	**dierais**	dad (no **deis**)
darían	**den**	**dieran**	**den**
diría	**diga**	**dijera**	
dirías	**digas**	**dijeras**	di (no **digas**)
diría	**diga**	**dijera**	**diga**
diríamos	**digamos**	**dijéramos**	**digamos**
diríais	**digáis**	**dijerais**	decid (no **digáis**)
dirían	**digan**	**dijeran**	**digan**
estaría	**esté**	**estuviera**	
estarías	**estés**	**estuvieras**	está (no **estés**)
estaría	**esté**	**estuviera**	**esté**
estaríamos	**estemos**	**estuviéramos**	**estemos**
estaríais	**estéis**	**estuvierais**	estad (no **estéis**)
estarían	**estén**	**estuvieran**	**estén**
habría	**haya**	**hubiera**	
habrías	**hayas**	**hubieras**	
habría	**haya**	**hubiera**	
habríamos	**hayamos**	**hubiéramos**	
habríais	**hayáis**	**hubierais**	
habrían	**hayan**	**hubieran**	
haría	**haga**	**hiciera**	
harías	**hagas**	**hicieras**	**haz** (no **hagas**)
haría	**haga**	**hiciera**	**haya**
haríamos	**hagamos**	**hiciéramos**	**hayamos**
haríais	**hagáis**	**hicierais**	haced (no **hayáis**)
harían	**hagan**	**hicieran**	**hayan**
iría	**vaya**	**fuera**	
irías	**vayas**	**fueras**	**ve** (no **vayas**)
iría	**vaya**	**fuera**	**vaya**
iríamos	**vayamos**	**fuéramos**	**vayamos**
iríais	**vayáis**	**fuerais**	id (no **vayáis**)
irían	**vayan**	**fueran**	**vayan**
oiría	**oiga**	**oyera**	
oirías	**oigas**	**oyeras**	**oye** (no **oigas**)
oiría	**oiga**	**oyera**	**oiga**
oiríamos	**oigamos**	**oyéramos**	**oigamos**
oiríais	**oigáis**	**oyerais**	**oíd** (no **oigáis**)
oirían	**oigan**	**oyeran**	**oigan**

	Infinitive	INDICATIVE			
		Present	Imperfect	Preterite	Future
14	poder (o:ue)	**puedo**	podía	**pude**	**podré**
		puedes	podías	**pudiste**	**podrás**
	Participles:	**puede**	podía	**pudo**	**podrá**
	pudiendo	podemos	podíamos	**pudimos**	**podremos**
	podido	podéis	podíais	**pudisteis**	**podréis**
		pueden	podían	**pudieron**	**podrán**
15	poner	**pongo**	ponía	**puse**	**pondré**
		pones	ponías	**pusiste**	**pondrás**
	Participles:	pone	ponía	**puso**	**pondrá**
	poniendo	ponemos	poníamos	**pusimos**	**pondremos**
	puesto	ponéis	poníais	**pusisteis**	**pondréis**
		ponen	ponían	**pusieron**	**pondrán**
16	querer (e:ie)	**quiero**	quería	**quise**	**querré**
		quieres	querías	**quisiste**	**querrás**
	Participles:	**quiere**	quería	**quiso**	**querrá**
	queriendo	queremos	queríamos	**quisimos**	**querremos**
	querido	queréis	queríais	**quisisteis**	**querréis**
		quieren	querían	**quisieron**	**querrán**
17	saber	**sé**	sabía	**supe**	**sabré**
		sabes	sabías	**supiste**	**sabrás**
	Participles:	sabe	sabía	**supo**	**sabrá**
	sabiendo	sabemos	sabíamos	**supimos**	**sabremos**
	sabido	sabéis	sabíais	**supisteis**	**sabréis**
		saben	sabían	**supieron**	**sabrán**
18	salir	**salgo**	salía	salí	**saldré**
		sales	salías	saliste	**saldrás**
	Participles:	**sale**	salía	salió	**saldrá**
	saliendo	salimos	salíamos	salimos	**saldremos**
	salido	salís	salíais	salisteis	**saldréis**
		salen	salían	salieron	**saldrán**
19	ser	**soy**	**era**	**fui**	seré
		eres	**eras**	**fuiste**	serás
	Participles:	**es**	**era**	**fue**	será
	siendo	**somos**	**éramos**	**fuimos**	seremos
	sido	**sois**	**erais**	**fuisteis**	seréis
		son	**eran**	**fueron**	serán
20	tener (e:ie)	**tengo**	tenía	**tuve**	**tendré**
		tienes	tenías	**tuviste**	**tendrás**
	Participles:	**tiene**	tenía	**tuvo**	**tendrá**
	teniendo	tenemos	teníamos	**tuvimos**	**tendremos**
	tenido	tenéis	teníais	**tuvisteis**	**tendréis**
		tienen	tenían	**tuvieron**	**tendrán**

	SUBJUNCTIVE		IMPERATIVE
Conditional	**Present**	**Past**	
podría	**pueda**	**pudiera**	
podrías	**puedas**	**pudieras**	**puede** (no **puedas**)
podría	**pueda**	**pudiera**	**pueda**
podríamos	podamos	**pudiéramos**	podamos
podríais	podáis	**pudierais**	poded (no **podáis**)
podrían	**puedan**	**pudieran**	**puedan**
pondría	**ponga**	**pusiera**	
pondrías	**pongas**	**pusieras**	**pon** (no **pongas**)
pondría	**ponga**	**pusiera**	**ponga**
pondríamos	**pongamos**	**pusiéramos**	**pongamos**
pondríais	**pongáis**	**pusierais**	poned (no **pongáis**)
pondrían	**pongan**	**pusieran**	**pongan**
querría	**quiera**	**quisiera**	
querrías	**quieras**	**quisieras**	**quiere** (no **quieras**)
querría	**quiera**	**quisiera**	**quiere**
querríamos	queramos	**quisiéramos**	queramos
querríais	queráis	**quisierais**	quered (no **queráis**)
querrían	**quieran**	**quisieran**	**quieran**
sabría	**sepa**	**supiera**	
sabrías	**sepas**	**supieras**	sabe (no **sepas**)
sabría	**sepa**	**supiera**	**sepa**
sabríamos	**sepamos**	**supiéramos**	**sepamos**
sabríais	**sepáis**	**supierais**	sabed (no **sepáis**)
sabrían	**sepan**	**supieran**	**sepan**
saldría	**salga**	saliera	
saldrías	**salgas**	salieras	**sal** (no **salgas**)
saldría	**salga**	saliera	**salga**
saldríamos	**salgamos**	saliéramos	**salgamos**
saldríais	**salgáis**	salierais	salid (no **salgáis**)
saldrían	**salgan**	salieran	**salgan**
sería	**sea**	**fuera**	
serías	**seas**	**fueras**	**sé** (no **seas**)
sería	**sea**	**fuera**	**sea**
seríamos	**seamos**	**fuéramos**	**seamos**
seríais	**seáis**	**fuerais**	sed (no **seáis**)
serían	**sean**	**fueran**	**sean**
tendría	**tenga**	**tuviera**	
tendrías	**tengas**	**tuvieras**	**ten** (no **tengas**)
tendría	**tenga**	**tuviera**	**tenga**
tendríamos	**tengamos**	**tuviéramos**	**tengamos**
tendríais	**tengáis**	**tuvierais**	tened (no **tengáis**)
tendrían	**tengan**	**tuvieran**	**tengan**

	Infinitive	INDICATIVE			
		Present	Imperfect	Preterite	Future
21	traer	**traigo**	**traía**	**traje**	traeré
		traes	**traías**	**trajiste**	traerás
	Participles:	trae	**traía**	**trajo**	traerá
	trayendo	traemos	**traíamos**	**trajimos**	traeremos
	traído	traéis	**traíais**	**trajisteis**	traeréis
		traen	**traían**	**trajeron**	traerán
22	venir (e:ie)	**vengo**	venía	**vine**	**vendré**
		vienes	venías	**viniste**	**vendrás**
	Participles:	**viene**	venía	**vino**	**vendrá**
	viniendo	venimos	veníamos	**vinimos**	**vendremos**
	venido	venís	veníais	**vinisteis**	**vendréis**
		vienen	venían	**vinieron**	**vendrán**
23	ver	**veo**	**veía**	**vi**	veré
		ves	**veías**	**viste**	verás
	Participles:	ve	**veía**	**vio**	verá
	viendo	vemos	**veíamos**	**vimos**	veremos
	visto	veis	**veíais**	**visteis**	veréis
		ven	**veían**	**vieron**	verán

Stem-changing verbs

	Infinitive	INDICATIVE			
		Present	Imperfect	Preterite	Future
24	contar (o:ue)	**cuento**	contaba	conté	contaré
		cuentas	contabas	contaste	contarás
	Participles:	**cuenta**	contaba	contó	contará
	contando	contamos	contábamos	contamos	contaremos
	contado	contáis	contabais	contasteis	contaréis
		cuentan	contaban	contaron	contarán
25	dormir (o:ue)	**duermo**	dormía	dormí	dormiré
		duermes	dormías	dormiste	dormirás
	Participles:	**duerme**	dormía	**durmió**	dormirá
	durmiendo	dormimos	dormíamos	dormimos	dormiremos
	dormido	dormís	dormíais	dormisteis	dormiréis
		duermen	dormían	**durmieron**	dormirán
26	empezar	**empiezo**	empezaba	**empecé**	empezaré
	(e:ie) (c)	**empiezas**	empezabas	empezaste	empezarás
		empieza	empezaba	empezó	empezará
	Participles:	empezamos	empezábamos	empezamos	empezaremos
	empezando	empezáis	empezabais	empezasteis	empezaréis
	empezado	**empiezan**	empezaban	empezaron	empezarán

	SUBJUNCTIVE		IMPERATIVE
Conditional	**Present**	**Past**	
traería	**traiga**	**trajera**	
traerías	**traigas**	**trajeras**	trae (no **traigas**)
traería	**traiga**	**trajera**	**traiga**
traeríamos	**traigamos**	**trajéramos**	**traigamos**
traeríais	**traigáis**	**trajerais**	traed (no **traigáis**)
traerían	**traigan**	**trajeran**	**traigan**
vendría	**venga**	**viniera**	
vendrías	**vengas**	**vinieras**	**ven** (no **vengas**)
vendría	**venga**	**viniera**	**venga**
vendríamos	**vengamos**	**viniéramos**	**vengamos**
vendríais	**vengáis**	**vinierais**	venid (no **vengáis**)
vendrían	**vengan**	**vinieran**	**vengan**
vería	**vea**	**viera**	
verías	**veas**	**vieras**	ve (no **veas**)
vería	**vea**	**viera**	**vea**
veríamos	**veamos**	**viéramos**	**veamos**
veríais	**veáis**	**vierais**	ved (no **veáis**)
verían	**vean**	**vieran**	**vean**

	SUBJUNCTIVE		IMPERATIVE
Conditional	**Present**	**Past**	
contaría	**cuente**	contara	
contarías	**cuentes**	contaras	**cuenta** (no **cuentes**)
contaría	**cuente**	contara	**cuente**
contaríamos	contemos	contáramos	contemos
contaríais	contéis	contarais	contad (no **contéis**)
contarían	**cuenten**	contaran	**cuenten**
dormiría	**duerma**	**durmiera**	
dormirías	**duermas**	**durmieras**	**duerme** (no **duermas**)
dormiría	**duerma**	**durmiera**	**duerma**
dormiríamos	**durmamos**	**durmiéramos**	**durmamos**
dormiríais	**durmáis**	**durmierais**	dormid (no **durmáis**)
dormirían	**duerman**	**durmieran**	**duerman**
empezaría	**empiece**	empezara	
empezarías	**empieces**	empezaras	**empieza** (no **empieces**)
empezaría	**empiece**	empezara	**empiece**
empezaríamos	**empecemos**	empezáramos	**empecemos**
empezaríais	**empecéis**	empezarais	empezad (no **empecéis**)
empezarían	**empiecen**	empezaran	**empiecen**

	Infinitive	INDICATIVE			
		Present	Imperfect	Preterite	Future
27	entender (e:ie)	**entiendo**	entendía	entendí	entenderé
		entiendes	entendías	entendiste	entenderás
		entiende	entendía	entendió	entenderá
	Participles:	entendemos	entendíamos	entendimos	entenderemos
	entendiendo	entendéis	entendíais	entendisteis	entenderéis
	entendido	**entienden**	entendían	entendieron	entenderán
28	jugar (u:ue) (gu)	**juego**	jugaba	**jugué**	jugaré
		juegas	jugabas	jugaste	jugarás
		juega	jugaba	jugó	jugará
	Participles:	jugamos	jugábamos	jugamos	jugaremos
	jugando	jugáis	jugabais	jugasteis	jugaréis
	jugado	**juegan**	jugaban	jugaron	jugarán
29	pedir (e:i)	**pido**	pedía	pedí	pediré
		pides	pedías	pediste	pedirás
	Participles:	**pide**	pedía	**pidió**	pedirá
	pidiendo	pedimos	pedíamos	pedimos	pediremos
	pedido	pedís	pedíais	pedisteis	pediréis
		piden	pedían	**pidieron**	pedirán
30	pensar (e:ie)	**pienso**	pensaba	pensé	pensaré
		piensas	pensabas	pensaste	pensarás
	Participles:	**piensa**	pensaba	pensó	pensará
	pensando	pensamos	pensábamos	pensamos	pensaremos
	pensado	pensáis	pensabais	pensasteis	pensaréis
		piensan	pensaban	pensaron	pensarán
31	reír(se) (e:i)	**río**	reía	reí	reiré
		ríes	reías	reíste	reirás
	Participles:	**ríe**	reía	**rió**	reirá
	riendo	reímos	reíamos	reímos	reiremos
	reído	reís	reíais	reísteis	reiréis
		ríen	reían	**rieron**	reirán
32	seguir (e:i) (gu)	**sigo**	seguía	seguí	seguiré
		sigues	seguías	seguiste	seguirás
		sigue	seguía	**siguió**	seguirá
	Participles:	seguimos	seguíamos	seguimos	seguiremos
	siguiendo	seguís	seguíais	seguisteis	seguiréis
	seguido	**siguen**	seguían	**siguieron**	seguirán
33	sentir (e:ie)	**siento**	sentía	sentí	sentiré
		sientes	sentías	sentiste	sentirás
	Participles:	**siente**	sentía	**sintió**	sentirá
	sintiendo	sentimos	sentíamos	sentimos	sentiremos
	sentido	sentís	sentíais	sentisteis	sentiréis
		sienten	sentían	**sintieron**	sentirán

	SUBJUNCTIVE		IMPERATIVE
Conditional	**Present**	**Past**	
entendería	**entienda**	entendiera	
entenderías	**entiendas**	entendieras	**entiende** (no **entiendas**)
entendería	**entienda**	entendiera	**entienda**
entenderíamos	entendamos	entendiéramos	entendamos
entenderíais	entendáis	entendierais	entended (no entendáis)
entenderían	**entiendan**	entendieran	**entiendan**
jugaría	**juegue**	jugara	
jugarías	**juegues**	jugaras	**juega** (no **juegues**)
jugaría	**juegue**	jugara	**juegue**
jugaríamos	**juguemos**	jugáramos	**juguemos**
jugaríais	**juguéis**	jugarais	jugad (no **jueguéis**)
jugarían	**jueguen**	jugaran	**jueguen**
pediría	**pida**	**pidiera**	
pedirías	**pidas**	**pidieras**	**pide** (no **pidas**)
pediría	**pida**	**pidiera**	**pida**
pediríamos	**pidamos**	**pidiéramos**	**pidamos**
pediríais	**pidáis**	**pidierais**	pedid (no **pidais**)
pedirían	**pidan**	**pidieran**	**pidan**
pensaría	**piense**	pensara	
pensarías	**pienses**	pensaras	**piensa** (no **pienses**)
pensaría	**piense**	pensara	**piense**
pensaríamos	pensemos	pensáramos	pensemos
pensaríais	penséis	pensarais	pensad (no penséis)
pensarían	**piensen**	pensaran	**piensan**
reiría	**ría**	**riera**	
reirías	**rías**	**rieras**	**ríe** (no **rías**)
reiría	**ría**	**riera**	**ría**
reiríamos	**riamos**	**riéramos**	**riamos**
reiríais	**riáis**	**rierais**	reíd (no **riáis**)
reirían	**rían**	**rieran**	**rían**
seguiría	**siga**	**siguiera**	
seguirías	**sigas**	**siguieras**	**sigue** (no **sigas**)
seguiría	**siga**	**siguiera**	**siga**
seguiríamos	**sigamos**	**siguiéramos**	**sigamos**
seguiríais	**sigáis**	**siguierais**	seguid (no **sigáis**)
seguirían	**sigan**	**siguieran**	**sigan**
sentiría	**sienta**	**sintiera**	
sentirías	**sientas**	**sintieras**	**siente** (no **sientas**)
sentiría	**sienta**	**sintiera**	**sienta**
sentiríamos	**sintamos**	**sintiéramos**	**sintamos**
sentiríais	**sintáis**	**sintierais**	sentid (no **sintáis**)
sentirían	**sientan**	**sintieran**	**sientan**

	Infinitive	INDICATIVE			
		Present	Imperfect	Preterite	Future
34	volver (o:ue)	**vuelvo**	volvía	volví	volveré
		vuelves	volvías	volviste	volverás
	Participles:	**vuelve**	volvía	volvió	volverá
	volviendo	volvemos	volvíamos	volvimos	volveremos
	vuelto	volvéis	volvíais	volvisteis	volveréis
		vuelven	volvían	volvieron	volverán

Verbs with spelling changes and reflexive verbs

	Infinitive	INDICATIVE			
		Present	Imperfect	Preterite	Future
35	conocer	**conozco**	conocía	conocí	conoceré
	(c:zc)	conoces	conocías	conociste	conocerás
		conoce	conocía	conoció	conocerá
	Participles:	conocemos	conocíamos	conocimos	conoceremos
	conociendo	conocéis	conocíais	conocisteis	conoceréis
	conocido	conocen	conocían	conocieron	conocerán
36	creer (y)	creo	creía	**creí**	creeré
		crees	creías	**creíste**	creerás
	Participles:	cree	creía	**creyó**	creerá
	creyendo	creemos	creíamos	**creímos**	creeremos
	creído	creéis	creíais	**creísteis**	creeréis
		creen	creían	**creyeron**	creerán
37	cruzar (c)	cruzo	cruzaba	**crucé**	cruzaré
		cruzas	cruzabas	cruzaste	cruzarás
	Participles:	cruza	cruzaba	cruzó	cruzará
	cruzando	cruzamos	cruzábamos	cruzamos	cruzaremos
	cruzado	cruzáis	cruzabais	cruzasteis	cruzaréis
		cruzan	cruzaban	cruzaron	cruzarán
38	destruir (y)	**destruyo**	destruía	destruí	destruiré
		destruyes	destruías	destruiste	destruirás
	Participles:	**destruye**	destruía	**destruyó**	destruirá
	destruyendo	destruimos	destruíamos	destruimos	destruiremos
	destruido	destruís	destruíais	destruisteis	destruiréis
		destruyen	destruían	**destruyeron**	destruirán
39	enviar	**envío**	enviaba	envié	enviaré
	(envío)	**envías**	enviabas	enviaste	enviarás
		envía	enviaba	envió	enviará
	Participles:	enviamos	enviábamos	enviamos	enviaremos
	enviando	enviáis	enviabais	enviasteis	enviaréis
	enviado	**envían**	enviaban	enviaron	enviarán

	SUBJUNCTIVE		IMPERATIVE
Conditional	**Present**	**Past**	
volvería	**vuelva**	volviera	
volverías	**vuelvas**	volvieras	**vuelve** (no **vuelvas**)
volvería	**vuelva**	volviera	**vuelva**
volveríamos	volvamos	volviéramos	volvamos
volveríais	volváis	volvierais	volved (no volváis)
volverían	**vuelvan**	volvieran	**vuelvan**

	SUBJUNCTIVE		IMPERATIVE
Conditional	**Present**	**Past**	
conocería	**conozca**	conociera	
conocerías	**conozcas**	conocieras	conoce (no **conozcas**)
conocería	**conozca**	conociera	**conozca**
conoceríamos	**conozcamos**	conociéramos	**conozcamos**
conoceríais	**conozcáis**	conocierais	conoced (no **conozcáis**)
conocerían	**conozcan**	conocieran	**conozcan**
creería	crea	**creyera**	
creerías	creas	**creyeras**	cree (no creas)
creería	crea	**creyera**	crea
creeríamos	creamos	**creyéramos**	creamos
creeríais	creáis	**creyerais**	creed (no creáis)
creerían	crean	**creyeran**	crean
cruzaría	**cruce**	cruzara	
cruzarías	**cruces**	cruzaras	cruza (no **cruces**)
cruzaría	**cruce**	cruzara	**cruce**
cruzaríamos	**crucemos**	cruzáramos	**crucemos**
cruzaríais	**crucéis**	cruzarais	cruzad (no **crucéis**)
cruzarían	**crucen**	cruzaran	**crucen**
destruiría	**destruya**	**destruyera**	
destruirías	**destruyas**	**destruyeras**	**destruye** (no **destruyas**)
destruiría	**destruya**	**destruyera**	**destruya**
destruiríamos	**destruyamos**	**destruyéramos**	**destruyamos**
destruiríais	**destruyáis**	**destruyerais**	destruid (no **destruyáis**)
destruirían	**destruyan**	**destruyeran**	**destruyan**
enviaría	**envíe**	enviara	
enviarías	**envíes**	enviaras	**envía** (no **envíes**)
enviaría	**envíe**	enviara	**envíe**
enviaríamos	**enviemos**	enviáramos	enviemos
enviaríais	**enviéis**	enviarais	enviad (no enviéis)
enviarían	**envíen**	enviaran	**envíen**

	Infinitive	INDICATIVE			
		Present	Imperfect	Preterite	Future
40	graduarse (gradúo) **Participles:** graduando graduado	**gradúo** **gradúas** **gradúa** graduamos graduáis **gradúan**	graduaba graduabas graduaba graduábamos graduabais graduaban	gradué graduaste graduó graduamos graduasteis graduaron	graduaré graduarás graduará graduaremos graduaréis graduarán
41	llegar (gu) **Participles:** llegando llegado	llego llegas llega llegamos llegáis llegan	llegaba llegabas llegaba llegábamos llegabais llegaban	**llegué** llegaste llegó llegamos llegasteis llegaron	llegaré llegarás llegará llegaremos llegaréis llegarán
42	proteger (j) **Participles:** protegiendo protegido	**protejo** proteges protege protegemos protegéis protegen	protegía protegías protegía protegíamos protegíais protegían	protegí protegiste protegió protegimos protegisteis protegieron	protegeré protegerás protegerá protegeremos protegeréis protegerán
43	tocar (qu) **Participles:** tocando tocado	toco tocas toca tocamos tocáis tocan	tocaba tocabas tocaba tocábamos tocabais tocaban	**toqué** tocaste tocó tocamos tocasteis tocaron	tocaré tocará tocarás tocaremos tocaréis tocarán
44	vestirse (e:i) **Participles:** **vistiendo** vestido	**me visto** **te vistes** **se viste** nos vestimos os vestís **se visten**	me vestía te vestías se vestía nos vestíamos os vestíais se vestían	me vestí te vestiste **se vistió** nos vestimos os vestisteis **se vistieron**	me vestiré te vestirás se vestirá nos vestiremos os vestiréis se vestirán

	SUBJUNCTIVE		IMPERATIVE
Conditional	**Present**	**Past**	
graduaría	**gradúe**	graduara	
graduarías	**gradúes**	graduaras	**gradúa** (no **gradúes**)
graduaría	**gradúe**	graduara	**gradúe**
graduaríamos	graduemos	graduáramos	graduemos
graduaríais	**graduéis**	graduarais	graduad (no **graduéis**)
graduarían	**gradúen**	graduaran	**gradúen**
llegaría	**llegue**	llegara	
llegarías	**llegues**	llegaras	llega (no **llegues**)
llegaría	**llegue**	llegara	**llegue**
llegaríamos	**lleguemos**	llegáramos	**lleguemos**
llegaríais	**lleguéis**	llegarais	llegad (no lleguéis)
llegarían	**lleguen**	llegaran	**lleguen**
protegería	**proteja**	protegiera	
protegerías	**protejas**	protegieras	protege (no **protejas**)
protegería	**proteja**	protegiera	**proteja**
protegeríamos	**protejamos**	protegiéramos	**protejamos**
protegeríais	**protejáis**	protegierais	proteged (no **protejáis**)
protegerían	**protejan**	protegieran	**protejan**
tocaría	**toque**	tocara	
tocarías	**toques**	tocaras	toca (no **toques**)
tocaría	**toque**	tocara	**toque**
tocaríamos	**toquemos**	tocáramos	**toquemos**
tocaríais	**toquéis**	tocarais	tocad (no **toquéis**)
tocarían	**toquen**	tocaran	**toquen**
me vestiría	**me vista**	**me vistiera**	
te vestirías	**te vistas**	**te vistieras**	**vístete** (no te **vistas**)
se vestiría	**se vista**	**se vistiera**	**vístase**
nos vestiríamos	**nos vistamos**	**nos vistiéramos**	**vistámonos**
os vestiríais	**os vistáis**	**os vistierais**	vestíos (no os **vistáis**)
se vestirían	**se vistan**	**se vistieran**	**vístanse** Uds.

Sección de consulta
Reference Section

MATERIAS	ACADEMIC SUBJECTS
la administración de empresas	business administration
la agronomía	agriculture
el alemán	German
el álgebra	algebra
la anatomía	anatomy
la antropología	anthropology
la arqueología	archaeology
la arquitectura	architecture
el arte	art
la astronomía	astronomy
la biología	biology
la bioquímica	biochemistry
la botánica	botany
el cálculo	calculus
el chino	Chinese
las ciencias políticas	political science
la computación	computer science
las comunicaciones	communications
la contabilidad	accounting
la danza	dance
el derecho	law
la economía	economics
la educación	education
la educación física	physical education

la enfermería	nursing
el español	Spanish
la filosofía	philosophy
la física	physics
el francés	French
la geografía	geography
la geología	geology
el griego	Greek
el hebreo	Hebrew
la historia	history
la informática	computer science
la ingeniería	engineering
el inglés	English
el italiano	Italian
el japonés	Japanese
el latín	Latin
las lenguas clásicas	classical languages
las lenguas romances	romance languages
la lingüística	linguistics
la literatura	literature
las matemáticas	mathematics
la medicina	medicine
el mercadeo/la mercadotecnia	marketing
la música	music
los negocios	business
el periodismo	journalism

el portugués	Portuguese
la psicología	psychology
la química	chemistry
el ruso	Russian
los servicios sociales	social services
la sociología	sociology
el teatro	theater
la trigonometría	trigonometry
la zoología	zoology

LOS ANIMALES	ANIMALS
la abeja	bee
la araña	spider
la ardilla	squirrel
el ave (f.), el pájaro	bird
la ballena	whale
el burro	donkey
la cabra	goat
el caimán	alligator
el camello	camel
la cebra	zebra
el ciervo, el venado	deer
el cocodrilo	crocodile
el cochino, el cerdo, el puerco	pig
el conejo	rabbit
el coyote	coyote
la culebra, la serpiente,	snake

la víbora	
el elefante	elephant
la foca	seal
la gallina	hen
el gallo	rooster
el gato	cat
el gorila	gorilla
el hipopótamo	hippopotamus
la hormiga	ant
el insecto	insect
la jirafa	giraffe
el lagarto	lizard
el león	lion
el lobo	wolf
el loro, la cotorra, el papagayo, el perico	parrot
la mariposa	butterfly
el mono	monkey
la mosca	fly
el mosquito	mosquito
el oso	bear
la oveja	sheep
el pato	duck
el perro	dog
el pez	fish
la rana	frog

el ratón	mouse
el rinoceronte	rhinoceros
el saltamontes, el chapulín	grasshopper
el tiburón	shark
el tigre	tiger
el toro	bull
la tortuga	turtle
la vaca	cow
el zorro	fox

EL CUERPO HUMANO Y LA SALUD

THE HUMAN BODY AND HEALTH

EL CUERPO HUMANO	*THE HUMAN BODY*
la barba	beard
el bigote	mustache
la barriga, la panza, la guata	belly, tummy
la boca	mouth
el brazo	arm
la cabeza	head
la cadera	hip
la ceja	eyebrow
el cerebro	brain
la cintura	waist
el codo	elbow
el corazón	heart
la costilla	rib
el cráneo	skull

el cuello	neck
el dedo	finger
el dedo del pie	toe
la espalda	back
el estómago	stomach
la frente	forehead
la garganta	throat
el hombro	shoulder
el hueso	bone
el labio	lip
la lengua	tongue
la mandíbula	jaw
la mejilla	cheek
el mentón, la barba	chin
la muñeca	wrist
el músculo	muscle
el muslo	thigh
las nalgas, el trasero, las asentaderas	buttocks
la nariz	nose
el nervio	nerve
el oído	(inner) ear
el ojo	eye
el ombligo	navel, belly button
la oreja	(outer) ear
la pantorrilla	calf

el párpado	eyelid
el pecho	chest
la pestaña	eyelash
el pie	foot
la piel	skin
la pierna	leg
el pulgar	thumb
el pulmón	lung
la rodilla	knee
la sangre	blood
el talón	heel
el tobillo	ankle
el tronco	torso, trunk
la uña	fingernail
la uña del dedo del pie	toenail
la vena	vein

LOS CINCO SENTIDOS	*THE FIVE SENSES*
el gusto	taste
el oído	hearing
el olfato	smell
el tacto	touch
la vista	sight

LA SALUD	*HEALTH*
el accidente	accident
alérgico/a	allergic
el antibiótico	antibiotic

la aspirina	aspirin
el ataque cardiaco, el ataque al corazón	heart attack
el cáncer	cancer
la cápsula	capsule
la clínica	clinic
congestionado/a	congested
el consultorio	doctor's office
la curita	adhesive bandage
el/la dentista	dentist
el/la doctor(a), el/la médico/a	doctor
el dolor (de cabeza)	(head)ache, pain
embarazada	pregnant
la enfermedad	illness, disease
el/la enfermero/a	nurse
enfermo/a	ill, sick
la erupción	rash
el examen médico	physical exam
la farmacia	pharmacy
la fiebre	fever
la fractura	fracture
la gripe	flu
la herida	wound
el hospital	hospital
la infección	infection
la inyección	injection

el insomnio	insomnia
el jarabe	(cough) syrup
mareado/a	dizzy, nauseated
el medicamento	medication
la medicina	medicine
las muletas	crutches
la operación	operation
el/la paciente	patient
el/la paramédico/a	paramedic
la pastilla, la píldora	pill, tablet
los primeros auxilios	first aid
la pulmonía	pneumonia
los puntos	stitches
la quemadura	burn
el quirófano	operating room
la radiografía	X-ray
la receta	prescription
el resfriado	cold (illness)
la sala de emergencia(s)	emergency room
saludable	healthy, healthful
sano/a	healthy
el seguro médico	medical insurance
la silla de ruedas	wheelchair
el síntoma	symptom
el termómetro	thermometer
la tos	cough

la transfusión	transfusion
la vacuna	vaccination
la venda	bandage
el virus	virus
cortar(se)	to cut (oneself)
curar	to cure, to treat
desmayar(se)	to faint
enfermarse	to get sick
enyesar	to put in a cast
estornudar	to sneeze
guardar cama	to stay in bed
hinchar(se)	to swell
internar(se) en el hospital	to check into the hospital
lastimarse (el pie)	to hurt (one's foot)
mejorar(se)	to get better; to improve
operar	to operate
quemar(se)	to burn
respirar (hondo)	to breathe (deeply)
romperse (la pierna)	to break (one's leg)
sangrar	to bleed
sufrir	to suffer
tomarle la presión a alguien	to take someone's blood pressure
tomarle el pulso a alguien	to take someone's pulse
torcerse (el tobillo)	to sprain (one's ankle)
vendar	to bandage

EXPRESIONES ÚTILES PARA LA CLASE	USEFUL CLASSROOM EXPRESSIONS
PALABRAS ÚTILES	*USEFUL WORDS*
ausente	absent
el departamento	department
el dictado	dictation
la conversación, las conversaciones	conversation(s)
la expresión, las expresiones	expression(s)
el examen, los exámenes	test(s)
la frase	sentence
la hoja de actividades	activity sheet
el horario de clases	class schedule
la oración, las oraciones	sentence(s)
el párrafo	paragraph
la persona	person
presente	present
la prueba	quiz
siguiente	following
la tarea	homework
EXPRESIONES ÚTILES	*USEFUL EXPRESSIONS*
Abra(n) sus libros.	Open your book(s).
Cambien de papel.	Change roles.
Cierre(n) su(s) libro(s).	Close your books.
¿Cómo se dice ___ en español?	How do you say ___ in Spanish?
¿Cómo se escribe ___ en español?	How do you write ___ in Spanish?

¿Comprende(n)?	Do you understand?
(No) comprendo.	I (don't) understand.
Conteste(n) las preguntas.	Answer the questions.
Continúe(n), por favor.	Continue, please.
Escriba(n) su nombre.	Write your name.
Escuchen la cinta (el disco compacto).	Listen to the tape (compact disc).
Estudie(n) la lección tres.	Study lesson three.
Haga(n) la actividad (el ejercicio) número cuatro.	Do activity (exercise) number four.
Lea(n) la oración en voz alta.	Read the sentence aloud.
Levante(n) la mano.	Raise your hand(s).
Más despacio, por favor.	Slower, please.
No sé.	I don't know.
Páse(n)me los exámenes.	Pass me the tests.
¿Qué significa ___?	What does ___ mean?
Repita(n), por favor.	Repeat, please.
Siénte(n)se, por favor.	Sit down, please.
Siga(n) las instrucciones.	Follow the instructions.
¿Tiene(n) alguna pregunta?	Do you have any questions?
Vaya(n) a la página dos.	Go to page two.

COUNTRIES & NATIONALITIES	**PAÍSES Y NACIONALIDADES (GENTILICIOS)**	
NORTH AMERICA	***NORTEAMÉRICA***	
Canada	**Canadá**	**canadiense**
Mexico	**México**	**mexicano/a**
United States	**Estados Unidos**	**estadounidense**
CENTRAL AMERICA	***CENTROAMÉRICA***	
Belize	**Belice**	**beliceño/a**
Costa Rica	**Costa Rica**	**costarricense**
El Salvador	**El Salvador**	**salvadoreño/a**
Guatemala	**Guatemala**	**guatemalteco/a**
Honduras	**Honduras**	**hondureño/a**
Nicaragua	**Nicaragua**	**nicaragüense**
Panama	**Panamá**	**panameño/a**
THE CARIBBEAN	***EL CARIBE***	
Cuba	**Cuba**	**cubano/a**
Dominican Republic	**República Dominicana**	**dominicano/a**
Haiti	**Haití**	**haitiano/a**
Puerto Rico	**Puerto Rico**	**puertorriqueño/a**
SOUTH AMERICA	***AMÉRICA DEL SUR***	
Argentina	**Argentina**	**argentino/a**
Bolivia	**Bolivia**	**boliviano/a**
Brazil	**Brasil**	**brasileño/a**
Chile	**Chile**	**chileno/a**
Colombia	**Colombia**	**colombiano/a**

Ecuador	**Ecuador**	**ecuatoriano/a**
Paraguay	**Paraguay**	**paraguayo/a**
Peru	**Perú**	**peruano/a**
Uruguay	**Uruguay**	**uruguayo/a**
Venezuela	**Venezuela**	**venezolano/a**
EUROPE	***EUROPA***	
Armenia	**Armenia**	**armenio/a**
Austria	**Austria**	**austríaco/a**
Belgium	**Bélgica**	**belga**
Bosnia	**Bosnia**	**bosnio/a**
Bulgaria	**Bulgaria**	**búlgaro/a**
Croatia	**Croacia**	**croata**
Czech Republic	**República Checa**	**checo/a**
Denmark	**Dinamarca**	**danés, danesa**
England	**Inglaterra**	**inglés, inglesa**
Estonia	**Estonia**	**estonio/a**
Finland	**Finlandia**	**finlandés, finlandesa**
France	**Francia**	**francés, francesa**
Germany	**Alemania**	**alemán, alemana**
Great Britain (United Kingdom)	**Gran Bretaña (Reino Unido)**	**británico**
Greece	**Grecia**	**griego/a**
Hungary	**Hungría**	**húngaro/a**
Iceland	**Islandia**	**islandés, islandesa**
Ireland	**Irlanda**	**irlandés, irlandesa**
Italy	**Italia**	**italiano/a**

Latvia	**Letonia**	**letón, letona**
Lithuania	**Lituania**	**lituano/a**
Netherlands (Holland)	**Países Bajos (Holanda)**	**holandés, holandesa**
Norway	**Noruega**	**noruego/a**
Poland	**Polonia**	**polaco/a**
Portugal	**Portugal**	**portugués, portuguesa**
Romania	**Rumania**	**rumano/a**
Russia	**Rusia**	**ruso/a**
Scotland	**Escocia**	**escocés, escocesa**
Serbia	**Serbia**	**serbio/a**
Slovakia	**Eslovaquia**	**eslovaco/a**
Slovenia	**Eslovenia**	**esloveno/a**
Spain	**España**	**español(a)**
Sweden	**Suecia**	**sueco/a**
Switzerland	**Suiza**	**suizo/a**
Ukraine	**Ucrania**	**ucranio/a, ucraniano/a**
Wales	**Gales**	**galés, galesa**
Yugoslavia	**Yugoslavia**	**yugoslavo/a**
ASIA	***ASIA***	
Bangladesh	**Bangladesh**	**bangladesí**
Cambodia	**Camboya**	**camboyano/a**
China	**China**	**chino/a**
India	**India**	**indio/a**
Indonesia	**Indonesia**	**indonesio/a**

Iran	**Irán**	**iraní**
Iraq	**Iraq, Irak**	**iraquí**
Israel	**Israel**	**israelí**
Japan	**Japón**	**japonés, japonesa**
Jordan	**Jordania**	**jordano/a**
Korea	**Corea**	**coreano/a**
Kuwait	**Kuwait**	**kuwaití**
Lebanon	**Líbano**	**libanés, libanesa**
Malaysia	**Malaisia**	**malaisiano/a**
Pakistan	**Pakistán**	**pakistaní**
Russia	**Rusia**	**ruso/a**
Saudi Arabia	**Arabia Saudí**	**saudí**
Singapore	**Singapur**	**singapurés, singapuresa**
Syria	**Siria**	**sirio/a**
Taiwan	**Taiwán**	**taiwanés, taiwanesa**
Thailand	**Tailandia**	**tailandés, tailandesa**
Turkey	**Turquía**	**turco/a**
Vietnam	**Vietnam**	**vietnamita**
AFRICA	***ÁFRICA***	
Algeria	**Argelia**	**argelino/a**
Angola	**Angola**	**angolano/a**
Cameroon	**Camerún**	**camerunés, camerunesa**
Congo	**Congo**	**congolés, congolesa**
Egypt	**Egipto**	**egipcio/a**
Equatorial Guinea	**Guinea Ecuatorial**	**ecuatoguineano**

Ethiopia	**Etiopía**	**etíope**
Ivory Coast	**Costa de Marfil**	**ivoriano/a**
Kenya	**Kenia, Kenya**	**keniano/a**
Libya	**Libia**	**libio/a**
Mali	**Malí**	**malinqués, malinquesa**
Morocco	**Marruecos**	**marroquí**
Mozambique	**Mozambique**	**mozambicano**
Nigeria	**Nigeria**	**nigeriano/a**
Rwanda	**Ruanda**	**ruandés, ruandesa**
Somalia	**Somalia**	**somalí**
South Africa	**Sudáfrica**	**sudafricano/a**
Sudan	**Sudán**	**sudanés, sudanesa**
Tunisia	**Tunicia, Túnez**	**tunecino/a**
Uganda	**Uganda**	**ugandés, ugandesa**
Zambia	**Zambia**	**zambiano/a**
Zimbabwe	**Zimbabue**	**zimbabuense**
AUSTRALIA AND THE PACIFIC	***AUSTRALIA Y EL PACÍFICO***	
Australia	**Australia**	**australiano/a**
New Zealand	**Nueva Zelanda**	**neozelandés, neozelandesa**
Philippines	**Filipinas**	**filipino/a**

MONEDAS DE LOS PAÍSES HISPANOS

CURRENCIES OF SPANISH-SPEAKING COUNTRIES

PAÍS *COUNTRY*	*MONEDA* *CURRENCY*
Argentina	**el peso**
Bolivia	**el boliviano**
Chile	**el peso**
Colombia	**el peso**
Costa Rica	**el colón**
Cuba	**el peso**
Ecuador	**el sucre, el dólar estadounidense**
El Salvador	**el colón, el dólar estadounidense**
España	**el euro**
Guatemala	**el quetzal, el dólar estadounidense**
Honduras	**el lempira**
México	**el peso**
Nicaragua	**el córdoba**
Panamá	**el balboa, el dólar estadounidense**
Paraguay	**el guaraní**
Perú	**el sol**
Puerto Rico	**el dólar estadounidense**
República Dominicana	**el peso**
Uruguay	**el peso**
Venezuela	**el bolívar**

EXPRESIONES Y REFRANES	EXPRESSIONS & SAYINGS
EXPRESIONES Y REFRANES CON PARTES DEL CUERPO	*EXPRESSIONS & SAYINGS WITH PARTS OF THE BODY*
A cara o cruz	Heads or tails
A corazón abierto	Open heart
A lo hecho, pecho	What's done is done./Don't cry over spilled milk.
A ojos vistas	Clearly, visibly
Al dedillo	Like the back of one's hand
¡Choca/Vengan esos cinco!	Put it there!/Give me five!
Codo con codo	Very closely/Cheek by jowl
Con las manos en la masa	Red handed
Costar un ojo de la cara	To cost an arm and a leg
De rodillas	On one's knees
Duro de oído	Hard of hearing
En cuerpo y alma	In body and soul
En la punta de la lengua	On the tip of one's tongue
Darle a la lengua	To chatter/To gab
En un abrir y cerrar de ojos	In a blink of the eye
Entrar por un oído y salir por otro	In one ear and out the other
Estar con el agua al cuello	To be up to one's neck with/in
Estar para chuparse los dedos	To be delicious/To be finger-licking good
Hablar entre dientes	To mutter/To speak under one's breath
Hablar por los codos	To talk a lot
Hacer la vista gorda	To turn a blind eye on something

Hombro con hombro	Shoulder to shoulder
Llorar a lágrima viva	To sob/To cry one's eyes out
Metérsele (a alguien) algo entre ceja y ceja	To put an idea in someone's head
Mirar por encima del hombro	To look over one's shoulder
No pegar ojo	Not to be able to sleep/To stay up all night
No tener corazón	Not to have a heart
No tener dos dedos de frente	Not to have an ounce of common sense
Ojos que no ven, corazón que no siente	Out of sight, out of mind
Perder la cabeza	To lose one's head
Quedarse con la boca abierta	To be thunderstruck
Romper el corazón	To break someone's heart
Tener buen/mal corazón	Have a good/bad heart
Tener un nudo en la garganta	Have a knot in your throat
Tomarse algo a pecho	To take something too seriously
Venir como anillo al dedo	To fit like a charm/To suit perfectly
EXPRESIONES Y REFRANES CON ANIMALES	*EXPRESSIONS & SAYINGS WITH ANIMALS*
A caballo regalado no le mires el diente.	Don't look a gift horse in the mouth.
Comer como un cerdo	To eat like a pig
Cuando menos se piensa, salta la liebre.	Things happen when you least expect it.
Es una mosquita muerta.	Butter wouldn't melt in his/her mouth.

Llevarse como el perro y el gato	To fight like cats and dogs
Perro ladrador, poco mordedor./Perro que ladra no muerde.	His/her bark is worse than his/her bite.
¿Quién le pone el cascabel al gato?	Who will bell the cat?
Ser una tortuga	To be a slowpoke
EXPRESIONES Y REFRANES CON ALIMENTOS	*EXPRESSIONS AND SAYINGS WITH FOOD*
Agua que no has de beber, déjala correr.	If you're not interested, don't ruin it for everybody else.
Al pan, pan y al vino, vino.	Not to mince words.
Como agua para chocolate	Ready to explode/At the boiling point
Con pan y vino se anda el camino.	Things never seem as bad after a good meal.
Contigo pan y cebolla.	You are all I need.
Dame pan y dime tonto.	I don't care what you say, as long as I get what I want.
Descubrir el pastel	To let the cat out of the bag
Dulce como la miel	Sweet as honey
Estar en el ajo	To be in the know
Estar en la higuera	To take the lid off something
Estar más claro que el agua	To be clear as a bell
Ganarse el pan	To earn a living/To earn one's daily bread
No hay miel sin hiel.	There's no rose without a thorn./There's always a catch.
No sólo de pan vive el hombre.	Man doesn't live by bread alone.

Pan con pan, comida de tontos.	Variety is the spice of life./All work and no play makes Jack a dull boy.
Ser agua pasada	To be water under the bridge
Ser más bueno que el pan	To be gorgeous
Temblar como un flan	To shake/tremble like a leaf
Expresiones y refranes con colores	*Expressions and sayings with colors*
Estar verde	To be inexperienced/wet behind the ears
Poner los ojos en blanco	To roll one's eyes
Ponerle a alguien un ojo morado	To give someone a black eye
Ponerse rojo de ira	To turn red with anger
Ponerse rojo	To turn red/To blush
Ponerse verde de envidia	To be green with envy
Quedarse en blanco	To go blank
Verlo todo de color de rosa	See the world through rose-colored glasses
Refranes	*Sayings*
A buen entendedor, pocas palabras bastan.	A word to the wise is sufficient.
Ande o no ande, caballo grande.	Bigger is always better.
A quien madruga, Dios le ayuda.	The early bird catches the worm.
Cuídate, que te cuidaré.	Take care of yourself, and then I'll take care of you.
De tal palo tal astilla.	A chip off the old block.
Del dicho al hecho hay mucho trecho.	Easier said than done.

Dime con quién andas y te diré quién eres.	A man is known by the company he keeps.
El saber no ocupa lugar.	You can never know too much.
Lo que es moda no incomoda.	No discomfort is too great in the name of fashion.
Más vale maña que fuerza.	Brains is better than brawn.
Más vale prevenir que curar.	Prevention is better than cure.
Más vale solo que mal acompañado.	Better alone than with a bad companion.
Más vale tarde que nunca.	Better late than never.
Mucho ruido y pocas nueces.	All talk and no action.
No es oro todo lo que reluce.	All that glitters is not gold.
Poderoso caballero es don Dinero.	Money talks.
Por la boca muere el pez.	Talking too much can be dangerous.
Vale más una imagen que mil palabras.	A picture is worth a thousand words.

COMMON FALSE FRIENDS

False friends are Spanish words that look similar to English words but have very different meanings. While recognizing the English relatives of unfamiliar Spanish words you encounter is an important way of constructing meaning, there are some Spanish words whose similarity to English words is deceptive. Here is a list of some of the most common Spanish false friends.

actualmente ≠ actually

actualmente = nowadays, currently

actually = **de hecho, en realidad, en efecto**

aprobar ≠ approve

aprobar = to pass (an exam)

approve = **consentir, estar de acuerdo**

argumento ≠ argument

argumento = plot

argument = **discusión, pelea**

armada ≠ army

armada = navy

army = **ejército**

asistir ≠ assist

asistir = to attend, to go to

assist = **ayudar, colaborar**

balde ≠ bald

balde = pail, bucket

bald = **calvo/a**

batería ≠ battery

batería = drum set

battery = **pila**

bravo ≠ brave

bravo = wild, fierce

brave = **valiente**

cándido/a ≠ candid

cándido/a = innocent

candid = **sincero/a**

carbón ≠ carbon

carbón = coal

carbon = **carbono**

casual ≠ casual

casual = coincidental

casual = **informal, despreocupado/a**

casualidad ≠ casualty

casualidad = coincidence

casualty = **víctima**

colegio ≠ college

colegio = school

college = **universidad**

collar ≠ collar

collar = necklace

collar = **cuello (de camisa)**

comprensivo/a ≠ comprehensive

comprensivo/a = understanding

comprenhensive = **completo, extensivo**

constipado ≠ constipated

estar constipado/a = to have a cold

to be constipated = **estar estreñido/a**

crudo/a ≠ crude

crudo/a = raw, undercooked

crude = **burdo/a; grosero/a**

desgracia ≠ disgrace

desgracia = misfortune

disgrace = **deshonra, vergüenza**

divertir ≠ divert

divertirse = to enjoy oneself

to divert = **desviar**

educado/a ≠ educated

educado/a = well-behaved

educated = **culto/a, instruido/a**

embarazada ≠ embarrassed

estar embarazada = to be pregnant

to be embarrassed = **tener vergüenza**

eventualmente ≠ eventually

eventualmente = possibly

eventually = **finalmente, al final**

éxito ≠ exit

éxito = success

exit = **salida**

físico/a ≠ physician

físico/a = physicist

physician = **médico/a**

fútbol ≠ football

fútbol = soccer

football = **fútbol americano**

lectura ≠ lecture

lectura = reading

lecture = **conferencia**

librería ≠ library

librería = bookstore

library = **biblioteca**

máscara ≠ mascara

máscara = mask

mascara = **rímel**

molestar ≠ to molest

molestar = to bother, to annoy

molest = **abusar**

oficio ≠ office

oficio = trade, occupation

office = **oficina**

rato ≠ rat

rato = while

rat = **rata**

realizar ≠ realize

realizar = to do

to realize = **darse cuenta**

red ≠ red

red = net

red = **rojo**

remover ≠ remove

remover = to stir; to turn over

remove = **sacar, quitar**

revolver ≠ revolver

revolver = to stir; to rummage through

revolver = **revólver**

sensible ≠ sensible

sensible = sentitive

sensible = **sensato/a, razonable**

suceso ≠ success

suceso = event

success = **éxito**

sujeto ≠ subject

sujeto = fellow, guy

subject = **tema, asunto**

LOS ALIMENTOS	FOODS
FRUTAS	*FRUITS*
la aceituna	olive
el aguacate	avocado
el albaricoque, el damasco	apricot
la banana, el plátano	banana
la cereza	cherry
la ciruela	plum
el dátil	date
la frambuesa	raspberry
la fresa, la frutilla	strawberry
el higo	fig
el limón	lemon, lime
el melocotón, el durazno	peach
la mandarina	tangerine
el mango	mango
la manzana	apple
la naranja	orange
la papaya	papaya
la pera	pear
la piña	pineapple
el pomelo, la toronja	grapefruit
la sandía	watermelon
las uvas	grapes

VEGETALES	*VEGETABLES*
la alcachofa	artichoke
el apio	celery
la arveja, el guisante	pea
la berenjena	eggplant
el brócoli	broccoli
la calabaza	squash, pumpkin
la cebolla	onion
el champiñón, la seta	mushroom
la col, el repollo	cabbage
la coliflor	cauliflower
los espárragos	asparagus
las espinacas	spinach
los frijoles, las habichuelas	beans
las habas	lima beans
las judías verdes, los ejotes	string beans, green beans
la lechuga	lettuce
el maíz, el choclo, el elote	corn
la papa, la patata	potato
el pepino	cucumber
el pimentón	bell pepper
el rábano	radish
la remolacha	beet
el tomate, el jitomate	tomato
la zanahoria	carrot

El pescado y los mariscos	*Fish and Shellfish*
la almeja	clam
el atún	tuna
el bacalao	cod
el calamar	squid
el cangrejo	crab
el camarón, la gamba	shrimp
la langosta	lobster
el langostino	prawn
el lenguado	sole, flounder
el mejillón	mussel
la ostra	oyster
el pulpo	octopus
el salmón	salmon
la sardina	sardine
la vieira	scallop

La carne	*Meat*
la albóndiga	meatball
el bistec	steak
la carne de res	beef
el chorizo	hard pork sausage
la chuleta de cerdo	pork chop
el cordero	lamb
los fiambres	cold cuts; food served cold
el filete	fillet
la hamburguesa	hamburger

el hígado	liver
el jamón	ham
el lechón	suckling pig; roasted pig
el pavo	turkey
el pollo	chicken
el puerco	pork
la salchicha	sausage
la ternera	veal
el tocino	bacon

OTRAS COMIDAS	*OTHER FOODS*
el ajo	garlic
el arroz	rice
el azúcar	sugar
el batido	milkshake
el budín	pudding
el cacahuete, el maní	peanut
el café	coffee
los fideos	noodles, pasta
la harina	flour
el huevo	egg
el jugo, el zumo	juice
la leche	milk
la mermelada	marmalade; jam
la miel	honey
el pan	bread
el queso	cheese

la sal	salt
la sopa	soup
el té	tea
la tortilla	omelet (Spain); tortilla (Mexico)
el yogur	yogurt

Cómo describir la comida	*Ways to Describe Food*
a la plancha, a la parrilla	grilled
ácido/a	sour
al horno	baked
amargo/a	bitter
caliente	hot
dulce	sweet
duro/a	tough
frío/a	cold
frito/a	fried
fuerte	strong, heavy
ligero/a	light
picante	spicy
sabroso/a	tasty
salado/a	salty

DÍAS FESTIVOS	HOLIDAYS
Enero	*January*
Año Nuevo (1)	New Year's Day
Día de los Reyes Magos (6)	Three Kings Day (Epiphany)
Día de Martin Luther King, Jr.	Martin Luther King, Jr. Day
Febrero	*February*
Día de San Blas (Paraguay) (3)	St. Blas Day (Paraguay)
Día de San Valentín, Día de los Enamorados (14)	Valentine's Day
Día de los Presidentes	Presidents' Day
Carnaval	Carnival (Mardi Gras)
Marzo	*March*
Día de San Patricio (17)	St. Patrick's Day
Nacimiento de Benito Juárez (México) (21)	Benito Juárez's Birthday (Mexico)
Abril	*April*
Semana Santa	Holy Week
Pésaj	Passover
Pascua	Easter
Declaración de la Independencia de Venezuela (19)	Declaration of Independence of Venezuela
Día de la Tierra (22)	Earth Day

Mayo	*May*
Día del Trabajo (1)	Labor Day
Cinco de Mayo (5) (Mexico)	Cinco de Mayo (May 5th)
Día de las Madres	Mother's Day
Independencia Patria (Paraguay) (15)	Independence Day (Paraguay)
Día Conmemorativo	Memorial Day

Junio	*June*
Día de los Padres	Father's Day
Día de la Bandera (14)	Flag Day
Día del Indio (Perú) (24)	Native People's Day

Julio	*July*
Día de la Independencia de los Estados Unidos (4)	Independence Day (United States)
Día de la Independencia de Venezuela (5)	Independence Day (Venezuela)
Día de la Independencia de la Argentina (9)	Independence Day (Argentina)
Día de la Independencia de Colombia (20)	Independence Day (Colombia)
Nacimiento de Simón Bolívar (24)	Simón Bolívar's Birthday
Día de la Revolución (Cuba) (26)	Revolution Day (Cuba)
Día de la Independencia del Perú (28)	Independence Day (Peru)

Agosto	*August*
Día de la Independencia de Bolivia (6)	Independence Day (Bolivia)
Día de la Independencia del Ecuador (10)	Independence Day (Ecuador)
Día de San Martín (Argentina) (17)	San Martín Day (anniversary of his death)
Día de la Independencia del Uruguay (25)	Independence Day (Uruguay)

Septiembre	*September*
Día del Trabajo (EE. UU.)	Labor Day (U. S.)
Día de la Independencia de Costa Rica, El Salvador, Guatemala, Honduras y Nicaragua (15)	Independence Day (Costa Rica, El Salvador, Guatemala, Honduras, Nicaragua)
Día de la Independencia de México (16)	Independence Day (Mexico)
Día de la Independencia de Chile (18)	Independence Day (Chile)
Año Nuevo Judío	Jewish New Year
Día de la Virgen de las Mercedes (Perú) (24)	Day of the Virgin of Mercedes (Peru)

Octubre	*October*
Día de la Raza (12)	Columbus Day
Noche de Brujas (31)	Halloween

Noviembre	*November*
Día de los Muertos (2)	All Souls Day
Día de los Veteranos (11)	Veterans' Day
Día de la Revolución Mexicana (20)	Mexican Revolution Day
Día de Acción de Gracias	Thanksgiving
Día de la Independencia de Panamá (28)	Independence Day (Panama)

Diciembre	*December*
Día de la Virgen (8)	Day of the Virgin
Día de la Virgen de Guadalupe (México) (12)	Day of the Virgin of Guadalupe (Mexico)
Januká	Chanukah
Nochebuena (24)	Christmas Eve
Navidad (25)	Christmas
Año Viejo (31)	New Year's Eve

NOTE: In Spanish, dates are written with the day first, then the month. Christmas Day is **el 25 de diciembre**. In Latin America and in Europe, abbreviated dates also follow this pattern. Halloween, for example, falls on 31/10. You may also see the numbers in dates separated by periods: 14.2.01. When referring to centuries, roman numerals are always used. The 16th century, therefore, is **el siglo XVI**.

PESOS Y MEDIDAS

WEIGHTS & MEASURES

LONGITUD

LENGTH

El sistema métrico *Metric system*		***El equivalente estadounidense*** *U.S. equivalent*
milímetro = **0,001 metro** millimeter = 0.0001 meter		= 0.039 inch
centímetro = **0,01 metro** centimeter = 0.01 meter		= 0.39 inch
decímetro = **0,1 metro** decimeter = 0.1 meter		= 3.94 inches
metro meter		= 39.4 inches
decámetro = **10 metros** dekameter = 10 meters		= 32.8 feet
hectómetro = **100 metros** hectometer = 100 meters		= 328 feet
kilómetro = **1.000 metros** kilometer = 1,000 meters		= .62 mile

U.S. system ***El sistema estadounidense***		*Metric equivalent* ***El equivalente métrico***
inch **pulgada**		= 2.54 centimeters **= 2,54 centímetros**
foot = 12 inches **pie = 12 pulgadas**		= 30.48 centimeters **= 30,48 centímetros**
yard = 3 feet **yarda = 3 pies**		= 0.914 meter **= 0,914 metro**
mile = 5,280 feet **milla = 5.280 pies**		= 1.609 kilometers **= 1,609 kilómetros**

Superficie			*Surface Area*
El sistema métrico *Metric system*			***El equivalente estadounidense*** *U.S. equivalent*
metro cuadrado square meter			= 10.764 square feet
área	=	**100 metros cuadrados**	
are	=	**100 square meters**	= 0.025 acre
hectárea	=	**100 áreas**	= 2.471 acres
hectare	=	**100 ares**	

U.S. system ***El sistema estadounidense***	*Metric equivalent* ***El equivalente métrico***
yarda cuadrada = 9 pies cuadrados = 0,836 metros cuadrados square yard = 9 square feet = 0.836 square meters	
acre = 4.840 yardas cuadradas = 0,405 hectáreas acre = 4,840 square yards = 0.405 hectares	

Capacidad			*Capacity*
El sistema métrico *Metric system*			***El equivalente estadounidense*** *U.S. equivalent*
mililitro milliliter	=	**0,001 litro** 0.001 liter	= 0.034 ounces
centilitro centiliter	=	**0,01 litro** 0. 01 liter	= 0.34 ounces
decilitro deciliter	=	**0,1 litro** 0.1 liter	= 3.4 ounces
litro liter			= 1.06 quarts
decalitro dekaliter	=	**10 litros** 10 liters	= 2.64 gallons

hectolitro	**=**	**100 litros**	
hectoliter	=	100 liters	= 26.4 gallons
kilolitro	**=**	**1.000 litros**	
kiloliter	=	1,000 liters	= 264 gallons

U.S. system ***El sistema estadounidense***			*Metric equivalent* ***El equivalente métrico***
ounce **onza**			= 29.6 milliliters = 29,6 mililitros
cup **taza**	= 8 ounces **= 8 onzas**		= 236 milliliters **= 236 mililitros**
pint **pinta**	= 2 cups **= 2 tazas**		= 0.47 liters **= 0,47 litros**
quart **cuarto**	= 2 pints **= 2 pinta**		= 0.95 liters **= 0,95 litros**
gallon **galón**	= 4 quarts **= 4 cuartos**		= 3.79 liters **= 3,79 litros**

Peso ***El sistema métrico*** *Metric system*			*Weight* ***El equivalente estadounidense*** *U.S. equivalent*
miligramo **milligram**	**=** **=**	**0,001 gramo** **0.001 gram**	
gramo gram			= 0.035 ounce
decagramo dekagram	**=** =	**10 gramos** 10 grams	= 0.35 ounces
hectogramo hectogram	**=** =	**100 gramos** 100 grams	= 3.5 ounces
kilogramo kilogram	**=** =	**1.000 gramos** 1,000 grams	= 2.2 pounds

tonelada (métrica)	= **1.000 kilogramos**	
metric ton	= 1,000 kilograms	= 1.1 tons

U.S. system ***El sistema estadounidense***		*Metric equivalent* ***El equivalente métrico***
ounce **onza**		= 28.35 grams ***= 28,35 gramos***
pound **libra**	= 16 ounces **= 16 onzas**	= 0.45 kilograms ***= 0,45 kilogramos***
ton **tonelada**	= 2,000 pounds **= 2,000 libras**	= 0.9 metric tons ***= 0,9 toneladas métricas***

TEMPERATURA

Grados centígrados
Degrees Celsius

To convert from Celsius to Fahrenheit, multiply by 9/5 and add 32.

TEMPERATURE

Grados Fahrenheit
Degrees Fahrenheit

To convert from Fahrenheit to Celsius, subtract 32 and multiply by 5/9.

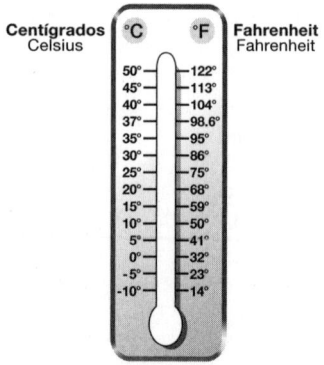

NOMBRES DE PILA ESPAÑOLES	SPANISH PERSONAL NAMES

Note: Not all Spanish names have English equivalents.

NOMBRES FEMENINOS	*WOMEN'S NAMES*
Alba	Elba
Alicia	Alice, Alicia
Amanda	Amanda
Ana	Ann, Anne
Araceli (Celi)	
Asunción (Asun)	
Asunta	
Aurora	Aurora, Dawn
Beatriz (Bea, Beti, Biata)	Beatrice
Belén	
Berta	Bertha
Blanca	Blanche
Carlota	Charlotte
Carolina (Carol)	Caroline
Catarina (Cati)	Catherine, Catharine
Cecilia	Cecile
Celia	Celia
Claudia	Claudia
Consuelo	
Diana	Diane
Dorotea	Dorothy
Elena	Helen, Ellen

Elia	
Elvira	Elvira
Emilia	Emily
Encarna	
Ester	Esther
Estrella	Stella, Estelle
Eva	Eve
Gemma	
Gertrudes	Gertrude
Gloria	Gloria
Inés	Inez
Irene	Irene
Isabel	Elizabeth
Josefa	
Josefina (Pepi, Fina)	Josephine
Juana	Joan, Joanne, Jane
Judith	Judith
Julia	Julia, Julie
Julieta	Juliet, Juliette
Laura	Laura
Leonor	Leonore
Lidia	Lydia
Lourdes	
Luisa	Louise
Manuela (Manola, Manoli)	
Margarita (Marga)	Margaret

María	Mary, Marie
Marta	Martha
Mercedes (Merche)	
Mónica	Monica, Monique
Montserrat (Montse)	
Noelia	
Norma	Norma
Olga	Olga
Paloma	
Patricia (Pati)	Patricia
Paula	Paula
Raquel	Rachel
Rocío	
Rosa	Rose
Rosalía	Rosalie
Rosana	Rosana, Roseanne
Rosario	
Sandra	Sandra
Sara	Sarah
Silvia	Sylvia
Sofía	Sophia
Sonia	Sonya
Susana (Susi)	Susan
Teresa	Theresa
Verónica	Veronica
Victoria (Vicki)	Victoria

Violeta	Violet
Zoe	Zoe
Nombres masculinos	*Men's names*
Alberto	Albert
Alejandro	Alexander
Álex	Alex
Alfonso	Alphonse
Alfredo	Alfred
Andrés	Andrew
Ángel	
Antonio (Toni)	Anthony
Aquiles	Achilles
Arturo	Arthur
Augusto	August
Bernardo	Bernard
Camilo	
Carlos	Charles
César	
Cristiano	Christian
Cristóbal	Christopher
Damián	Damian
David	David
Diego	James
Eduardo	Edward
Emilio	Emil
Enrique	Henry, Eric

Ernesto	Ernest
Esteban	Stephen
Eugenio	Eugene
Evaristo	
Federico (Fede)	Frederick
Felipe	Philip
Fernando	
Francisco (Paco)	Francis
Gerardo	Gerard
Gregorio	Gregory
Guillermo	William
Gustavo	Gustav
Ignacio (Nacho)	Ignatius
Jaime	James
Javier (Javi)	Xavier
Jeremías	Jeremiah, Jeremy
Jesús	
Joaquín	
Jorge	George
José (Pepe)	Joseph
Juan	John
Julián	Julian
Julio	Julius
Justino	Justin
León	Leo, Leon
Leonardo	Leonard

Lucas	Luke
Luis	Louis
Manolo	
Manuel	
Marcelo	Marcel
Marcos	Mark
Mariano	
Miguel	Michael
Oscar (Óscar)	Oscar
Pablo	Paul
Patricio	Patrick
Pedro	Peter
Rafael (Rafa)	Raphael
Raimundo	Raymond
Ramón	Raymond
Ricardo	Richard
Roberto	Robert
Santiago	James
Sebastián	Sebastian
Sergio	Serge
Simón	Simon
Sixto	
Teodoro	Theodore
Tomás	Thomas
Vicente	Vincent

Compound Women's Names

In Spanish-speaking countries women frequently have names that are a combination of **María** and another name, as in **María Dolores** or **Ana María**, for example. Women with such names are rarely known as **María** but are addressed using the second name in the combination or a nickname derived from both names. **María del Carmen**, therefore, might be called **Carmen** or perhaps **Maricarmen**. Below are listed common combinations with **María**, followed by nicknames derived from them.

Note: **María** is not strictly a woman's name in the Spanish-speaking world. Some men's names contain **María**. **José María**, for example, is a common name.

María Ana (Ana, Mariana)

María Antonia (Antonia, Tonia, Toñi)

María Concepción (Concha)

María Cristina (Cristina, Cris, Tina)

María de los Ángeles (Ángeles, Mariángeles)

María del Carmen (Carmen, Maricarmen, Mámen)

María del Mar (Marimar)

María Dolores (Dolores, Mariló, Loles, Lola, Lolita)

María Elena (Elena)

María Eugenia (Eugenia, Maru, Genia)

María Inmaculada (Inma)

María Isabel (Isabel, Isa, Maribel, Mabel)

María Luisa (Luisa, Marilú)

María Nieves (Nieves, Marinieves)

María Pilar (Pilar, Pili, Maripili, Mapi)

María Reyes (Reyes, Marirreyes)

María Rosa (Marisa)

María Soledad (Marisol)

María Teresa (Teresa, Tere, Maritere, Maite)

Ana María (Ana, Anamari)

Ángela María (Ángela)

Eva María (Eva)

Rosa María (Rosa, Rosamari)

Compound Men's Names

José Manuel (Josema)

José María (Josema, Chema)

José Miguel

Juan Antonio

Juan Carlos (Juanca)

Juan José (Juanjo)

Juan Luis (Juanlu)

Juan Manuel (Juanma)

Juan Pablo (Juanpa)

Miguel Ángel

NÚMEROS

NUMBERS

Números ordinales

Ordinal numbers

primero/a	**1º/1ª**	first	1st
segundo/a	**2º/2ª**	second	2nd
tercero/a	**3º/3ª**	third	3rd
cuarto/a	**4º/4ª**	fourth	4th
quinto/a	**5º/5ª**	fifth	5th
sexto/a	**6º/6ª**	sixth	6th
séptimo/a	**7º/7ª**	seventh	7th
octavo/a	**8º/8ª**	eighth	8th
noveno/a	**9º/9ª**	ninth	9th
décimo/a	**10º/10ª**	tenth	10th

Fracciones

Fractions

$\frac{1}{2}$	**un medio, la mitad**	one half
$\frac{1}{3}$	**un tercio**	one third
$\frac{1}{4}$	**un cuarto**	one fourth (quarter)
$\frac{1}{5}$	**un quinto**	one fifth
$\frac{1}{6}$	**un sexto**	one sixth
$\frac{1}{7}$	**un séptimo**	one seventh
$\frac{1}{8}$	**un octavo**	one eighth
$\frac{1}{9}$	**un noveno**	one ninth
$\frac{1}{10}$	**un décimo**	one tenth
$\frac{2}{3}$	**dos tercios**	two thirds
$\frac{3}{4}$	**tres cuartos**	three fourths (quarters)
$\frac{5}{8}$	**cinco octavos**	five eighths

Decimales		*Decimals*	
un décimo	0,1	one tenth	0.1
un centésimo	0,01	one hundredth	0.01
un milésimo	0,001	one thousandth	0.001

OCUPACIONES	OCCUPATIONS
el/la abogado/a	lawyer
el actor, la actriz	actor
el/la administrador(a) de empresas	business administrator
el/la agente de bienes raíces	real estate agent
el/la agente de seguros	insurance agent
el/la agricultor(a)	farmer
el/la arqueólogo/a	archaeologist
el/la arquitecto/a	architect
el/la artesano/a	artisan
el/la auxiliar de vuelo	flight attendant
el/la basurero/a	garbage collector
el/la bibliotecario/a	librarian
el/la bombero/a	firefighter
el/la cajero/a	bank teller, cashier
el/la camionero/a	truck driver
el/la cantinero/a	bartender
el/la carnicero/a	butcher
el/la carpintero/a	carpenter
el/la científico/a	scientist
el/la cirujano/a	surgeon

el/la cobrador(a)	bill collector
el/la cocinero/a	cook, chef
el/la comprador(a)	buyer
el/al consejero/a	counselor, advisor
el/la contador(a)	accountant
el/la corredor(a) de bolsa	stockbroker
el/la diplomático/a	diplomat
el/la diseñador(a) (gráfico/a)	(graphic) designer
el/la electricista	electrician
el/la empresario/a de pompas fúnebres	funeral director
el/la especialista en dietética	dietician
el/la fotógrafo/a	photographer
el/la higienista dental	dental hygienist
el hombre/la mujer de negocios	businessperson
el/la ingeniero/a en computación	computer engineer
el/la intérprete	interpreter
el/la juez	judge
el/la maestro/a	elementary school teacher
el/la marinero/a	sailor
el/la obrero/a	manual laborer
el/la oficial de prisión	prision guard
el/la obrero/a de la construcción	construction worker
el/la optometrista	optometrist
el/la panadero/a	baker
el/la paramédico/a	paramedic

el/la peluquero/a	hairdresser
el/la piloto	pilot
el/la pintor(a)	painter
el/la plomero/a	plumber
el/la político/a	politician
el/la programador(a)	computer programer
el/la psicólogo/a	psychologist
el/la quiropráctico/a	chiropractor
el/la redactor(a)	editor
el/la reportero/a	reporter
el/la sastre	tailor
el/la secretario/a	secretary
el/la supervisor(a)	supervisor
el/la técnico/a (en computación)	(computer) technician
el/la fisioterapeuta	physical therapist
el/la vendedor(a)	sales representative
el/la veterinario/a	veterinarian